Teaching and learning in the early years

2nd edition

Edited by David Whitebread

RoutledgeFalmer
Taylor & Francis Group

LONDON AND NEW YORK

First published 1996
by Routledge
Reprinted 1997, 1998, 1999

Reprinted 2001, 2002 (three times)
by RoutledgeFalmer
11 New Fetter Lane, London EC4P 4EE

Simultaneously published in the USA and Canada
by RoutledgeFalmer
29 West 35th Street, New York, NY 10001

Second edition first published 2003

RoutledgeFalmer is an imprint of the Taylor & Francis Group

Typeset in Palatino by M Rules
Printed and bound in Great Britain by
St Edmundsbury Press, Bury St Edmunds, Suffolk

British Library Cataloguing in Publication Data
A catalogue record for this book is available from the British Library

Library of Congress Cataloging in Publication Data
A catalog record for this book has been requested

ISBN 0–415–28048–6

Teaching and learning in the early years

2nd edition

This book provides a broad-ranging and up-to-date review of current thinking and best practice within nursery and infant education. The book is based on the basic truth that an effective early years curriculum must start with the children, their needs and their potential. The best teaching must have a strong element of fun, wonder and excitement, and play is a crucial part of this.

This new edition has been fully revised and updated in light of the introduction of the Foundation Stage and Early Learning Goals. The authors review all major areas of the Early Years curriculum and a range of basic issues and principles, including:

- an analysis of current research into how children learn
- discussions of issues such as classroom organisation, curriculum management, and assessment
- a detailed section on play and language
- chapters covering individual curriculum areas, including new chapters on children's art, ICT and PSHE

Each chapter combines a review of important principles with practical and inspiring classroom examples. The book is essential reading for all Early Years trainee teachers.

David Whitebread is a senior lecturer in psychology and early years education at the University of Cambridge Faculty of Education. His most recent publication is *The Psychology of Teaching and Learning in the Primary School* (RoutledgeFalmer, 2000).

DEDICATION

This book is dedicated to Dorothy Glynn (nee Gardner), who was the professional tutor on my PGCE course at Clifton College, Nottingham, during the academic year 1973–4. It was Dorothy who persuaded me to focus on the early years, and who was an inspiration to me and all her students with her deep love and enthusiasm for young children. She had been inspired, in her turn, by the work of Susan Isaacs. I thus like to think that we are continuing a long tradition of recognising that early years education must start with the needs and potentialities of the young child, and that this book will help to inspire others to continue it further.

CONTENTS

PART B Play and language

PART C The wider curriculum

PART D   The way forward

FIGURES

CONTRIBUTORS

Tandy Adlam did the BEd at University of Cambridge Faculty of Education and has since taught a variety of age groups in Cambridge schools, including four years at Colleges Nursery School, Cambridge. She is currently working at home as the mother of two wonderful children who have learning difficulties.

Holly Anderson is joint language coordinator in the University of Cambridge Faculty of Education and teaches language and professional studies to early years students. A nursery and infant teacher for 18 years, she became a language advisory teacher before moving into ITT in 1992. She has been the UK leader of a cross-cultural research project looking at early years provison in Norway and the UK. Her publications are in the area of early years language education, the most recent being Anderson and Styles (eds) (2000) *Teaching Through Texts*, Routledge.

Helen Arnold sadly died recently. When she wrote this chapter she worked part-time as a senior lecturer in language and psychology at Homerton College. She wrote extensively for children and teachers over many years. Her publications include *Listening to Children Reading* (Hodder & Stoughton) and *Reading for Learning* (Macmillan/Nelson). She was general editor and part author of the Scholastics *Literacy Boxes* series of children's information books.

Jane Bower has been a practising primary teacher since 1979, becoming co-ordinator of expressive arts for four primary schools in Cumbria in 1988, and later arts advisory teacher for Key Stages 1 and 2 in Cambridgeshire.

Her published writing began with stories for BBC's *Playschool* in 1983. She now writes regularly on primary art for *Child Education, Early Years Educator* and other early years journals and has produced teaching packs for a variety of publishers. Jane also works as an artist in residence, undertaking ceramic and mural commissions working alongside children in schools. She is currently working part-time as an art teacher for reception and Key Stages 1 classes in a local school.

Helen Bromley is a former infant teacher with 16 years' experience. She is now a freelance early years consultant delivering INSET throughout the country, most particularly on play, communication, language and literacy. She contributes regularly to *Early Years Educator Magazine* and her first book, *Book Based Reading Games* was published by the Centre for Language in Primary Education earlier this year.

Helen Broomby was until recently employed by Cambridgeshire County Council as the care and education training manager for the Cambridgeshire Care and Education Partnership, where she had a strategic role for training all childcare and education practitioners and for ensuring the high quality of training. She has over 30 years' experience of early years work in a range of diverse settings and as a trainer of early years practitioners in both qualifications and continual professional development. She has undertaken research projects, training and consultancy for national bodies including the National Early Years Network and the Daycare Trust. Helen is committed to the promotion of a positive ethos for the personal, social, health and well-being of young children.

Penny Coltman did a degree in agricultural zoology at Leeds University before originally training as a secondary science teacher. She worked as a Key Stage 1 teacher at Gt Chesterford C of E Primary School, Essex for eight years, where she was the maths and science coordinator. She is now a lecturer in early years science in the University of Cambridge Faculty of Education. She has published extensively in *Child Education* and other early years journals, works as a consultant for the BBC on schools programmes, and has been involved in writing several published schemes for early years science.

Dianne Conway studied geography as a special subject alongside her early years education course at Whitelands College, London. She has taught for 22 years across Key Stage 1 and until recently was geography coordinator at Stapleford Community Primary School, Cambridgeshire. She is currently supply teaching and teaches geography for early years students in the University of Cambridge Faculty of Education.

Ros Daniels worked at Hare Street Infant School in Harlow and at the University of Cambridge Faculty of Education on the BEd Professional Studies course, lecturing with a colleague on behaviour management. She has published an article on planned activity time (PAT) in *Child Education* (1995, with Jackie Lamb and Debbie Barnes) and an article on behaviour in Bill Roger's book *Behaviour Management* (1995).

Mary Jane Drummond taught in infant and primary schools in London and Sheffield, and was headteacher of an infant school. She spent four years at Leeds University working on the schools council project 'Communication skills in early childhood', directed by Joan Tough. She has taught at the former Cambridge Institute of Education, and now within the University of Cambridge Faculty of Education, since 1985, where she has developed a range of multi-disciplinary early years courses. She has worked with the Early Childhood Unit at the National Children's Bureau and acted as a consultant for a number of LEAs. She has published widely on a range of early years issues, including *Assessing Children's Learning* (David Fulton, 1993).

Jane Edden is a retired senior lecturer in music education, previously at Homerton College. She has taught music to children in a variety of schools both in this country and in Trinidad. As primary music specialist for Cambridgeshire she was co-author of *Managing Music with Infants*, and she contributed a chapter to Eve Bearne's book *Use of Language Across the Primary Curriculum* (Routledge, 1998).

Lesley Hendy is a former senior lecturer in drama and education at Homerton College, and is now a Senior Research Associate for the University of Cambridge Faculty of Education. Before retraining as a drama specialist, she worked as a nursery and infant teacher and was a headteacher of a first school. Over the past few years she has specialised in drama for the early years, in which field she has published widely. Her latest publication is *Supporting Drama and Imaginative Play in the Early Years* (Open University Press, 2001).

Holly Linklater studied theology and religious studies (BA Hons) at Cambridge University. She then did a sabbatical year as president of Cambridge University Students' Union before finally studying for a PGCE at Homerton College. She is now reception teacher and early years co-ordinator in a small school in Essex, occasionally lecturing at Homerton and writing for and about early years and Key Stage 1.

Rachel Sparks Linfield is director of studies at St John's College School, Cambridge and a teacher of 4- to 5-year-olds. Before this she worked as a senior lecturer in primary science at Homerton College, Cambridge and as a Key Stage 2 class teacher. She is a member of the editorial board of *Primary Science Review* and for four years was the assistant editor. She has written a number of books for early years teachers and non-fiction books for Key Stage 2 children.

Patricia Maude has taught physical education for many years to children and teachers in primary schools and to trainee teachers in the former Homerton College, now within the University of Cambridge Faculty of Education. She has also contributed to conferences both in the UK and abroad. Recent publications include a chapter concerned with the language of physical education in Eve Bearne's book *Use of Language across the Primary Curriculum* (1998, Routledge) and two books, *Gymnastics* (1997, Hodder Primary PE) and *Physical Children, Active Teaching* (2001, Open University Press). In the New Year's Honours 2000, she received an MBE for services to physical education.

Annie Owen worked as a classroom teacher for nine years, and then as an advisory teacher before coming to Homerton College, where she worked until recently as a senior lecturer in maths education before taking up her current post at the London Institute of Education. She has written several mathematics books for the primary years and contributes regularly to *Junior Education*. Recently she has contributed extensively to a range of published primary maths schemes.

Pam Pointon worked as a classroom teacher for 13 years and then as a Research Fellow at the Centre for Global Education, University of York. She is currently a lecturer in primary geography at the University of Cambridge Faculty of Education. Her current research interests include work concerned with classroom environments.

Sallie Purkis was formerly a senior lecturer in history at Homerton College and is now better known as a consultant, reviewer and writer on primary history. She is a regular contributor to *Junior Education*, and a reviewer for the *TES* and *Teaching History*. She is a consultant and author of teachers' notes for the BBC (*Watch* and *Radio History*) and Thames TV (*Seeing and Doing*). She has published extensively on primary history including a wide-ranging series of Key Stage 1 and 2 children's history books for Longmans.

Laurie Rousham was a teacher and a Headteacher in primary schools in Suffolk from 1972-90, teaching children aged 4-11. Having worked as a senior lecturer in mathematics education at Homerton College, he is now a

Numeracy Consultant for Suffolk LEA. He has published articles and reviews for the *Times Education Supplement*, *Child Education* and *Junior Education* and has extensively researched the effects of calculator use on the mathematical education of young children.

John Siraj-Blatchford is a senior lecturer in science and technology education in the University of Cambridge Faculty of Education. He has been involved in research projects concerned with young children's technological literacy for a number of years and is currently co-director of the developmentally appropriate technology in early childhood (DATEC) project, a research and development project, funded by the EU. He has published extensively in relation to early years science, technology and ICT and is currently working on a book with David Whitebread concerned with supporting ICT in the early years.

Paul Warwick is currently a senior lecturer in primary science and professional studies in the University of Cambridge Faculty of Education. Before this he worked as deputy headteacher of a primary school and then as a primary science support teacher for Cambridgeshire LEA. He has published articles in *Questions* and *Primary Science Review*. His most recent area of research has concerned the use of writing frames as a learning and assessment tool in primary science lessons.

David Whitebread is a senior lecturer in psychology and early years education in the University of Cambridge Faculty of Education. Until recently he was also coordinator of the primary PGCE course. Before coming to Cambridge he taught in several primary schools, mostly in Leicestershire, for about 12 years. About half of this time he taught in Key Stage 1. His doctoral dissertation was concerned with the development of children's problem-solving abilities. He has published extensively on psychological approaches to young children's learning in relation to a variety of areas. His most recent publication is *The Psychology of Teaching and Learning in the Primary School* (RoutledgeFalmer, 2000). Currently he is involved in research with Essex EYDCP to establish guidelines for effective pedagogy in the foundation stage and with Cambridgeshire EYDCP to investigate the development of independent learning in the Foundation Stage.

Sally Wilkinson taught in primary schools in Suffolk for eight years, teaching children aged 4 to 9. She now works as an advisory teacher for English and is a literacy consultant for Suffolk LEA. She has published articles in *Primary English, English in Education* and is currently working on two projects producing English resource materials for Year 2 and Key Stage 2 teachers.

ACKNOWLEDGEMENTS

Vygotsky's model of the 'zone of proximal development', Figure 1.1, is reproduced with permission from *Understanding Children's Development 2nd edition* (p. 353) by Peter K. Smith and Helen Cowie, 1991, Oxford: Blackwell Publishers. **Bruner's nine glasses problem**. Figure 1.2, is reprinted with permission from *Studies in Cognitive Growth* (p. 156) edited by J.S. Bruner *et al.*, 1966, New York: John Wiley & Sons Ltd. **The growth of neural connections in the brain**, Figure 1.4, from *Mapping the Mind* by R. Carter, 1998, London: Weidenfeld & Nicolson, is reproduced with permission from Moonrunner Design Ltd. **Tandy Adlam's nursery class**, Figure 2.1 and **Plan of Tandy Adlam's nursery classroom**, Figure 2.2, are reproduced with grateful thanks to Sue Bainbridge, headteacher, Colleges Nursery School, Cambridge. **Children in Holly Linklater's class holding a tea party for Biff, Chip and Kipper**, Figure 2.4 and **Plan of Holly Linklater's reception classroom**, Figure 2.5, are reproduced with grateful thanks to Henry Weir, headteacher, Debden Primary School, Debden. Figures 4.2 to 4.8 are reproduced with grateful thanks to Kay. Dimelow, headteacher, Huntingdon Nursery School, Huntingdon. **The regular sequence of motor development in infants**, Figure 10.1, from *Understanding Child Development 1st edition* (p.202) by Spencer A. Rathus, 1998, is reprinted with permission of Brooks/Cole, an imprint of the Wadsworth Group, a division of Thomson Learning. **A beginning thrower**, Figure 10.2, and **A beginning and advanced runner**, Figure 10.3, are reprinted with permission from K.M. Haywood and N. Getchell, 2001, *Life Span Motor Development 3rd edition* (Champaign, IL: Human Kinetics). The figures **A beginning thrower and a beginning runner** were originally redrawn from film tracing provided by the Motor Development and Child Study Laboratory, University of

Wisconsin-Madison. **An advanced 6-year-old-kicker**, Figure 10.4, and **The leap**, Figure 10.5, are reproduced by permission of PCET Wallcharts Ltd, 27 Kirchen Road, London W13 OUD and Jan Traylen. Photographs are by Jan Traylen, 1994, from wallcharts entitled *Games Skills* and *Gymnastic Skills*. **Snake paintings**, Figure 12.1 and **Sewn pizzas**, Figure 12.2, are reproduced with grateful thanks to Anne Horler, principal, Horler's Preparatory School, Comberton. We would also like to thank Birmingham City Council, Curriculum Support Service for allowing us to use Figures 16.4 to 16.6. This material comes from *Harborne Infant School Local History Project*. **Goodey's (1973) model of geographical experiences**, Figure 17.1, is reproduced by permission of the University of Birmingham Centre for Urban and Regional Studies. The diagram, originally titled **Child in information space**, is from *Perception in the Environment: An Introduction to the Literature*, occasional paper n.17 by B. Goodey, 1973 (p. 7). The extract on p. 313 from *Geography in the National Curriculum: Non-statutory Guidance for Teachers*, 1991 (p. 4) is reproduced by permission of the copyright holder, the Curriculum Council for Wales, Cardiff. The extract on p. 315 from *Geography for Ages 5–16*, DFES, London, 1990, extract from *Geography from 5–16*, DES, London, 1986, and p. 316 **Aims for geographical education**, from *Geography for ages 5–16*, DES, London, 1990 are all reproduced with permission. Crown copyright is reproduced with the permission of the controller of HMSO, Norwich. **Exploring the seaside; a geographical enquiry**, Figure 17.3, from *Non-statutory Guidance for Geography*, 1991, is reproduced by permission of the Curriculum Council for Wales, Cardiff.

PREFACE

When I wrote the preface for the first edition of this book six years ago, I commented that we found ourselves publishing at a time of critical importance for early years education in the UK and maybe in other parts of the world as well. At long last the crucial importance of good quality early years education was finally being recognised, research evidence that children's success in school and other aspects of their life can be significantly enhanced by quality educational experiences when they are very young was finally being taken seriously.

As a consequence, in 1996 a number of changes in the educational provision for young children were beginning to emerge and there have certainly been very significant developments in the UK in the intervening period. Through the creation of Early Years Care and Education Partnerships, educational provision has, for the first time, been provided for all 3- and 4-year-olds. There have, of course, been considerable battles about an appropriate curriculum for this age range. However, the establishment of a distinct Foundation Stage, covering the nursery and reception years, with its own Early Learning Goals and curriculum guidance, has been a huge step forward. The emphases on play, on personal, social and health education and on children's self-initiated activities have been widely welcomed.

However, the situation for 5-7-year-olds is not nearly so promising. There has been mounting concern about the effects of the introduction of the literacy and numeracy strategies at Key Stage 1. While both these strategies are bristling with ideas for good practice, the overall effect of the introduction of literacy and numeracy 'hours' into many Key Stage 1 classrooms has resulted in an unrelieved diet of seat-based, teacher-directed tasks throughout the morning that does not meet the needs of many 5–7-year-olds. Imaginative play, for example, has more or less disappeared beyond the reception year. Opportunities for these young children to develop independent learning skills are also not very evident.

Further than this, there has been inevitable downward pressure on reception class teachers to introduce elements of the literacy and numeracy hours with their children, to 'prepare' them for Key Stage 1. By contrast, many early years educators would argue that 5–7-old-children would benefit from the extension of the principles of the Foundation Stage to cover all children aged 3–7 years, and that the formal learning of literacy and numeracy is best left for Key Stage 2. Evidence from the experience of different practices in other European countries, where this later introduction of formality is the norm, would seem to strongly support this position.

What is clearly the case, however, is that all these concerns and developments have led, as I hoped they would in 1996, to an increase in the status and numbers of well-qualified early years teachers working with our young children. Resources are now being made available by the UK government to ensure that our young children are being educated by teachers and other educators who are better trained and more professionally prepared than ever before. I would also like to think, of course, that this book will help to enhance the quality of their preparation for the endlessly fascinating and challenging task of educating 3–7-year-old children.

The original impetus to produce this book arose from a perceived absence of published material written in a way that would interest and serve the needs of our early years trainees. We wanted to produce a book which introduced and discussed general principles of early years education, but at the same time showed how these translated into practical activities in the classroom. The spirit of this book is that with thought and imagination young children can be taught in ways which incorporate the demands of the early learning goals and the national curriculum, but which do much more. The book is intended to convey the strong research base related to children's learning and development upon which all good early years teaching must be founded. It is also intended to demonstrate that the best teaching of young children must have a strong element of fun and wonder and excitement.

All sound teaching of young children is based upon understandings about how young children learn, and the book begins with an analysis of current research in this area. Principles which derive from this research inform the subsequent sections of the book concerned with different aspects of early years teaching and the early years curriculum.

There follows a section on basic principles and approaches that discusses issues related to the management of the early years learning environment. This is followed by a series of chapters concerned with play and language, the basics of early years education. A further section examines the wider curriculum of the arts, maths, technology and science, the social sciences and physical education. Each chapter examines basic principles and illuminates them with inspiring, practical examples of classroom activities.

In this second edition, of course, there has been extensive revision and updating in many chapters. In my introductory chapter, for example, I have briefly reviewed recent work on the brain and its implications for early years education. The chapter on writing now contains examples of word-processing. There are also three completely new chapters, concerned with PSHE, one of the areas of learning in the Foundation Stage, with ICT (the impact of which has mushroomed in the last six years) and with children's art.

The book is principally directed at early years trainee teachers, but it is also hoped contains material that will be of interest to the whole range of teaching and non-teaching professionals and other adults concerned with the education of young children. The term 'educator' has been used throughout the book in preference to 'teacher' in an attempt to include and recognise this wider group of adults working in early years education.

British nursery and infant education has long enjoyed an international reputation for high quality. This book is most of all a reaffirmation of this tradition and an attempt to help maintain and improve the quality of the education offered to our young children.

David Whitebread
January 2002

CHAPTER 1

Introduction

YOUNG CHILDREN LEARNING AND EARLY YEARS TEACHING

David Whitebread

There has traditionally been a strong association between understandings about child development and early years teaching. This book is written, however, at a particularly exciting time in this regard. The relationship between developmental research and the practices of teaching young children is currently a rich area of growth and development. This book is an attempt to distil the current state of knowledge about the ways in which young children (up to the age of 7) develop and learn, to show how educational principles derive from this, and to illustrate these principles with practical examples drawn from work in early years classrooms. In this introductory chapter I want to show how psychological research concerned with child development informs the principles of practice exemplified throughout the rest of the book.

There is a long tradition of ideas about children and their learning in early years education. In the nineteenth and early twentieth centuries these were largely developed by a number of outstanding and inspiring educators. Tina Bruce (1987) has provided an excellent review of the ideas of Froebel, Montessori, Steiner and others, derived ten common principles of early years education and attempted to show how these relate to modern research. These principles emphasise the holistic nature of children's learning and development (as distinct from learning separated out into subjects), the importance of developing autonomy, intrinsic motivation and self-discipline through the encouragement of child-initiated, self-directed activity, the value of firsthand experiences and the crucial role in children's development of other children and adults.

As we shall see, many of these ideas have been reinforced by modern psychological research; they have also been extended and developed in interesting and important ways. Much of current thinking about children's learning has been influenced by the work and ideas of three outstanding developmental psychologists – Jean Piaget, Lev Vygotsky and Jerome Bruner – and so it is with their contributions that we begin.

Piaget

The first major developmental psychologist to influence classroom practice was, of course, Jean Piaget. His ideas were welcomed enthusiastically in the 1960s because they were a reaction to the 'behaviourist' view of learning current within psychology and education at the time, with which people were increasingly unhappy. The behaviourist view placed the child in a passive position and viewed learning simply as a combination of imitation and conditioning by means of external rewards and reinforcements. This model works quite well as a way of explaining how you can teach parrots to roller-skate, but it is a woefully inadequate explanation of the range and flexibility of the achievements of the human child.

A huge amount has been written about Piaget's theory and its influence upon primary education. Brainerd (in Meadows, 1983) and Davis (1991) provide good reviews of the impact on education. On the positive side, the most important contribution of Piaget's work was to alert educators to the child's active role in their learning, and the importance of mental activity (see Howe, 1999). Piaget showed how children actively attempt to make sense of their world and construct their own understandings.

On the negative side, Piaget's emphasis on stages of development appears to have been ill-founded and resulted in serious underestimation of the abilities of young children (see Wood, 1998). The work of Margaret Donaldson (1978) and many other developmental psychologists subsequently has demonstrated that Piaget's tasks (such as his famous conservation tasks) were difficult for young children for a whole range of extraneous reasons unconnected to the child's understanding of the underlying concept. These tasks were too abstract and did not make sense to young children, they over-relied on rather sophisticated linguistic competence, and they were embedded in misleading social contexts. Interestingly, one of the major areas of discovery as regards young children's learning in recent years has related to their peculiar sensitivity to these kinds of contextual factors. This is an issue to which I want to return later in the chapter and, as we shall see, it has important implications for early years teaching.

More recent evidence has suggested that young children arrive at school with many more capabilities than was previously thought, and was suggested by Piaget. The pioneering work of Tizard and Hughes (1984) in the area of language, and of Gelman and Gallistel (1978) in relation to young children's understandings about number, are good examples here. Both suggested that children's abilities were being systematically under-appreciated by teachers, for much the same reasons as they had been by Piaget. In school, children were being faced by ideas or tasks taken out of any meaningful context, and for no clear purposes, and they were finding them difficult. In the home environment, when the same ideas or tasks occurred naturally, embedded in real meaning and purposes, the same children understood and managed them with ease.

Vygotsky

Piaget has also been criticised for under emphasising the role in children's learning of language and of social interaction with other children and with adults. The ideas of the Russian psychologist, Lev Vygotsky, have been an important influence in this area (see Smith, Cowie and Blades, 1998, for an introduction and Moll, 1990, for an extensive review of educational implications).

Piaget had emphasised the importance of the child interacting with the physical environment, and his followers in the educational sphere argued that the role of the teacher should be that of an observer and a facilitator. The general view of this approach was that attempting to directly teach or instruct young children was a mistake. It was claimed that whenever teachers attempted to teach children something, they simply deprived the children of the opportunity to discover it for themselves.

This view was partly a reaction against the simplistic 'behaviourist' model that children only learnt what they were taught. To some extent, however, it can be seen to have thrown the baby out with the bath water. More recent research inspired by the work of Vygotsky has argued that there is a much more central role for the adult, and, indeed, for other children, in the processes of learning. This role is not as an instructor delivering knowledge, however, but rather as a 'scaffolder' (a metaphor suggested by Jerome Bruner; see Smith, Cowie and Blades 1998, pp. 437–41) supporting, encouraging and extending the child's own active search for understanding.

Perhaps the most significant idea within Vygotsky's model of human learning is that of the 'zone of proximal development', as illustrated in Figure 1.1. Faced with any particular task or problem, children can operate at one level on their own, described as their 'level of actual development'. But they can perform at a higher level when supported or 'scaffolded' by an adult or more experienced peer, described as their 'level of potential development'. The 'zone of proximal development' (or ZPD) is that area of learning described by

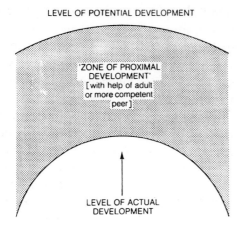

LEVEL OF POTENTIAL DEVELOPMENT

'ZONE OF PROXIMAL
DEVELOPMENT'
[with help of adult
or more competent
peer]

LEVEL OF ACTUAL
DEVELOPMENT

the difference between these two levels of performance or understanding. Vygotsky and his followers have argued, therefore, that children learn most effectively through social interaction, when they are involved in jointly constructing new understandings within their ZPD.

Figure 1.1 *Vygotsky's model of the 'zone of proximal development'*

Bruner

This view has been supported by evidence of the significant role of language within learning. The work of Jerome Bruner has been influential in regard to this issue (see, for example, Wood, 1998, for a discussion of Bruner's ideas on language and thought). Bruner described language as a 'tool of thought', and demonstrated in a range of studies the ways in which language enables children to develop their thinking and perform tasks which would otherwise be impossible. In his famous 'Nine glasses problem' (see Figure 1.2), for example, he showed that children who could describe the patterns in a 3 x 3 matrix of glasses (which were taller or shorter one way and thinner or fatter the other) were also able to transform the matrix (i.e. arrange the glasses in a mirror image pattern). Children without the relevant

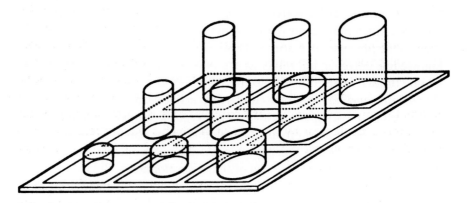

Figure 1.2 *Bruner's nine glasses problem*

language to call on, however, were only able to reproduce the pattern exactly as they had seen it.

It is now widely recognised that providing children with a relevant vocabulary and requiring them to formulate their ideas in discussion, is a vital element in helping children to develop flexibility in thinking and construct their own understandings about the world.

This has led to the recognition that a certain style of interaction between adults and children, and between pairs or small groups of children, can be enormously beneficial to learning. Paul Light (in Meadows, 1983) has provided a useful review of research indicating that this style involves dialogue between adults and children in which there is 'co-construction' of meanings. Forman and Cazden (1985) have reviewed work demonstrating the help to learning provided by collaboration and dialogue between children.

Jerome Bruner's other major contribution to our understandings about young children as learners is encapsulated in his phrase 'the spiral curriculum'. This is his view that, in principle, anything can be taught to children of any age, provided it is presented in a way that is accessible to them. Thus, having encountered a set of ideas at a practical level when they are young, they will use this knowledge to help them understand the same ideas at a more symbolic or abstract level when they are older. So learning is viewed as a spiral in which the same point is returned to and revisited but each time at a higher or deeper level. He demonstrated this by, for example, successfully teaching 8-year-old children to understand quadratic equations. He achieved this by providing them with the practical example of working out the area of rectangles (see Wood, 1st Edn,1988, ch. 7, for a review of this work).

Bruner's view about the constraints upon children's learning is very much in line with a whole range of contemporary research. Piaget's earlier notion that children are limited in what they can understand by certain kinds of logical deficiencies in their reasoning powers has been largely dismissed. As Margaret Donaldson (1978) argued, research shows that adults make the same kinds of logical errors as children, and have difficulties with the same kinds of reasoning problems. Children's learning is now seen as being limited much more simply by their lack of experience and of accumulated knowledge. This makes it more difficult for them to see what is relevant in any new situation, and to see what is the best way to proceed. When this is made clear by the context in which a task is presented, however, children's potential for learning is phenomenal and often way beyond our normal expectations, as Bruner ably demonstrated.

The current view of children as learners, therefore, is one that recognises their considerable appetite and aptitude for learning. However, it is also important to recognise the nature of children's limitations and their particular needs if they are to flourish. These needs are both emotional and intellectual. As we shall see, research evidence suggests that to become effective learners young children need love and security, and they need intellectual challenge. In the remainder of this chapter I want to examine these needs and their implications for educational environments. The chapter concludes with a brief look at emerging knowledge about the brain and some tentative thoughts about implications for early years education. Then finally, lest we forget the importance of the enterprise upon which we are embarked, there is a short discussion of the evidence concerning the impact of quality early years education on children's later development.

The need for love and security

On the emotional side, in order to develop into effective learners within the school context it is clear that young children need love and security. An important element in the tradition of early years education has always been a recognition of the need to consider the whole child. Children's learning and intellectual development is inseparable from their emotional and social development. In their early years, as well as mastering fundamental skills and understandings, young children are also forming their basic attitudes to themselves as people and as learners. The basic attitudes they form at this stage have major implications for their future educational progress.

An enormous body of research evidence collected by developmental psychologists supports this view. High self-esteem and feelings of self-efficacy are strongly related to educational success, and low self-esteem and what has been termed 'learned helplessness' are equally related to educational difficulty. It is difficult to attribute cause and effect here, but there is clearly a positive cycle of mutual interaction between self-belief and achievement and, sadly, a negative downward spiral associated with self-doubt and failure. Rogers and Kutnick (1990) have provided a useful survey of work in this area and its important implications for teachers.

Essentially, there are three aspects to this. If they are to thrive emotionally and intellectually, young children need to feel **love and self-worth**, they need to feel **emotionally secure** and they need to feel **in control**.

Love and self-worth

Psychologists have investigated in considerable detail the ways in which young children's sense of self develops in the first few years of life. From the earliest emergence within the first year of bodily awareness, and the recognition of the distinction between self and not-self, young children's sense of self becomes rapidly differentiated. They develop a self-image of them-selves as individuals, a self-identity of the sort of people they are and to which groups they belong (child, boy/girl, race, types of ability and so on), a distinction between their private and public selves (with an increasing number of roles within which they see themselves – son/daughter, sibling, friend, pupil), an ideal self to which they aspire, feelings of self-esteem and of self-worth.

In all this a crucial element is the ways in which they are viewed and treated by significant others in their lives. The metaphor has been developed by psychologists working in this area of the self as a mirror. Children's views about themselves develop as a reflection of the views transmitted to them by others in social interaction. This has also often been referred to as the Pygmalion effect, after the famous play by Shaw. In the play a flower girl is treated by everyone as a lady (after some grooming by Professor Higgins) and so she starts to view herself as a lady, and becomes one. All the evidence suggests that children who develop positive self-images and feelings of self-worth are those who have been surrounded in their earliest years by unconditional love and emotional warmth. Their parents or other carers have transmitted to them very powerfully that they are valued by others, and so they come to value themselves.

Emotional security

Alongside positive attitudes to themselves, young children need to develop feelings of trust in relation to their environment. The significance of feelings of emotional security was first highlighted by Harlow's famous experiments in the 1950s with baby monkeys. The initial experiments offered the babies a choice of two substitute but inanimate 'mothers', one which was soft and cuddly and another which was metal and hard but provided milk. The babies spent the vast majority of their time cuddling up to the soft model. Perhaps even more significantly, Harlow discovered that babies provided with a cuddly 'mother' of this kind became much more adventurous in exploring their environment than babies who were deprived of this obvious source of comfort.

In the 1950s the view was advanced by Bowlby that the emotional secu-rity needed by young children should ideally be provided by the biological mother or, failing that, by one constant adult figure in the child's life. In his excellent review of this and subsequent research, however, Rudolph Schaffer (1977) demonstrated that care did not need to be provided by one particular adult continuously. Rather, the quality and consistency of care emerged from research to be the crucial factors. The quality of care appears to be mostly a matter of how responsive the adult is to the child. The consistency of care is vital in giving the child a sense that their world is predictable. This has two elements, first that the same actions by the child produces the same response by the adult, and second that transitions between adult carers are handled carefully so that the child understands the programme of events.

Young children's almost obsessive concern for fairness (with rules applied consistently) and their strong preference for routine can be seen as clear outcomes of their need for emotional security. Their love of hearing familiar stories endlessly repeated is possibly a manifestation of the same phenomenon. This need for their experience to be predictable and to follow clear rules is very much linked to their need intellectually to make sense of their world, to which we return later. Emotionally, it is also strongly linked to their need to feel in control, to which we turn now.

Feeling in control

We have probably all played that game with young children of a certain age where the child performs an action, we respond in some way, and the child laughs (the 'dropping things out of the pram' game is a good example). Immediately the child does it again, we repeat our response and there is more laughter. And so it goes on, and on, and on. The adult always tires of this game before the child does because the child is in the process of discovering something really wonderful. He or she is in control of the world, and can make things happen.

This feeling of empowerment is fundamental to children developing positive attitudes to themselves, and particularly to themselves as learners. Within modern developmental psychology there has been a huge amount of research about this aspect of emotional development and its relation to motivation. This research has been concerned with examining what is called 'attribution theory' because it is concerned with the causes to which children attribute their successes and failures. Where children feel that their performance is determined by factors within their control (for example, how much effort they put into a particular task) they will respond positively to failure and try harder next time, believing all the time in their own ability to be successful in the task. Where they feel that their performance is determined by factors outside of their control (for example, their level of ability, or luck) they will respond negatively to failure and give up, believing that they will not succeed however much they try. It is clear that such 'learned helplessness' is extremely damaging to children's development as learners.

This model of 'attributions' explains well how poor self-esteem can result in lack of motivation, which in turn leads to lack of effort and consequent poor performance, confirming the children's view of themselves. Failing children thus becomes locked into a destructive self-fulfilling prophecy. In order to avoid this it is clearly vital that adults working with young children do everything in their power to give them the feeling of being in control.

Research on parenting styles is quite helpful here. Broadly speaking, researchers have found that it is possible to categorise parenting styles into three broad types. First, there is the 'autocratic' style, where rules are entirely constructed by the parent and enforced arbitrarily and inconsistently without explanation. At the opposite extreme there is the 'laissez-faire' style where there are no rules to which the child is expected to conform. Both these styles communicate low expectations to the child, a lack of responsiveness and consistency, and children suffering under these kinds of regimes typically have low self-esteem and little emotional security.

The third style is what might be termed 'authoritative' or 'democratic'. Here there are rules to which the child is expected to conform, they are applied consistently and they are discussed and negotiated with the child. Under this kind of regime children typically have high self-esteem and feel in control.

Implications for the early years teacher

- Create an atmosphere of emotional warmth, within which each child feels individually valued.
- Communicate high expectations to all children.
- Praise and recognise children's achievements, particularly when they are the result of a special effort.
- Run an orderly classroom that has regular classroom routines.
- Always explain to the children the programme of events for the day and prepare them for transitions.
- Put children in control of their own learning; allow them to make choices.
- Exercise democratic control; involve children in decisions about classroom rules and procedures and enforce rules fairly.
- Criticise a child's actions, but never the child.

The need for intellectual challenge

While it is clear that there is an intimate link between emotional and intellectual development, love and security on their own are not enough. Young children also need intellectual challenge. As we have reviewed, Piaget first argued, and it is now widely accepted, that children learn by a process of actively constructing their own understandings. All the evidence suggests that a learning environment that helps children to do this will, not surprisingly, be one which challenges them intellectually and stimulates them to be mentally active. It also turns out to be crucial, once again, that the children are put in control. Such an environment will provide **new experiences**, embedded in **meaningful contexts**, opportunities for **active styles of learning**, involving children in **problem-solving, investigations** and opportunities for **self-expression**, and, perhaps most crucially of all, opportunities for learning through **play**.

Play

If we are to understand anything about the ways in which young children learn, we must understand first the central role of play. The distinction between work and play is entirely misleading in the context of young children's learning, for much of the evidence suggests that play is when children do their real learning (see Moyles, 1989). Children's language development, for example, is commonly associated with playful approaches and activities – making up nonsense words, verbal jokes and puns, silly rhymes and so forth are all much enjoyed and of great benefit.

It was Bruner (1972), in a famous article entitled 'The nature and uses of immaturity', who first pointed out the relationship across different animal species between the capacity for learning and the length of immaturity, or dependence upon adults. He also pointed out that as the period of immaturity lengthens, so does the extent to which the young are playful. He argued that play is one of the key experiences through which young animals learn, and also the means by which their intellectual abilities themselves are developed. The human being, of course, has a much greater length of immaturity than any other animal, plays more and for longer, and is supreme, of course, in our ability to learn.

The crucial aspect of human intellectual ability that enables us to learn so effectively, Bruner argues, is our flexibility of thought. Play, he suggests, is all about developing flexibility of thought. It provides opportunities to try out possibilities, to put different elements of a situation together in various ways, to look at problems from different viewpoints. He demonstrated this in a series of experiments (e.g. see Sylva, Bruner and Genova, 1984) where children were asked to solve practical problems. Typically in these experiments, one group of children was given the opportunity to play with the objects involved, while the other group was 'taught' how to use the objects in ways which would help solve the problem. When they were then asked to tackle the problem, similar numbers of children in the two groups were completely successful. However, the 'taught' children who failed to solve the problem gave up very quickly. By contrast, the children who had the experience of playing with the materials persevered longer when their initial attempts did not work, were much more inventive in devising a range of strategies to solve the problem, and generally came much closer to a solution. Crucially, while the 'taught' children appeared to be just learning, or failing to learn, one specific 'menu' to solve one specific problem, the children who played were learning far more generalisable skills, and far more positive attitudes to problem-solving. They were, indeed learning how to learn.

Observation of children at play gives some indication of why it might be such a powerful learning medium. During play children are usually totally engrossed in what they are doing. It is quite often repetitive and contains a strong element of practice. During play children set their own level of challenge, and so what they are doing is always developmentally appropriate (to a degree that tasks set by adults will never be). Play is spontaneous and initiated by the children themselves; in other words, during play children are in control of their own learning.

Mari Guha (1987) has argued that this last element is particularly significant. There are many examples in psychological research of tasks where being in control has turned out to be crucial for effective learning. Guha cites, for example, experiments concerned with visual learning in which subjects are required to wear 'goggles' that make everything look upside down. They are then required to sit in a wheelchair and learn to move safely through an environment. The results of such experiments show that subjects moving themselves around the environment (and having a lot of initial 'crashes') learn to do this much more quickly than those who are wheeled safely about by an adult helper.

The parallels here with Bruner's 'play' and 'taught' groups are striking. The implications for how we can most effectively help young children to learn are also striking. A simple model which suggests that children learn what we teach them is clearly unsustainable. There is a role for the adult, however, in providing the right kind of learning environment, and this clearly needs to provide opportunities for play. Whenever a new material or process is introduced, for example, it is clear that children's learning will be enhanced if they are first allowed to play with them. When new information is being introduced, children need to be offered opportunities to incorporate this into their play also. As we discussed earlier, there is also a role for the adult in 'scaffolding' children's experiences within the learning environment, and various ways of participating and intervening in children's play can be enormously beneficial. Manning and Sharp (1977) have provided a very thorough and practical analysis of ways in which educators can, by these means, usefully structure and extend children's play in the classroom.

New experiences

Anyone who has spent any time at all with young children, and attempted to answer all the questions they keep asking, will be well aware of their apparently insatiable curiosity. I am reminded of the manic robot Johnny 5 in the film *Short Circuit* who continually and voraciously craves 'input'. Part of the notion of young children as active learners is a recognition of their compelling need for new experiences. Providing that they feel emotionally secure, as we have discussed, they will enthusiastically explore their environment and are highly motivated by novelty.

From the psychological perspective this is not surprising. It is one of the other distinguishing features of the human brain that it does, indeed, require a certain level of input. Unlike almost all other animals, we are very easily bored. If insufficient new information is being provided by the environment, furthermore, the human brain will provide its own amusement. Everyday, we all daydream. In extreme circumstances (for example, in sensory deprivation experiments where the subject is kept motionless in a completely dark, soundproof booth) this can result in powerful hallucinations.

Within psychological research this kind of work has underpinned a well-established relationship, known as the Yerkes–Dodson law, linking individuals' state of arousal and their performance on a task. Too little stimulation produces boredom and too much stimulation produces anxiety. Both are dysfunctional in terms of performance on a task, and of learning.

Thus, while we need to ensure that children feel in control of their classroom environment, we also need to ensure that they find it a stimulating, exciting and motivating place to be. We must never underestimate young children's abilities to absorb new information and to cope with new ideas. Young children, for example, love being introduced to new vocabulary, especially if the words are long and/or difficult (e.g. tyrannosaurus, equilateral, strato-cumulus, etc.). Further, there is an age-related factor here, whereby typically our optimum level of stimulation decreases as we get older. The chances are, therefore, that if you as an adult are feeling really comfortable with the pace of events in a classroom, some of the children will be bored!

Meaningful contexts

The dominant model in contemporary psychological research concerned with human learning is that of the child as an active information processor. As such, the child attempts to make sense of, and derive meaning from, experience by means of classifying, categorising and ordering new information and relating it to what is already known. This inductive style of learning involving the identification of patterns and regularities from the variety of our experience is a very dominant aspect of human functioning. The astonishing facility with which children learn their first language, by working out the rules for themselves (aided by a little 'motherese') is a good example of the power of inductive processes.

This search for patterns and regularities within the variety of experience has important implications for the ways in which young children make sense of new experiences. They expect to find pattern and regularity, and they expect new experiences to fit together in some way with what they already know. This was beautifully illustrated by an experiment in which young children were asked 'bizarre' questions, such as 'Is milk bigger than water?' and 'Is red heavier than yellow?' (see Hughes and Grieve in Donaldson, Grieve and Pratt, 1983). What happened was that the children answered the questions and did so in ways which illustrated their attempt to make sense of them in terms of the context in which they were asked and their own previous experience. Thus, they might reply that 'Milk is bigger than water because it's creamier' or 'Red is heavier than yellow because the yellow is a little plastic box and the red paint's got a big plastic box'.

As Hughes et al. point out, what the children were doing in response to these bizarre questions is what they do all the time when they are faced with new information or problems. It is for this reason that children's performance and understanding is always likely to be enhanced when tasks are presented in ways that help young children to make sense of them in the light of what they already know. In other words, tasks need to be placed in contexts that are meaningful to young children.

As we noted earlier, many of Piaget's tasks have been criticised precisely on the grounds that their meaning was not clear and children misinterpreted them in their attempts to make sense of them, based upon their previous experience. Donaldson (1978) reviewed a number of alternative versions of Piagetian tasks where an attempt had been made to place them in meaningful contexts and thus make their purpose more intelligible to young children.

For example, Piaget's famous number conservation task consisted of showing the child two equal rows of buttons (as shown in Figure 1.3, Part 1) and asking the child whether there are more white buttons or black buttons, or whether they are the same. One of the rows was then transformed by the experimenter (as shown in Figure 1.3, Part 2) and the question was repeated. Piaget found that many young children could correctly recognise that the first two rows contained the same number, but said there were more white buttons in the second condition. He concluded that these young children were overwhelmed by their perceptions and that they lacked the logical understanding of the conservation of number.

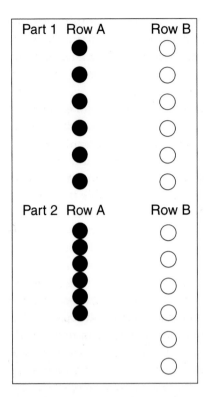

Figure 1.3 *Piaget's number conservation problem*

When this task was repeated, however, by a colleague of Margaret Donaldson's, the transformation of one of the rows of buttons was effected by a 'naughty teddy' glove puppet. In these circumstances many more young children were able to say that the two rows still contained the same number.

Donaldson concludes that the introduction of the naughty teddy changes the meaning for the child of the second question. This question is made sense of by the children in relation to the social situation and their own previous experience. When the adult transforms the pattern and repeats the question, this means to some children that their first answer was wrong and the adult is helping them to see the correct answer. In the amended version, the second question is a cue to check that the naughty teddy hasn't lost or added any buttons during his mischief.

The lessons for the early years teacher are clear. Young children do not passively receive the information we provide for them. They are engaged continually in a process of active interpretation and transformation of new information. If we want to help them to make sense of their educational experiences we must ensure that we place new tasks in contexts that will enhance their meaning for young children. This often means actively making links with what the children already know and presenting the activity in the context of a story or game. As a consequence of children's limited symbolic understandings, it also means that hands-on experiences, where the children are gaining information directly through their senses, is always likely to be more effective. It is also a rationale for organising activities within the meaningful context of children's interests or a cross-curricular topic.

If children are to use their powerful inductive processes to find patterns and regularities in their experience, it is also important to present the same ideas, concepts or processes in a variety of such meaningful contexts. Only in this way can children begin to disentangle what is relevant and what is irrelevant in relation to any particular idea. Children who are taught one way of carrying out a particular process are often left confused about the essential nature of the task. I have been told by young children that you cannot add together two numbers written side by side, you have to put one of them underneath the other. I also remember one of my own young daughters, on returning from a visit to the science museum, telling me excitedly about this machine she had seen (which sounded like an internal combustion engine from her description). When asked what she thought it was for, she replied that there was a lot of gravel all around it, so she thought it might be making that. Now she has seen lots of machines in different contexts, she has induced that the gravel around museum exhibits is usually purely cosmetic.

Mental activity

An important feature of the human brain is that we all find enjoyment in mental activity. As we have discussed, it was Piaget who first drew attention to the fundamental relationship between mental activity and learning. The kind of mental activity we need for learning can be stimulated in two main ways, through problem-solving and self-expression. Both of these processes require us to restructure what we know and to make use of it in new ways. It is well established within modern developmental psychology that this kind of restructuring is required to integrate new information into our existing conceptual framework. In a very important sense, this is the essence of real learning.

Within a number of areas of research, the relationship between mental activity and learning has been clearly demonstrated. For example, within memory research, a range of research has confirmed what is known as the 'generation effect'. Information that has at least been partly generated or transformed in some way is always more memorable than that which has been simply received. It is for this reason that teaching spellings by providing anagrams from which the children have to generate the words is always more effective than simply giving a list of the words. Michael Howe (1999) usefully reviews a number of experiments that have demonstrated this point, and that suggest more active ways of presenting information to young children.

Problem-solving is fundamental to human intellectual functioning. It is part of our need to make sense of our experience and gain control over our environment. Robert Fisher (1987, 1990), amongst others, has argued that as educators we can most effectively harness the power of young children's abilities to learn by presenting new ideas and information as problems to be solved, or areas to be investigated, for purposes that are meaningful and real to the children. He has also produced excellent reviews of the justification and practice of this kind of approach within primary education.

Within the purely cognitive sphere, however, it is also important because of the processes of cognitive restructuring involved. There is good evidence to suggest that the process of self-expression is important in helping children to understand and make sense of their experiences. The Vygotskian notion of learning through the co-construction of meanings in social situations (as reviewed by Light, in Meadows, 1983) and Bruner's notion of language as a 'tool of thought' are important here. In their explorations of young children's use of language in the home and school, Tizard and Hughes (1984) have presented evidence of children engaging in processes of intellectual search through talk. The kinds of meaningful dialogues with adults that are likely to stimulate this kind of mental activity, however, they found to be much more common in the home environment than in the school. They argue that as educators we must find means of developing quality conversations between ourselves and the children in our classrooms.

One way into this kind of activity that would appear to be well worth pursuing is that offered by the 'philosophy for children' approach originally developed by Matthew Lipman and reviewed by Costello (2000). In essence, this approach consists of posing children with moral or ethical problems through the contexts of stories and then engaging them in philosophical debate about the issues raised. Children are encouraged to clarify their meanings, make explicit their assumptions, expose ambiguities and inconsistencies and so on. Exciting work has been done by using picture books with very young children (see, for example, Murris, 1992). Young children reveal impressive abilities to reason, argue and use talk to communicate meaning through this kind of activity, and develop a range of vital intellectual skills in the process.

One of the clear disadvantages of the classroom environment relative to the home is, of course, to do with the adult–child ratio. For this reason, it is also important to stimulate challenging talk between the children. As a consequence, a range of educators have urged the more extensive use of collaborative groupwork in primary classrooms (see, for example, Dunne and Bennett, 1990). As we reviewed earlier, research adopting a Vygotskian perspective (Forman and Cazden, 1985) has demonstrated the various ways in which peer interaction during collaborative groupwork can enhance performance and stimulate learning. Requiring children to work in groups to solve problems, carry out investigations, or produce an imaginative response in the form of writing, drama, dance or whatever is potentially of enormous benefit.

It is important to recognise that the value of self-expression is not limited to the medium of language. Requiring children to transform their experiences into various 'symbolic' modes of expression is likely to aid the processes of learning. When children draw, paint, dance, construct, model, make music and, indeed, play, they are engaged in the active process of making sense of their world in a way that is unique and individual to them, of which they are in control. The sheer vigour and enthusiasm with which young children engage in these kinds of activities is an important pointer to their significance.

Although I have attempted to separate out different elements in the psychological processes which relate to children's need for intellectual challenge, I must conclude by emphasising the powerful ways in which all these elements are of a piece. When children are playing, they are also nearly always problem-solving, or investigating, or engaging in various forms of self-expression. Play often helps children to place new information in meaningful contexts.

It is also important to recognise the ways in which intellectual challenge contributes to emotional or affective elements of children's development. It is no accident that humans find activities of the type we have discussed here immensely enjoyable. Adults at play, for example, are often enjoying the mental challenge of solving problems (crosswords, jigsaws, puzzles, games) or of expressing themselves (music, art, drama). With enjoyment comes concentration, mental effort, motivation and achievement. Self-expression is important in its own right because it builds upon and enhances children's sense of individuality and self-worth. Children who have experienced the excitement of finding things out for themselves or of solving problems are learning to take risks, to persevere and to become independent learners.

Implications for the early years teacher

- Provide opportunities for play of all kinds.
- Provide vivid, first hand, new experiences.
- Place tasks in meaningful contexts; help children to make sense of new experiences by relating them to what they already know.
- Introduce the same idea in a variety of meaningful contexts.
- Organise tasks to stimulate mental activity; adopt problem-solving and investigational approaches wherever possible.
- Provide opportunities for self-expression: when children have learnt something new, give them a chance to make something of their own from it.
- Provide opportunities for meaningful conversations between groups of the children, and between the children and adults.

The brain and early education

I have referred here and there in this chapter to evidence about the ways in which the human brain learns and develops. Following the huge expansion of research in neuroscience during the 1990s – dubbed the 'decade of the brain' – we now know enormously more about brain functioning and development than we did even when the first edition of this book was published six years ago. Neuroscientists and educators are increasingly talking to one another and some commentators have rushed to justify particular educational arguments by reference to brain research.

At this stage, we need to approach neuroscientific evidence with a good deal of caution, however. Serious research into the brain is still very much in its infancy and the one finding about the human brain that is incontrovertable is that it is enormously complex. The possibilities for misinterpretation and oversimplification are legion. Talk of 'educating the left side of the brain' or the 'brain-friendly' classroom is dangerously premature.

However, a number of useful reviews have already been compiled of evidence that is of relevance to early education (Blakemore, 2000) and education generally (Byrnes, 2001). Such evidence as we have so far does, at least, seem to support a number of important, general positions in regard to early education:

- The brain develops and learns by forming vast numbers of connections between brain cells in 'neural networks'; this supports the inductive nature of human learning and its implications for experiential learning, play and meaningful contexts.
- The overwhelming majority of these connections are formed in the first few years of life (see Figure 1.4) causing the human brain, uniquely, to quadruple in size between birth and 6 years of age; babies literally build their own brains, and the environments in which they do so are clearly significant.
- Processing in the young brain is quite generalised; specifically adapted regions gradually form over the first few years; consequently, requiring young children to learn in ways which depend upon later emerging functions is futile and potentially counter-productive; there are important implications here for the introduction of formal, disconnected learning and of tasks involving the manipulation of symbolic representations such as letters and numerals.

As we learn more about the early development of the brain, it will clearly be of interest to early years educators. Those readers who wish to be better informed at this stage might like to look at Rita Carter's (1998) excellent and well-illustrated introduction.

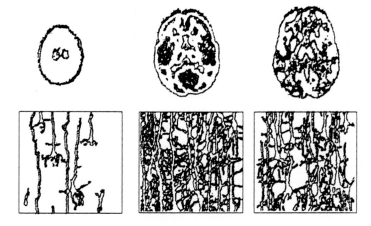

Neural connections are sparse at birth (left), but new connec-
tions are made at a terrific rate during infancy and by the
age of six (middle) they are at maximum density. Thereafter
they decrease again as unwanted connections die back.
(right.) Adults can increase neural connections throughout
their life by learning new things. But if the brain is not
used the connections will become further depleted.

Figure 1.4 *The growth of neural connections in the human brain (from Carter, 1998)*

The impact of quality in early years education

It is now well established that children's educational experience in the early years has both immediate effects upon their cognitive and social development and long-term effects upon their educational achievements and life prospects. Sylva and Wiltshire (1993) have reviewed a range of evidence which supports this position. This evidence includes studies of the Head Start programmes in the USA, the Child Health and Education Study (CHES) of a birth cohort in Britain and Swedish research on the effects of day care.

To begin with these various studies appear to produce inconsistent findings. Early studies of the Head Start programmes suggested immediate cognitive and social gains, but little lasting effect. The CHES study, on the other hand, found a clear association between pre-school attendance and educational achievements at age 10. Further analysis, however, reveals that lasting long-term effects are dependent upon the quality of the early educational experience. Sylva and Wiltshire note particularly the evidence of long-term impact achieved by High/Scope and other high-quality, cognitively orientated pre-school programmes.

What emerges as significant about these particularly effective early educational environments is very much in line with the kinds of directions indicated in this chapter. These environments offered real intellectual challenge in the ways we have discussed, with the adult educators very much in the Vygotskian role of 'scaffolding' the children's experiences. Within this framework, the children are put very much in control of their own learning.

In the High/Scope regime, for example, the central model of learning is the 'plan, do and review' cycle. Children plan their activities for the session or the day in a small group with an adult educator. They then move off to carry out the planned activities, and later return to review progress again with their small group and the adult educator. This pattern builds in purposeful adult–child and child–child conversations which seem to Sylva and Wiltshire to be 'an embodiment of Vygotsky's notion of effective instruction within the zone of proximal development' (1993, p. 36).

This way of working also places the responsibility very much on individual children for their own learning. What all the high-quality early years regimes identified by Sylva and Wiltshire did was to help children develop what they term a 'mastery' orientation to learning and to themselves. This relates very closely to the emotional issues we discussed earlier in the chapter. Children in high-quality early years environments developed feelings of high self-esteem, with high aspirations and secure feelings of self-efficacy. Such children grew to believe that, through effort, they could solve problems, understand new ideas, develop skills and so on. They felt in control of their environments and confident in their abilities.

These are some of the themes that this chapter has attempted to illuminate, and which permeate all the other chapters of this book. If we wish to provide quality learning environments for our young children, these need to be informed by understandings about how young children learn and develop. The rest of the present volume is dedicated to indicating how these understandings can be translated, imaginatively and reflectively, into the everyday practice of the early years classroom.

References

Blakemore, S.J. (2000) *Early Years Learning, Report 140*, POST (Parliamentary Office of Science & Technology).

Bruce, T. (1987) *Early Childhood Education*, London: Hodder & Stoughton.

Bruner, J.S. (1972) 'The nature and uses of immaturity', *American Psychologist*, 27, 1–28.

Byrnes, J.P. (2001) *Minds, Brains, and Learning*, London: Guilford Press.

Carter, R. (1998) *Mapping the Mind*, London: Weidenfeld & Nicolson

Costello, P. J. M. (2000) *Thinking Skills and Early Childhood Education*, London: David Fulton.

Davis, A. (1991) 'Piaget, teachers and education: into the 1990s', in P. Light, S. Sheldon and M. Woodhead (eds) *Learning to Think*, London: Routledge.

Donaldson, M. (1978) *Children's Minds*, London: Fontana.

Donaldson, M., Grieve, R. and Pratt, C. (eds) (1983) *Early Childhood Development and Education*, Oxford: Basil Blackwell.

Dunne, E. and Bennett, N. (1990) *Talking and Learning in Groups*, London: Macmillan.

Fisher, R. (1987) *Problem-solving in Primary Schools*, Oxford: Basil Blackwell.

Fisher, R. (1990) *Teaching Children to Think*, Oxford: Basil Blackwell.

Forman, E.A. and Cazden, C.B. (1985) 'Exploring Vygotskian perspectives in education: the cognitive value of peer interaction', in J.V. Wertsch (ed.) *Culture, Communication and Cognition*, Cambridge: Cambridge University Press.

Gelman, R. and Gallistel, C.R. (1978) *The Child's Understanding of Number*, Cambridge, MA: Harvard University Press.

Guha, M. (1987) 'Play in school', in G.M. Blenkin and A.V. Kelly (eds) *Early Childhood Education*, London: Paul Chapman.

Howe, M.J.A. (1999) *A Teacher's Guide to the Psychology of Learning, 2nd Edn*, Oxford: Basil Blackwell.

Manning, K. and Sharp, A. (1977) *Structuring Play in the Early Years at School*, Cardiff: Ward Lock Educational/Drake Educational Associates.

Meadows, S. (ed.) (1983) *Developing Thinking*, London: Methuen.

Moll, L.C. (ed.) (1990) *Vygotsky and Education*, Cambridge: Cambridge University Press.

Moyles, J.R. (1989) *Just Playing? The Role and Status of Play in Early Childhood Education*, Milton Keynes: Open University Press.

Murris, K. (1992) *Teaching Philosophy with Picture Books*, London: Infonet Publications.

Rogers, C. and Kutnick, P. (eds) (1990) *The Social Psychology of the Primary School*, London: Routledge.

Schaffer, R. (1977) *Mothering*, London: Fontana.

Smith, P.K., Cowie, H. and Blades, M. (1998) *Understanding Children's Development, 3rd Edn*, Oxford: Basil Blackwell.

Sylva, K., Bruner, J.S. and Genova, P. (1984) 'The role of play in the problem-solving of children 3–5 years old', in P. Barnes, J. Oates, J. Chapman, V.

Lee and P. Czerniewska (eds) *Personality, Development and Learning*, Sevenoaks: Hodder & Stoughton.

Sylva, K. and Wiltshire, J. (1993) 'The impact of early learning on children's later development: a review prepared for the RSA inquiry "Start Right"', *European Early Childhood Education Research Journal*, 1, 17–40.

Tizard, B. and Hughes, M. (1984) *Young Children Learning*, London: Fontana.

Wood, D. (1988, 1998) *How Children Think and Learn, 1st/2nd Edn*, Oxford: Basil Blackwell.

Basic principles and approaches

CHAPTER 2

Spinning the plates

ORGANISING THE EARLY YEARS CLASSROOM

Holly Anderson with Tandy Adlam, Penny Coltman,
Ros Daniels and Holly Linklater

Imagine being a juggler spinning plates. The act is a familiar one; it has been performed on stages up and down the country ever since music hall was popular entertainment. The plates spin round, the juggler runs from pole to pole twirling, maintaining momentum, sometimes increasing speed in the nick of time just as a plate begins to fall. For Early Years educators the management of a classroom can seem like this, juggling the needs and interests of all the children, making sure each one is gainfully occupied. Planning a motivating and purposeful activity for a small group takes an understanding of how children learn, and how teachers can affect that learning; whole class teaching, with all the children involved in the same activity, demands a range of complex skills too; but managing to organise groups of children and individuals so that each child is working at a suitable activity with the right amount of support seems to be the hardest to achieve.

It is easy to see the results of poor management. Children stand around in queues waiting for a small amount of attention from the teacher, frustration arises because children are overdependent on adult support and are unable to function without constant intervention, equipment is lost in the general chaos of a badly organised classroom; all these features cause problems for children and staff alike. However it seems as if the more talented the teacher, the more difficult it is to see the amount of thought and planning that goes on behind the scenes to facilitate the whole range of pupil/teacher interactions. Good teachers make the plate spinning seem easy, almost as if good management is by accident rather than design. The focus for this chapter therefore is to make explicit such skills, to explore how the organisation of the rooms and the management of children, resources and adults can support the education of the children within them.

Curriculum planning is easier to show than classroom management, and yet it is management which reflects the underlying philosophy of what is an appropriate learning environment and reveals our attitude to children as learners, as well as highlighting aspects of the curriculum and the way it is taught. To examine this, it is important to consider first what those of us working with young children feel we should be creating, and why.

Meeting children's needs and practical constraints

In the first chapter in this book Whitebread refers to love and security, making sense, self-expression and new experiences as four basic needs young children have. Other early years educationalists would agree with this, supporting the notion that children should be involved in motivating, purposeful tasks and be encouraged to become independent learners. Links between home and school are seen as important to children's educational success as well as providing security of continuity. Much value is placed on what children bring to school. The work of the National Writing Project (1989), for example, has shown the amount of literacy knowledge children acquire from living in a print-rich environment. This has complemented and reinforced the findings of researchers such as Tizard and Hughes (1984) and Gordon Wells (1987) who showed the subtle complexities of dialogue at home where there is a shared context and frame of reference.

However, in spite of this consensus, there are a number of constraints placed on teachers which make it difficult to put theory and belief into practice. Variables such as the age of the children, the number of children in each class (which at the time of writing is causing much concern with predictions that more and more primary children will be taught in classes of over 30, some over 35), the number of adults working with the children, the support offered by parents, the type of building, the size and shape of the room, the priorities identified by the school, even the type of school (nursery, infant or primary) all affect decisions about class management and organisation.

More recently, the statutory demands imposed by the National Curriculum and the National Literacy and Numeracy Strategies have begun to have an impact too, with studies showing that these do not fit easily into a developmental, holistic approach to teaching and learning (Blenkin and Kelly, 1994; Cox and Sanders, 1994; Whitehead, 1999). Neither does testing at seven, or six in many cases for the youngest Year 2 children, particularly when viewed alongside the importance attached to the results and the possibility of them being used in league tables. This can lead to pressures to implement a subject driven curriculum, and the reception class teacher can find herself at the beginning of the school year with a class of over 30 children, many of whom are under five. It is no wonder that concern is being expressed, not least from the teachers themselves (Pascal, 1990; David, 1991; Anning, 1991; Bennett et al., 1992).

There is evidence that we need to share our educational beliefs with the parents of the children we teach, to counteract the growing trend in which parents are attaching more importance to formal acquisition of reading and writing in the early years (DES, 1990; Cox and Sanders, 1994). To quote from Angela Anning:

> In one sense, infant teachers are simply responding to the demands of society, or more specifically of parents, to get on with 'proper' schooling. On the whole parents favour the old elementary school tradition of instruction in the 3Rs – reading, writing and arithmetic. Froebel, Steiner, Montessori and discovery learning are seen by the majority of parents as the province of a minority of intellectuals and middle-class romantic liberals who mostly have a shrewd knowledge of how to work the education system anyway. 'Normal' parents are suspicious of learning through play.
>
> (Anning, 1991, p. 17)

It is clear that a partnership in which the school values what children bring from home and parents support the school's approach to education is something we must continue to work towards.

Educational principles and classroom practice

Just how are schools managing to balance the needs of the children they teach with these demands from outside and other constraints? What influence have pioneers such as Montessori and Froebel had on current practice? (see Anning, 1991 for a description of ideologies). How are schools creating an environment in which the children have freedom of movement and opportunities to learn through play in the way Piaget (1962) and others have suggested is essential for cognitive development? If we believe in Bruner's (1977) notion of 'scaffolding' and Vygotsky's (1978) emphasis on working alongside children in their 'zone of proximal development', how do we find time to play with the children, supporting and extending their learning? How can those adults working in reception classes build on the good practice that is found in many nursery schools and classes? Bearing in mind that children in most other European countries do not start formal schooling until six – seven in Scandinavia – how do schools in the UK cater for the needs of children of this age? With the Foundation Stage (children of five and below) now preceding Key Stage 1, is there a difference in the way classrooms are organised as the children move from Reception into Years 1 and 2? What about those children in vertically grouped classes – is there a marked difference in the education of the four- , five- , six- and seven-year-olds?

In an attempt to answer some of these questions, this chapter looks at four early years teachers and how they manage their classes. Each one approaches her own situation from a different starting point, raising further questions to be considered. These have been put as a focus for discussion so that readers can reflect on some of the underlying issues which need to be explored. Inevitably, there is variety in the ways classes are run, not least because of the different ages of the children and the type of school and environment. However, through each narrative a similar thread emerges – a commitment to the children and a determination that the curriculum should work for the children rather than against them.

A nursery class

The first account is from Tandy Adlam, a teacher in a city nursery school. She teaches the youngest of the children in this chapter, all the children being four and under, so for many it will be their first step away from home, the first time they compete for adult attention in a large group, the first time they play alongside other children. These factors have implications for the choices Tandy makes. The type of school also has a bearing; as a nursery school, the adult/pupil ratio is controlled by legislation, and most of the people working with the children are trained, either as nursery nurses or nursery teachers. This too will affect the way that adults are used, as will the fact that the school is organised on High/Scope lines (see Brown, 1990). On reading the account, it is interesting to see how people as a resource are managed and how the classroom organisation helps the children adjust to being in a large group away from the familiar home setting.

Tandy's school

The nursery in which I work is purpose built with a large, accessible garden, catering for 40 children at any one time. Sometimes activities can spill into an adjoining community room, but for the most part all activities take place in the main nursery room and garden.

There are two teachers, two nursery nurses and a full-time learning-support assistant who work as a team, taking a High/Scope approach to classroom organisation. Although the staff plan the curriculum together and work with all the children in the nursery at certain times, each member of staff has particular responsibility for a certain group of children. This means that the children have the security of small group situations and the knowledge that particular adults are responsible for them, so they know who to go to if they are upset, for example. It also means that each member of staff can develop close relationships with the children in their group and monitor the children's progress very closely (see Figure 2.1).

Figure 2.1 *Tandy Adlam's nursery class: the children enjoy the security of working in a small group*

Tandy's classroom

The room is divided into different areas to provide opportunity for the following activities to take place at the same time: painting, collage work and model making, drawing and writing, water play, wet and dry sand play, role play, woodwork, puzzles and games, as well as construction and block play (see Figure 2.2).

Resources

There is low-level storage furniture in each area containing a selection of equipment, allowing children to choose items they need independently (see Figure 2.3). All equipment is stored in containers labelled with pictures and

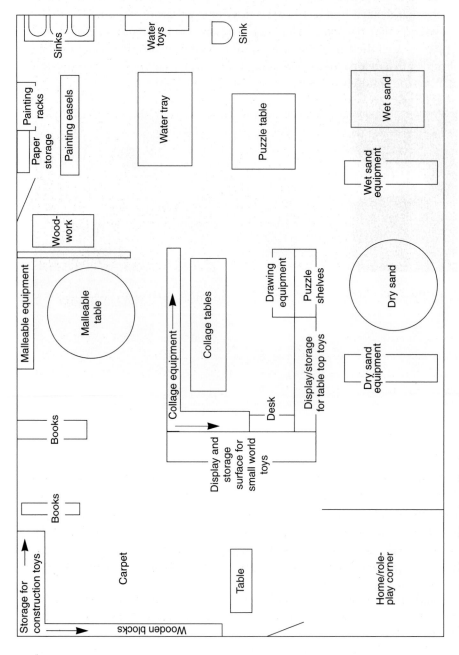

Figure 2.2 *Plan of Tandy Adlam's nursery classroom*

Figure 2.3 *Low-level storage of equipment to allow children independent access*

words, so that children can tell what is inside and replace things easily. The selection of equipment available in an area is changed weekly, to give the children varied experience in each area and to provide for progression in that area during the year.

The pattern of the day

Each morning, before the children arrive, staff set up equipment and prepare activities indoors and out. The outdoor space offers opportunities for learning which both complement, contrast with and extend indoor activities. For example, children can climb, build very large structures and dig outdoors, but equally can enjoy exploring percussion instruments, books and painting in the garden. Equipment in all the areas is varied regularly – for example, the children might have buckets, spades and moulds in the sand followed by funnels, sieves and tubes.

Staff observations of the children usually inform the provision of activities – for example, when the children were interested in the police cars that went by, staff set up a police station.

When the families arrive at the nursery they are welcomed by the adults linked to the group, known as their 'keyworkers'. The children plan what they would like to do, either indoors or outdoors, with their keyworker, recording their task pictorially and setting about the task independently. In this way the staff are free to support children who need help settling into an activity. At the end of this extended free choice session, the children tidy the nursery and outdoor area, returning to their keyworkers for snack and 'recall' time. They discuss what they have been doing with the other children in the group, which encourages them to use descriptive language and consider the processes they have employed to complete certain activities. It also encourages them to listen to one another.

Recall is followed by small group time, when the children engage in an activity initiated by their keyworker. This might be a music or dance session, or a maths, art or science activity; this gives the staff an opportunity to extend the children's learning, encourage them to explore ideas or materials, and teach them new skills. When planning small group activities, staff refer closely to the individual records which they keep for each child. These records show progress in different High/Scope skill areas, such as communication, language and literacy, movement, or attributes such as initiative or social relations. This allows staff to pinpoint areas where children show an interest or need support, and to provide appropriate activities. At the end of small group time, children enjoy a story together before going home.

Key points

So, in Tandy's school:

- The whole staff is involved in planning, supporting and recording children's learning.
- Each member of staff is 'keyworker' to a group of children, so that the children, although working with different adults, have the security of a central relationship.
- The children move freely between areas and are encouraged to manage their own time, making decisions about their own learning.
- Language is seen as central to learning, with children describing both plans and activities to each other in small groups.

A reception class

Next is Holly Linklater, a newly qualified reception class teacher in a village primary school. Her children are older, and in statutory school, but are still mainly under five in the autumn term when they all begin school. This means that at first they follow the Curriculum Guidance for the Foundation Stage rather than the National Curriculum, although, as in most nursery and reception classes, preparation for Key Stage 1 is seen as important. The permitted pupil–teacher ratio is higher than in a nursery class so inevitably there are fewer adults per child than in Tandy's class. However Holly, like Tandy, does have a trained nursery nurse working with her (not uncommon, but by no means the norm in infant classrooms). The physical environment, though, is quite different from that of Tandy's class, being in an old Victorian school building, so on reading this account it is interesting to see how the building has affected organisation. An outdoor area is used less than in Tandy's nursery class, but is still planned for and equipped with resources for the children.

Reception realities

I teach in a small rural primary school that serves the families of the surrounding villages together with the families posted at the local Army barracks. The breadth of experience shared amongst the children considerably enriches the character of the school. My class currently receives 60 per cent of its pupils from the barracks. Inevitably there is a significant turbulence factor with families moving after a maximum of two years throughout the year.

Like many reception teachers I welcome all of my class into full-time education at the beginning of the autumn term. I have a trained nursery nurse working with me, and depending on the size of my class I may have additional support from teaching assistants. We also welcome parent helpers twice a week once all of the children have settled in.

Due to a building project my classroom is currently situated in the Victorian part of the school. The room does not ideally cater for the needs of young children and the outdoor facilities are somewhat limited. However, what I hope I can illustrate is that even if the odds are against you the children's curriculum entitlement can still be met: reality can be beaten with enough imagination!

Rationale

'The time for all serious effort is when we are young.'
'Undoubtedly.'
'Arithmetic and geometry and all the other studies leading to dialectic should be introduced in childhood, though we mustn't exercise any form of compulsion in our teaching.'
'Why?' he asked.

'Because a free man ought not to learn anything under duress. Compulsory physical exercise does no harm to the body, but compulsory learning never sticks in the mind.'
'True.'
'Then don't use compulsion,' I said to him, 'but let your children's lessons take the form of play. You will learn more about their natural abilities that way.'
'There's something in what you say.'

(Plato, 1974)

One might say that since Plato made this observation in the fourth century BCE, we have come full circle! Certainly the rationale behind the early learning goals does not stray far from this principle. Children have a natural propensity to learn, which to them is to play. Our role as early years educators is to build on this. There is great emphasis in the guidance for the foundation stage on the importance of respecting the children's roots, working with their parents as partners, allowing the children space to show you their different starting points within a curriculum that is relevant and appropriate, planned and purposeful. Theoretically at least this then leaves you and your colleagues time to observe and respond, to scaffold the children's education in an environment where they feel confident to take risks and make 'mistakes' without the fear of failure. I have certainly found that the more confident and secure the children are, the easier it is for me to support and extend their learning towards and beyond the early learning goals.

Ready, steady, go!

Before you let any children into your classroom it is essential that you feel prepared. The speed at which reception children work through activities invariably leaves very little time for thought. The key to a good day is to be 'poised and ready' before it begins, and be prepared to be flexible!

The Curriculum Guidance for the Foundation Stage is a flexible document sympathetic to teaching a developmentally appropriate curriculum. Consequently I find that the nature of my planning and the structure of the day for my reception children changes significantly over the year. Initially the children work through a series of 'ongoing activities', gradually working towards a much more structured routine, including a full literacy and numeracy hour: part of the crucial preparation for Key Stage 1.

The number of extra adults that you may have working in your class obviously influences the nature of the class routine. As my class grew over the year (up to 32 at one point!) I was fortunate to attract extra assistance. It was important to ensure that the assistant's time was carefully planned so that the children could gain maximum benefit from their being with us. Furthermore, I maintain that careful planning needs to include periods when they simply 'join in' with the movement in the classroom as so much of reception children's learning is spontaneous.

Routines

Planning and establishing a daily and weekly routine is enormously important, for your sanity as a teacher and the children's sense of security. The routine should take into account both the children's needs: not sitting on the carpet for too long, and your needs: being able to set out activities. I always start the day with the children by writing a list on the board of 'things to do today'; typically it would look like this:

- Register
- ERR*
- Literacy
- Activities
- Assembly
- Playtime
- ERR*
- Snacktime
- Numeracy
- Activities
- Quiet reading
- Prayer
- Lunchtime
- Playtime
- Register
- ERR*
- PE
- Playtime
- Storytime
- Home time
  *ERR: Early Reading Research, a 12-minute teaching session focusing on phonics and sight vocabulary

The children are empowered by being 'in the know', and love crossing items off as we go along. The list quickly puts paid to perpetual questioning such as 'When is it lunchtime?' or 'When can we do show and tell?' It puts a lot of children at ease, enabling them to make the most of each activity rather than worrying about what might happen next, as well as giving a sense of timing.

In the early days it is a great antidote to feeling homesick as it is made clear at the beginning of the day that you are going to let them go home! As the year progresses I incorporate times for those keen on watching the clock.

I keep the list the same every day as much as I can; for example, I do not state what the 'activities' for numeracy will consist of until numeracy time. After a few days the children soon learn the list from memory and can follow it on the board with very limited reading skills.

A key part of the day for my reception class is snacktime, which serves a great many functions. As we have a long morning (lunch is at 12.30 pm) the milk and light snack on offer (in addition to the fruit that they may bring from home to eat at playtime) is always very welcome. Moreover, we have found that children eat more of their lunch if they have had something to eat mid-morning. However, perhaps most important is the opportunity that it allows for the children to sit quietly at a table and talk to their friends, and to carry out positions of responsibility such as giving out cups, collecting in placemats. An excellent way of covering the curriculum for personal, social and emotional development, speaking and listening . . . as well as lots of others! On Fridays we have special snack time usually involving some form of cooking. This session offers an excellent way of pulling together literacy or numeracy themes of the week. Some of the most successful snacktimes so far have been when we made porridge (eaten in the Three Bears' House), winter soup (Stone Soup), toast (spreading skills), currant buns (sold for the sum of 1p!). Parents are asked to make a small termly voluntary contribution, and the milk is heavily subsidised by the County Council.

Resources

The vast majority of learning in the Foundation Stage is made through practical activities, and in turn this means that reception classes are generally faced with serious storage issues! It is essential that all resources are easily accessible to you, but not necessarily to the children. For example, bubble blowing is an activity that I like to control with regard to when and where it takes place; consequently that box is on a higher shelf. However, the cars, Lego, colouring pencils and jigsaws are freely accessible to the children at all times, lessons or wet play times. Such an arrangement not only enables the children to be independent at activity time, but it also ensures that they can be totally responsible for tidying up.

As well as deciding where and how resources are stored in the classroom, a similar degree of consideration needs to be given to the outdoor area. For health and safety reasons (and an awkward shed) the teacher on duty has to get out and put away the ride-on toys, but the children are responsible for the key to the shed; they quickly learn that a misplaced key means less fun at playtime! In addition to the large equipment, in the small playhouse we keep a bucket of building blocks, cars and road mat, as well as role-play resources. As a rule, the more constructive activities that are provided, the fewer 'incidents' have to be resolved by the adults supervising!

Room for everyone

On his first trip to the staff room, to use the microwave, one boy in my class enquired as to where the teachers' beds were. Although today it is unlikely that a teacher officially lives at school, it does sometimes feel like it, and the classroom is usually required to serve functions that extend beyond those that the children experience. However, to the same extent it does also need to feel like their space, too. On visiting my classroom David Whitebread commented that I had obviously made the fatal mistake of letting children in. I took this as a compliment. The 'jungle vines' that twist down the length of the classroom supporting snakes of words that begin with 's', and parrots with carefully folded paper wings do not interfere with my need to plan, liaise and coordinate. Likewise my box of 'very important pieces of paper' and shelves of policies and guidelines do not inhibit the children's learning; if anything each supports the other. The classroom needs to reflect the partnership that is undertaken between teachers, pupils, parents and the wider school community.

Display space needs to be considered along the same lines as the organisation of resources. A narrow board next to the door makes an excellent area for me to pin up planning for the week, the duties rota, lists of who is collecting which child on which day. Boards that are unfeasibly high for four-year-olds are preserved for displaying work for parents to admire, whereas those that can be viewed without a periscope are of a more interactive nature. Incidentally, if, like me, you find yourself with a classroom whose display boards, by modern standards, appear more suited to giraffes than children, the backs of bookcases can be monopolised to great effect.

In order to cut down on the amount of time that needs to be spent on displays, on my largest board I have tended to construct a main piece (such as a large palm tree). The children's work (pictures of jungle animals) is added over the course of the term. Questions such as 'How many elephants can you see?' can be added, and the fact that the display is continually under development means that it's always worth looking at!

Running a large class, and latterly sharing a room, I quickly learnt that not an inch of space could afford to be wasted, and compromises had to be carefully considered. The sand pit and easel live outside, and we all wear an extra layer of clothing because of having to have the door open. Some tables and chairs have been sacrificed to ensure that we have a large carpet area for construction activities, and role-play area. With a limited amount of furniture rearrangement just over half of the class can be seated; but in the main 'hot desking' around the table for eight means that there is such novelty to sitting down, the level of concentration is far higher than might usually be expected!

Ideally, I would like to provide space for Duplo castles and the train set to be set up all day allowing for extended play – children can greatly benefit from opportunities to reflect on and return to activities. I would certainly recommend that those with large classrooms resist the temptation to overfill the space, but rather allow the children to express some of their natural creativity. It never ceases to amaze me the number of different roles that two large cushions can take on: space rockets, pirate ships, hospital beds, cars . . .!

Recording and reporting

During the reception year a huge amount of the children's achievements will go unrecorded, not through any failing of the teacher, but by virtue of the nature of what is achieved. However, there are a number of devices that can be employed to make tracking progression, parent's evenings and writing reports a little easier.

A method that I use a lot to monitor skills is to use a class list with jotting space. This is particularly useful for ongoing activities, such as computer programs, enabling any passing adult to make notes focusing, for example, on mouse control. Also by incorporating a tick box for the children next to their name, it is an excellent way of keeping track on who has had a turn.

The 'stepping stones' laid out in the Curriculum Guidance for the Foundation Stage break down the Early Learning Goals very thoroughly and can be photocopied and used for the 'highlighter' method of assessment, perhaps in conjunction with reviewing medium term planning.

Reflection

I am still fortunate enough to believe that working in a reception class is one of the most rewarding jobs. The transformations that you are privileged enough to observe, as well as the challenges that you have to overcome on a daily basis rarely leave you wondering whether or not you have achieved anything that day. Moreover, as an early years teacher, if it suddenly snows you are encouraged to abandon your planning and take the children outside (just make a note that that is what you did!). It is this flexibility within the framework of the Foundation Stage that should ensure that the year is thoroughly enjoyable for you and your class! (see Figure 2.4).

Figure 2.4 *Children in Holly Linklater's class holding a tea-party for Biff, Chip and Kipper (characters from a popular reading scheme)*

Key points

Holly's account emphasises:

- Ways in which she encourages children to take responsibility for themselves and the classroom environment and equipment. The layout of the room, the way in which equipment is stored and labelled, are all designed to this end.
- That curriculum subjects are covered, but the way it is delivered changes over the year in order to ensure that the teaching is developmentally appropriate for the children.
- That flexibility of working is important within a clear structure; this gives children a feeling of empowerment but also security.
- The importance of respecting and building on the children's home experiences.
- The importance of creating a partnership between teachers, pupils, parents and the wider community (including the relationship between the teacher and other adults helping in the classroom).

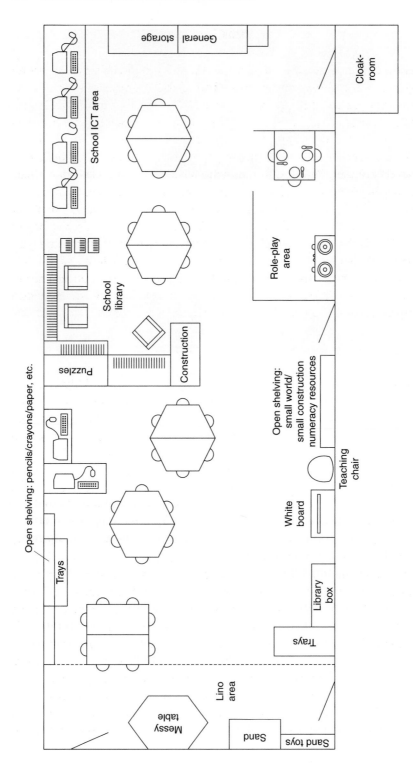

Figure 2.5 *Plan of Holly Linklater's reception classroom*

A Year 2 class

The Rumbold report (DES, 1990) stated the need to provide a child-centred curriculum for those under five. The Curriculum Guidance for the Foundation Stage upholds this view and has enabled those working in reception classes to justify the type of environment Holly has described for them, rather than perhaps those working with older children. To see whether there is a marked change in organisation to ensure curriculum demands are met, Penny Coltman, who teaches a Year 2 class in a village church school, now describes her situation. These children, in a primary school similar in size to Holly's are firmly part of the establishment, old hands in the system with two years of full-time education already behind them. This is the year in which they will take national tests in all three core subject areas, so specific aspects of the curriculum need to be taught. Will there be more emphasis on subjects rather than social and emotional needs? Will there be a marked separation between 'work' and 'play'? How does Penny cater for the needs of her six- and seven-year-olds?

Penny's classroom

For two years I shared a teaching post with a compulsive and highly expert furniture mover. Every possible permutation of space, table and storage unit was arranged, employed for about half a term or so and then rearranged. It was a remarkable learning experience. Through this process of regular experiment I discovered that the way to achieve the maximum floor area for children to use is to have as few tables as possible. Floor space is one of the most valuable commodities in the classroom. We sit together on the floor for stories, news times or for decision-making meetings. The children build imaginative layouts on the floor using roads and cars or sets such as Playmobil, and sometimes parts of the floor are covered with enormous PVC cloths, providing an extensive surface for painting or modelling. For these reasons the 29 children in this class work mostly at three large tables positioned around a central space (see Figure 2.6). The ' teacher's desk' is merely a utilitarian piece of furniture in which personal equipment is stored. It is in no way central to the room and the ' teacher' is very rarely to be found anywhere near it. Its chair has long since been commandeered for the computer, providing an ideal height from which children can use a keyboard in comfort. Equipment is there to be used, and so storage is all at child height and clearly labelled. Children are encouraged to see for themselves when materials and apparatus are required, and to collect, use and return it independently. This principle would apply equally to glue pots, number lines or hand lenses.

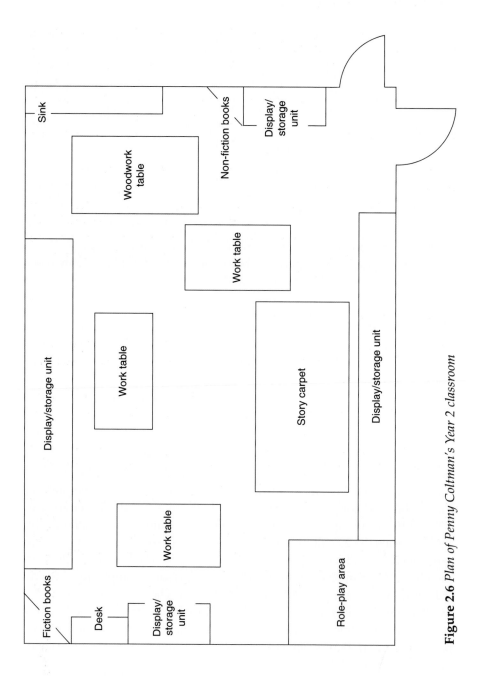

Figure 2.6 *Plan of Penny Coltman's Year 2 classroom*

Children's seating

At the beginning of each year the children are allocated places, after lengthy consultation with their previous teacher to ensure that friends are together where possible. This provides a touch of security for children entering a new room. There is a place ready, with a named pencil waiting, and no need to wander around the room looking for a friend or a spare seat. Over the ensuing weeks these placings will evolve rapidly as children ask to move. Such requests are a courtesy and are always granted unless there is simply not enough space on the desired table.

These places are used at the beginning of the day for registration (knowing approximately where children should be helps to quickly identify absentees), and for a fair proportion of the day's work. Seating will be changed for the literacy and numeracy hours, in which children work in differentiated groups, and on any occasion during the day when children are engaged in cooperative activities and may be working with other friends, either by their choice or mine.

Organisation of activities

Usually all the class will be working on similar tasks at any given time, which might be differentiated by complexity, recording method or outcome. Balance of curriculum is a constant consideration. Some areas are allotted fixed times, usually because of external factors. Maths and English are always at the same times in Key Stage 1 because of the literacy and numeracy hours, enabling children to be moved between classes for fine tuning of differentiated lessons. The set times have the added advantage of enabling parents to come in to help. Conversely, other areas of the curriculum are varied through the week, and there is no fixed daily or weekly routine. Activities are fitted in so as to provide the children with a varied diet. The result of this ranges from a quiet calm in which everyone is reading, drawing or writing, to a wonderful impression of organised chaos as we indulge *en masse* in craft, art or technology. The moment at which a brilliant end product arises like a phoenix from this turmoil of activity is one of life's pleasures, and the grand clearing up operation is a lesson in itself. Being 'in charge of the bin bag' is seen as a highly prestigious position!

Role-play, fantasy and self-esteem

Developing a sense of cohesion within the class is one of the central aspects of my philosophy as a teacher and various techniques are used to promote this. One of the most important is the use of role-play and fantasy in the classroom, in which aspects of current topics are adopted and extended as classroom themes. A major project at the beginning of each term is the construction of a new topic-related role-play area in a sunny corner of the room. These areas are built for the children to play in, by the children themselves. They are large scale and bold in design providing a visual focus that has immediate impact on entering the room. This collaborative construction not only acts as a topic stimulus but involves all the children in a practical and purposeful design and technology exercise that encourages the exploration and development of some imaginative and at times sophisticated engineering ideas. The proportionately large amount of space allocated to these areas, which has included teepees, tree houses, castles and hot air balloons, as well as more conventional shops and homes, is a reflection of the high status attributed to role-play in the classroom. Children in Year 2 are still very much in need of all the opportunities to explore concepts through enactment, benefiting from the associated linguistic activities and interactions.

Role-play will also become an integral part of the working day, permeating even the mundane and routine. An illustration of this approach was within a recent topic on sea travel. Every member of the class worked together to build a role-play area in the form of a pirate ship, The Red Shark. In the interests of democracy the name of the ship was chosen by ballot. From this moment our classroom ceased to exist as we became crew members. Each child (and their teacher!) chose a suitably bloodthirsty pirate name by which they were addressed at all times, including registration. We adjourned to the 'main deck' for assemblies, and to 'the heads' when we needed the lavatory. Those of us who brought sandwiches for lunch had 'ship's biscuits', and the rest ate 'hot rations' in the 'galley'. We regularly 'cleaned the decks', were visited by either landlubbers, enemy crew or captains from other ships, and the biggest treat of all, for those who had achieved beyond the call of duty, was to be forced to 'Walk the Plank!' At the end of the half-term topic we celebrated with a pirate feast for which the crew prepared an amazing variety of theme-related food (see Figure 2.7).

Activities like this are not only great fun, but they also encourage a sense of pride and ownership as children develop a perception of their classroom as a place over which they have some influence and control. Similarly as collaborative skills develop, so does an awareness of collective responsibility and caring, not only for the environment, but for each other. Courtesy within the classroom and empathy towards each other are qualities that are actively encouraged by example and request. The contributions made by children with learning difficulties to cooperative projects are just as valued as those made by the very able. Role-play in particular is an area in which children with special needs may shine. The consequent fillip to the self-esteem of these children, and the benefits of this to their progress is unquestionable.

Figure 2.7 *Penny Coltman's Year 2 class: the importance of role-play and fantasy*

Involving parents

A happy and open relationship with parents, based on confidence and trust, is crucial to the building of a successful relationship with their children. Good communication is essential and parental visits to the classroom in the mornings as children are delivered are seen as valuable contact times, as are moments by the school gates at the end of the day. This is complemented by use of the usual reading record as an all purpose two-way news channel.

Parents are invited and indeed encouraged to be involved in many classroom activities. For example, several groups of children working on mathematics at the same time can be impossibly demanding on teacher input. Parents who have been suitably briefed provide a first point of reference to children playing a number game or solving a spatial problem. The regular contributions of volunteer parents working with me in listening to children read, result in every child in the class receiving uninterrupted hearing time at least three times a week, with more for those in difficulty. Sometimes the bonuses are unexpected. On countless occasions parents who have become involved as helpers have proved to be invaluable sources of both inspiration and practical support. In many ways parents are among the most valuable of available resources, and it is a great pity that this degree of voluntary support within the nation's classrooms is given so little formal recognition.

Key points

Penny, working with older children in a Year 2 class, displays some similarities of approach to those of Tandy and Holly:

- The children are given as much freedom of choice and independence in their learning as possible.
- With the older children there is still space for floor activities.
- A role-play area is seen as enhancing learning across many curriculum areas.
- A concern is still clear to ensure that the children feel emotionally secure.

But also some differences:

- Alone with no other trained staff, she has to rely on parent volunteers for help so she includes this in her organisation, making it as easy as possible for those who can spare some time to work with her and the children.
- With older children, the range of needs widens, so support from parents and even across classes is considered, enabling activities to be structured to best meet these needs. The timetable is planned with this in mind, as is the grouping of the children.
- Groups are flexible and designed for different purposes, but are often meant to reinforce collaboration. Although it is important to allow younger children opportunities to work together, it is as the children get older that more weight is given to collaborative learning.

A vertically grouped class

So all three teachers so far have very similar values. This is echoed in the final description by Ros Daniels who teaches a vertically grouped Key Stage 1 class in a large town. In an infant school the whole staff can work together on designing a curriculum appropriate to the needs of the young children they teach. Ros and her colleagues have wanted to find ways in which to give the children in their care security and self-esteem, at the same time making learning both challenging and purposeful for all three year groups in each class.

Ros's infant school

During the last few years we, as a staff of a large infant school with a nursery class and hearing impaired unit, have developed a system that we feel meets the requirements of the national curriculum while at the same time being compatible with child-centred teaching and learning. Our policies are written by the whole staff and reflect the overall positive approach we have in our school towards all aspects of the children's learning and development. We have chosen to use developmental approaches in many areas of the curriculum; as a result no formal schemes are used in any subject areas and we encourage the children to take responsibility for their own learning during a daily timetabled session called 'planned activity time' (PAT). The children in the hearing impaired unit, taught a natural aural approach, integrate as fully as possible in the other classes, thus learning with the other children. As a staff we are constantly discussing the best ways to meet the needs of the children, and we decided last year to restructure the classes so that we each now teach a vertically grouped class of Reception, Year 1 and Year 2 children.

The class rules

A key element in our philosophy is a positive behaviour policy based upon rights, rules and responsibilities, with the emphasis on the children taking control of their own behaviour within a highly structured environment (see Figure 2.8). Each class draws up its own set of rules which are then published so that the children know exactly what is expected of them. They can then enjoy their rights within this structured and clear framework and are consequently encouraged to take responsibility for themselves.

This independence and responsibility is achieved in a variety of ways. For example, the children go to the toilet without asking permission by placing their name card in a chart and they can have a drink in the classroom whenever they are thirsty. A sound chart is a visible reminder for the children to work within the agreed sound level.

The pattern of the day

We feel the children need security as well as ownership. The way we negotiate the rules reflects both of these, as does the way we plan each day. This is a typical day in school:

THE FRAMEWORK OF OUR BEHAVIOUR POLICY

*These 3 strands of discipline should work together to
create a caring community atmosphere.*

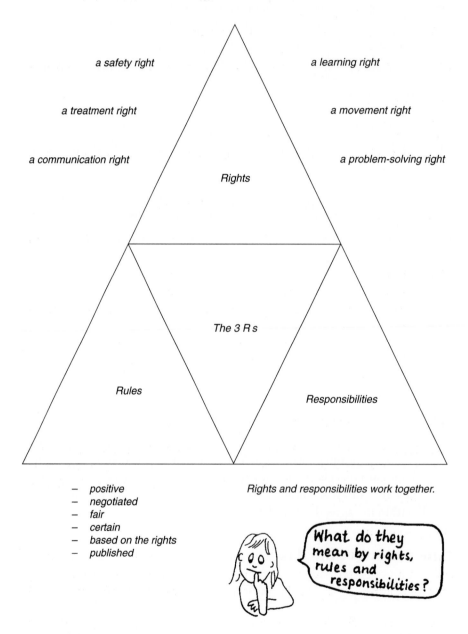

a safety right   *a learning right*

a treatment right   *a movement right*

a communication right   *a problem-solving right*

Rights

The 3 R s

Rules   *Responsibilities*

- *positive*   *Rights and responsibilities work together.*
- *negotiated*
- *fair*
- *certain*
- *based on the rights*
- *published*

What do they mean by rights, rules and responsibilities?

Figure 2.8 *The 3 Rs: rights, rules and responsibilities*

Time	*Activity*
8.50	Children arrive at school and are individually welcomed. Books in book bags are changed ready to take home
9.10	Register involving children (e.g. finish the sentence 'I would like to . . . I like it when . . .'
9.20	Spelling activities, often with a partner (look, cover, write, check; multisensory sheets)
9.40	Maths activities (a variety on offer to meet different needs and abilities)
10.15	Playtime
10.35	Assembly
11.00	Planned activity time (PAT) Planning – verbal, storyboarding, design sheets, listing equipment, pictures Activity Recall/review in large group or with partners
12.00	Lunchtime
1.10	Register involving children (e.g. 'my favourite story is . . .) and friendship circles (self-esteem activities)
1.30	Writing workshop and sharing of writing
2.15	Reading session, apprenticeship approach (children read in a variety of ways in terms of groupings. Usually a collaborative partnership)[1]
2.45	Gathering together on the carpet in the reading area. Story: from the author of the week (e.g. Jan Ormerod)
3.00	Hometime

Whole class activities and groupwork

Each day has timetabled sessions that have a clearly defined beginning and end. In addition to this are curriculum input sessions that may be whole class activities or direct teaching of skills to a specific group of children. Examples of these are:

Writing workshops

These sessions vary in length and format. They involve the children in both collaborative and individualised writing activities. It is a designated writing time for children and adults. Many writing contexts are offered, from journal

[1] Ros's timetable offers scope for both a 'literacy hour' and 'numeracy hour' to be included. In the morning she gives time for maths and word level work, in the afternoon her activities focus on writing and reading at text and sentence level.

writing to writing in role, writing books and letters; giving a wide range of choices across a variety of genres.

A science input on air

The children are grouped according to their experience and provided with appropriate activities based upon the theme of air. Most of these sessions end with a sharing of all the activities engaged in by the class. These will include illustrative and investigative activities. These activities are recorded by an adult in each child's science diary with a diagnostic comment in shorthand.

Planned activity time

Alongside this teaching we operate PAT which encourages the children to take control of their own learning. This is a daily timetabled session in which children cannot be withdrawn by an adult for any reason. Although the children decide for themselves what they want to do, it is in no way a traditional 'choosing' time. Children are required to:

- initiate and plan their chosen activity;
- organise themselves;
- follow through their activity;
- review, recall and record their activity.

The children decide which of the classroom areas to work in and this is recorded and monitored by the teacher. They can spend between three and six sessions, by negotiation, in any one area and the children are encouraged to have autonomy over their work; the adult's role is that of facilitator and enabler.

The classroom environment

In order to work as we do, the classroom needs to be organised to give maximum space to the children and provide a range of starting points for their ideas. Interactive displays in the school, thematic collections of carefully selected resources, entice the children to explore a range of ideas. Simple stick puppets in a display, for example, encourage the children to re-enact the stories contained in surrounding books.

As another example, we used the story of 'Mrs Wishy Washy' (from the Streakiest books) to create a display which included fluffy slippers, a mob cap, an apron and a scrubbing brush, then provided a duck, a pig and a cow for the children to wash. Tabard costumes with animal headbands enabled the children to dress up as animals to enact the story and animal puppets invited a puppet show version to be created. A display such as this could also extend to

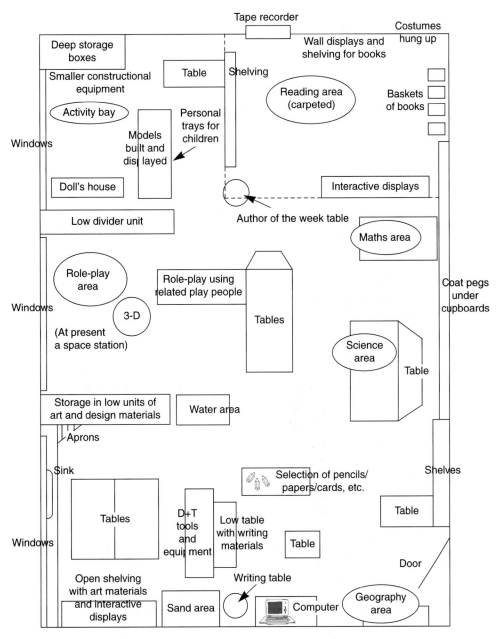

Figure 2.9 *Plan of Ros Daniel's vertically grouped classroom*

a wider theme on farm animals, or keeping clean. We recently used this story to test out washing powders on muddy clothes! These displays provide a fundamental part of the children's learning, contributing to their independence.

Core areas in the classroom also give opportunities for children to create their own learning environment at whatever level is appropriate for them. The classroom (see Figure 2.9) therefore contains:

A reading area with:

- baskets of books
- baskets of props, puppets and toys to use with the books
- 2-D displays on inboard
- tape recorder and tapes
- collections of stories
- author of the week
- wall diary, etc.

A writing area with:

- hats (writing in role)
- pens, paper, felts
- paper: sizes, colours, shapes
- diaries
- telephones
- message pads
- menu layouts
- plans
- maps
- post box
- stamps
- sellotape, etc.

A role-play area (changed half-termly), for example:

- castle
- museum
- art gallery
- rainforest
- cave
- jungle
- underwater
- world
- space

- North Pole
- pirate ship

A sand area with a range of equipment to encourage storymaking:

- animals
- dinosaurs
- wood
- string
- tools
- lollipop sticks
- playpeople
- trucks
- pulleys, etc.

A water area with a range of equipment to encourage storymaking:

- water animals
- ice animals
- boats
- divers
- containers
- syringes
- shells
- pipes

An activity bay with:

- a range of small world role-play and constructional equipment (e.g. Playpeople contexts)

There are also art, design and making, science and maths areas all containing an interactive display plus a range of appropriate equipment and resources, and we create a number of cross-curricular areas to link with the current topic or interests when the need arises.

These areas provide a stimulating and enticing environment which, supported by the way we organise the timetable, gives the children control and motivation in their learning. We are fully committed to empowering the children and have adopted policies and practices which will allow this. By encouraging the children to take responsibility for their own learning we are enabling them to become both autonomous and confident learners – surely an essential aim at Key Stage 1.

Key points

Ros Daniels' approach again has similarities with the others:

- An emphasis on children developing autonomy and responsibility as learners: PAT time has similarities with the High/Scope
  organisation and she encourages her infant children to plan
  their work in the way that Tandy Adlam does with her nursery
  class.
- As with Penny's Year 2 class, specific curriculum areas are identified in the classroom organisation and there is a greater sense
  of the timetable including maths and English activities. This
  appears to be a response to the more structured needs of the
  older children.
- An emphasis on children developing positive attitudes to themselves and to others.
- A concern to offer children as wide a range as possible of experiences and good-quality resources.

The early years tradition and classroom organisation

What is striking is the extent to which all four teachers have, directly or indi-
rectly, been influenced by a tradition of early years practice observed and
described so eloquently by Susan Isaacs working in the early part of the
twentieth century. Her philosophy is described thus:

> It is significant that Susan Isaacs saw the role of the teacher as not
> only supportive but interventionalist. The teacher must 'have the right
> answer ready for an intellectual problem' and is there to 'meet' the
> children's free enquiry and activity with careful structuring of learning
> experiences and situations. Though she valued observation of young
> children as highly as Maria Montessori and appreciated the values of
> the maternal nurturing role, she saw the role of the teacher as far more
> specialised, positive and active in promoting the child's learning.
>
> (Anning, 1991, p. 15)

In the words of a teacher, Evelyn Lawrence, who worked at her school:

> the children do what appeals to them at the moment. The work of the
> educator is to select his material, and at times indirectly suggest

activities that the child will of his own accord do things which are useful for his work. Lately one or two of the children have drawn up rough outlines of their day's work. . . . They are urged to answer their own questions, with the teachers to help them discover where the answers are to be found.

(Drummond, 1993, p. 18)

This child-centred, developmental pedagogy is not easy to maintain, as Drummond goes on to explore; there are tensions in balancing the needs of the individual with the needs of the group, especially when a statutory curriculum imposes its own restrictions. The teachers in this chapter show how much their organisation plays a part in supporting them, in partnership with a number of other adults, to meet the children's needs in both affective and cognitive domains. The way the classrooms are managed enables the adults to have opportunities to be facilitators, enablers and instructors. Andrew Pollard and his co-writers (1993) see this teaching and learning process as a social construction of meaning, and suggest that there are three important conditions for this model of teaching to be put into effective practice:

- provision of a classroom context in which children are enabled to control and manage the construction of meaning and understanding;
- effective assessment and communication with the children so that relevant adult support and instruction is identified;
- provision of appropriate adult support and instruction for the subjects which form the curriculum.

(Pollard in Campbell (ed.), 1993, p. 36)

There is no one way to organise a classroom; there are so many variables, so many factors to consider. However, by examining the practice of four early years specialists, a number of practical issues have been raised in the context of specific situations, which it is hoped will provide a framework through which the rest of the book can be viewed. Each of the teachers in this chapter manages to keep the plates spinning and puts the needs of the children at the centre of her plans, creating an environment in which all the children have some freedom to explore aspects of their world which fascinate, perplex and challenge them.

Pointers for organising the early years classroom

Points to take into account when considering how to use and organise the available resources in your classroom:

- Make the spaces in your classroom as flexible as possible; provide some usable floor space; be prepared to experiment with different arrangements.
- Provide children with opportunities to work in a variety of ways (alone, in groups, with an adult, etc). The degree of structure and direction in tasks will depend upon the age range of the children.
- Provide flexibility and choice of activities.
- Give children responsibility and independence, including access to the resources they will need and opportunities to make decisions.
- Set and maintain clear rules and structures so that children have security.
- Make sure all adults are clear about their roles, and involve them in decision-making.

References

Anning, A. (1991) *The First Years at School, Education 4 to 8*, Milton Keynes: Open University Press.

Bennett, S., Wragg, E., Carre, C. and Carter, D. (1992) 'A longitudinal study of primary teachers' perceived competence in, and concerns about, National Curriculum implementation', *Research Papers in Education*, 7 pp. 53–78.

Blenkin, G. and Kelly, V. (eds) (1994) *The National Curriculum and Early Learning, an Evaluation*, London: Paul Chapman Publishing Ltd.

Brown, M. (1990) *An Introduction to High/Scope Approach to the National Curriculum*, Ypsilanti, MI: High/Scope Press.

Bruner, J. (1977) *The Process of Education*, Cambridge, MA: Harvard University Press.

Cox, T. and Sanders, S. (1994) *The Impact of the National Curriculum on the Teaching of Five Year Olds*, London: Falmer Press.

David, T. (1991) *Under Five – Under Educated?*, Buckingham: Open University Press.

DES (1990) *Starting with Quality* (The Rumbold Report), London: HMSO.

Drummond, M.J. (1993) *Assessing Children's Learning*, London: David Fulton.

National Writing Project (1989) *Becoming a Writer*, Walton-on-Thames: Nelson.

Pascal, C. (1990) *Under Fives in the Infant Classroom*, Stoke on Trent: Trentham Books.

Piaget, J. (1962) *Play, Dreams and Imitation in Childhood*, London: Routledge and Kegan Paul.

Plato (1974) *The Republic*, trans. with an introduction by Desmond Lee (2nd edn), London: Penguin, part IIX, 536d–7a.

Pollard, A., Osborn, M., Abbott, D., Broadfoot, P. and Croll, P. (1993) 'Balancing priorities: children and the curriculum in the nineties', in R.J. Campbell (ed.) *Breadth and Balance in the Primary Curriculum*, London: Falmer Press.

Tizard, B. and Hughes, M. (1984) *Young Children Learning: Talking and Thinking at Home and at School*, London: Fontana.

Vygotsky, L. (1978) *Mind in Society: The Development of Higher Psychological Processes*, Cambridge, MA: Harvard University Press.

Wells, G. (1987) *The Meaning Makers: Children Learning Language and Using Language to Learn*, Sevenoaks: Hodder & Stoughton.

Whitehead, M. (1999) A Literacy Hour in the nursery? The big question Mark, *Early Years* Vol. 19, Number 2.

CHAPTER 3

'My mum would pay anything for chocolate cake!'

ORGANISING THE WHOLE CURRICULUM: ENTERPRISE PROJECTS IN THE EARLY YEARS

Penny Coltman and David Whitebread

In the last few years, with the introduction of a statutory national curriculum in maintained schools in England and Wales, there has inevitably been huge controversy about the curriculum. As regards its impact on the education of children in the 3- to 8 year age range, some commentators have taken the extreme view that the national curriculum is fundamentally at odds with early years education (eg Blenkin and Kelly, 1994). Others have argued, however, that while there are dangers and difficulties, with imagination early years educators can be true to their principles, stay within the law, and provide the young children in their care with an appropriate, rich and stimulating curriculum (see, for example, the Early Years Curriculum Group, 1989). This is the position taken within the present chapter. We want to discuss what the principles for such an early years curriculum might be, and then to demonstrate how these might be brought to life through one particular approach involving the use of Enterprise projects.

The national curriculum and the early years curriculum

This chapter is not intended as a critique of the national curriculum. However, its introduction in England and Wales has raised a number of issues which need to be addressed when we come to think about organising a curriculum for young children. These issues can be identified in terms of dangers or problems, on the one hand, and benefits, on the other hand, inherent in the national curriculum approach.

Dangers and problems of the national curriculum

There are a number of dangers in the approach to the curriculum underlying the national curriculum. We want to just mention three:

The early years and Key Stage 1

There has been a lack of clarity, and some consequent debate about precisely when young children should begin the national curriculum. As a result, in some schools children have been introduced to elements of the national curriculum during their reception year (i.e. the year in which children become 5 years old), as they become 'ready', while in other schools the national curriculum has not been begun until Year 1 (i.e. the year which all children begin as 5-year-olds). Whichever date is taken, however, there is a very real danger of 'downward' pressure on the early years curriculum. Early years educators working with 3–5-year-olds may be encouraged to view their work as a 'preparation' for the national curriculum, and this can have a distorting influence. The more recent introduction of the foundation stage, covering the nursery and reception years, with its own curriculum guidance (QCA, 2000), might have helped here, but its beneficial effect has been badly damaged by the insistence that reception children should be introduced to the literacy and numeracy strategies (DfEE, 1998, 1999).

In particular, there is a danger that this kind of pressure can result in young children being hurried on to tasks for which they do not have the prerequisite skills and understandings. Particular concern has been expressed about the influence on 4-year-olds in reception classes (e.g. see Cleave and Brown, 1991, whose book provides an excellent outline of an appropriate curriculum for 4-year-olds). Here there is some evidence that children have been provided with a diet of seat-based, pencil and paper types of tasks at too early a stage. This kind of inappropriate provision can result in a loss of confidence amongst young children, and the development of entirely unhelpful anxieties about certain kinds of tasks (e.g. reading and writing, written numbers, etc.). In the home context young children learn very effectively through various informal means when no one is deliberately attempting to 'teach' them anything. Continuity in terms of the ways in which young children are expected to learn is just one of the features of good links between the worlds of home and school that need to be in place if young children are to thrive in their first years in school.

We know from a range of research (e.g. Bennett et al., 1984) that it is enormously difficult to set tasks that are at precisely the appropriate level for each of the individual children in a primary school classroom. It is clearly vital that educators of young children make their judgements about appropriate tasks entirely on the basis of their understandings about young children's learning, and their knowledge of the particular children. Pressure to 'prepare' pre-school, nursery and reception children for Key Stage 1 can be entirely counter-productive. Indeed, The Early Years Curriculum Group (2002) have recently argued that our children would be better served if the principles of the foundation stage (including learning through play, supporting child-initiated activities, allowing children time to explore ideas in depth, and adopting a more cross-curricular approach to learning) were translated upwards into Key Stage 1.

A curriculum of separate subjects

A number of features of the ways in which the national curriculum was established have been unhelpful in relation to the early years. From the outset the curriculum was conceived as consisting of a list of separate subjects. The curriculum for each of these subjects has been drawn up and revised by committees which have been dominated by subject specialists with higher education and secondary school backgrounds. It has been a major source of concern that separating out the curriculum into subjects in this way can lead to an 'artificiality' or lack of coherence in the educational experience offered to the young child. There is a strong tradition amongst early years educators that young children need an integrated curriculum, and this is a view supported by recent research (reviewed in Chapter 1) emphasising the significance of 'meaningful contexts' for young children's learning. While the national curriculum may have been presented as separate subjects, it is therefore vitally important that an integrated, topic-based approach is maintained within the early years. Palmer and Pettitt (1993), amongst others, have demonstrated very well how such an approach can be developed that is compatible with the national curriculum. The enterprise projects described within the present chapter are a particular example of a method of providing young children with a powerful, holistic experience which nevertheless covers a wide range of curriculum areas.

The 'delivery' model

The language of the national curriculum documents has also reflected a bias towards an inappropriate model of teaching and learning in relation to the early years. These documents talk of the educator 'delivering' the curriculum to the children. Concerns about this model, and a perceived emphasis (particularly in earlier versions of the national curriculum) on subject knowledge have led to worries about the young child being placed in an unhelpfully passive learning role. As has also been reviewed in Chapter 1, there is clear evidence from research that young children learn most effectively by means of 'active' styles of learning.

Allied to this concern has been the danger of a kind of 'tick list' approach to the curriculum. Once a particular aspect of the curriculum has been 'delivered' to the children, and some rudimentary assessment has been made that they have 'received' it, this aspect can be ticked off as having been covered, and we do not need to worry about it any more. In fact, of course, as anyone who has ever worked with young children is only too aware, the relationship between what we as educators attempt to 'teach' a child and what that child actually learns from the experience is often far more complex. Certainly, the development of skills and understandings by young children involves a highly active and complex set of processes that we are far from understanding. It is clear, also, that there are many and various ways and styles of learning, so that an activity or experience which might be highly effective for one child will be no help whatsoever to another. Effective teaching is, therefore, likely to involve constant revisiting of areas through a diversity of meaningful tasks which engage, in a variety of ways, the active involvement of young learners.

Benefits of the national curriculum

On the other hand, the introduction has brought a number of direct and indirect benefits to early years education. Once again, we want to mention three:

Skills and understandings in the Foundation Stage and Key Stage 1

The concerns about the overloading of the curriculum with subject content have not been nearly so great in the early years as they have at later stages. On the whole, the curriculum at the Foundation Stage and Key Stage 1 has been a helpful description of the skills and understandings that might reasonably be expected of young children. If anything, the main criticism would be that in some areas the abilities of young children have been underestimated. Nevertheless, the statement of the curriculum contained in the foundation stage and Key Stage 1 statutory orders has largely given official recognition to a process of change in the early years curriculum from 'product' and towards 'process' that has been proceeding and gathering pace throughout the second part of the twentieth century. Fisher (1987) has neatly described this gradual but inexorable change in practice as one which:

> moves from simply teaching the children the facts of language, mathematics, history, geography, science and other 'disciplines', towards

encouraging children to be scientists, historians, geographers, linguists and mathematicians, through the use of appropriate problem-solving skills and processes.

(Introduction)

A broad and balanced curriculum

As well as giving official backing to modern early years practice in terms of styles of teaching and learning, the curriculum guidance for the Foundation Stage and the Key Stage 1 national curriculum has confirmed the expansion of the curriculum for young children from the traditional 'three Rs' to a broader and more balanced diet. This, once again, is the culmination of a process that has been developing officially and unofficially for many years. The areas of learning and experience identified by HMI (DES, 1985) in an earlier attempt to define the school curriculum (linguistic and literary, mathematical, aesthetic and creative, human and social, physical, scientific, technological, moral and spiritual) had already been widely accepted and used by early years educators (e.g. ILEA, 1987; Drummond et al., 1989). To some extent, these have now been enshrined in the six areas of learning within the Foundation Stage. While there may be concerns about the separation of the curriculum into distinct subjects, the requirement to introduce young children to skills and under-standings under such a wide range of subject headings does help to ensure, as Palmer and Pettitt (1993) have argued, that all children receive the broad and balanced curriculum to which they are entitled. Regrettably, the current pressure to introduce the literacy and numeracy 'hours' into reception classrooms can result in a backward-looking narrowing of the curriculum, but it is to be hoped that this will be resisted.

Re-evaluation of young children's learning

Some aspects of the introduction of the national curriculum have obliged early years educators to re-evaluate their understandings about children's learning. The concomitant new arrangements for assessment have obliged teachers to make assessments of children's skills and understandings in a much more analytical manner than hitherto. This has resulted in wide dis-cussion amongst teachers and other early years educators concerning such matters as the validity and reliability of different kinds of evidence for chil-dren's learning, the sequence of children's learning in different areas, different levels of learning or understanding, and so on.

The arrangements for school inspections, organised by OFSTED (Office for Standards in Education), have obliged teachers to produce plans that, more explicitly than before, identify the intended 'learning outcomes' of the various activities and tasks for the children, and to think critically about the quality of learning taking place in their classrooms. As Anning (1991) has argued, there are a range of influences on early years educators' beliefs and understandings about young children's learning. They are influenced by the traditional beliefs and values of early years education as identified so helpfully, for example, by Bruce (1987). They are also influenced by their social and cultural surroundings, by the findings of developmental psychologists, by their own experiences as a learners, and by their experience of working on a daily basis with young children. What is clear, however, is that the quality of early years education can only be enhanced by these beliefs and understandings being made explicit, being articulated, and being constantly re-evaluated and examined in the light of new evidence.

There is no doubt that the last few years have been ones of considerable turmoil in education, and that teachers and other educators have been pulled in different directions, often as a consequence of muddle and lack of forethought amongst those in positions of power. However, now that the dust has settled to some extent, a clearer picture is emerging, and it is not one that is entirely incompatible, in the present authors' view, with early years principles. One example of this might be the role afforded to play as a learning medium in early years classrooms. The important role of 'active', self-directed modes of learning, often in the form of one or other kind of play, has long been recognised by early years educators. There appears, however, possibly under the pressure referred to above to 'prepare' children for the national curriculum, and the literacy and numeracy strategies, to have been a decline in the provision for play within early years classrooms. It is significant, if perhaps a little ironic, that in an OFSTED report on teaching in reception classes (OFSTED, 1993), which was generally very complimentary, the one area of concern expressed related to the lack of opportunities for children to learn through appropriately structured play. It is to be hoped that the new emphasis on learning through play set out in the curriculum guidance for the foundation stage will give reception and other early years educators the strength to provide appropriately in this regard for their young children.

Principles for an early years curriculum

Through all this debate, in the view of the present authors, there are a number of important principles that should guide the content and organisation of the early years curriculum. These principles derive from the evidence about children's learning, and from the collective experiences and views of early years educators, as discussed in Chapter 1. Despite the dangers, the national curriculum is not necessarily incompatible with these principles, but they should guide the way it is taught and managed.

At this point it is worth reminding ourselves about the needs of young children identified in Chapter 1. For the curriculum to be effective and appropriate, it needs to take into account these needs. As was argued there, to learn effectively young children need a curriculum and a style of teaching which provides them with emotional security and feelings of being in control. Young children need a curriculum that starts with what they understand and can do already, and helps them make sense of their world by providing them with meaningful tasks, which require their active engagement, and which give them opportunities to express their understandings in a variety of media, principally through imaginative play and talk. Young children's natural curiosity can be stimulated to help them learn effectively by providing novel first hand experiences and opportunities to explore, investigate and problem-solve.

From these understandings we have derived four principles which we believe should guide the organisation and management of the early years curriculum. These principles are as follows. Young children's learning will be enhanced when:

1 the content of the curriculum is **'meaningful'** to them and related to their existing knowledge and interests
2 they are **active participants in their learning** rather than just passive recipients; they should have opportunities to make their own decisions about their learning
3 they are encouraged to indulge their natural inclination to engage in **imaginative play** related to significant life experiences
4 they are **emotionally secure** because there is continuity and good communication between the worlds of home and school.

Enterprise projects

These principles clearly support an integrated, topic-based approach, and this can be carried out in a whole variety of ways. In the remainder of this chapter, however, we want to demonstrate one kind of approach that seems to embody these principles in a particularly powerful way. This approach consists of what has been termed Enterprise projects (see DES, 1990, for a general review of this kind of work in primary schools). In essence these consist of using some kind of adult enterprise or place of work as a starting point, and enabling children to explore and investigate it, partly by carrying out a similar kind of enterprise themselves.

Over a period of five years the authors carried out an enterprise project each year with classes of young children ranging from reception to Year 2.

These have been focused on a bakery, puppet theatres, a newspaper, a museum, and a fashion show. The details of some of these projects have been reported elsewhere (Coltman and Whitebread, 1992; Whitebread et al., 1993, 1994, 1995). What follows is a description of these projects and an analysis of the ways in which such projects provide a powerfully effective curriculum for children in the early years, particularly in relation to the four principles identified above.

All the projects involved the following basic elements:

- a visit to a local workplace to find out, by a variety of means, about the kinds of work carried out and the people who worked there;
- the children engaging in a related, small, real enterprise of their own, which involved research, planning, production, advertising, accounting, etc.;
- opportunities for the children to represent their experiences for themselves in a variety of ways, through talk, play, drawing, modelling and writing;
- a fixed 'end point' in the form of an event towards which children could work and to which friends and families could be invited.

Learning through 'meaningful' work

The first principle is concerned with the extent to which the content of the curriculum is 'meaningful' to young children and related to their existing knowledge and interests. This also relates to the links between home-based styles of learning that are informal and for real purposes and school-based styles of learning which sometimes suffer by comparison by being formal and purposeless from the child's point of view. Research in relation to both language (Tizard and Hughes, 1984) and mathematics (Hughes, 1986) has demonstrated that most children find the informal, 'real' world of the home and the community a much more conducive environment for learning than the artificial and, from the child's point of view, 'meaningless' tasks of traditional schooling. This has led to a developing new pedagogy which emphasises the importance of children within school carrying out tasks for 'real' purposes within the context of real world situations and problems (see, for example, Hall, 1989, in relation to language and Atkinson, 1992, in relation to maths).

This 'authenticity' was established within the enterprise projects we carried out in a number of ways:

- **The localness of the workplaces** visited gave them a meaningfulness to the children through familiarity. The local newspaper was taken by many of the children's families, many had already visited the local museum and some of the children's friends and relations worked at the local bakery.

- **Projects related to the children's interests:** for example the bakery mainly made Christmas puddings; the puppet show gave them an opportunity to re-enact one of their favourite stories (Cinderella and Snow White were chosen, somewhat adapted to give everyone a part!); the contents of the newspaper they produced contained items of interest to them: reviews of latest children's films, a fashion page complete with photographs of

House for sale. 5 bedrooms.
Dining room. Conservatory.
2 toilets. Kitchens. Large
pond in garden. Quiet area.
Good Price.
£80,000.

A lovely house with a large garden.
Close to the shops. Near to a school.
It has 1 main bedroom and a lounge.
1 roof garden and your own little
parking space next to the house.
Price £40,000.

This house has 2 bedrooms.
1 pool. Room under stairs.
Double glazing. Double bed.
A vase of flowers. It's a
bargain.
Price 70,000.

1 bed. home. Ballet room.
Disco room. 1 big bathroom
and a nice size kitchen.
Swimming pool and stable.
Come soon.
Price £100,000.

Figure 3.1 *The children advertise their own houses for sale*

6–7-year-old 'models' (an interest later developed in the fashion show project), 'Aunt Sherry's Problem Page' (Dear Aunt Sherry, my brother is a
pain in the neck!), and a page of Houses for Sale (the children's own
houses, drawn and described by them – see Figure 3.1); the museum set up
by the children exhibited artefacts provided by themselves, their families,
village friends and the school and focused on the history of the school and
the village.

- **A wide range of opportunities for learning through 'real' work provided:**

Writing for real purposes: the children wrote scripts, programmes, posters,
price lists, guidebooks, official invitations to special guests, press releases,
a whole newspaper, and, most excitingly as it turned out, a range of business letters. These included letters accompanying the donations to
charities, but also letters to local businesses selling advertising space in
the class newspaper, bids for an Arts Grant to support the puppet theatre

Back to the Past Museum Company.
(a division of Class 4 enterprises).

27.1.94.

Dear Sir,

Please may you consider sponsoring our posters for our
Back to the Past museum. We estimate the cost
will be about 10 pounds. Your company logo will
appear on all posters and we anticipate a large
crowd of people attending.

Thankyou for your kind attention.

Yours Faithfully,

Matthew Paddick,

(Company Secretary.)

Figure 3.2 *Writing for real purposes: Matthew writes applying for sponsorship*

companies, and for sponsorship for the class museums and the fashion show (see Figure 3.2). All these letters received formal and entirely business-like replies which were much treasured by the children.

Real maths: a lot of book-keeping and accounting, of course (see Figure 3.3), but also measuring ingredients for refreshments when parents and friends were invited in for the grand launch or opening; handling real

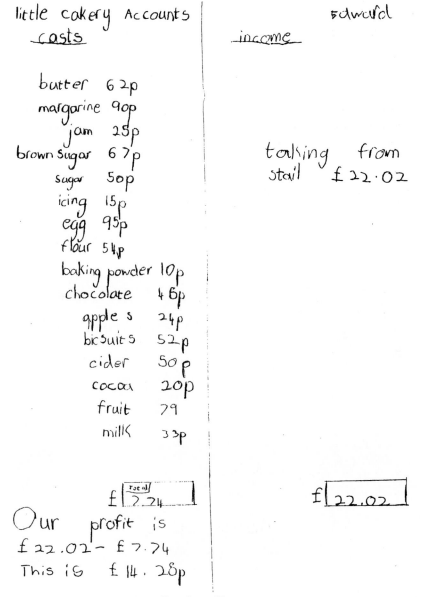

Figure 3.3 *Real maths: Edward's cake stall accounts*

money when children sold tickets, postcards, programmes, etc.; setting out the seats in the 'auditorium' for the puppet shows, with tickets corresponding to numbered seats; measuring and making patterns and costumes to fit for the fashion show; making decisions about what to charge for various items in all the projects.

Genuine economic transactions: real money was used throughout; all costs were charged, but all the projects managed to make a good profit! The children were confronted with the simple realities of costs, prices, consumer preferences, profits and losses throughout the projects. Our records are full of fascinating discussions we held with children, particularly when they had to make decisions about pricing, for example. How much profit was it fair to make? What price would people pay for a newspaper? Children had to use their real world knowledge to help them solve these problems. On one occasion a child volunteered that his mum would pay anything for chocolate cake!

Work roles and processes emulated authentically: work roles were made explicit to the children. To help with this process, for example, badges for cook, market researcher, editor, museum guide, designer and so on were often worn by the children when they carried out these roles. Processes seen by the children on visits were emulated in ways which made them

Figure 3.4 *Authentic work processes: Robert uses a computer graphics package to design his T-shirt*

as real as possible. Good examples of this would be the cataloguing procedures developed during the museums project, the computer booking system developed during the puppet theatre project, the operation of a real telephone by the children during the newspaper project on which they took calls to a 'tele-sales' service, and computer aided design for T-shirts in the fashion show (see Figure 3.4).

Children being 'active' learners and empowered to make their own decisions

Our second principle concerns children being active participants in their learning rather than just passive recipients and having opportunities to make their own decisions about their learning. An 'active' style of learning is an intrinsic aspect of enterprise projects because the children are actually experiencing adult activities first hand, and not simply being told about them. What goes along with this is that we must always be open to the children taking the initiative. A good example of this was a poster designed by one of the children. This was done in the evening at home inspired by a day of designing the role-play area to accompany the fashion show project, and proudly brought into school the next morning. On another occasion, during the puppet theatre project, a child on her own initiative brought into the class a large cardboard box that had contained her family's new washing machine. She explained that this was to be made into a puppet theatre. The provision of opportunities for imaginative play is also an important aspect of this 'active' involvement of children, and we will come on to this next.

What is significant here, however, are the opportunities enterprise projects offer, because of their intrinsically open-ended and problem-solving character, for children to take decisions and so develop feelings of empowerment. Tizard and Hughes (1984), amongst others, have pointed out how so much of what happens between adults and children in the home is child-initiated, whereas this is very much not the case often in the classroom. The consequent loss of feelings of control, self-efficacy and self-esteem for the young child can be very damaging. Research has consistently shown that self-esteem is whittled away by the difficulties many children face in relation to school learning. The strong relation between self-esteem and school achievement is well documented.

All the projects were set up in such a way as to allow the children considerable opportunities to make decisions and develop a real feeling of ownership and empowerment. The children made choices collectively about such matters as the name of the cake stall they set up and ran, which story to do as a puppet play, how to spend the profit made by their enterprise, and so on. Individually and in small groups they made a whole range of sophisticated decisions – about what to charge for postcards on sale in the museum 'shop', about the content and layout of their page in the class newspaper, about how many tickets to print for the puppet show, what information to include in the programmes, and so on. Many of these decisions involved considerable research and discussion. The mechanism of company board meetings was also used within some of the projects as a way of helping the children to review progress and discuss and plan the work still to be done.

While, of course, they had their plans for the projects, the teachers involved always attempted, as a further way of empowering the children, to respond to and support initiatives coming from them. This is sometimes referred to as the 'dead bird' model of the curriculum, because children are inclined to bring in this kind of fascinating object, and the skilful early years educator has always made the most of such opportunities. But it is a feature of the curriculum which has been under threat from the pressures of the national curriculum, and which it is desperately important that we preserve.

There are numerous examples of this from all the projects, but let us just mention two from the fashion show. Sometimes occasions arise because children, stimulated by their involvement in the project, bring in items with rich possibilities. During the fashion show project, a child arrived one day with a box full of Victorian hats, and the whole day was given over to examining them, finding out about how they were made, what they were made of, who wore them. Pictures were drawn, the children made their own Victorian hats, and so on.

Other occasions arise when an activity introduced by an adult is developed by the children in unexpected ways. An example of this arose when, as part of the fashion show project, an activity was introduced involving drawing a 2-D scale drawing of the catwalk. This activity, which was planned to take about an hour, lasted for two days, as the children transformed it into a 3-D modelling activity. Having completed the 2-D drawing children began to add stand-up proscenium arches, which needed buttresses. Then they raised the catwalk plans on to box bases to show the height, added model pot plants, audiences on seats and delightfully accurate paper puppets of themselves in costume (initially on straws, but later on strings to facilitate twirling). With their models complete the children then gave miniature performances of the show to a tape of the music.

Opportunities for imaginative play

This last example leads us very well into our third curriculum principle. Once again, as was reviewed in Chapter 1, there has been renewed interest in the ways that children's natural playfulness, usually given full rein in the home but very much curtailed within the school context, enhances the quality of their learning. Learning through play supports the strategies developed under the previous two headings. It helps children to derive meaning from their experiences. One of the main factors in the efficacy of play is also its self-directedness; play gives children control over their own learning.

The play corner in the classrooms during the projects was transformed into an imaginary cake shop, a practice puppet booth, a box office, a newspaper office, a museums office (see Figure 3.5) and a boutique. These were designed and largely built by the children, and played in to the point of destruction. During the puppet theatre project, for example, following the visit to the theatre, some of the children suggested that they turn part of the classroom into a box office. The teacher set about discussing with the class how they would go about rearranging the classroom to accommodate this. Tables were moved, chairs piled up and carpets rearranged. A table was needed for the booking lady, a door for people to walk in, somewhere to display the puppets, a noticeboard for the posters, and so on. When the general environment of the box office had been created, discussion followed of what was needed to equip it. A telephone was installed, a computer, paper, pencils, pens, diary, tickets and a telephone book. From then on throughout the project there were always children in the box office busily taking telephone calls, writing messages, issuing tickets, taking money, making programmes and posters, putting up notices and signs and generally becoming thoroughly involved in the exciting new world of theatre management!

This kind of play was engaged in by the children throughout each of the projects with energy and enthusiasm. As the projects developed it was notable the extent to which new elements of the project, and

Figure 3.5 *Role-play: the museum office*

new information that had been made available to the children, was incorporated in their play.

Integrating the worlds of school and community

The final feature of the projects was the extent to which the divisions between the school and the outside adult community were broken down. As we have discussed, there is an important aspect of this to do with styles of learning, but continuity and good communication between the worlds of home and school is also a vital component in providing young children with emotional security in the classroom.

There were a number of aspects of this attempt at integrating the worlds of school and adult community within the projects:

- The children visited an adult place of work, and often one where adults they knew worked; our observations of the adults explaining their work to the children suggested this was an intense and satisfying experience for both parties.
- Adults visited the classroom to explain their work to the children, and also to work alongside the children with their enterprises; this also, of course, supported the authenticity of the children's enterprises (see Figure 3.6).

Figure 3.6 *Adults working alongside the children: the local museum warden discusses one of the class's collection with Sam*

- The children interacted with adults in the local community in a business-like manner (formal letters requesting sponsorship, selling advertising space, inviting local dignitaries to open the Grand Launch, giving interviews to the local press about the projects, etc.).
- The projects generated an enthusiasm which led to an enormous involvement of the parents and the wider community in all kinds of ways – loaning resources (exhibits for the museum), helping with making (puppets, costumes, cakes), helping with research (important people being interviewed for the newspaper, and as a source of local history for the museum), attending the Grand Opening or Launch, providing expertise (photographs of the children as models for the fashion page, and the village policeman setting up a mock robbery, both for the newspaper), offering sponsorship, providing ideas and moral support.

The involvement and enthusiasm of the children and of the local communities for these enterprise projects has been particularly rewarding. An atmosphere of real teamwork was generated in which young children, parents, teachers and community shared the pleasure of cooperative purpose and achievement. The museum exhibitions, for example, were so popular that, when they were taken down in school, they had to be immediately

This is the Roman pot found in Great Chesterford.

Figure 3.7 *Alexander's postcard: one of half a dozen that sold like hot cakes at the local museum*

remounted within the local museum which received large numbers of interested visitors, many of whom purchased some of the postcards designed and made by the children (see Figure 3.7). The video of the fashion show quickly sold out with copies being sent as far away as the Orkneys and Northern Norway!

Planning and assessment

Carrying out the kind of projects described in this chapter with young children can be an enormously rewarding and effective way of organising and developing the curriculum. As with any high-quality teaching, however, it depends vitally upon detailed planning based upon careful assessments of the children's needs and abilities. We therefore need to conclude with some remarks about these crucially important aspects of the early years educator's work.

Progression

The topic-based approach to the curriculum has commonly been criticised because of the lack of progression in activities. One argument for teaching a more subject-based curriculum has been that it enables concepts and skills to be introduced and then built upon more systematically. It is, however, perfectly possible to build progression into the activities within a topic, given careful task analysis and planning. As part of the planning for the kind of enterprise projects described in this chapter, for example, it is important to analyse the planned activities in terms of different areas of the curriculum (see Figure 3.8). This ensures a good range and balance of skills is being addressed. It also leads on to an analysis of the nature of the skills and understandings to be taught. That the activities are placed in the meaningful context provided by the topic or project, however, enhances the children's understandings about their purpose and thus supports rather than detracts from the real progression in learning. Here are a couple of examples from the fashion show project:

Letter writing

Introduced with letters to Father Christmas (not part of the project), which were chatty, informal, and concluded with 'love from . . .'.

Developed within the project with formal, thank you letters to some people from Marks & Spencer's children's clothes department who had been into school to talk to the children about the design process; these letters had a more formal layout with the school address, proper indentation, the date, began with 'Dear Sir' and concluded with 'Yours sincerely . . .', but the content was very straightforward.

Concluded with formal letters with more complex content; these involved applying for sponsorship, inviting special guests to the fashion

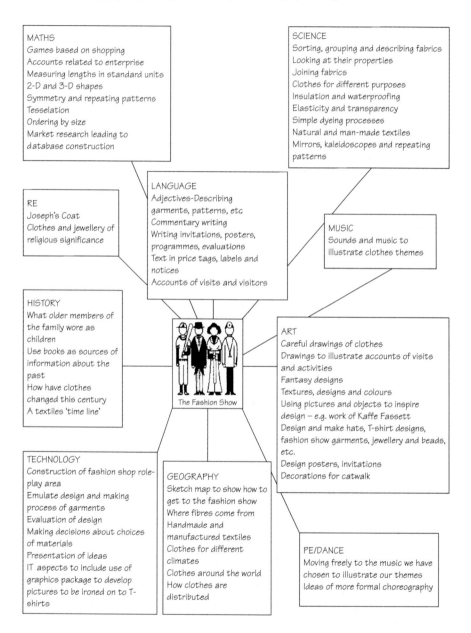

MATHS
Games based on shopping
Accounts related to enterprise
Measuring lengths in standard units
2-D and 3-D shapes
Symmetry and repeating patterns
Tesselation
Ordering by size
Market research leading to database construction

SCIENCE
Sorting, grouping and describing fabrics
Looking at their properties
Joining fabrics
Clothes for different purposes
Insulation and waterproofing
Elasticity and transparency
Simple dyeing processes
Natural and man-made textiles
Mirrors, kaleidoscopes and repeating patterns

RE
Joseph's Coat
Clothes and jewellery of religious significance

LANGUAGE
Adjectives-Describing garments, patterns, etc
Commentary writing
Writing invitations, posters, programmes, evaluations
Text in price tags, labels and notices
Accounts of visits and visitors

MUSIC
Sounds and music to illustrate clothes themes

HISTORY
What older members of the family wore as children
Use books as sources of information about the past
How have clothes changed this century
A textiles 'time line'

The Fashion Show

ART
Careful drawings of clothes
Drawings to illustrate accounts of visits and activities
Fantasy designs
Textures, designs and colours
Using pictures and objects to inspire design – e.g. work of Kaffe Fassett
Design and make hats, T-shirt designs, fashion show garments, jewellery and beads, etc.
Design posters, invitations
Decorations for catwalk

TECHNOLOGY
Construction of fashion shop role-play area
Emulate design and making process of garments
Evaluation of design
Making decisions about choices of materials
Presentation of ideas
IT aspects to include use of graphics package to develop pictures to be ironed on to T-shirts

GEOGRAPHY
Sketch map to show how to get to the fashion show
Where fibres come from
Handmade and manufactured textiles
Clothes for different climates
Clothes around the world
How clothes are distributed

PE/DANCE
Moving freely to the music we have chosen to illustrate our themes
Ideas of more formal choreography

Figure 3.8 *Analysis of planned activities for the fashion show project by subject*

show, sending a charity donation (to Radio Cambridgeshire's Send-a-Cow appeal on this occasion !) and so forth (Figure 3.2 is a good example of this stage); invariably replies were received to these letters, also written very formally.

Tessellation

Introduced by looking at patchwork patterns on fabrics and tessellating squares, rectangles and hexagons of different patterns; all these shapes tessellate with themselves in any orientation.

Developed by looking at pattern cutting for various shapes which tessellate when the shape is rotated, e.g. T-shirt, sock, skirt (see Figure 3.9).

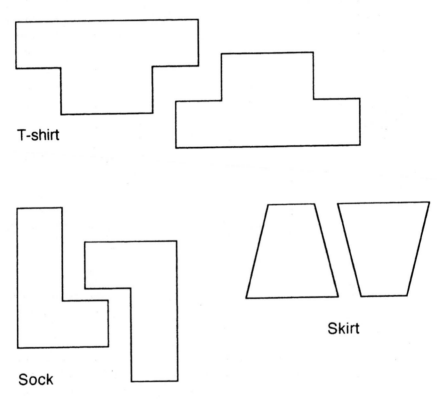

T-shirt

Sock

Skirt

Figure 3.9 *Tessellating T-shirt, sock and skirt patterns*

Concluded by looking at real dressmaking patterns that did not tessellate and attempting to fit them on to rectangles of fabric in the most economical way (i.e. fitting in the most patterns with least waste, as we had seen at the clothes factory we visited).

Assessment

Early years educators have always placed great emphasis on making careful observations and assessments. In order to make assessments of an individual child's understanding or level of skill, it is important to plan activities that will enable the extent to which a child has made the new understanding or skill their own to be seen. This involves another kind of progression from *structured or closed activities* to introduce the new skills or concepts developing on to more *open-ended activities* that give the child opportunities to use what they have learnt in their own innovative ways.

It is entirely possible to build this kind of progression of activities into enterprise projects. The meaningful context, furthermore, provides a real purpose to the activities, and the child's real level of skill or understanding can be much more validly revealed than when they are carrying out an activity simply for its own sake, where the child's motivation and understanding of the requirements of the task are sometimes open to question. More open-ended activities reveal a child's thinking and abilities much more clearly than closed tasks, particularly of the 'Blue Peter' variety where all the child has to do is follow instructions. They also provide children with opportunities to express themselves, to gain feelings of ownership, and to have a more memorable, first hand experience. This is, of course, often what is happening, as we have reviewed, when children engage in imaginative play related to significant new experiences, and their play can be an important source for observations and assessments for this reason.

Within the enterprise projects many of the activities were planned with this kind of assessment in mind. Here are two examples, both from the fashion show project:

Measuring materials for costumes

Structured or closed activities in which the children were taught various techniques for measuring themselves, including the use of appropriate measuring units and instruments.

Open-ended activities where the children were required to use their measurements of themselves to measure out materials so that their costumes would be the right size; choice of method of measurement was left to the children.

Emergent writing

Structured or closed activities in which the children were taught the names of different garments, how to write out sizes, amounts of money, addresses and so forth.

Open-ended activities in the role-play area, the 'Clothes R Us' boutique, including, for example, the provision of an order book in which children, role-playing as shop assistants, could write out orders taken from other children role-playing as customers (see Figure 3.10).

Differentiation

Having planned for a progression in the children's understandings and skills, and made assessments of their responses to the various activities, it is, of course, vital to differentiate the activities so that each child can succeed at an appropriate level. There are numerous ways in which this can be done, and once again this needs to be planned. Here are some suggested means of doing this and some examples from the enterprise projects:

- **Outcome:** perhaps the simplest form of differentiation is to set up an activity so that the requirements are the same for all the children, but it is so open-ended that they can respond at their own level; *examples*: designing a poster, making a model catwalk.

- **Support:** once again, the requirements can be the same, but the level of the outcome needs to be similar, so this common level of achievement is reached by means of variable levels of adult support; *examples*: making a costume, baking a cake.

- **Recording method:** the activity may be the same for everyone, but the children may be required to record what they have done in more or less sophisticated ways; *example*: a science activity on the qualities of different textiles recorded by sticking samples of the textiles on paper, by drawings, or by descriptive writing.

- **Complexity:** finally, the children may be given tasks to do that are all related to the same skill or concept, but that are at different stages in the progression of work planned; *example*: mapwork related to the destinations of different garments made at the clothes factory involving activities at three levels:
  - countries located on world map and drawings of garments attached
  - journey of garments to Hong Kong investigated and a list made of the continents they travel through
  - journey of garments through the UK to the port investigated; compass directions, road numbers and towns travelled through recorded.

As suggested above, differentiating the presentation and demands of a task by these means should lead to its successful completion by every pupil. In

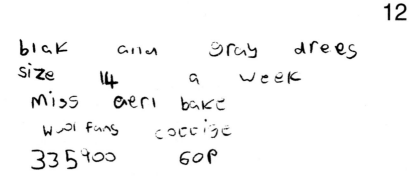

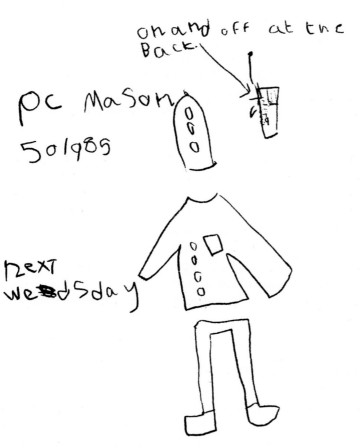

Figure 3.10 *Writing in the role-play area as a means of assessment: orders placed in the 'Clothes R Us' order book*

planning for this, one approach is to think about the various 'sub-tasks' involved and to then view them in reverse order. It is the actions needed to complete the task, the fastening of the final button on the coat, which children must be encouraged to complete without aid, however small this step may be. Once that step is mastered the starting point for the task can be moved back until the child is managing all the steps from start to finish.

Thus, in writing a story there is little joy for a child with difficulties in meeting the differentiated expectations of a teacher by managing the scribing of 'Once upon a time' . . . and no more. It is the satisfaction of writing 'and they all lived happily ever after' that offers the real sense of achievement. The learner has independently added the last piece of jigsaw, and hence has ownership of the completed puzzle.

Conclusion

Within education there is growing interest currently related to developing more experiential, problem-solving approaches to teaching and learning across the curriculum (Fisher, 1987, provides a good review of work in primary schools). We have attempted to show that enterprise projects can provide an excellent basis for this kind of development. There was an intensity of 'real' learning for the children within these projects that was very special. The enthusiasm with which the children, their teachers, parents and other members of the local communities still recall the projects, in some cases now after several years have elapsed, is a testimony to their significance for all who participated in them. We have attempted to demonstrate in this chapter that such projects form an excellent basis for organising an appropriate and effective early years curriculum. Through this kind of project it is possible to meet the needs of young children. They arrive at school confident and expert learners in the informal context of their home environment. Through the kind of curriculum organisation proposed here they are enabled to make the transition to becoming equally effective and assured in the environment of the school.

Pointers for organising the early years curriculum

- With thought and imagination, it is possible to organise the early years curriculum in ways which are compatible with the demands of the national curriculum, and with our understandings about how children learn.

- Young children's learning will be enhanced when:
  1 the content of the curriculum is **'meaningful'** to them and related to their existing knowledge and interests
  2 they are **active participants in their learning** rather than just passive recipients; they should have opportunities to make their own decisions about their learning
  3 they are encouraged to indulge their natural inclination to engage in **imaginative play** related to significant life experiences
  4 they are **emotionally secure** because there is continuity and good communication between the worlds of home and school.
- These principles can be embodied powerfully within enterprise projects.
- The success of this model of curriculum organisation depends upon:
  1 clearly identified **progressions** of related activities
  2 **assessment** of children's level of understanding or skill using **open-ended activities**
  3 **differentiation** of activities so that each child can succeed at an appropriate level.

References

Anning, A. (1991) *The First Years at School*, Buckingham: Open University Press.

Atkinson, S. (ed) (1992) *Mathematics with Reason*, London: Hodder & Stoughton.

Bennett, N., Desforges, C., Cockburn, A. and Wilkinson, B. (1984) *The Quality of Pupil Learning Experiences*, London: Lawrence Erlbaum.

Blenkin, G. and Kelly, V. (eds) (1994) *The National Curriculum and Early Learning, an Evaluation*, London: Paul Chapman Publishing Ltd.

Bruce, T. (1987) *Early Childhood Education*, London: Hodder & Stoughton.

Cleave, S. and Brown, S. (1991) *Early to School: 4 Year Olds in Infant Classes*, London: Routledge.

Coltman, P. and Whitebread, D. (1992) The little bakery: an infant class develops EIU, *Economic Awareness*, 5, 1, pp. 3–9.

DES (1985) *The Curriculum from 5 to 16*, Curriculum Matters 2, HMI Series, London: HMSO.

DES (1990) *Mini-Enterprise in Schools: Some Aspects of Current Practice: A Report of HMI*, London: HMSO.

DfEE (1998) *The National Literacy Strategy: Framework for Teaching*, Suffolk: DfEE.

DfEE (1999) *The National Numeracy Strategy*, Suffolk: DfEE.

Drummond, M.J., Lally, M. and Pugh, G. (eds) (1989) *Working with Children: Developing a Curriculum for the Early Years*, Nottingham: National Children's Bureau/Nottingham Educational Supplies.

Early Years Curriculum Group (1989) *Early Childhood Education: The Early Years Curriculum and the National Curriculum*, Stoke-on-Trent: Trentham Books.

Early Years Curriculum Group (2002) *Onwards and Upwards: Building on the Foundation Stage*, Early Years Curriculum Group.

Fisher, R. (ed.) (1987) *Problem Solving in Primary Schools*, Oxford: Basil Blackwell.

Hall, N. (1989) *Writing with Reason*, Sevenoaks: Hodder & Stoughton.

Hughes, M. (1986) *Children and Number*, Oxford: Basil Blackwell.

ILEA (1987) *The Early Years: A Curriculum for Young Children*, London: ILEA Centre for Learning Resources.

OFSTED (1993) *First Class: The Standards and Quality of Education in Reception Classes*, London: HMSO.

Palmer, J. and Pettitt, D. (1993) *Topic Work in the Early Years*, London: Routledge.

QCA (2000) *Curriculum Guidance for the Foundation Stage*, London: QCA.

Tizard, B. and Hughes, M. (1984) *Young Children Learning*, London: Fontana.

Whitebread, D., Coltman, P. and Farmery, J. (1993) Project File: a puppet theatre, *Child Education*, 70, 6, 31–8.

Whitebread, D., Coltman, P. and Bryant, P. (1994) Project File: a class museum, *Child Education*, 71, 12, 27–34.

Whitebread, D., Coltman, P. and Davison, S. (1995) Project File: infant newshounds, *Child Education*, 72, 1, 29–36.

CHAPTER 4

'We are passing the smile around'

PERSONAL, SOCIAL AND HEALTH EDUCATION IN EARLY YEARS

Helen Broomby

Introduction

PSHE is one of the most fundamental areas of learning and development. It is the base from which all else is built, from which children can flourish or flounder. Without personal, social and health development all further layers of learning may be skewed and thwarted. For here, we are talking about children's basic social and emotional needs, their self-worth and self-belief. It is now accepted that whatever cognitive powers we inherit they cannot be utilised fully if our personal and social health needs are not nurtured.

Additionally, the realisation of the child's development in PSHE enables children to play an active part in their world and to form a sound basis for citizenship. They develop the competence and motivation to 'make a difference'. They learn to contribute to the world in which they live.

We know from a wealth of research that children learn best through active learning, through physical engagement with materials and through engaging with people. There is nothing more potent in this experiential learning than that which is negative; a damning word, an experience that suggests failure, a gesture that underlines rejection. On the other hand a friendly smile or a kind word can be very effective.

The nature of the interactions between child and carer/adult is a crucial and controlling factor in that child's development. Babies are acutely sensitive to every move and gesture made by the people around them, they depend on this instinctively for their survival. They study the moves and read the signs that tell them who they are and what is expected of them. Babies and children learn through this method from the moment of their first breath. They learn from every move, every glance and every word. They learn about how to be and how to behave, they learn what you think of them, how important they are, how they fit into the family and later into school and society. They learn both the positive and unfortunately the negative.

Adults respond differently to the realisation of the weight of this responsibility, especially when their involvement is with young children still in the formative stages of their development. For some adults, the tendency would be to ignore the responsibility and others may become over-anxious about their handling of young children. Neither is a good option. Both reactions are based on the adult's own experiences, and these experiences need to be considered if they hamper effective working with young children. These considerations underlie a need for an approach that takes account of adults' responses and children's needs. I discuss in this chapter the need for a whole school approach that supports both the children and the adults.

Context

In addition to the above thoughts, the contrasting theories of the nature versus nurture debate, the political dimension of women in society and mothers' role within the home, the personal and private versus the public and the political have swung back and forth over the years. The blame for the 'poor upbringing', low self-esteem and anti-social behaviour of the children has often rested within the personal dimension of the home and primarily with the mother. At other times it has rested with schools and society. We need to take regard of this and be mindful to accept responsibility and to avoid blame. People as parents, guardians, teachers or carers all come with their own histories and experience but they also come from within a culture, a society that for that period in time has fostered a particular aspect or approach. As teachers or carers of children we are working within an establishment with particular social constraints, the schools are an element of the society that we are creating for children. They are also highly significant in the development of those children.

If the above observations are taken as given, PSHE must be seen as an ongoing developmental partnership between the family, including the child, and the school or pre-school setting. This includes *all* those engaged with the children during the normal course of the working day. It refers not only to the relationships taking place within the classroom but also those relationships between the child and non-teaching staff.

In what follows, I will first consider the importance of and some practicalities in developing a whole school approach and then turn to considerations as to how PSHE can be embedded both as day-to-day practice and as a discrete curricular subject. The benefits of a reflective style cannot be underestimated. Too often we are preoccupied, not able to make the time. Nonetheless, it helps to work within a reflective style and most of all a style that avoids much of the blame that can be used to absolve schools of their responsibility. The systems, the policies and procedures we set up need to reflect the acceptance and inclusion of all children, an appreciation of difference and enhancement of the self-esteem of the children. It is as part of that society and the expected socialization of the children that we are considering within this chapter.

The whole school approach

In adopting a reflective style it helps first to examine the nature of your own personal history and that of the society and its expectations, especially in relation to assumptions about children and childcare practices. An exercise of this sort is the opening to the development of a whole school approach. These considerations need a personal response from all members of staff and after discussion a whole school view.

What future, what type of society, what sort of people do we want to develop? What sort of school, what sort of teachers and what sort of children? How can we establish an ethos and values that will achieve this future?

It is crucial that schools allocate time to discussing, establishing and agreeing the ethos and values to which the whole team feel they can work. This must be done with everyone in the school including the classroom assistants, caretaker, secretaries, school meals staff, playground supervisors, school nurse, parents.

> *I overheard a conversation between a small group of reception class children who were talking about the order of who was in charge, who told who what to do. The group agreed that the teacher tells the children what to do and the headteacher tells the teacher what to do. When I asked then who tells the headteacher what to do, the answer was 'the school caretaker'.*

The people who make a difference to the school as perceived by the children are often not the same as those that the adults think of first. The good practice in the classroom will be undermined if the experience is not carried throughout the whole school day, through the mealtime into the playground and through all of the school years. Many of the problems experienced by children happen in the playground.

What is a whole school approach?

Once established, the ethos and values and policy need to be what informs every aspect of the school. The messages related throughout every aspect of school life need to project a consistent ethos of respect, consideration, inclusion and equality. The notices on the wall, the letters home, the manner in which different types of families are treated and the way in which we speak to children in the playground are all part of this work.

The policy is undermined by the actions of those not subscribing to the ethos of the whole school approach. The policy will need to be reviewed regularly as new members of staff join the team or there are new government requirements. Creative ways need to be found to safeguard this way of working to ensure that full account is taken of the children's needs. A school that has discussed this fully and developed the ethos of a whole school approach will be in a better position to protect it.

In the absence of this an ad-hoc system will emerge. With basic philosophical gaps in the system, fragmentation will occur, with a consequent lack of consistency of approach. Individual teachers will bring to bear their own particular agendas and methods of working. This may work within the four walls of the classroom but will need to be re-negotiated as the children move into the shared space of the playground or the dining hall. This is where many of the difficulties of the lack of policy will emerge. With a set of agreed principals embedded in policy practitioners have a framework within which to work.

As part of this whole school approach, PSHE needs planning for progressive incremental steps throughout the school. The importance of the subject will be severely undermined if exactly the same format is repeated each year. Valuable as it is, how many times can children engage with a project about Me and My Family? Schemes of work for progression need agreement across the whole school and if at all possible with the pre-school settings.

Circle time

Early years settings have for many years understood the value of circle time as a sociable activity for children. This time is used to encourage children to talk to the group and to listen to each other, to sing and read stories together. This practice has in recent years been developed into practice for group discussion and PSHE activities for older children. Jenny Mosley (1996) in her book *Quality Circle Time in the Primary Classroom* provides extensive circle time activities on, for example, feelings, being kind, friendship and cooperation. Mosley promotes circle time as part of a whole school approach with all classes participating in their own circle time meetings and extends this idea to encompass the notion of a school circle time. Circle time is one part of developing the time to work on the issues of this programme. To be effective the learning needs to be integrated and applied consistently across the school day using a variety of different activities and methods.

In a school where all children, whatever their background, are valued and have a clear understanding and respect for one another, appreciation of differences and an understanding of acceptable behaviours and ways of relating to each other, the aim is that they will begin to adopt the values underpinning this approach as a framework for social interaction.

Circle time activities

The magic box

Tell the children there is a picture of a very special person inside. Each has a look inside the box but must not say anything and pass the box on until every child has had the chance to look inside the box. They are then asked who was the special person. What the children see inside the box is a mirror.

Figure 4.1 *Circle time: 'We are passing the smile around', by Becky, aged 6*

I am good at . . .

Ask the children to think about all the things that people may be good at and give some examples to get them started. When you have lots of suggestions introduce the self-portrait activity. Children paint self-portraits and label them. Use smaller pieces of paper for drawings and descriptions of all the things they are good at. Glue the pictures around the edge of their self-portraits. In the circle time each child holds his or her picture and in turn names the things they have drawn around their self-portrait, 'I am good at.'

Guess the feeling

One child leaves the circle, the rest of the class choose one emotion, e.g. happy, sad, cross, excited, etc., and think of ways to show this emotion. The person comes back and has to guess which emotion has been chosen.

Pass the smile around the circle (see Figure 4.1).

Personal development

Curry and Johnson (1990) offer a useful description of four areas that make up personal development: acceptance, power and control, moral worth and competence. Children need to feel accepted for who they are first by the important people in their lives and later by their peers, friends and teachers. Young children experiment with power and control over their immediate environment, their relationships and they eventually develop self-control. Moral worth is about the development of right and wrong and the emergence of conscience. Competence is about the child's increasing skills and abilities to achieve in all aspects of their development. There are significant considerations that will be developed further under the following headings: self-esteem, behaviour and the development of independence.

Self-esteem

The concept of self is being developed during the first and second year of life. Initially the baby is not aware of the difference and separateness of the adult feeding him or her. The child has to discriminate between what is 'me' and 'not me'. Where do I begin and others end? The physical nature of the boundaries begins with this experience and develops into more involved, complex and sophisticated ideas about the self. In this very early interaction there are three important lessons being learned.

One is about acceptance, essential for self-esteem; the second is about boundaries; and the third is about the relationships between self and others that will run throughout the whole of their lives. Acceptance is essential to self-esteem.

The development of positive self-esteem is, in my view, the most valuable gift you can give to a children. This will affect their capacity for development in every aspect of their lives: the personal, social, intellectual, emotional and physical, at home, at school, at work, and at play. Children need to feel sure of themselves in order to engage fully in any activity. They need to feel confident of their self-worth to be able to take risks and face challenges (see Figure 4.2). They need to be given permission to make mistakes and to know that this will not destroy them. They need to feel totally accepted for who they are, no more, no less. They need to feel tolerated when their actions push us to the limits. They need to know that we can separate who they are from any unacceptable behaviour.

Figure 4.2 *'I can do it. Look at me': physical skills help increase confidence*

At this point it is worth taking note of the work of Goleman (1996) and Rogers (1961). Goleman argues that our view of human intelligence is far too narrow, and what he refers to as 'emotional intelligence' is closely linked to success in later life. He presents a powerful argument which asserts that the emotional lessons a child learns actually sculpt the brain's circuitry. It seems to me that we cannot afford to ignore this aspect of development. Rogers says that not only is the development of self-esteem central to all other forms of learning but that people will learn only if they feel that the learning helps to construct or maintain their sense of self, and makes a strong case that people will reject or block learning that is perceived as threatening to themselves.

If we accept these arguments, the remit for our work is set. We must ensure that children's emotional well-being is taken into account for them to make full use of their cognitive abilities to becoming thinking beings. We would be well advised, concludes Goleman, to pay more attention to this aspect of children's development, which will cascade into every other aspect of human development and life. What can we do that will help children fare better in life?

How do we enhance children's self-esteem?

There are a number of books that are particularly good on this subject, one of which is *Self-Esteem* and *Successful Early Learning* by Rosemary Roberts (1995). In addition, I offer a few general principles:

- Avoid using raised voices, put-downs, sarcasm and humiliation – even those glares used to silently make children feel bad about themselves.
- Be open, clear and simple about what is expected.
- Children on the whole want to please, use that as a starting point.
- Offer realistic praise for effort and achievement.
- Offer encouragement.
- Provide opportunities for children to comment on the things they have done well.
- Make sure the tasks you request are within the capabilities of the children – build on success.
- Practise the use of positive language.
- Develop full use of drama and role-play to develop confidence.

Behaviour

A happy and accepting atmosphere in the classroom helps children to learn. If you are positive about your work and enjoying what you are doing this will emanate to the children. There is nothing so infectious as an atmosphere – either good or bad. It is unrealistic to think people are happy all of the time, but a genuine interest in the children and in what you are doing will go a long way in producing positive results.

How can we help children in dealing with powerful emotions?

Young children experience very powerful emotions. Sometime these feelings can be uncontrollable, unpredictable and frightening for the child. Children's lives can be traumatic and life can demand a lot from them. We know that it helps children to be able to talk about their feelings, but this demands a great deal of sophistication and maturity. It is important to introduce children to the language of emotions: happy, sad, angry, frustrated, disappointed, afraid and so on, and to help them to identify their feelings. When children experience feelings it can be difficult for them to understand what is causing the feelings but they are uncomfortable with the sensation. Identifying feelings and naming them helps provide a context for understanding and expressing the feelings and offers a sense of control. There are lots of card games and books produced now along these lines (e.g. 'Angry Arthur'). As with all other aspects of learning the adults' role is then to work with the children to extend the emotional language. This is by far the most crucial aspect of emotional development.

- Observe children to note any changes in behaviour;
- listen to what children say;
- develop active listening skills in the children;
- provide games that extend emotional language;
- provide books and stories that identify and express feelings;
- allocate time for children to engage in pretend play;
- provide sensory play materials which can be either soothing, e.g. water, or a release of tension, e.g. clay;
- provide therapeutic experiences, e.g. small world play to re-enact situations;
- verbalise your own feelings and thinking, helping children to understand the process you use.

It is difficult for children in isolation to deal with feelings of rejection, pain, separation and loss. These can be the result of a family breakdown or a bereavement. At such times when the whole family needs support, the child is often left struggling to understand what is happening. Schools may be the only constancy in their lives. Children react differently to these life situations. With some children we will be in no doubt that something is wrong, but with others we may need to watch more closely to notice the quiet withdrawing. We will need to think about how best to approach this at a time of crisis with a particular child; as the class develops the language and expressive skills they will have some useful tools when difficulties arise.

Children who are not allowed to express their negative feelings may be in danger of what Roberts (1995) calls a kind of 'emotional helplessness'. Feelings do not cease to exist simply because they are denied. The tendency is for them to become more powerful. Emotional development is about learning how to accept and manage feelings and how to respond appropriately.

Very young children experiment with their ability to control, they play with situations that help them understand the control they exert over their environment. They also do this in relationship to the adults and other children in their lives. This is developed further into helping them to deal with their emotions. For a child to develop self-control they need to have these feelings acknowledged.

Steps in helping children to deal with difficult behaviour:

- To maintain good eye contact, get down to the child's height and look directly into their eyes;
- keep your tone of voice quiet and calm;
- ask what is wrong and what would make them feel better;
- listen to what they have to say and repeat this to them with the other considerations they need to think about;
- help them learn to negotiate about what they can do or may not be able to do;
- help them to reach an agreement about what they may be able to do later or another day.

Adults taking these actions not only prevent a public humiliation but help the children resolve the problem and advance children's emotional literacy. They also give them some techniques for dealing with strong or difficult feelings.

Children need to feel safe and secure in their environment and in their relationships. We need to establish a classroom in which the rules and boundaries are clear. All children have the right to feel safe and that includes feeling safe from humiliation and teasing and harmful words as well as from physical danger.

Is it as simple as teaching children right from wrong?

There are many reasons why children's behaviour may become difficult and some are explained by powerful emotions. However, most ongoing difficulties are rooted in poor self-esteem. Essentially we need to try to understand why children are behaving in a particular way and question whether it is a temporary change or a longer term problem. Children can learn the rules of what is acceptable and what is not; children with poor reasoning ability and poor self-esteem may tend to quote the rules but will not internalise them without a lot of support and providing lots of thinking and reasoning.

The development of the concept of right and wrong is quite complex and some children take longer than others in reaching this stage of moral development. The aim must always be to work towards children having their own internal sense of right and wrong. This works best if boundaries are clear and rules are applied consistently.

A strong moral sense develops from the ability to empathise with others. The development of empathy is based on children's ability to see things from someone else's point of view. This can be encouraged in the following ways:

- Dramatic play helps children to put themselves in the shoes of others, aid understanding, test the ways groups work and what part they have in them. They can change roles and try out something else, e.g. being the leader of the group or the youngest.

Figure 4.3 *'Can I help you?': encouraging children to look out for others*

- Play games that encourage children to look out for others and develop their skills in asking what others need (see Figure 4.3). Develop the thinking about what it might be like to be in someone else's position.
- Encourage sensitivity, helping children to see just how much someone needs and not taking over from them.
- Read stories and discuss the motivation or view of the different characters.

Educators have expressed concerns over children's behaviour in the classroom. Some put this down to the increased demand for higher attainment targets in schools and others to social problems. It is important that we continue to question the cause in the knowledge that as part of the adult world we are creating the situation in which the children behave in a particular way. We need to take account of this in the schools and in the wider communities and ensure that we have good systems in place to support and protect children in developing emotionally and socially.

In helping children to integrate with their peers and become socially competent we must be aware that we respect the individual differences of children, the uniqueness that makes them who they are. The aim is not to make all children behave in the same way, nor to conform to the social pressures of the group. How then do we get this balance right? Our approach and attitudes will determine how children will respond to each other's differences through our example and the accepted ethos of inclusion.

Listening skills

Listening is a skill that needs to be learned. There are lots of games that you can play to enhance listening skills. For example:

- Encourage children to listen to the sounds around them and try to guess what they are.
- Supply tapes that have recordings of different sounds for children to identify.
- Listen to stories and music and talk about what they have heard.
- Develop the skill of listening to each other. The circle time is one opportunity for this. Each child should have the chance to speak and be listened to. It may be best to do this in small groups at first as young children will find it hard to concentrate if you try to go around the whole class to hear what they have to say. Many classes devise some simple rules to make sure children do not speak when someone else is speaking; they often agree that the child speaking will hold an object to indicate it is their turn to talk and will then pass it on to the next speaker. Children should be able to say no if they do not wish to take part.

- Use games so that children can talk to the one next to them and ask them about a subject, then the listener can tell the group. Some children find it hard to give this amount of effort and time to listening to another child. It will need to be developed slowly.

Conflict management

Dealing with conflict is for many adults very difficult. Some people become over-aggressive and others withdraw and avoid conflict. It is hardly surprising that if adults have such difficulty with this we also have difficulty in passing on useful messages to children about how to deal effectively with conflict. We need to move to a better acceptance of conflict as a natural and healthy part of life through which we can learn something about ourselves and others. Very young children are often better at this than adults. Children as young as 2 often squabble but then soon forget about it. At some stage children are taught that the conflict itself is wrong – that their ability to express themselves is stifled as they get older and that 2-year-olds' methods are no longer sociably acceptable. At this key point in the child's development we are in a position to provide them with the skills and techniques that will set them up for life. If we work with children expressing their feelings and finding ways to understand each other's points of view, we can help them begin to resolve conflicts.

Wear (2000) identifies three lessons: those of compromise, mediation and negotiation that we need to learn to defuse difficult situations. To help children learn these skills try the following procedure when a conflict arises:

1 Cool off: ask the children to take deep breaths, ask what they are feeling, talk about what happened (language listening skills)
2 Talk about what they each want out of the situation.
3 Agree to try to work together. Share points of view and listen to the other person.

Learning to compromise

They may agree to disagree, to walk away, or to take responsibility for finding a joint solution to the problem. Finding a way through may first involve generating many possible solutions, then deciding together which is the best one. In a win/win situation it may not be anyone's first choice, but it may be the only one that they can live with. This serves to empower the sense that they have choices about how they act, that there are different ways forward out of a difficult situation, and positive outcomes are possible. Practising listening and cooperative skills and avoiding insults and put-downs are also important elements of children's learning in this area.

Learning to negotiate

We see children who are socially adept managing to negotiate with others to get what they want.

> *A young child is sitting on the step with his younger brother who has hold of the toy he wants to play with. The older brother tries to take the toy but the youngest is not going to let go so easily. The older child picks up a toy that he thinks the younger one will like. 'look at this, you like playing with this truck don't you, remember we made it go fast down the slope.' He reaches over to remove the toy from the child's hand. Still not giving up. 'Look what it will do, just let me have this for a while and I will give it back to you.'*

What a lot of learning has gone into this action. What an excellent young negotiator and what an asset he will be to the adult world when he grows up. These lessons are there in everyday life, and real incidents and events can be used as examples to illustrate a specific issue and to promote discussion and request possible solutions during circle time. Remember younger children will need props to assist conceptualising the scene. You can do this with puppets and get the children to repeat phrases that will help the character in the play to negotiate a positive solution.

Learning to mediate

With younger children and in the classroom it is usually the adult who becomes the mediator in a conflict. Children can be helped to develop the ability to resolve their own conflicts. This is a tactic used with discretion with an adult keeping a watchful eye to make sure it doesn't get out of control. Lorna Farrington in *Playground Peacemakers* (2000) provides a progressive programme of activities designed to be used as part of a whole school approach to conflict resolution. Farrington outlines the success of working with children to become mediators in disputes. These playground peacemakers are coached to mediate between the parties. Teachers report fewer fights and fewer verbal squabbles. Those who are not involved in the conflict, but who in the past might have helped to inflame the situation, have a more positive role to be helpful and constructive.

Independence

Between the ages of 3 and 7 years, there is an enormous amount of development taking place on the road to children becoming independent, autonomous people managing their own personal care and in control of their own learning and able to make decisions. Many 3-year-old children have developed an awareness of themselves and their own identity. Their motor skills are developing and they are increasingly gaining control of their movements. Fine motor skills are the last to develop and take a good deal of muscle development for children to be able to gain the very delicate movements needed to undertake such tasks as sewing, writing with a fine pencil and fastening small buttons. It is far better to provide a child with the right tools and equipment graded in size, e.g. thick pencils, large buttons, to enable them to manage and succeed with the task than to leave them to struggle with it. It is crucial that we observe the children carefully to be aware of their physical development (see Chapter 10). Children from a very young age can be very independent if provided with the correct equipment. If necessary the tasks can be broken down into stages to maintain the sense of them trying to do things for themselves. It is well researched now that children on transition from one setting or school to another effectively lose approximately a year, and there can be a tendency to assume they are not as capable as they are.

How do we develop the skills of independence?

Much self-reliance in the early stages depends on the ability of children to do practical things for themselves. By achieving these small tasks children gain confidence to try other things.

- Observe, know what skills they have.
- Break the task up into steps to assist in independence.
- Encourage self-reliance.
- Check that the furniture, storage units are at the right level and height.
- Check that you have a good range of graded tools, scissors, pencils, wood-work tools, puzzles, cooking equipment, etc.
- Check that the children can manage the fastenings on dressing-up clothes.
- Provide materials that help children to practise using practical skills such as fastening buttons or tying laces.
- Provide activities that build fine manipulative muscles, such as play-dough.
- Request that young children are dressed in clothes that encourage them to manage themselves to the toilet, e.g. elasticated trousers.
- Provide hand-washing sink, soap and towel in easy reach, encourage cleaning the basin after washing painted hands.
- Facilitate dressing and undressing. Lots of time needed for this, changing for games, outdoor shoes, etc.
- Develop physical abilities of children in the gym and playground gradually to maintain confidence.

Developing independent thinking

Children are thinking and problem-solving from a very young age. If they have engaged in active learning they will already be proficient independent thinkers. Children working out which beaker fits into which adopt a process of problem-solving, first of all by trial and error, and once they have worked it out by looking and thinking. The further children go into the formal school years the more we need to work on maintaining their capacity and capability to be in control of their own learning and to extend their skills to be independent thinkers.

If children are used to the teacher telling them what to do and expecting a particular outcome they will exert a lot of effort in interpreting the instructions and trying to get it the way you want it rather than by applying their own judgement and thinking about how the task could be achieved. Our role here is to pose the problem to be solved or the task to be undertaken and let the children work out their own way of doing it.

> *One of my students provided an excellent example of this with a group of 5–6-year-olds who were learning about the properties of different materials. She provided them with a doll that she sat in the middle of the table and told them a story about the doll packing to go on holiday. They were to help design a hat for the doll to take on holiday. There was lots of conversation about the different kinds of hats that the doll may take. It could be a hat to protect the doll from the sun, and they came up with ideas about what that might be. Alternatively it could be a rain hat. They talked about what they would need to think about in making a rain hat. The project was very successful and all of the children fully engaged in the task they had in hand. They drew their designs (one child even drew a flow chart of how he was going to approach the task) and chose the materials from a wide selection. The range of hats produced was astounding, every one with a unique design. There were sun hats with neck flaps, some with peeks, some with frilly shades, some with netting 'to keep the flies out'. The fabrics for the rain hats were tested for waterproofing by running them under the water before they started. The problems solved on the way were numerous. One child had designed the hat flat and when she tried it on the doll she realised it wouldn't go on – there needed to be space for the head. She thought about it and decide it needed more space so she found a bigger piece of cloth and made the hat with tucks in it so the head could fit.*

The children here learned not just from their own discoveries but also from each other, they learned about design, planning, the properties of the materials, what would stick and alternative glues, staples, etc. They also came up with ideas to stiffen the rim. There were endless problem-solving experiences, lots of learning, it was fun and very memorable.

Children need to know their way around the classroom, they need to feel that it is theirs to use. They need to be in charge of tidying it up and knowing where everything goes and be responsible for checking and reporting when materials are getting low or broken. Everyone should be part of the routine for keeping the room clean, and again, cleaning utensils need to be child size.

Social development

Social development includes issues that are both general and specific. Our considerations here need to extend to the wider community for which we are preparing children. In providing them with the knowledge, skills, attitudes and understanding for creating a healthy society and a positive view of the diversity of people within it, we hope to generate a tolerant and inclusive school and future. We need to foster this by providing a positive view of children from a variety of different backgrounds, families, cultures and dis/abilities.

In what follows, Setting the scene, I consider the need to create a welcoming environment and agree the rules with the children. This is followed by three main threads: Working together; Relationships; Citizenship.

Setting the scene

Children need to feel valued by, and safe and secure with the adults and children around them. They need a sense of belonging, to feel they have a place in the group and that they are important. They need to know they can trust the adults to take care of them in every aspect of their being. Adults are very powerful in this situation and the atmosphere we establish will set the framework for how the children behave towards one another and develop an understanding of what is acceptable and what is not.

Creating a welcoming environment

Most schools now have a settling-in policy for working with new children that reflects the importance of the partnership with parents. Many schools will visit the children at home or at their pre-school setting prior to their first day. This visit is invaluable. It establishes a strong link with home and acknowledges the child's prior experiences as important. It also provides you with an opening for conversations with the child. Many settings have a staggered intake for new children and call upon the established children to assist with the new children and to help them to become familiar with the setting, to show children around and take them to lunch. It is an excellent two-fold venture: in addition to the obvious benefits to the child who is new, it provides a real opportunity for children to help a younger child and in turn, enhances their self-esteem.

- Make sure all the children have a place in the group. Having their photographs included on a welcome poster instantly gives the children a place in the group.
- Provide a welcome in different languages.
- Provide a welcome that lets children and parents feel that you really are pleased to see them.
- Give yourself time to prepare the classroom in advance of the children arriving so that you can focus your attention on the children and parents.
- Look after yourself so that you can make sure you are fresh and ready for the day.
- Be sure to talk to all of the children as they arrive.
- Show respect for all children and their parents.
- Make sure that you have a good range of multicultural resources and check the images portrayed within books and on posters.

Remember that children learn from watching us. They are very good at reading body language and will follow our signals. If we are seen to respect all children and all families it will establish important messages from the outset.

Agreeing the rules with the children

Children need to feel safe and secure both in themselves and in the group. This is provided by the boundaries that we operate within that give us a feeling of being in control and equally provide a certain element of predictability about the control of the group. This way it is not so threatening (see also Chapter 1). Roberts (1995) identifies the following three rights that apply to children and adults: the right to feel safe, the right to learn (and to teach) and the right to be treated with dignity and respect.

Additionally, children need to know and understand what is expected of them and for what reasons. They will engage with this better if they have a part in thinking it through. If the children have had the chance from the outset to consider the options, think about what is important, and what sort of class they want to be part of, it will make more sense to them. It offers children a framework in which to understand and be part of creating the boundaries of the group.

For children where this approach of discussing and negotiating is similar to their experience at home it will be easy for them to adopt. For other children this will be much more difficult and you can see them struggling to understand this new approach. However, the more open, defined, verbalised and repeated the messages are the more it will begin to make sense and assist with the developing reason. One model for establishing the principals and guidelines is through a class discussion.

Activity

Discuss with the children and develop ways of working. Ask the children some guiding questions in order to draw out some guidelines for them to agree.

- What do you think makes a classroom feel friendly? What could we do?
- What do you think we could do to make sure everyone gets time to talk and for us to listen?
- How do you think it would feel if some children in the class made fun of you? How do you think we should behave to each other?
- What do you think could happen if you run in the classroom? How can we make sure people don't get hurt?
- What would you like to happen if . . . you fall over, you are having trouble tying your shoelace, you feel upset, you cannot reach the toy you want?
- What do you think would be a good way to help a new child to settle in the class?
- If someone was being mean to you, what do you think you should do? What do you think others around you could do to help you?

The outcomes from this discussion should be recorded in simple statements and displayed in language accessible to the children. Get the children to draw pictures and illustrate their own posters depicting their statements. Possible outcomes for example, might be:

we work together;
we listen to each other;
we take turns and share (see Figure 4.4);
we walk in the classroom;
we help each other;
we are kind to each other;
we look out for each other;
we are friendly to one another.

Figure 4.4 *'Sharing' by Rosie Alsop, aged 7*

The way we work with the children from here on in will be based on this initial task. This is just a starting point. For this to be fully adopted as a way of being in the school it needs to be followed up by activities throughout the year. The verbalisation of the agreement and the reasoning behind it will help the children to become familiar with this way of thinking. If the group of children hear the same messages repeated when they go into assembly, the playground or the dinner hall, they will begin to feel a sense of security in the consistency and fairness this offers. The discussions need to develop in complexity and become more sophisticated as the group moves through the school.

Working together cooperation

How do we help children to develop the skills of cooperation?

We are as human beings essentially sociable. Children are interested in each other, and social interaction can be encouraged and facilitated by the way the teacher sets the scene and manages the classroom. However, for some children this is not so easy. This lack of ease may be developmental.

We must take into account the maturity of the child, and his or her experience. Some theories show a child moving from solitary play through to cooperative play (Piaget, 1896–1980). Critics of this view have since argued that the stages are not so clearly defined or distinct. Babies are certainly sociable beings and from a very young age will play turn-taking games in passing you a toy and taking it back. This is clearly evident in conversation with babies where the baby has learned long before words are formed, that there is a sequence taking place. They gurgle in response to the carer and then wait their turn. The baby is playing sociably.

During the age group 3–7 years there is a huge development of fantasy/dramatic play/imaginative play which involves children in playing out a whole scene together. This is a very elaborate form of cooperative play. Children learn significantly from these interactions (see Figure 4.5).

Figure 4.5 *Children playing out a scene together and learning to cooperate*

It is well documented that when children are experiencing shock or trauma they will revert to the things that give them comfort and are less demanding. This may involve becoming more solitary for a period.

Classroom organisation

The room organisation of the day and the classroom need to be considered for their added value in social interaction. This may be through organising for close proximity or ease of eye contact. This is best done by providing:

- seats set facing diagonally opposite, round or square tables;
- play equipment chosen to encourage cooperation and positioned to take into account what the children can see to encourage them to talk and think together, e.g. paint easels side by side, water tray positions opposite (see Figure 4.6);
- a well-resourced role-play area with lots of opportunities to move freely and play cooperatively;
- floor space for construction, rail tracks, large puzzles;
- comfortable book corner and communal listening bay for sharing stories;
- opportunities for joint creative projects;
- comfortable, sociable meal time.

There appear to be fewer opportunities now for children to engage in unsupervised play in their free time. Increased amounts of time allocated to organised activities (e.g. music lessons) or in isolated activities such as watching TV leave less time for engagement in cooperative play and less opportunity to test out their social skills. We need to ensure that this is happening during the school day by making sure the opportunities exist and engage children fully in group activities, games and lessons.

Working things out together	Cooperative play	Taking turns
Building/ construction	Parachute game	Card games
Large puzzles	Role-play	Computerised toys
Playing music	Drama	Bikes
		Skipping
		Team games

Relationships

What part can we play in helping children to make friends?

Social intelligence is an aspect that Goleman (1996) states as being crucial for our success and levels of fulfilment in virtually all aspects of our lives, from making friends to holding down a job. When children are asked to comment on what is important to them at school it is friends they talk about. Peers are important to us.

Figure 4.6 *Play equipment chosen and positioned to encourage cooperation and social interaction; standing around the water tray and sharing a tandem*

Friendships provide us with a sense of ourselves and our self-worth.
For some children making friends does not come naturally. One child
in ten has a social learning deficiency. They do not know how to act in
social situations and have limited and isolating responses to others.
They are basically not fun to be with and do not know how to make
others feel good. They are more likely to brag, sulk, cheat, and give up
when losing. They have poor empathy skills.

(Wear, 2000, p. 95)

We have considered the need for children to have a sense of belonging
to a group which comes from feeling accepted for who they are. Belonging
can then be difficult if a child has already developed 'social learning
deficiencies'. We have to accept that some children are not as easy to like
as others. Children in the group will watch your response to these children
and will learn from how you are with them. You will need to find positive
ways of working with all children. Some of the social lessons need to be
explicit and reinforced.

How do we encourage friendships between children and assist in the
development of social skills? One significant aspect of our practice should be
the positive reinforcement of friendly actions and social skills amongst the
children (see Figure 4.7). Here are some examples:

Salim was kind to me when I fell over.
Carol helped me to do the puzzle.
Beth lent me her pencil.
Jason said he liked it when I said thank you.
Nadia looked after the rabbit.
Afsi asked if I wanted to have a ride in the cart while she pulled it.
Paul let me have a go with his new toy.
Ben invited me to play with him in the skipping game.
Kate saw what a mess I had made with the paints and offered to help me
to clean it up.

Encourage children to see what others need and prompt them to offer support.

*'Jess look, Sam is trying to put the rabbit back in the hutch, do you think he
could do with some help?'*
   'I'll hold the door open for him.'

Systematic approaches to teaching social skills are often highly effective in
changing behaviour. Wear (2000) found that social skills training that
included the teacher modelling behaviour and giving clear and positive

Figure 4.7 *Friendships provide us with a sense of self-worth; we should encourage and praise friendly actions*

feedback on children's attempts to practise them worked better than attempts to teach attitudes and values alone.

Citizenship and involvement

How can we help to develop the citizens of the future?

Children need to have an active part to play in their world. Each is an important member of the group and each has a useful contribution to make. Children who are damaged by lack of self-worth will have difficulty in believing this message. Children need to learn that they can make a difference and that their contribution counts for something for them to develop a sense of responsibility towards the social classroom and the people around them.

Where children have been engaged in putting forward their ideas for making the classroom, school or play area better, and they have been taken seriously, they have learned some very valuable lessons in social responsibility. There are lots of examples to draw on to illustrate this from children's suggestions on how to make a better cage for the classroom pet to live in, to a better play space in the playground, to how to prevent bullying. In some schools, children as young as seven are actively involved in formal meetings of the school council, being elected by the class to represent their views at the meeting and reporting back. The most popular topic for discussion always seems to be the toilets! Maybe the planners could learn something from this.

The degree to which children will take responsibility will be incremental but even the smallest task needs to be seen as important – whether it is watering the plants, helping to clear away or listening to a younger child read.

Health

It is well documented that much can be done during these early years to positive effect. In the UK, The White Paper on *Excellence in Schools* (DfEE, 1997) outlines the government's intention to help all schools to become healthier schools and that education has a role to play in promoting better health and emotional well-being for all children, in particular those who are socially and economically disadvantaged. A healthy school is one that is successful in helping pupils to do their best and to build on their achievements. It promotes physical and emotional health by providing accessible and relevant information and equipping pupils with skills and attitudes to make informed decisions about their health (DfEE 1999).

> So what do children need to know about health and keeping safe?
> How can we best promote an understanding of these issues with children in the early years?
> How can we assist in their developing the skills to make decisions about healthy living and keeping safe?
> What role do the parents and families have?

What do children need to know about health and keeping safe?

There is a wealth of texts on what children need to know about health and keeping safe in the primary years. *Health for Life Ages 4–7* by Noreen Wetton and Trefor Williams (2000) is particularly well considered about this in the early years and full of ideas for activities. To summarise, children need information that is appropriate to their age. Children between the ages of 3 to 8 years are very capable of absorbing huge amounts of basic information about their bodies, naming parts of the body and differences between people: hair, skin colour, gender, what we put into our bodies, e.g. food, drinks, medicine, etc. and what we put on our bodies, e.g. clothes, hats, sun cream.

Children need to know that their bodies need good food and exercise to be healthy. They need to know that there are dangers and they will have a better understanding of some of these dangers more than others. They need to know what things feel like and what makes them feel good, what makes them feel bad and what is that strange feeling when you are not quite sure, but you don't feel comfortable. This sense is one that we need to work on with young children to help them to take notice of and to trust their instincts.

We are laying the foundations of an understanding of good health by providing information and encouraging decision-making skills that assist in children's ability to make healthy lifestyle choices.

How can we best promote an understanding of these issues with children in the early years?

Children need guiding into thinking about which are good things that the body needs and which are not good things (see Figure 4.8). They will have an understanding of what it feels like if they hurt themselves and will be

Figure 4.8 *Good things that the body needs: 'Would you like some fruit?'*

able to make suggestions about how to protect themselves from danger, e.g. from sharp objects, traffic or falling.

The best way to promote this understanding with young children is to make sure that what we do starts from what they know, e.g. themselves. Start with the feelings they have and can identify and develop from this (emotional literacy again). We need to make sure that the work we do with children is developmental and progressive. We would do well to acknowledge Bruner's notion of the 'spiral curriculum' here. The curriculum and information needs to be progressive but also needs to be repeated at different levels of understanding to a greater depth and packaged differently. The youngest children need to work things out by repeatedly playing through ideas. They need the opportunity to repeat games themselves in order to make sense of them. We know that the more tangible and hands on the activities are the greater their assimilation of understanding.

Ideas for health education activities

- Circle time rounds: 'I am healthy when . . .', 'Being healthy is . . .', 'What do healthy people do?'
- Change places if . . . (teacher calls out examples of healthy things, e.g. if you had cereals for breakfast, if you brushed your teeth this morning) – children stand up and change places.
- Draw pictures of themselves doing something healthy.
- Sort out pictures of food into healthy and not so healthy and make a collage.
- Keeping safe: My name is . . . and I live at . . . (name of the road or town); make card with their name, address and phone number on it; paint pictures of their front door with the number on and make a class display.
- Ask the children to name all the things they feel they have to keep safe from and talk about, add to the list to make sure they include fire, water, sun, road and home safety. Ask the children to draw pictures. Back in the circle, lay three large sheets of paper on the floor each with a title in the middle: 'things', 'people' and 'places'. Discuss with the children the pictures they have drawn and get each one to place their picture on the poster.

- Books and stories.
- Role-play area – dolls, hospital, etc.
- Card games of body parts.
- Road safety tracks.
- Swimming pool safety.
- Naming feelings: what makes me happy/sad angry/upset is . . .
- Puppets.

- Small world play.
- Visitors, traffic control, fire brigade, police, nurse.
- Circle time discussion on:
  - What happens when you are tired? . . . Your body needs sleep.
  - What happens when you are hungry? . . . Your body needs food.
  - What happens when you stay underwater for a long time? . . . Your body needs air.
  - What happens when it is a rainy day and you cannot go out to play? . . . Your body need exercise.
  - Saying No!

We could also develop children to practise the skills they need to deal with difficult situations and to call on others to help them. This is part of developing a caring environment. This can be particularly helpful if we as adults take a stance against bullies. The whole staff approach is important here. The days have gone when it used to be considered character building to leave children to deal with bullies on their own. Many schools have effective anti-bullying policies in place. Bullies can operate only if everyone turns a blind eye. If the culture of the school is to take this seriously and to develop a supportive ethos, the bullies will eventually lose their lifeline. We need to develop in children an ability to ask for help. This needs playing out and re-enacting. Role-play and drama are very useful here. Some children will need lots of experiential rehearsal of this situation to be able to assert themselves.

How can we assist in their developing the skills to make decisions about healthy living and keeping safe?

We need to give children the resources to deal with life situations. Decision-making is a key skill here. Children need to feel they have power to make decisions. They need to use their knowledge and their understanding and they need to be able to make the decisions to promote their health. We need to develop decision-making at a basic level before this can be drawn into play at more complex levels. Lorna Farrington talks about children in the early years spending 75 per cent of their day in making decisions and higher up the school only 5 per cent of their time. We need to turn this around. We know that this is an important skill to develop and we need to reconsider the school day to ensure we are extending this skill as children move through the school.

What role do the parents and families have?

Parents/carers need to be fully aware of the issues that are being discussed with the children. It is a good school policy which states prior to entry that certain issues will be part of this curriculum. We engage parents in this from the outset in the interest of informing and protecting children.

The lives and culture of families will play a significant role in the lives of the children in regard to healthy lifestyles or otherwise. Children are not easily in control of what they eat, the types of food bought for the family, the approaches to exercise, the use of leisure time, the ability to express individual preferences, or to reject what parents do themselves. However, most parents want what is best for their children and are delighted when the school takes some responsibility for this. Many parents have had to battle with schools to take these issues seriously especially over the provision of school meals. Parents have a huge job on their hands to compete with advertising that becomes ever more invasive in enticing children to want things that we know are not good for promoting health and are delighted that schools will support them in this. There is no point in teaching good nutrition and good eating habits in the classroom and then providing children with very poor and unhealthy food at lunchtime.

Some parents may need to understand why the programme encourages children to think for themselves and to question when they would prefer that children simply learn to do as they are told. Families need to be aware when children will be considering issues relating to children keeping safe. This may include dealing with some delicate issue; it may really need a specific meeting with parents to discuss the issues and let them know how the subject will be approached and what will be discussed. It is important that parents are involved in this discussion. They may have to pick up on issues or questions with the child at home and need some preparation for this.

Conclusion

Children learn as much, if not more, from the way in which we behave towards them as from the content of the lessons and activities. The approaches we use and the attitudes and respect we show children in their early years will affect their ability to learn and their growth into effective citizens.

Pointers for PSHE in the early years

- The links between PSHE and children's learning has been well established by research.
- The quality of the relationship between the adults and children is crucial.

- The partnership between the family and school is important.
- The benefits of a whole school approach to PSHE cannot be underestimated.

Social

- Creating a welcoming environment and agreeing the rules sets the scene.
- The processes involved in developing these principles are learning experiences in themselves.
- There are vital aspects of the social component of the PSHE programme and approach which help children to cooperate, to develop friendships and to develop citizenship skills.

Personal

- Personal development is best founded on a firm basis of positive self-esteem.
- Adults need to help children to identify, understand and develop skills to cope with powerful emotions.
- A unified and sympathetic whole school approach to behaviour is vital.
- The development of listening skills, conflict management skills, learning to negotiate and to mediate are all essential life skills.
- The development of independence and independent learning needs to be progressive.

Health

- A healthy school enables children to give their best and build on their achievements.
- The safety of the child is paramount.
- A major goal is to develop children's understanding of health issues as a precursor to their making informed and important decisions.
- In health, as in all other social and personal development issues there is a need for continuing dialogue with the children's families.

References

Curry, N. and Johnson, C. (1990) *Beyond Self-esteem: Developing a Sense of Human Value*, Washington, DC: NAEYC.

DfEE (1997) White Paper on *Excellence in Schools*, Nottingham: DfEE Publications.

DfEE (1999) *National Healthy Schools Standard Guidance*, Nottingham: DfEE Publications.

Farrington, L. (2000) *Playground Peacemakers, Peaceful Conflict Resolution for Schools Using The Mediation Way For Teachers in Key Stage 1*, Plymouth, UK: Loxley Enterprises.

Goleman, D. (1996) *Emotional Intelligence – Why It Can Matter More Than IQ*, London: Bloomsbury.

Mosley, J. (1996) *Quality Circle Time In The Primary Classroom* Volume 1, Wisbech, UK: LDA.

Roberts, R. (1995) *Self-esteem and Successful Early Learning*, London: Hodder & Stoughton Educational.

Rogers, C. (1961) *On Becoming a Person*, London: Constable.

Wear, K. (2000) *Promoting Mental, Emotional and Social Health, A Whole School Approach*, London: Routledge.

Wetton, N. and Williams, T. (2000) *Health For Life Ages 4–7*, Cheltenham: Thornes Nelson.

Further reading

James, F. and Browsword, K. (1994) *A Positive Approach*, Twickenham, UK: Blair Publications.

Laishley, J. (1987) *Working with Young Children*, Second Edition, London: Hodder & Stoughton.

Roffey, S., Tarrant, T. and Majors, K., (1994) *Young Friends: Schools and Friendship*, London: Cassell.

CHAPTER 5

'Is it like the school bus?'

ASSESSMENT IN THE EARLY YEARS

Rachel Sparks Linfield and Paul Warwick

For those concerned with developing children's learning in the early years, assessment has always been seen as:

> an integral part of the educational process, continually providing both 'feedback' and 'feedforward'.
>
> (DES, 1987, para. 4)

Early years educators monitor their pupils' development to inform their day-to-day teaching and to allow them to report learners' achievements. They use formative assessment, where the emphasis is on planning the next steps to be taken with a child, and summative assessment to provide a snapshot of the child's achievements and abilities at a particular stage. In doing this they have made assessment all-embracing, attempting to build a picture of the whole child, believing that:

> The process of assessing children's learning – by looking closely at it and striving to understand it – is the only certain safeguard against children's failure, the only certain guarantee of children's progress and development.
>
> (Drummond, 1993, p. 10)

In this chapter we use case study evidence to illustrate some of the assessment principles and practices adopted by successful early years educators. In doing so, we make a distinction between assessment *for* learning (formative assessment), which involves the use of classroom assessment to improve learning, and assessment *of* learning (summative assessment), which measures what pupils know or can do. We will be placing greatest emphasis on assessment for learning, central to which are the following principles.

Assessment for learning:
- is embedded in the teaching and learning process of which it is an essential part;
- shares learning goals with pupils;
- helps pupils to know and recognise the standards to aim for;
- provides feedback that leads pupils to identify what they should do next to improve;
- has a commitment that every pupil can improve;
- involves both teacher and pupils in reviewing and reflecting on pupil performance and progress;
- involves pupils in self assessment.

(QCA website, 2001)

Assessment *for* learning in the early years

The findings of Black and Wiliam (1998), developed by Shirley Clarke's work with thousands of primary school teachers (2001), provides a series of strategies for developing effective formative assessment. Key points for early years educators include:

- the necessity of sharing learning intentions with pupils;
- the need to use questioning and discussion to support learning;
- the desirability of encouraging pupils to make assessments of their own work;
- the importance of positive feedback and marking;
- the need to develop individual target setting;
- the vital requirement to adjust teaching to take account of learning.

We will now consider each of these strategies.

Sharing learning intentions

Educators understand the necessity of defining clear learning objectives to ensure that both teaching and assessment are focused. However, it is also essential that these learning intentions are shared with the children, in terms that help them to make sense of the purpose of the task. Giving instructions for how a task is to be carried out is different from stating the learning intentions of the task, and children need both if they are to feel the sense of success that accompanies learning. For example, the following instructions might be given for painting a rainbow:

'Today I want you to paint a picture of a rainbow. Here is a chart of the rainbow colours that we have been looking at this week. You should have a piece of white paper, a long, flat-headed brush and some paints. Paint the most beautiful rainbow that you can.'

Whilst there is nothing really wrong with these instructions, they do not give the learning intention of the task. The instructions are likely to lead pupils to ask a number of questions such as:

• Must I fill the paper?
• Must I only do a rainbow?
• What does beautiful mean – really bright or soft colours?

These questions reflect pupils' uncertainty about what the teacher is looking for. Typical manifestations of this uncertainty include:

• Children asking for the instructions to be repeated.
• Time-wasting tactics.
• Do nothing, wait until a neighbour starts and then copy.

The essential adjunct to the instructions is therefore a statement of learning intentions for the task. For example: 'I would like you to show that a rainbow is made of different bands of colour, and that those colours go in the same order no matter how big or small the rainbow is that you paint.' Educators should, as far as possible, avoid including the learning intentions *within* the instructions as this can be muddling for a child. Where educators and children have a clear, shared understanding of the learning intentions assessment will have greater meaning.

Using questioning and discussion to support learning

Educators are adept at using a variety of questions for different purposes. Early years pupils benefit from questioning that will allow them to articulate *their* ideas. Only then can this information be used in teaching that is targeted to develop learning.

The following transcripts illustrate clearly how questioning and discussion can be used to ascertain different starting points for teaching and learning for different pupils. A class of 4–5-year-olds was working on a project entitled 'All

Figure 5.1 *A picture containing living and non-living things*

Around Me'. Children had been on walks and collected items for their '-interest table'. They had looked at the local countryside and had made drawings of all that they had seen. The teacher became aware that children talked about living things but was uncertain that all her class used the phrase 'living thing' to mean the same thing. During an afternoon of 'All Around Me' activities she showed the picture reproduced in Figure 5.1. and asked children to pick out living and non-living things. Transcripts of three of the conversations are given. The children had all been in the reception class for two terms.

Conversation 1 between teacher (T) and girl aged 5 (G).

T   What in the picture is living?
G   Nothing, it's only a picture.
T   Pretend it isn't a picture but it's outside.
G   It's all living. The hedgehog, the sun, the tree, the apple, the mummy, the smoke – it's moving.
T   Is the car living?
G   Yes, it's all real. Not pretend. It's real.

This conversation indicates that this child believed 'living' to mean 'real'.

Conversation 2 between teacher (T) and girl aged 5 years 3 months (G).

T   What can you see in the picture that is living?
G   The people.
T   Anything else?
G   The butterfly. The hedgehog, I think it's living but it looks funny. Is it supposed to be real?
T   I think it's supposed to be like the hedgehogs we find outside. Not like the toy one in our book corner.

G   Hedgehogs outside aren't always living. I saw one 'deaded' in the road. A car had 'runned' over it.

T   Are the apples living?

G   No. The tree is.

T   Why do you say that?

G   The tree can grow until it gets cut down. The apples just fall off.

Here the child had a concept of living to do with growth. She readily recognised animals as living but was confused about apples.

Conversation 3 between teacher (T) and boy aged 4 years 7 months (B).

T   Can you see two things in this picture that are living?

B   Mmm. The butterfly?

T   And?

B   The children.

T   Can you see anything that is not living?

B   The hedgehog might be dead. The car might have gone over it.

T   Is –

B   But I don't think so. I think it's happy.

T   Is the house living?

B   People might live in it.

T   Is the tree living?

B   No.

T   Why not?

B   It just grows. It's not 'alive'.

T   How do you mean, 'it's not alive'?

B   It can't walk.

In this conversation the boy readily identified humans and animals as living. Trees, however, were not viewed as alive. As a result of these, and similar conversations, the teacher realised that within her reception class the word 'living' held many different meanings. The majority saw animals and humans as living but did not view plants in the same way. For some 'living' was synonymous with 'can move'. The teacher followed up the conversations with more experiences of 'living things'. The discussions provided clear evidence of understanding and misunderstanding of a concept. They demonstrate the importance of listening to children for assessing understanding.

While considering the use of questioning and discussion in obtaining evidence for formative assessment, it seems sensible to go further and to consider how both the products of pupils' work and observations of pupils at work can be used in combination with questioning and discussion to build a more rounded profile of the learner.

In the following example (taken from Sparks Linfield 1994) a class of 5–6-year-olds were asked to observe a straw in a glass of water and to draw what they had observed. The teacher hoped that the children would notice that the straw appeared to bend. The teacher let four children at a time observe and draw and to use the drawings as evidence of observing the bent straw. The following conversations, however, again show the importance of talking to children and watching them at work. The drawings produced by one group of pupils appear in Figure 5.2.

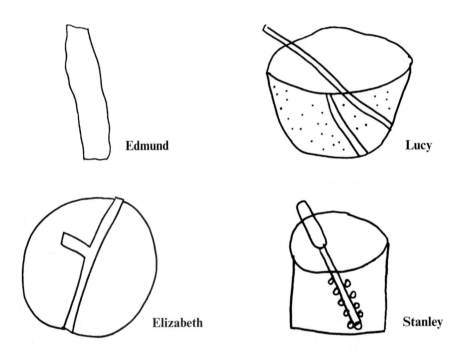

Figure 5.2 *Four children's drawings of a straw in a glass of water*

The drawings produced by Lucy and Elizabeth seem to reflect knowledge that the straw appears to bend. Edmund, though, seems to have only seen a straight straw. Observation of the children at work, and discussion with them, however, showed otherwise.

The teacher was, in the words of Clayden and Peacock (1994), observing 'with a purpose'. While watching the children she realised that Stanley was not drawing what he had observed. Instead, he tried to copy Lucy's drawing and then decided to draw the pipette he had used in a previous experiment.

The teacher was most impressed by Lucy when she saw the elliptical bowl. They discussed her finished picture:

T   What have you drawn?
L   The straw.
T   What's under the straw? [*She pointed at what she imagined was the straw's reflection.*]
L   It's that mark on the table. I did it when I was colouring.
T   And the dots? [*She thought they were bubbles.*]
L   That's pen on the table. Shall I get a cloth to wipe it off?

This conversation showed that what the teacher was seeing in the picture was not what Lucy had intended. The final surprise came through talking to Edmund.

T   Can you see the straw in the glass?
E   Yes.
T   Does it look like the one out of the water?
E   No, the one in the water's bent.
T   Why haven't you drawn it bent?
E   'Cos it's only pretend. Really the straw is straight.

Edmund had not only observed the bent straw but also knew this was just an optical effect. Without discussion, this knowledge would not have been evident. The experience of watching the children at work and of discussing their drawings raises the question of how often through looking at 'written' evidence we make the assumption that children have understood a concept when discussion would prove otherwise. Equally, how often do we think children have not understood when actually they do? Frequently children perceive things differently from adults. Many children use drawings to record what they 'know' rather than what they 'see'. Clearly discussion has much to offer here to valid assessment.

Pupil self-assessment

It may seem that a call to involve early years pupils in the assessment of their own work is an unnecessary burden on the already over loaded educator. However, we believe that self-assessment by pupils 'far from being a luxury, is in fact an essential component of formative assessment' (Black and Wiliam, 1998, p.10). If sharing learning intentions with pupils is likely to promote learning, encouraging pupils to respond to how well *they* feel those intentions have been met is surely equally important. The role of the educator is to train pupils to look for specifics

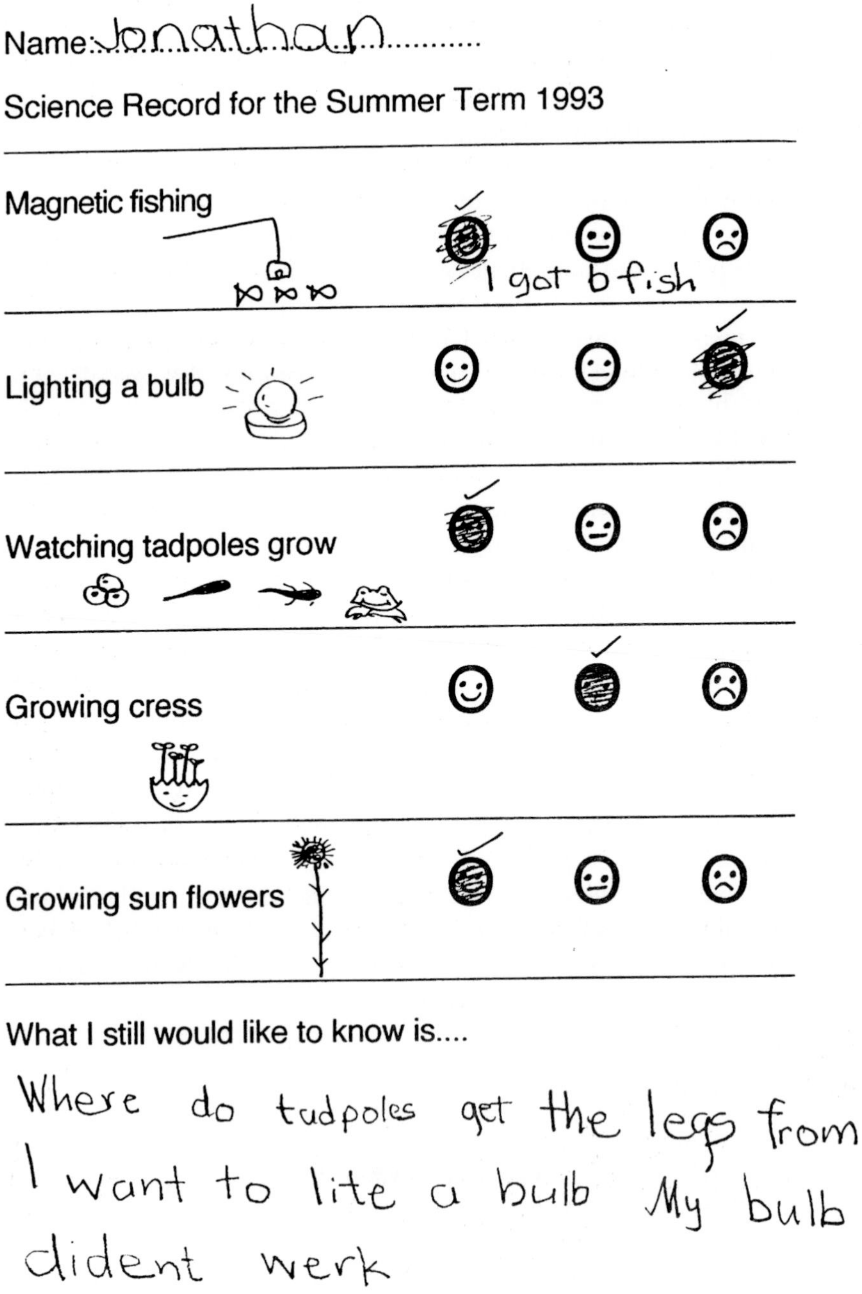

Name: Jonathan

Science Record for the Summer Term 1993

Magnetic fishing

I got 6 fish

Lighting a bulb

Watching tadpoles grow

Growing cress

Growing sun flowers

What I still would like to know is....

Where do tadpoles get the legs from
I want to lite a bulb My bulb
dident werk

Figure 5.3 *Self-assessment by Jonathan, aged 6*

related to learning intentions and to comment on these, however simply. Much is written and discussed on the subject of allowing pupils to take ownership of their work. Modelling by the educator of the process of commenting on a task is one way that self-assessment can be encouraged, and allows for a substantive development for pupils in adopting such ownership.

Positive pupil attitudes to work are clearly essential if motivation is to be maintained, self-esteem is to be enhanced and learning progress is to be made. Many pupils' enjoyment of assessing their own performance is enhanced if they feel they can convey how they feel about the work they are undertaking, as well as commenting on their progress. Whilst simply talking to children can provide evidence of positive or negative attitudes, the example in Figure 5.3 (see p.124) shows a 'smiley face' assessment, completed by a 6-year-old boy, forming part of a review of work. Self-assessment such as this can help children to take responsibility for their own learning and to develop their autonomy. Children who are unable to complete such sheets unaided enjoy working with an adult or older child to scribe for them.

Another means of children themselves contributing to an assessment of their understanding comes through the use of concept mapping. Many educators will already be familiar with concept maps as a means of assessing children's knowledge prior to an activity. As envisaged by Novak and Gowin (1984) they are a method of constructing hierarchies of concepts with 'propositional links' showing how those concepts are related. With young children, however, it is more sensible to simplify concept mapping, making it a method of showing links between concepts but ignoring the hierarchical structure of those concepts. To give an example, consider the words 'tree' and 'water'; how are these related? Using an arrow to show the nature and direction of the relationship, the simple map illustrated in Figure 5.4 might be produced.

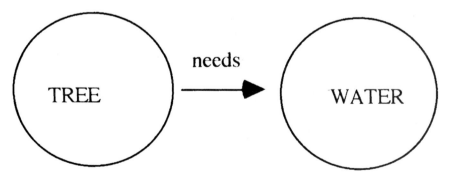

Figure 5.4 *A concept map showing the relationship between 'tree' and 'water'*

This simple idea can be extended by the educator to establish the initial understanding that children have of key ideas they will encounter in a lesson or through a topic. The concept maps in Figure 5.5 and 5.6 were drawn by two 6-year-old children prior to carrying out some work with plants. They were based upon the following words provided by the teacher – seed, flower, bulb, water, light, bud, stalk (see p.127).

The understanding expressed by the children in the two maps is substantially different. This suggests that even if similar activities were carried out by these children the educator would have different expectations of them and would be likely to question them in a manner more focused to their level of understanding. This technique is an important one for any educator with a broadly constructivist view of learning, where the notion of children constructing their own sense of the world is central (see Chapter 1). For the constructivist 'what is already in the learner's mind matters' (Ollerenshaw and Ritchie, 1993) since it will provide a basis for subsequent teaching and for the conceptual change that results. Harlen (2000) points out how easy even very young children find the technique, and in assessing pre- and post-teaching maps the educator is able not only to see how the child's concepts have developed, but also to assess the effectiveness of the work that has been carried out.

It will be apparent that children need to be taught this technique and need to understand particularly how important the 'joining words' are in making the whole thing have meaning. It will also be apparent that concept maps used with children after work on a topic provide just one more method by which they can, with help, reflect upon their own learning. As with all methods used for recording children's thoughts it should not be used too frequently. This is not just to prevent fatigue on the part of the children; concepts maps are time-consuming for the educator and the children to analyse and should be seen as only one tool in the assessment armoury.

Some modifications to the technique may help to make it more manageable. The creation of group or class concept maps is a beneficial way of encouraging discussion and can provide a basis in itself for the children to challenge one another's ideas. In some respects this is rather like the use of 'floor books' (instead of recording ideas in a list, here where the educator lists the children's ideas in a large book as they gather round on the floor). However, the educator has specific concepts that form the basis of creating the map and the children are encouraged to discuss possible linkages. Carrying out this exercise both before and after a lesson or longer topic can be, as suggested above, most revealing. A further refinement with younger children is to create 'picture concept maps'. Moving around pictures rather than words and articulating relationships between

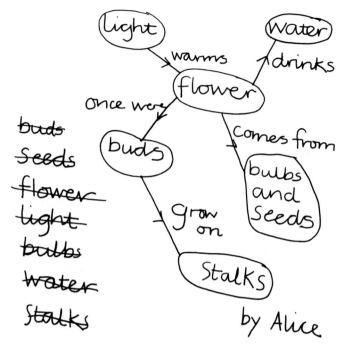

Figure 5.5 *A concept map by Alice, aged 6*

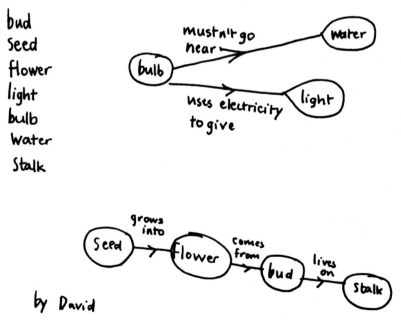

Figure 5.6 *A concept map by David, aged 6*

them can help some children, and not only those who might be bilingual or who might have problems with reading, to express properly the extent of their understanding.

Feedback, marking and individual target setting

Feedback for very young children will inevitably be oral, with written feedback being incorporated as children are increasingly able to interpret symbols, such as smiley faces, and read comments used by the educator. There are, however, several important principles that should be applied to all feedback, some of which relate to target setting.

Feedback needs to be provided as promptly as possible, and for young pupils this can often mean during the course of an activity. It needs to be positive, reflecting on success in relation to the learning intentions of the task. Stating the next achievable target should also be part of the purpose of feedback. Obviously, with young pupils, any targets will be stated in very simple terms and pupils will need to be reminded of them in future work. This is where recording of assessment information is so important, as no educator can expect to hold essential 'next steps' for all pupils in their head. Equally important, however, is the view of assessment as a sampling process, whereby the focus shifts from pupil to pupil and from one area of the curriculum to another. It is impossible to give detailed feedback and targets to all pupils for all work undertaken, just as it is impossible to engage all pupils in self-assessment for all tasks. Provided that the key issues we have discussed relating to effective assessment for learning are borne in mind, however, pupil learning is likely to be promoted in any educational setting.

Adjusting teaching to take account of learning

There is an intimate and unbreakable link between effective teaching and effective planning and assessment. The three, together, form a cycle of action that should lead to the curriculum being increasingly refined for the pupil. When working with early years children it is vital that the assessments and subsequent changes to the curriculum consider the whole child. A child who is assessed as having weak fine motor skills may be unable to complete a practical activity but have the conceptual understanding to follow what is happening. At such times, the careful matching for both skills and understanding can lead to more productive and enjoyable learning.

The curriculum context for planning and assessment in the early years

In England, the curriculum context within which assessment happens in the early years is provided at the Foundation Stage (3–5 years) by the *Curriculum Guidance for the Foundation Stage* (DfEE/QCA, 2000) and at Key Stage 1 (5–7 years) by the *National Curriculum for Key Stage 1* (DfEE/QCA, 1999). Although the curricula in these phases of education differ in structure, the broad principles underlying assessment *for* learning are relevant to both and, equally, remain relevant in different national settings. Educators will be aware that any statutory national curriculum and government non-statutory curriculum guidance will never provide for the totality of pupils' learning experiences. However, for those countries where they exist, they clearly offer an important framework that must be considered in planning and assessing.

Assessment *of* learning in the early years

From time to time it is necessary to assess for summative purposes some aspects of pupil development. This may result from the educator's desire to 'run a check' on the appropriateness of their own formative assessments, or it may be built into a school's assessment procedures. The experience in England is certainly that many schools link intermittent summative tasks to a rolling programme of analysis linked to national curriculum levels of attainment. Whatever the reasons for embarking upon what might be seen as more formal school-devised assessments, there are a number of principles and procedures that we feel should be adopted.

The first of these is that, for these summative assessments, the focus should be limited. The activity that the children are carrying out is likely to allow them to use a range of skills and concepts, yet for assessment purposes the educator should focus on just two or three assessment objectives, which in England may or may not relate to the foundation stage curriculum 'stepping stones' or to national curriculum programme of study statements. For example, in an activity on changing materials, the teacher may have an assessment question related to science processes:

Assessment question: Can the pupils recognise when a test or comparison is unfair?

Having defined what is to be assessed it is now possible to sort out some precise evidence, related to the specific activity, that will give a guide to whether the child is achieving the objective. In relation to our example it may be:

> *Evidence:* Child is able to articulate why items selected for melting must be the same size.

Having established up to four assessment questions to be answered (no more!), the educator will then give the task to the children and, working with them, will assess their performance. Again, in England, what the teacher at Key Stage 1 will need to consider is the extent to which pupils have made progress. In national curriculum terms, this may mean a movement within a level of attainment. For the Foundation Stage children might have moved 'up a stepping stone' or achieved development in relation to an early learning goal.

Statutory testing

The English system provides for statutory summative assessment at the end of the foundation stage (3–5 years) and Key Stage 1 (5–7 years). The subject of the validity, reliability and general usefulness (given the wealth of formative assessment evidence available for each child) of the end of Key Stage 1 national curriculum tests has been considered extensively over the last decade and more. As a means of providing a statistical analysis of 'value added', the tests in English and mathematics provide a useful device for governments, but they are a blunt instrument as performance across a range of criteria is summated into a single level of attainment in a subject.

The need for a 'baseline' from which to measure value added is clear in the context of national testing, and we have indicated that there may be some value in having devices to help summate achievement at particular points. Work in numerous Local Education Authorities in England shows how much has been done since the introduction of statutory baseline assessment for 4-to 5-year-old children in September 1998, to try to ensure that it is embedded 'within a process of quality assessment practice' (Threlfall and Woodbridge, 1999, p. 97). Baseline assessments at the age of 5 are now intended to provide the starting point for an evaluation of value added at Key Stage 1. It thus seems pertinent to raise some issues highlighted by research and writing on, and experience of, baseline assessments.

First, Drummond points to the fact that, although baseline assessment *can* be purposeful, it is essential to understand 'why it is more important to look at learning (rather than record) attainments, or levels of attainment'

(1999, p. 43). In supporting this view, Nutbrown (1998) examines two baseline assessment instruments and concludes that there were very real dangers of testing becoming the driving force of pedagogy in the early years. She contrasts the possible effects of this with a curriculum where effective formative assessment drives the curriculum. Further, she points out that baseline assessment, if seen as the starting point of the value-added ideal in the primary school, becomes 'a staging post of accountability' (Nutbrown, 1998, p. 60), rather than a genuine baseline that celebrates a range of pupil achievement. This concern has very real credence in a climate where early years educators are being asked to indicate 'literacy deficits' at the age of 5.

It may help here to highlight things that baseline assessments in the past often failed to reveal about pupils. The early baseline assessments for children starting school considered areas such as pre-reading skills, phonological awareness and numeracy skills. Educators were also asked to make observations regarding personal and social skills. The assessments often, however, did little to assess a child's 'readiness to learn'. Many early years educators are aware that a child who can listen, manipulate play dough, use a paintbrush, collaborate with peers and concentrate is likely to be ready to learn, regardless of the results of a formal baseline assessment. Many vital skills for learning have not been part of the remit of baseline assessments. In addition, many early years children have found the context and nature of questions used within baselines very different from their normal, day-to-day experiences of school. This is shown in the following transcripts of an end of reception year baseline assessment carried out with Ayesha, aged 4 years. The questions were accompanied by pictures in a book.

Educator:	If Jasmine wants to buy an apple which costs 5 pence which coin should she use? (*Ayesha is shown three coins.*)
Ayesha:	Who's Jasmine?
Educator:	She's the little girl in the question.
Ayesha:	I don't know a Jasmine. You usually use our names in stories and things. Could it be Alice in the question?

When the educator repeated the question using the name 'Alice' Ayesha answered correctly.

Educator:	If you had three apples and I had two apples how many would we have altogether?
Ayesha:	Actually I think you should have the three apples because you're bigger than me.

Again, the educator changed the wording of the question and Ayesha answered correctly.

Educator:	Fourteen people are riding on a bus. If three more get on, how many are riding on the bus now?
Ayesha:	Well if it was like the school bus that would be too many. Is it like the school bus?
Educator:	No, I expect it's a bit bigger.
Ayesha:	Would it have seat belts for everyone?
Educator:	Oh yes.
Ayesha:	Well then. (*Long pause.*) You'd prob'ly need eighteen belts then.
Educator:	Why?
Ayesha:	Seventeen for the people and the driver would need one too!

These transcripts show a child who is able to use her numeracy skills. They also reveal a child who engages with the context of the questions and is eager to make sense of her learning. Ayesha could not relate to the unknown Jasmine but willingly answered the question correctly when it featured her friend Alice. Similarly, her sense of fairness would not let her imagine having more apples than her teacher. Her final answer showed an ability to visualise and to relate her answer to the real world. She was lucky to be working with an educator who was willing to listen and also who had time to listen. When all the baseline assessments had been completed the educator commented that Ayesha had required a great deal more time than the majority of her class. She also said the value of the assessment was not Ayesha's final score but instead was what she had discovered about Ayesha's ability to reason. The educator made excellent use of the assessment opportunity and ensured that Ayesha's next targets matched her progress.

Hurst and Lally (1992) have commented:

> Assessment of young children must cover all aspects of a child's development and must be concerned with attitudes, feelings, social and physical characteristics. . . . Learning is not compartmentalised under subject headings for young children.
>
> (Hurst and Lally, 1992, p. 55)

Many early years educators show clear ability and commitment to assessments that involve the whole child. The following points are, we believe, central to effective assessment in the early years:

Pointers for assessment in the early years

- Be aware of the wide variety of opportunities for formative assessment.
- Plan for and take time to listen to and observe children.
- Appreciate that discussion holds the key to much effective assessment.
- Keep a notebook with a page for each child for formative assessment. Jot down useful observations and discussion points, dating each entry.
- Feed assessment information into planning for future teaching.

References

Black, P. and Wiliam, D. (1998) *Inside the Black Box: Raising Standards through Classroom Assessment*, London: King's College.

Clarke, S. (2001) *Unlocking Formative Assessment: Practical Strategies for Enhancing Pupils' Learning in the Primary Classroom*, London: Hodder & Stoughton.

Clayden, E. and Peacock, A. (1994) *Science for Curriculum Leaders*, London: Routledge.

DES (1987) *National Curriculum: Task Group on Assessment and Testing – a Report*, London: HMSO.

DfEE/QCA (1999) *The National Curriculum: Handbook for Primary Teachers in England*, London: HMSO.

DfEE/QCA (2000) *Curriculum Guidance for the Foundation Stage*, London: HMSO.

Drummond, M.J. (1993) *Assessing Children's Learning*, London: David Fulton.

Drummond, M.J. (1999) Baseline assessment: A case for civil disobedience?, in C. Connor (ed.) *Assessment in Action in the Primary School*, London: Falmer Press.

Harlen, W. (2000) *Teaching, Learning and Assessing Science 5–12*, London: Paul Chapman.

Hurst, V. and Lally, M. (1992) 'Assessment and the nursery curriculum', in G. Blenkin and A. Kelly (eds) *Assessment in Early Childhood Education*, London: Paul Chapman.

Novak, J. and Gowin, D. (1984) *Learning How to Learn*, Cambridge: Cambridge University Press.

Nutbrown, C. (1998) Early assessment – examining the baselines, in *Early*

Years: An International Journal of Research and Development, Vol. 19, No.1, Chester: Trentham Books.

Ollerenshaw, C. and Ritchie, R. (1993) *Primary Science: Making it Work,* London: David Fulton.

QCA (2001) Hyperlink – *http://www.qca.org.uk.*

Sparks Linfield, R. (1994) 'Straw Assessment', *Primary Science Review,* 35, 17.

Threlfall, S. and Woodbridge, J. (1999) Baseline assessment: Policy into practice, in C. Connor (ed.) *Assessment in Action in the Primary School,* London: Falmer Press.

PART B

Play and language

CHAPTER 6

'It is only a story, isn't it?'

INTERACTIVE STORY-MAKING IN THE EARLY YEARS CLASSROOM

Lesley Hendy

Children are born as storytellers. We have an innate need to tell, act out and listen to stories in order to shape our lives and give them meaning. As Bettleheim (1995) reminds us, 'Today, as in times past, the most important and also the most difficult task in raising a child is helping him to find a meaning in life.' Children's story-making is often hurriedly dismissed as either being appealing but rather shallow or lacking in coherent construction and limited in meaning. But as Engel (1995) suggests, 'Children's stories can be vital to us as parents, teachers and researchers because they give us insight into how children of different ages experience the world, and how a specific child thinks and feels' (p. 3).

One of the initial activities that can be observed in the behaviour of early childhood is the ability to play in the 'as if'. When you ask a group of adults what games they played as children they often reply, 'mummies and daddies', 'doctors and nurses', 'cowboys and Indians', 'shops', 'hairdressers', etc. All these games require children to substitute the real for the fictional; the play is about working 'as if' you were someone else, somewhere else, doing something else. This ability to use 'pretend play' begins before nursery age and often continues into puberty and sometimes beyond.

Children actively engage in story-making from as early as twelve months old. They are able to use 'pretend' play to act out their stories either by themselves or with others. Small children at play will often speak aloud their thoughts and provide actions to support them. As their lives change, the stories of their lives change accordingly. Many parents and teachers have experienced the 'make-believe' tea-party or the imaginary friends.

It could be said that the beginnings of drama can be found in these early types of story-making activities. These stories are 'played out' and the 'scripts' children use come from their experiences. Drama as used in early education, however, concerns the making of meaning rather than the making of plays. Young children are not creating 'roles' in the theatrical sense but enter these '"pretend" situations as themselves. As Hendy and Toon (2001) state, 'Pretend' play could be described as children engaging with a series of different behaviours and events. It is about trying out ideas, motivations and reactions to events in make-believe situations' (p. 22).

Pretend play, in this regard, has a very important part to play in a child's development. The introduction of the national curriculum sadly brought about a decline in 'pretend' play and especially the role-play area as an integral part of the curriculum. It is hoped that the establishment of the foundation stage will reverse this trend.

As schooling progresses, personal response through play and role-play is often regarded as unreliable and self-indulgent. By adulthood the wonderful spontaneity and creativity found in small children has been replaced by feelings of inadequacy and social foolishness. Mention the word 'drama' to gatherings of trainees or practising teachers and a perceptible apprehension travels through the group. 'I hope she isn't going to make us get up and do something' or 'I'm not making a fool of myself' are common comments often heard at the beginning of drama courses. For many the memory of reading Shakespeare around the class or participation in performance, requiring the learning and delivering of lines, has caused their adult misgivings.

In the last ten years or so, business and industry have rediscovered the use of role-play as an important constituent of management training. There are now few courses in which there is not an element of role-play used for team-building, the exploration of difficulties in groups or as a means of engaging in problem-solving and decision-making. These are precisely the things that the good early years specialist wants to encourage in his or her children's learning and development.

In this chapter, I shall outline some ways in which drama in the early years can be used as an effective learning medium, from adult intervention of play in the 'home/role-play corner' to actively making stories with children. I shall also discuss the use of 'drama strategies' as a way of providing time for reflection and widening experience within story-making. In doing so I hope to ease anxieties about drama and provide early years educators with a strong rationale for including drama as a teaching tool within the planning of the curriculum.

Why drama is important in the early years

As an integral part of the natural development of children's play, role-play offers us a ready-made medium in which we can engage with our children. Through the 'as if', i.e. the ability to function in an imaginary environment, children are given a different viewing point from which to consider, discover and make meaning of the world.

However, role-play as a feature of child play needs careful examination. We need to be aware that small children function in the 'as if' in two distinct ways. The first is *socio-dramatic play* in which they act out scripts from their real lives and the second is *thematic-fantasy* play where they create story from their imagination. It is important we provide opportunities for both as each requires a different mode of thought.

It was Bruner (1986) who first defined these two ways of thinking. His 'paradigmatic' mode that he described as being involved with logic, sequencing and the ability to be analytical can be detected in the socio-dramatic play of 'homes', 'hospitals', 'offices', etc. Bruner's 'narrative thinking', on the other hand, can be found in the creativity and construction of make-believe events found in thematic-dramatic play.

The inclusion of dramatic activity in the national curriculum 2000 Speaking and Listening at KS1 and KS2 would appear to be for the encouragement of purposeful language. Some significant research has shown the importance of role-play in the development of early language (Sylva, Bruner and Genova, 1976, Hutt, 1989, Kitson, 1994) and an OFSTED report *First Class* (OFSTED, 1994 p. 8) indicated that where 'drama and role-play were used effectively' there appeared to be 'better overall standards in literacy'.

Nonetheless, the use of drama should not be seen as exclusive to the development of language. The socio-dramatic aspects of 'pretend' play should be extended across the curriculum and used in any circumstances that require children to describe and communicate their findings and observations (science, maths, geography, history, design and technology). All aspects of the curriculum can be enhanced when children are given a fictional' as if' context in which to discuss and communicate what they know. They will need to use their logical and analytical abilities in 'as if' contexts that require natural laws to apply. The 'narrative' skills provided by thematic-dramatic play will develop creative thinking and strengthen work in the other arts.

Drama work, as well as giving opportunities to explore the curriculum in different ways, can also provide the teacher with the opportunity for group activity that involves social interaction and the exchange of ideas. Through such an activity children can pose and solve problems, make decisions and use their knowledge and skills to work as a group.

By bringing into the classroom the dimension of action, drama enhances learning through the use of PEOPLE–SPACE–TIME. Through the creation of a fictional world, children are given the opportunity of being who they like, where they like and when they like. For example, they could enter a fictional world as themselves, trying to find solutions to such matters as how to clean up their village as part of a project on the environment. They might be mice trying to reach the moon in order to see whether it is really made of cheese as part of a topic on the sun and moon. They could be a group of servants worried about the disappearance of Snow White or alternatively farmers trying to work out how you can remove milk from a broken-down milk tanker.

The use of fictional contexts puts children in control. By making use of their existing language, experience, motivations and interests, the teacher can intervene in the play to bring new shape and fresh ways of looking at things. These opportunities provide the teacher with a wide range of potential contexts otherwise unavailable in the normal classroom situation.

The overall purpose of drama as a way of learning should be to effect change that may occur in a number of ways. For example, it may, bring about a change in:

- the level of knowledge and understanding;
- ways of thinking;
- attitude;
- the expectation of what role-play can offer;
- existing language;
- awareness of the needs of others.

There may also be a change in the relationship that exists between language use and the control of knowledge. By providing opportunities for children to set the agenda and to learn about things that interest them the teacher has access to a wider curriculum. This can be achieved even within the constraints of existing curriculum requirements.

The general characteristics of drama as a learning medium can be described as:

- a method of teaching that helps present information and ideas within a different form of communication (sometimes children are the experts, the teacher the one who needs to be taught);
- a means of giving children some control over their learning, thereby giving them greater access to knowledge and ideas (children are given opportunities to choose the problems that have to be solved and the decisions to be made);

- a method of giving children a fictional situation in which they can respond outside the structure of the ordinary classroom (the shy child is given a context in which to act as someone else);
- an alternative means of describing and communicating that allows pupils to bring their own knowledge about the world into the classroom (children with specialised knowledge such as fishing or horse-riding are able to make a fuller contribution);
- a method of learning that allows pupils and teachers to function as equals;
- a method of providing a 'need to know' that can heighten the learning that has taken place or will take place back in the classroom (children often want to research into something that has arisen within a story).

If drama activity is about anything, it is about the learning and turning-points in life. Such moments can cause the participants to reflect on their actions and to rethink some of their ideas from within a safe environment. To sustain the action the players have to use both their factual and subjective knowledge. They will also be introduced to new material, both factual and objective, that they can use to help them solve problems and take decisions. This is where the teacher plays such a crucial role. As Readman and Lamont (1994, p. 16) reflect:

> It is the responsibility of the teacher to:
> – resist any assumptions about the kind of role(s) children might adopt;
> – select content areas which reflect genuine cultural diversity;
> – enable children to adopt roles which challenge any stereotypes;
> – offer children opportunities to work collaboratively.

Out of the home corner

In the early years classroom the most obvious place for a teacher to introduce new ways of using the 'as if' is in the home/role-play corner. Home/role-play corners in the classroom are usually the province of children only and sometimes it is important to allow the children to play alone. However, there are other times when an adult could enter the fantasy situation and play alongside them.

Knowing when and how to intervene constructively, without the children feeling the teacher is intruding, takes sensitivity and watchfulness. Initially just passing by and engaging in short conversations in role will help build trust. On a recent visit to an infant classroom where the teacher had set up a seaside cafe in her home corner, I was encouraged to buy chips and join a complaint about the lack of salt and vinegar!

When you gauge that the children are ready to accept you, an adult, into their make-believe world, more time can be spent with them in their home/role-play corners. By dropping 'home' and renaming it role-play area, many more possibilities become available. Role-play corners should be seen by the children as more than just places for dressing up and pushing the doll's pram. A home corner can confine the activities to socio-dramatic play only. By providing different types of environment, the children are given scope to engage in both socio- and thematic-dramatic play.

The creation of a role-play area could involve the class in making things to go in it and might require use of maths, design and technology or information technology. Often sterile play comes from the fact that the children have had no input into the design or management of the area.

Intervention by adults

Having joined the children at play and adopted a role within their make-believe, we can both initiate or respond in order to facilitate learning. Each intervention by the teacher varies the learning opportunities and the possible learning outcomes (Baldwin and Hendy, 1994). It is particularly effective if the teacher identifies and makes use of learning opportunities that arise naturally and are offered by the children themselves. It is important for children to feel some ownership of the story and that their contributions to the dramatic play are valued. The teacher may enter the story as the patient or the customer but they must treat the 'doctor' or 'dentist', 'travel agent' or 'greengrocer' with the same respect as if it were real life. This will help to develop the shared fiction in a more open way, and as other children hear the conversations, they can be encouraged to join in. The teacher's intervention will also help the children in role to become more committed to their part in the fiction. By using this approach, we are able to indicate to the children that their dramatic play is valued and highly regarded. We communicate that it is important to us and is a respected form of activity.

Types of role-play area

Role-play areas do not always have to represent familiar locations: any place and any time is possible. Some examples might be:

- places that take children back in time, such as castles, sailing ships, pirate ships, old houses to begin to give small children a sense of the past;
- time travel settings, such as a spaceship or a time machine;
- fairy story places, such as the Three Little Pigs' brick house, Little Red Riding Hood's cottage, Cinderella's kitchen or The Seven Dwarfs' house;
- places of the imagination, such as the all green room, the upside-down room, the room of dreams.

All these possibilities develop children's speaking and listening and allow exploration of other areas of the curriculum. What we choose to provide for our children will determine the learning opportunities we can exploit.

By entering children's dramatic play in this way, we are able to build up trust and commitment. We are able to add dimensions that children are usually unable to sustain for themselves. The ideas can be extended later when bigger group or whole-class drama is undertaken. Our interventions can add the dimension of persistence and consequence; what children do and say can be challenged, questioned and analysed, not just by the adult but by the children themselves.

The Greek word for drama means 'living through' and the action of the drama needs to be lived through by players using make-believe to create the setting for their pretend existence. Within this fantasy world, it is important that all agree to take part and share the same action. Adults must be careful never to begin in role without telling the children that they are doing so. Saying 'Can I play?' informs children of our intentions. All the players must employ knowledge they have brought with them from their real lives to help them in the pretend world. Life experience and factual knowledge are applied in an active way, frequently providing a genuine 'need to know'. It is important that children and adults are always aware that they are playing. They must be able to 'hold two worlds in their head at the same time' (Readman and Lamont, 1994 p. 27). All should be aware that at any time the make-believe can cease which paradoxically creates the safety. Vygotsky has described this ability to live in these two worlds as the 'dual affect'. Aristotle also described this phenomenon as 'metaxis' – the real world and the fantasy world of the drama coming together in the mind of the player.

Drama helps children to communicate in a more significant way and allows them to think more deeply about the consequences of their actions. The random 'play' shooting on the playground, for instance, can be challenged – shooting hurts people and this can be explored. Also, drama allows children to have new experiences and to test out their reactions in a safe environment. Children are repeatedly asked to interpret the actions of others, often in unfamiliar ways, and are given the opportunity to replay, change and reflect upon different parts of the action.

Using improvisation as the medium for dramatic activity

The term *improvisation* as the medium for dramatic activity often appears in documents and books. Within most groups, either students or early years educators, there is some common understanding as to what this term means but less understanding of how it works. It could best be defined as an active method of working which requires both children and teachers to enter a fictional world in which they will be able to:

- explore human relationships and behaviour;
- have a firsthand experience of events and ideas;
- have a genuine need to talk and listen;
- solve problems and make decisions;

sometimes as themselves or sometimes as other people.

In this fictional world, both dialogue and non-verbal action between participants is made up as the situation proceeds, as with ordinary conversations and actions in real life. The group does not have a pre-written script that is learnt, spoken and acted. Through the fictional context, the dialogue and non-verbal action can be steered to include anything the teacher or the children want to discuss or explore. This activity is known as 'continuous improvisation' as it carries on as long as all participants are able to sustain it. Drama in the classroom uses elements that are also to be found in theatrical action: human relationships and situations driven by tension and suspense caused by complications in the plot linked through place and time, using movement and language.

It is very difficult to sustain continuous improvisation for long periods of time. Young children can quickly become disengaged from it either because they feel their contribution is not being heard or they become absorbed in their own story-making. Maintaining improvisation with very large groups may not be easy and, with ever increasing class size, drama needs to be carefully planned and organised.

Drama strategies as a tool for planning

A drama strategy is a structuring device that helps the teacher focus the children on certain aspects of the story being made. Over recent years, the use of drama strategies has become an important aspect of drama planning and structuring. A teacher can interrupt the story by using a drama strategy to:

- help build a shared environment – Are we all in the same wood? What common understanding do we have about circuses? As we look at the island what do we all see?
- move the plot on through teacher narration if the story is not going any-where or has become rather circular in its development;
- look at something that has happened to help build group identity about the dilemma – this stops children's insatiable desire for 'what happens next'.

In some instances the group can go back and rerun a section that might be leading the children somewhere they do not want to go. 'Unlike real life', as one student observed, 'you can rewind and change what has just been done.'

Some useful drama strategies that work with early years

Most good books on educational drama contain descriptions and uses for drama strategies (Baldwin and Hendy, 1994; Neelands, 1990; Readman and Lamont, 1994; Toye and Prendiville, 2000; Woolland, 1993). The ones I have included are those I personally have found most suitable for work with early years children.

Teacher-in-role is possibly the drama strategy most familiar to educators. This is a very powerful tool as it allows the teacher to enter the fictional world alongside the children and to structure the story from within. When first introduced to this strategy, teachers-in-training can find the prospect of entering into the context with the children rather daunting; organising the action from the outside seems a much safer option. Those who are willing to undertake teacher-in-role and participate fully in the story-making find that this is one of the most effective and adaptable strategies they can employ.

Other strategies include:

- *still-image* – the group or smaller groups take up a pose to construct a pic-ture to describe what they want to say;
- *circle time* – the whole group gathers in a seated circle to discuss events and make group decisions: a useful device for calming and controlling the group;
- *what can you see?* – (more suitable for KS1) each child describes an en-vironment, an event, a person to build a group image;
- *thought-tracking* – individuals say aloud what they think and feel about an event, character or idea;

- *collective role-play* – several children take on the role of one character and support each other in what they say;
- *small-group work* – (more suitable for KS1) a small group of children are asked to create a small scene, with or without dialogue, to show what might have happened during an event or what might happen if an idea is carried out.

Planning dramatic activity

By using the elements of theatrical action, improvisation and drama strategies teachers have the tools to plan and structure story-making. The dramatic activity is based on creating a context for improvised situations to take place that can be enhanced by the use of other strategies. As has already been suggested, using drama for educational purposes is about making meaning for children rather than making plays.

The structuring of the story-making must provide a strong dilemma (tension and suspense) from which the children can build belief; in other words something must happen to engage their interest. The children need to be able to enter the role behaving 'as if' it were so. To work, the activity must provide enough stimulation for the children to have a common willingness to suspend disbelief.

Young children possess an innate ability to understand the structuring of stories. They instinctively know that once the story of the drama has started something is going to happen (Hendy, 1995). They know that the protagonists in the story will come across complications and dilemmas that have to be solved – Red Riding Hood meets a wolf who wants to eat her, the Three Little Pigs are chased by a wolf intent on destroying their homes and eating them. These dilemmas are strong and life threatening. This does not mean to say that all drama must be about life and death situations. But something must be happening that creates a powerful tension to hold the interest and create contexts in which new knowledge and understandings can take place.

Choosing the context

Choosing the context is an important factor in the planning for interactive story-making. Well-known children's stories are a good basis for starting as they often have interesting settings that capture the imagination of small children. Having selected the context it is worth identifying some of the learning areas that could be explored as the story develops. Stories set in woods or the outdoors might lead to environmental issues or aspects of geography. Stories set indoors might provide a background for work in science or maths, whereas stories set long ago might produce some interesting insight into history and things of the past.

After the theme has been selected key learning areas should be identified. These can be universal ideas such as:

- How do we find out about what people are like?
- How do we deal with people who are different?
- How do we deal with the things that frighten us?

or more curriculum-based learning such as:

- How do we describe similarities and differences between materials? (science)
- How do we design something which will carry us on the wind? (technology)
- Can we recount a story from our past? (history)
- How might we describe something that is 3-D in shape? (maths)

To answer some of these questions the story can be structured, through the use of improvisation and drama strategies, to explore the key learning areas. Using The Three Little Pigs as an example (see detailed plan in Figure 6.1), the universal question from this story might be:

- How do we cope with bullies and people who seem more powerful than us?

The curriculum-based questions might be focused on design and technology, maths, science and geography (see Figure 6.2).

The teacher needs to decide whether the storymaking is going to used to develop paradigmatic or narrative thinking. Stories that involve children pretending to be in familiar surroundings can be effective vehicles to introduce information or test their knowledge in maths, science, design and technology and other areas of the curriculum. Such stories could be termed *home stories* as they are based in reality and all the activities are controlled by natural laws, in other words there is *no magic*. Such interactive stories are a useful way of helping young children learn more about their world.

Fantasy stories, on the other hand, have a different feel and are rooted in the imagination. This kind of drama work can extend children's narrative thinking and imaginative powers, allowing the possibility of all worlds and ideas, however bizarre and extraordinary.

Inter-active Story-Making Plan for The Three Little Pigs to be used in a topic about Homes and Buildings

Learning Intentions	Planning	Making the Story
To encourage listening skills	My Story Teacher- role	Gather the children into sitting circle-time. Tell the children you are going to start the story as the mother of the Three Little Pigs. Leave the group and return looking very worried.Greet the children as if they were friends of your three sons. Tell them the first part of the three pigs story
To provide information about the building of homes To develop geographical vocabulary	Whole group-in-role Continuous Improvisation	Pack a basket with some food, lock your house and start on your journey. Tell the children you are nervous because you've not travelled outside your village before. Allow children to chose the way. As you walk along ask the children to identify the different geographical features that you pass like slopes, hills, roads, bridges, rivers etc. Arrive near the sea where the soil is very sandy. Mention the softness of the soil. Freeze the action. Tell the children that when you return, pushing an imaginary wheelbarrow you are the man who sold the pigs the straw.
To develop imaginative response To provide information about buildings and materials To provide opportunity for mathematical language	Teacher-in- role Whole group-in-role Continuous Improvisation	Enter as the man with the straw and greet the children by saying"Hello I haven't seen you around these parts. The Old Lady Pig looks tired. What are you doing here?" Encourage them to tell you about the Mother Pig's problem and get them to ask you whether you have seen the three little pigs. Tell the children you sold them some straw and you left them just here building a house out of it. There is no sign of them but notice there is straw blowing about. Ask the children to collect it up so it won't go to waste. Make them into bundles and put them in your wheelbarrow. You could use the opportunity to do some counting exercises. You sold them ten bundles but you've only picked up enough for eight, how many are missing? etc. Discuss with them whether sand is a very good place to build a house and whether straw is really a good material especially in a high wind. Take your leave of them and go out Freeze the action.
To provide opportunity to recall information	Teacher-in-role Meeting	Sit children in a circle.Tell them you are going back to be the Mother. Restart the action by coming into the circle and asking who they were talking to and what the had said to them. Try to steer the conversation onto the building of houses in the wrong place with the wrong materials. Freeze the action.
To provide opportunity to reflect on the story	Thought- tracking	Ask the children to close their eyes and as you go round the circle ask them to say aloud what they are thinking about their friends the three little pigs.
To provide opportunity to ask questions examine information and respond	Teacher-in-role Whole Group-in-Role Continuous Impro	Continue down the road, moving from the sea into some woods where you will meet the wood-cutter. Tell the children you can see a man through the trees. You are too tired to run could they go on ahead and speak to him for you. Freeze the action Move in front of the children and restart the action by miming wood cutting. Wait to see if they start to talk to you. Engage them in talk about house building with sticks and how you sold the pigs some sticks and they were going to build a house in the clearing over there. Take them to the clearing but find nothing but broken sticks scattered all around. Tell them your sorry but you have no idea where the pigs have gone but you told them it was a silly idea to build a house from thin sticks. Freeze the action
To develop understanding of other people's feelings	Simple Thought-tracking	Gather them into sitting-circle.Ask them to become the tired and worried Mother.Go round the group touching each child gently on the shoulder As you do so ask them to say aloud what the Mother pig is thinking as she watches the friends coming back without her children

Figure 6.1 *Interactive story making plan for The Three Little Pigs to be used in a topic about homes and buildings*

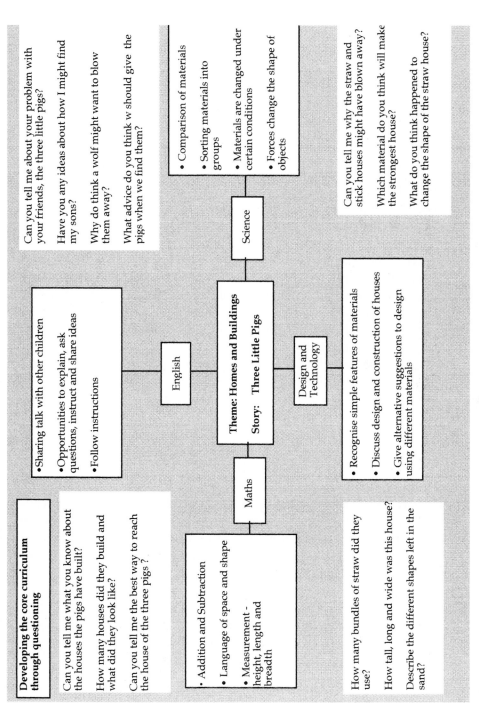

Figure 6.2 *Developing the core curriculum through questioning*

Planning must take into consideration the children's willingness to:

- adopt a role;
- make-believe with regard to actions and situations;
- make-believe with regard to objects;
- maintain the make-believe verbally;
- maintain the make-believe through movement;
- interact with the rest of the group;
- keep to the structure and the rules of playing.

Teachers must also plan with a commitment to their own participation in mind. Children are not able to engage in effective learning through drama unless the adult has:

- a genuine desire to work in this medium;
- an eagerness to enter the child's world, to believe in what they are doing and to take their work seriously;
- an understanding of how improvisation and drama strategies function and can be used;
- knowledge of the learning potential of any particular story together with ability to keep this to the fore;
- techniques to introduce problems for the group to solve;
- the willingness to take risks;
- the willingness to work beside the children and allow the group to make decisions.

Making the contract

It is important that before engaging in interactive story-making both children and adults enter into a contract that makes clear the plan of action, the expectations and the responsibilities of how to proceed when the story-making has begun. As has already been advised, never begin a story until all participants know what they are expected to do.

Some examples of active story-making

Working with a modern children's story

A trainee teacher recently decided to use Nick Butterworth's *After the Storm* as the basis for her drama. This story has the setting of a wood in which a storm has taken place and the animals have been left homeless. This story provided a richness of learning possibilities she could explore with her reception class. The class topic was animals so this story fitted well into the overall curriculum planning.

She began to examine her areas of learning. The wood setting would allow her to test out the children's knowledge of trees and animal habitats, work that they had already undertaken in the classroom. She wanted to discover how much knowledge the children had of life processes and living things. She wanted to see whether she could introduce some information about shape, space and measures as the children in their role as animals started to think about the design of their new homes. Design and making would be a strong feature of the story. Knowledge about environmental change (geography) could be discussed as the children made observations about their damaged habitat. By asking the children to remember what it had been like before the storm and to sequence the events before they heard the great wind she hoped to increase their sense of the past. Gradually, through careful planning, she was able to build up the learning potential inherent in the story.

Throughout she was keen to let the animals tell their own story but, by participating herself in the role of a water rat, she was able to question, pose problems and expand their understanding. Almost immediately the children created tension by the introducing the idea of the wolves. These animals were never seen but were present throughout, driving the animals to find a new home quickly before they were eaten. Not having the right tools or materials also became a major problem and slowed up progress on the new homes. Rescue came in the role of Wise Owl, a character again introduced by a child, who invited all the animals to his home in the tree and gave them tea.

Most of the story was created through continuous improvisation but the trainee introduced some other strategies to increase reflection and commitment. At the very beginning, the children were asked to stand quietly in a circle and look at the tree. The trainee went round to all the children in their role as an animal and asked them what could they see. Gradually they built up a group picture of the tree fallen in the wood. She then asked each of them to go and rescue something from their home. They returned to the circle and showed the others what they had rescued and what it meant to them. Many of these items were then used in the story. At the end of the story, all the children were asked to pretend to be a photograph (still-image) of their animals standing outside their new home. She subsequently read them the story and it became a big favourite with the class.

Working from children's ideas

When working from children's ideas the teachers have to be able to think on their feet and to seize learning opportunities as they arise. Such work is ideal for building group cooperation and extending the children's ability to solve problems and to take decisions. This does not mean that there is no previous planning involved but the planning will be of a more fluid nature, predicting beforehand what learning could be achieved if certain situations arise. With experience, teachers can engineer situations whatever line the story is taking. The following example comes from a story developed by a vertically grouped class who had been working on the theme of castles.

The session commenced with circle time. The children sat together with the adults and decided where they were, who they were and what they were doing. They wanted to be servants to a king and they were to be preparing a grand banquet. To start the action in a controlled manner each child was asked to enter the story space and take up a pose of the job they were doing (still-image) as if someone had painted a picture of them. When all the children were assembled the action began.

The story began slowly with all the children acting out mixing and peeling and roasting, etc. In my role as a new servant I asked for jobs to do and was told where everything was. I created problems by not doing my work well and was helped by the other servants. From this, I learnt a great deal about the children. Their knowledge of food preparation was very good and we had a long discussion about the best way to cook the potatoes. I asked questions about what I thought I knew about cooking and checked whether I was correct. In this instance, the children were the experts and I was the novice.

Before long the first major complication, the one that changes the course of the story-line, occurred. A child shouted 'fire' and before long we were running about trying to put out the flames. This was an opportunity to talk about the dangers of fire: How did it start? What happens when you get too near the flames? How do you deal with burns?, etc. Having dealt with this complication another arose. A second child told us that it was not the servants' carelessness that started the fire but a dragon the King had locked in the dungeon for burning people. The dragon was now crying and its tears had put out the flames.

As we sat down amongst the ruins of the King's banquet we discussed how we could help the sad dragon. Could we trust it not to burn us? How do you learn to trust people who have done you harm? Was the dragon really fierce or was she just afraid? Why might she have been burning villages and people before she was captured? After the discussion all the servants were asked to say aloud what they thought and felt about the dragon (thought-tracking) and the bravest were dispatched to release her from her prison. Questions in such stories are endless and can lead to many learning opportunities of a kind that are difficult to discuss in normal classroom situations as they do not necessarily arise.

To describe all the events in this story would take too long here, but suffice to say, some ninety minutes later the dragon had been taken home to her babies and the servants complete with cooked banquet returned to the castle to feed the King. Many areas of the curriculum were covered including maths – how big will we need to make our magic carpet to hold all the servants and the dragon? How can we measure the length of the dragon without a tape measure? Science – do dragons eat the same things as people? How fast did we need to run to get our magic carpet to fly? Geography – where in the world do dragons live? What sort of terrain will we be walking through if we land in the mountains? Music – let's make up a quiet song to sing to the dragon's baby to make her sleep.

The stories made up in this way are very special to children. I always make the point at the end to tell children that no one has ever heard this story before, it is new and it belongs to them. By writing these stories into book form they can make their own popular addition to the book corner.

Making use of a fairy story

Through the employment of teacher-in-role the Mother of the Three Pigs asked the children in role as the pigs' friends to help her search for them. By placing the context (the who, where, what and when) outside the events in the story already known by the children, the teacher gave herself more scope for exploration. It avoided the sometimes unproductive acting out of a familiar story. The children's knowledge of the original story helped them create a sequence of events, but more like detectives piecing together evidence on their journey.

The story began with circle time where the teacher told the children who she was going to be. She said when she returned to the circle she would be in role as the Mother of the Three Little Pigs and that they, the children, would be some of the pigs' friends. She asked them to close their eyes while she went out of the circle.

On returning she began to tell them about her children and how worried she was as they had been away for a very long time and she had received only one letter since they had left home. She reached into her pocket for a letter (which she had prepared earlier). She read it to the children. The letter said 'Hello Mum, we are fine. We have built a house made of straw and we are very proud of it. We have heard there is a wolf about so we will take care.' She asked the children questions about wolves and what they are like – should she be worried? Should she go and look for them? Would the children like to join her?

In small groups they drew maps of the landscape around the pigs' home using pictures and symbols to represent different places. These maps were used on the journey. Questions were asked about the locality – which way did they go? Did they go north, south, east or west? Did they go over the hills or through the woods? The path through the woods was chosen. As it grew dark they thought about a shelter for the night. Where will be the best place? How will they protect themselves from the wolf? Where will they find something to eat?

As the session progressed the children's interest was sustained by the teacher in her role as Mother. By introducing challenges and problems through effective questioning and leading discussion and by allowing children to direct the story and make it their own, she was able to exploit much of its learning potential. Through skilful use of drama strategies she created moments of reflection on events, people or ideas when and where they are needed.

The session ended as it had begun, in a circle time. The pigs had been found, the wolf was vanquished and all the participants were ready for bed.

Drama as a time saver

Contrary to popular thinking, teaching through drama is not a drain on precious classroom time. Through working in this active way teachers are given a powerful method of teaching and learning that is not always available in other forms of classroom organisation. Learning by doing, through the use of this interactive method encourages the retention of information. Recently a 7-year-old was able to tell me, in great detail, the events of an interactive story she had made two years previously in her reception class. Through the different modes of thinking and talking which story-making promotes, children are able to articulate what they know. With careful planning and structuring, drama, in the form of interactive story-making, provides a time-saving method of introducing children to new learning, challenging their assumptions and ideas and testing their existing knowledge within different contexts. This type of activity makes a significant contribution to children's social, emotional and cognitive development in their early years.

Pointers for early years drama

Some points to remember when using drama in the early years classroom:

- story-making is a natural activity in early childhood;
- drama in education is about making meaning rather than making plays;
- drama is a useful teaching tool across the curriculum and not exclusive to speaking and listening;
- the teacher as well as the children must be willing to 'suspend disbelief'and participate in the 'as if';
- planning for drama is strengthened by effective use of drama strategies;
- the context of the story must contain interesting complications and dilemmas;
- the context of the story should provide powerful learning situations;
- by its nature drama is an efficient and time-saving method of introducing new learning or testing old knowledge.

References

Baldwin, P. and Hendy, L. (1994) *The Drama Box*, London: HarperCollins.

Bettleheim, B. (1995) *The Uses of Enchantment: The Meaning and Importance of Fairy Tales*, Harmondsworth: Penguin.

Bruner, J. (1986) *Actual Minds, Possible Worlds*, Cambridge, MA: Harvard University Press.

Engel, S. (1995) *The Stories Children Tell*, New York: W.H. Freeman.

Hendy, L. (1995) 'Playing, role-playing and dramatic activity ', *Early Years*, 15, 2, pp. 13–22.

Hendy, L. and Toon, L. (2001) *Supporting Drama and Imagination Play in the Early Years*, Buckingham: Open University Press.

Hutt, C. (1989) 'Fantasy play', in S.J. Hutt, S. Tyler, C. Hutt and H. Christopherson (eds) *Play, Exploration and Learning*, London: Routledge.

Kitson, N. (1994) 'Fantasy play: A case for adult intervention', in J. Moyles (ed.) *The Excellence of Play*, Buckingham: Open University Press.

Neelands, J. (1990) *Structuring Drama Work*, Cambridge: Cambridge University Press.

OFSTED (1994) *First Class*, London: HMSO.

Readman, G. and Lamont, G. (1994) *Drama: A Handbook for Teachers*, London: BBC Education.

Sylva, K., Bruner, J. and Genova, P. (1976) 'The role of play in the problem-solving of children 3–5 years old', in J. Bruner, A. Jolly and K. Sylva (eds) *Play: Its Role in Development and Evolution*, Harmondsworth: Penguin.

Toye, N. and Prendiville, F. (2000) *Drama and Traditional Story for the Early Years*, London: Routledge.

Woolland, B. (1993) *The Teaching of Drama in the Primary School*, London: Longman.

CHAPTER 7

'Is there a seven in your name?'
WRITING IN THE EARLY YEARS

Sally Wilkinson

The aim of this chapter is to look at ways in which we as educators can provide opportunities that will nurture children as writers. Young children are constantly exposed to print in the environment in which they live, whether at home, playgroup, in the street or at school. They see adults and older children writing notes to each other, lists for a shopping trip, letters and e-mails. They begin to realise that these marks on paper and screen are regarded as important by those around them and can have many uses. Just as they learn to talk by experimenting with spoken language and imitating those around them, children will often experiment with marks on paper and on the computer screen. They will try out patterns and attempt to communicate through this medium themselves.

These independent marks are often referred to as 'emergent writing'. This term encompasses the vast number of ways in which young children use marks and letters to make meaning. As Yetta Goodman (1986) described, from a young age children engage in writing tasks for a wide variety of reasons, and by the age of 2 most children have begun to use symbols to represent real things. Therefore, by the time children enter a nursery or reception class they may already be very experienced emergent writers. They may be mark makers or they may be aware of the alphabetic nature of print. It is our job, as educators, to build on these skills, and the knowledge and understanding of writing that the children have. This involves adopting a developmental approach to writing whereby the children's emergent writing is acknowledged and they are encouraged to 'have a go' rather than copy from an adult model. The implications this has for how writing is approached in school, the contexts in which it happens and ways of encouraging children as independent writers will form the basis for this chapter.

Understanding children writing

Ann Browne, in her book *Helping Children to Write* (1993), correctly says that before we undertake the planning of a writing curriculum for young children we should have some understanding of what writing is for, how it is used and how it looks from the child's point of view. In his nursery class Josh has been looking at snails. Part of his response to this experience (see Figure 7.1) is to make sweeping circular marks across his paper that he says, as he does so, are the snails, and to make dots under this which he says is his writing. Josh is clearly showing, even in this early stage of his hand coordination development, that he knows that drawing and writing are formed by different sorts of marks.

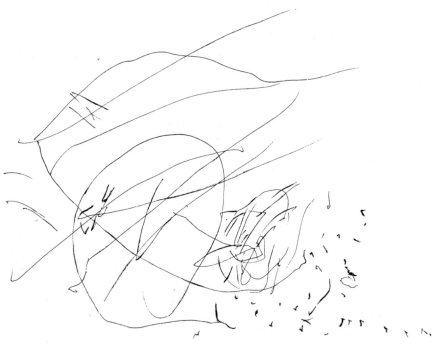

Figure 7.1 *Drawing and writing about snails by Josh, aged 3*

Other children of a similar age might respond with:

- marks mostly horizontal
- zig-zags
- single or linked round shapes
- straight and round marks imitating letter shapes
- large circular shapes

- one letter from their name repeated
- assorted letters from their name.

How children respond in these early stages varies greatly and is not part of a rigid hierarchy of stages. As the many examples of children's writing collected by teachers involved in the National Writing Project (1989) showed, some children experiment with all of the above, others with only one or two.

It does seem to be true, however, that the appearance of the marks in general reflects the children's cultural background, with marks being formed in the direction and following the orientation used by adults around them. Therefore, a child used to seeing adults using a Chinese script may well emphasise vertical marks in their writing. It is also often the case that children who prefer writing with their left hand, or who have not yet shown a preference, may start much of their mark making from the right-hand side of the paper.

Children whose mother tongue is not English may also include characters from their home language in their writing. In the piece of writing shown in Figure 7.2 Fatima is experimenting with a wonderful array of letter and character shapes based on written forms found in English and Bengali.

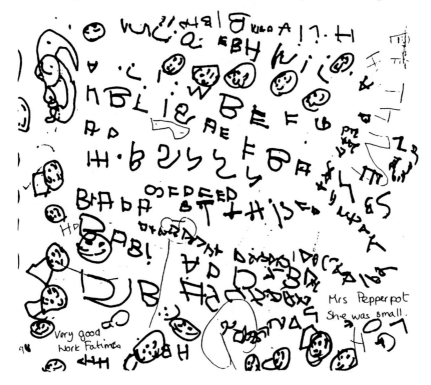

Figure 7.2 *Letter shapes drawn by Fatima showing the influence of English and Bengali written forms*

The way that writing is approached and organised in her class has meant that she is confident about herself as a writer and is willing to take risks with her writing. This piece of writing was in response to a story read by the class teacher who then wrote down what Fatima told her that the writing said. She praised Fatima for using so many different letters and characters and they talked about the ones Fatima liked the best.

Young children often develop knowledge and understanding about print long before they are able to demonstrate this through the marks they make on paper. Alex completed the two examples of writing shown in Figure 7.3 in the same week. The marks on the left were completed one morning in his nursery class. When making the marks with his pencil, he showed an under-standing of one-to-one correspondence as he told his teacher the letters as he wrote his name. However, his fine motor skills were not sufficiently devel-oped to allow him to represent actual letters. Later that week, when Alex was writing using a computer at home, he was able to demonstrate the full extent of his knowledge about print. First, he chose to type the alphabet in capital letters. (After typing the first 'a' he selected the Caps Lock, as he pre-ferred capitals.) Writing the alphabet involved much concentration as he sang an alphabet song after he typed each letter to help him remember which letter came next. He knew the name of each letter and could find them on the keyboard, but was not sure about all of the sounds they made. He could remember the visual appearance of mummy and daddy and write the numbers of two of his favourite types of train.

This opportunity to use a word processor, whether at home or in his nursery class, was very important to Alex for developing both his know-ledge about writing and his belief in himself as a writer. As with many

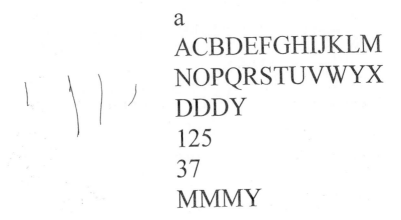

Figure 7.3 *Alex's writing by hand and using a word processor*

young children, boys in particular, Alex did not yet possess the physical skills to form the letters that he already knew. The computer therefore provided a very important avenue for his developing literacy skills.

The role of the educator

As can be seen from the examples so far, by encouraging children to write independently from the start, the role of the educator is altered significantly. Instead of spending time writing sentences for children to copy or answering requests for help with spelling, the educator has a more active role. Time can be spent talking with the children about their writing, observing the skills and knowledge they are using and joining with them as a fellow writer. As can be seen from Figure 7.4, the ways in which an educator can support and interact with children engaged in the writing process are many and varied.

What is certain is that the educator is at the centre of what happens in the classroom. We make decisions all the time, which influence not only the opportunities children have for writing in our classrooms, but also how they perceive the task of writing and themselves as writers. Writing needs to be presented as part of the whole language environment, a way of initiating or responding to communication and as something which can give pleasure for its own sake. The ways that activities are set up in the classroom should recognise that' reading, writing, talking about writing and talking in order to write must be continual possibilities; they overlap and interlock' (Smith, 1982, p. 202).

Talking about writing

Making time for talk at various stages of the writing process is one way of improving the quality of the content of the writing that the children produce. The importance of children being clear about what they want to say before they are asked to write is stressed in *Developing Early Writing* (DfEE, 2001). Encouraging children to tell their stories to a friend who would:

- say which parts they liked
- ask questions to clarify their understanding
- make suggestions of additions or parts to alter

means that a story is well established in a child's mind before a pen or pencil has been picked up. There is therefore less chance of the writer coming to the mental block of what to write next as they have already

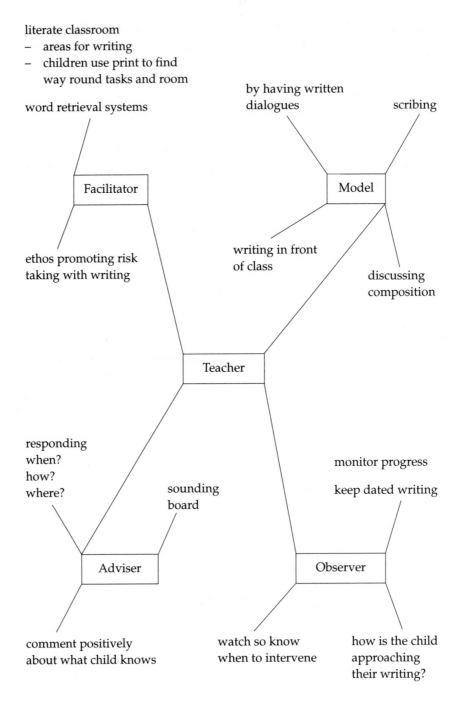

literate classroom
– areas for writing
– children use print to find
  way round tasks and room

word retrieval systems

by having written
dialogues

scribing

Facilitator

Model

ethos promoting risk
taking with writing

writing in front
of class

discussing
composition

Teacher

responding
when?
how?
where?

sounding
board

monitor progress

keep dated writing

Adviser

Observer

comment positively
about what child knows

watch so know
when to intervene

how is the child
approaching
their writing?

Figure 7.4 *Modes of interaction of the educator with children engaged in the writing process*

rehearsed it orally. Using talk in this way asks the children to draft their writing orally. This is an important stage on the way to their being able, when they are more exper ienced writers, to alter and improve their work on paper and respond to written comments given by peers. The latter idea, which involves partners responding to each other's work, is perhaps usually thought of as being appropriate only for older children. However, as was demonstrated during the National Writing Project (1989), with the support of an educator, young children are able to use talk and writing to comment on a partner's work in a way that extends that child's ideas or encourages them to develop their writing further.

Known texts and writing

As well as recognising the importance of talk to writing we also need to encourage children to draw on the stories, poems and factual texts that they have heard or have read for themselves. This knowledge, coupled with real life experiences, forms the nucleus of the store of ideas which they tap when involved in writing. Adult writers constantly use ideas that have their basis in something they have once read. So we should value examples in children's writing (such as that by Dale in Figure 7.5) which show through the language used or the ideas expressed that they have drawn on known texts or forms of writing.

> One day Sylvester was resting. Some beans rolled to Sylvester's basket. He was a cat.
> The beans grew and grew and grew into a Giant beanstalk. Sylvester woke up and suckering suckertash and he climbed the beanstalk . He climbed and climbed and climbed and climbded to the giants castle and when he went down he got knocked into China.

Figure 7.5 Sylvester the Cat *by Dale: writing showing the influence of known texts*

Shared writing

One of the ways that the educator can support and develop children's use of the language and formats of known texts is through shared writing with a group of children or the whole class. This methodology is emphasised in the National Literacy Strategy (DfEE, 1998) and consists of:

- demonstration and modelling of writing by the educator;
- scribing and developing ideas given by the children;
- supported composition by the children.

These elements may not all be present in one shared writing session and the educator may choose to develop a piece of writing over two or more days.

A group of children in a Year 2 class had been reading a talking book on the computer of the *Tortoise and the Hare*. Following on from the shared reading of the story the group made up their own fable with their own chosen characters, a spider and a cheetah. In shared writing the teacher began by demonstrating how to begin the story in the same style as the *Tortoise and the Hare* and then scribed the group's ideas for the story, helping the children use the story language they had heard in the talking book. Once the story was complete, it was read several times by the teacher and children together. Then pictures were drawn to go with each scene and scanned into *Clicker 4*, a computer program with a bookmaking facility. The children then wrote the part of the story that they had illustrated, with the support of word grids, to go on to the screen opposite their picture. Once all the pages were complete they were linked by the teacher to create the children's own talking book. Figure 7.6 shows one page from their finished book.

Writing areas

Careful thought needs to be given to the balance between the children writing in response to a stimulus initiated by the educator and providing opportunities for them to decide on the reason for writing. By setting up a writing or graphics area in the classroom we are providing time and space for children to experiment with a variety of writing materials. They will also be able to make decisions about what they would like to write and how it will be organised. Setting up an area does not require a large space or a major cash outlay. A table against a wall with a noticeboard for children to display their writing if they wish is fine. A plan of a typical area is shown in

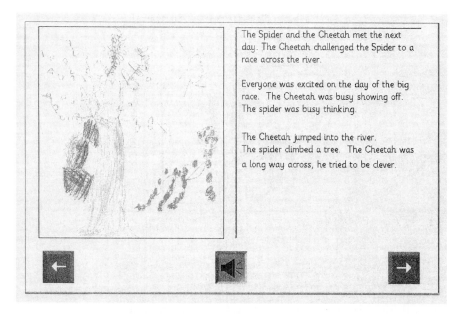

The Spider and the Cheetah met the next day. The Cheetah challenged the Spider to a race across the river.

Everyone was excited on the day of the big race. The Cheetah was busy showing off. The spider was busy thinking.

The Cheetah jumped into the river. The spider climbed a tree. The Cheetah was a long way across, he tried to be clever.

Figure 7.6 *A page from the talking book,* The Spider and the Cheetah

Figure 7.7. If the demand is great the children can always spill over on to neighbouring tables. Equipping the area with a variety of writing implements is more important than having large quantities all the same. The same is true of the materials that are provided for the children to write on; old envelopes, a pad of forms, different shapes, sizes and colours of paper can all be gathered through requests to businesses, shops and parents. The writing area can also reflect topics going on in the class. For instance, a topic on giants could mean that the writing area had giant size envelopes, paper and markers. A Year 1 class was helping to plan the planting for a flower bed in their school grounds, so the materials in their writing area included forms from seed catalogues, labels and diagrams of the school grounds for them to annotate. In settings where space is very limited a writing box can provide the same resources as a writing area. A plastic open toolbox with a carrying handle works well as children and educators can take it to where the writing will take place.

The writing area provides a low-risk environment in which children can rehearse favourite ways of writing, try new ideas and have control over the whole process from deciding on the purpose of their writing, to whether they will make a final neat copy. Sayarun, a Year 2 whose first language was Syleti, often spent her time in the writing area writing letters to other children in the class. She would choose as her recipients those whom she

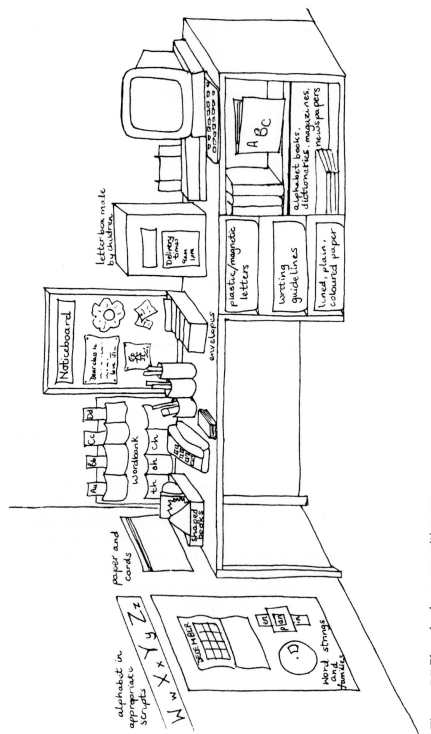

Figure 7.7 *Plan of a classroom writing area*

thought needed cheering up, someone she wanted to congratulate, or some-one who had not had a letter from the class postbox for a while. As her letter to her teacher shows (Figure 7.8), she understood many of the functions which letters could fulfil.

Notes

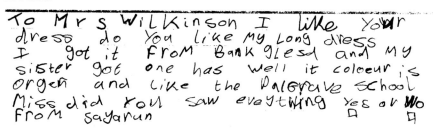

To Mrs Wilkinson I like your dress do you like my long dress I got it from Bank glesd and my sister got one has well it coloeur is orgeñ and like the Palgrave school Miss did you saw eveytwing yes or No from Sayarun

Figure 7.8 *Sayarun's letter to her teacher*

The postbox was an important feature of the writing area as it provided an authentic opportunity for writing to others, something that definitely motivated the children to write and influenced the quality of the writing that they produced.

Another child in the same class wrote his first truly independent piece of writing in the writing area. He had joined the Year 2 class from another school and was convinced that he could write only by copying an adult's model. At first much of his time in the writing area was spent drawing or on the phone to his grandmother. After a few weeks he posted his first letter and sent it to his teacher (Figure 7.9).

Figure 7.9 *Lee's first letter*

She was overjoyed to receive it and was also able to see from it what Lee understood about print. He had used letters from his name and had included mathematical signs as well. His drawing also began to include examples of environmental print such as car registrations, street signs and shop names. Lee spent time at weekends out with his father on his ice-cream van and was very interested in and knowledgeable about cars. It was not surprising, therefore, that these examples of environmental print were an important part of his first independent writing attempts.

Writing and role-play

Letters and postboxes also became an important focus for a Year 1 class who had been watching videos and listening to and reading stories about Postman Pat. An area of their classroom became Greendale Post Office and letters from the writing area and home corner were brought from the letter-box to the post office for sorting. The children also took on the roles of post master or mistress and customers, providing opportunities for form filling, marking of parcels and list making. Since the post office also sold cards, envelopes, writing paper and pens, these could be purchased and used in the writing area or home corner to generate more post for Greendale staff to collect, sort and deliver.

In role-play situations it is important that the children have some under-standing of the context in which their writing takes place and the forms of writing that might be expected to take place there. Therefore, setting up some types of role-play area might involve the children being taken on a visit to see what sort of things are needed in the area and what people do who work in, for instance, a vet's surgery. Prior to setting up a travel agency in their classroom, one reception class visited a local travel agency and saw all the brochures, forms and computers that were used when peo-ple came to book a holiday. They asked the staff what they said to the customers and watched while information was filled in on the computer and forms. Back in the classroom they equipped their travel agents with the following:

telephone	booking forms	pens
computer	tickets	pencils
diaries	timetables	ruler
note pads	labels	stapler
fax machine	posters	envelopes
(cardboard box		
with slits in)		

When the children were playing in the travel agents an adult sometimes joined in with them, taking on the role of a customer or one of the staff of the travel agents. The way in which the children were able to use writing in their play was expanded both by their visit to the travel agency and by an adult modelling the ways in which writing could occur. The children acting as customers would fill in forms on brochures and write notes in the home corner to remind them of what they wanted to ask the travel agents. Those being staff in the travel agent would type details into the computer, make notes, complete forms and fill in information in their diaries.

Providing authentic writing experiences, such as those above, in role-play means that the children are more likely to base their writing on realistic models of writing. The example in Figure 7.10 is from a nursery class and shows Chloe making the choice of an appropriate piece of paper for writing a shopping list from a selection of paper of various sizes available to them. She then wrote her list in the home corner (notice how many of their chosen letters are from their names) and took it with them when they went shopping in the class shop.

Figure 7.10 *Chloe's shopping list*

Purposes and audiences for writing

The importance of children having real reasons for writing in a range of forms and for a range of audiences has been a major topic of discussion in recent years. *The National Curriculum for English* (DfEE, 2000) sets out very clearly the range of purposes and audiences that children should have experience of during Key Stage 1.

When considering who the audience is for a piece of writing, it may be that for children writing in the writing area the answer could be a friend in the class who will receive their card or letter, someone at home or themselves. The value of the latter should not be underestimated, as providing an opportunity for children to write without any obligation for them to show their writing to anyone else can contribute immensely to their writing development. The relaxing environment of the writing area can free some children to write in ways that they are not able to do when an educator has expectations of their achievement. Daniel was in Year 2 and his teacher felt that even though he had mastered the technical side of writing, she did not often succeed in motivating him to want to write. For Daniel the freedom to write for himself and about whatever he wanted was essential. His story (Figure 7.11) began from a blank flap book that was part of the stock of the writing area and represents his greatest writing achievement during his first term in the class.

The examples of children writing during role-play showed how important it is for children to write in authentic situations, so that their play echoes the purposes for which writing is used in the real world. They can also gain much from writing to imaginary audiences such as when a reception class received a letter from Roger, the robot that they had made from junk materials. They corresponded with Roger (in fact their class teacher) for several weeks, with the children asking Roger many questions about himself and responding to enquiries from him about themselves. The way in which children respond to their audience in this situation can vary. Some are happy to believe that Roger can write although others may be more sceptical. Even if the latter is true, the children are usually still willing to enter into correspondence if they know their letters will receive a reply.

Another way of providing opportunities for children to experiment with forms of writing that they do not usually have the opportunity of using is through writing in role to an imagined audience. Excellent stimuli for this are picture books such as *The Jolly Postman* and *Each Peach Pear Plum* (both by Janet and Allan Ahlberg). The former contains many examples of different reasons for writing that can lead the children to develop their own letters, catalogues and postcards. In the example in

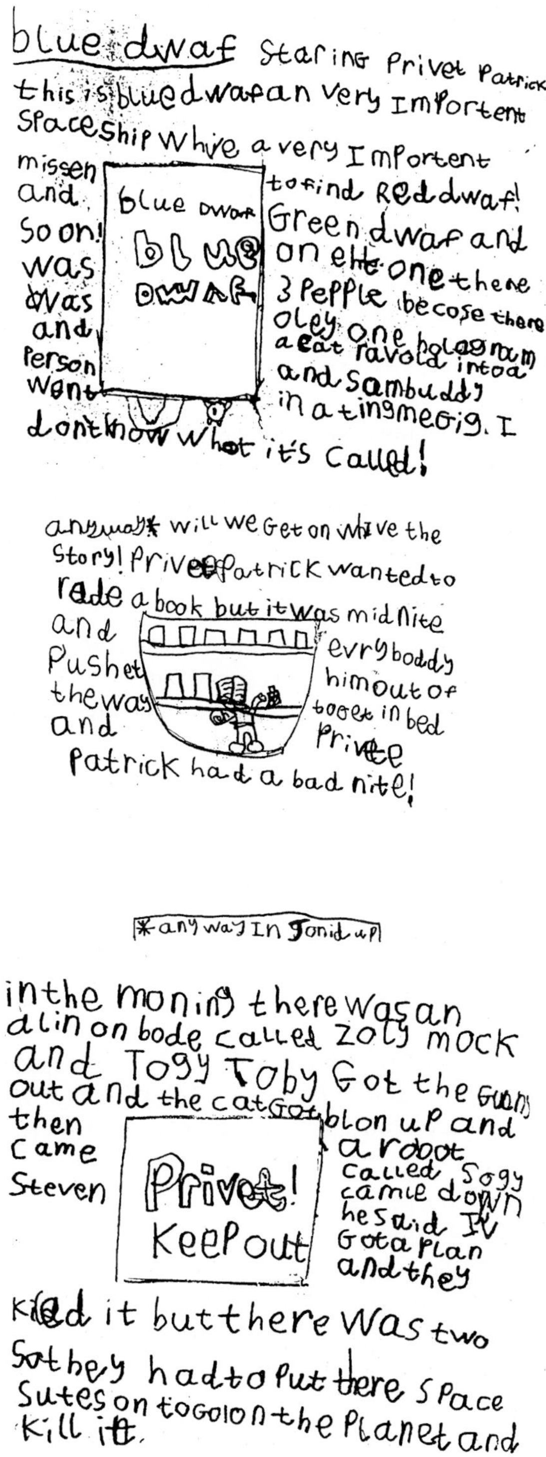

blue dwaf staring Privet Patrick!
this is bluedwafan very importent
spaceship whive a very importent
missen and. [blue dwor BLUE DWAF] tofind Reddwaf!
and. Green dwaf and
so on! on eht one there
was 3 peple becose there
was oley one holagram
and a eat ravold intoa
person and sambuddy
wont in a tingmeoig. I
donthow whot it's called!

anywa* will we Get on whive the
story! Priveppatrick wantedto
rade a book but it was mid nite
and evryboddy
Pushet himout of
the way booek in bed
and Privee
Patrick had a bad nite!

*any way In Jonid up]

inthe moning there was an
alin on bode called zoty mock
and Togy Toby Got the Guon
out and the cat Got blon up and
then a rooot
Came [Privet! Keepout] called sogy
Steven camie down
he said I
Gota plan
andthey
kld it butthere Was two
Sothey hadto Put there sPace
Sutes on toGolon the Planet and
kill it.

Figure 7.11
*Daniel's story on a
self-chosen theme!*

Figure 7.12 Darren's letter to BB Wolf draws directly on one in *The Jolly Postman* from Red Riding Hood's solicitors. Simon's, on the other hand, shows him devising the whole of the scenario for himself. He was invited to write something that could have been posted to one of the characters in *Each Peach Pear Plum* and he chose to write a postcard to Bo-Peep from her lost sheep. The way that he manages to express succinctly all that is necessary is just right for a postcard, and the explanation of where the sheep have gone is so appropriate!

Making books

Bookmaking gives children an excellent reason for writing. Seeing their book published, either within the class or for a wider school audience, is tremendous for developing children's self-esteem and their image of themselves as writers. Often the books made by them and their peers are the ones that are the most popular in the book corner and are returned to over and over again. The actual recording of the text of a book can be done in several ways and does not have to be completed by the children. The role of the educator may be to lead the composition of the text in shared writing sessions or to act as a scribe for a group of children, rereading for them what they have composed so far and encouraging contributions from the whole group.

Collaborative writing

Sometimes being alone with a piece of paper is a daunting experience. Young children can feel that they don't have any ideas or are unsure of committing them to paper. Collaborating with other children means they can build on each other's ideas, discuss possible options and make adjustments together. It is another way in which talk becomes central to the writing process. The actual recording of the writing could be carried out by:

- the educator acting as scribe for the group;
- jointly by all the children in the group;
- by one or two children decided on by the group;
- by a child nominated as scribe by the educator;
- by an older child working with a younger child.

Children in a nursery class took turns to put their hands in a feely bag containing fruit and vegetables such as a pineapple, fennel and broccoli. As they

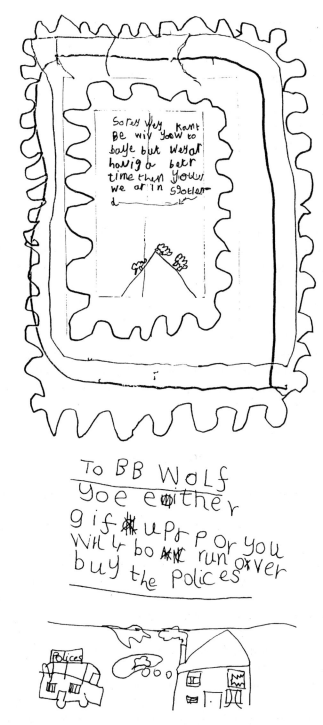

Figure 7.12 *Letters to BB Wolf and Bo-Peep by Darren and Simon*

- younger child developing the ideas of the older child;
- younger child doing most of the writing, asking questions of the older child.

The educators involved set up the pairings very carefully so that the children working together were able to relate to each other socially. Where the older children were leaders in the partnerships, they provided invaluable one-to-one interaction, developing their own skills as encourager and questioner as they sought to extend their younger partner's ideas. This can be seen in an excerpt of conversation between Ruby, a Year-2 – bilingual – speaker and Seema, Year 6:

Seema: What do you think should happen next?
Ruby: It flies. He (the bird) eats the food.
Seema: (writing) The bird flies up to the tree and eats the food.

What happens to the two girls?

Ruby: They go home.

Conclusion

This chapter has considered young children writing in a variety of settings and for a range of purposes and audiences. Central to all these has been the understanding the educator has of the sorts of responses to expect from the children, which reveal the knowledge, skills and understanding they have about writing. The educator provides writing opportunities which build on these, involving the children in using writing in play situations, writing areas, and when working collaboratively with others. These and other experiences will allow children to develop as confident, motivated writers willing to take risks with their writing. So instead of classrooms where children ask educators:

'Can you write that for me?'

what can be heard are enthusiastic emergent writers saying:

'I can write that myself!'

Pointers for writing in the early years

Young writers need:

- to have an environment to write in which provides real purposes for writing;
- to have ownership of their writing;
- to be able to choose what to write about and for what reasons;
- to have their attempts valued whatever their stage of development;
- to have experiences which link writing with talking and reading;
- to see adults writing;
- opportunities to write in collaboration with others.

References

Browne, A. (1993) *Helping Children to Write*, London: Paul Chapman Publishing.

Department for Education and Employment (DfEE) (1998) *The National Literacy Strategy:* Framework for Teaching, DfEE.

Department for Education and Employment (DfEE) (2000) *National Curriculum for English*, DfEE and QCA.

Department for Education and Employment (DfEE) (2001) *Developing Early Writing*, DfEE.

Goodman, Y. (1986) 'Writing development in young children', *Gnosis*, No. 8, March.

National Literacy Strategy (1998) *Framework for Teaching*, DfES.

National Writing Project (1989) *Becoming A Writer*, Walton-on-Thames: Nelson.

Smith, F. (1982) *Writing and the Writer*, London: Heinemann Educational.

Vygotsky, L. (1978) *Mind in Society*, London: Harvard University Press.

Further reading

Czerniewska, P. (1992) *Learning About Writing*, Oxford: Blackwell.

Hall, N. (ed.) (1989) *Writing With Reason*, London: Hodder & Stoughton.

CHAPTER 8

'What's that dog thinking, Mrs Bromley?'

PICTURE BOOKS AND LEARNING TO READ

Helen Bromley

Supporting young children with their development as readers should be an exciting prospect for all those working with children in the early years. Building on the knowledge of reading that they bring with them, sharing well-loved favourite texts, introducing and discussing new authors and titles, and, most of all, watching the children's excitement grow as the world of the reader opens up to them (see Figure 8.1).

My own memories of school reading are not exciting. I can vividly recall being sent to the headmistress' study to read some of my *Happy Venture Reader* book to her. Although I can remember Dick, Dora, Nip and Fluff, it is not with any particular affection. They are remembered more as distant relations who had to be tolerated, rather than as good friends. The books with which I formed the closest ties had been introduced to me at home, courtesy of the local library: *Little Bear* (Holmelund Minarik, 1957), *Fox in Socks* (Seuss, 1965) and many others. This was in the late 1950s. Since then there has been an explosion in the publishing of books for children, providing educators with a rich and varied selection to use in the classroom.

Liz Waterland (1992) talks about the difference between 'free range' and 'battery' books. The difference between these being that free range books are written by authors and illustrators who have had freedom to carefully choose and compose their books from the imagination, whilst battery books are products of a factory-type approach to literature. 'There is a hint of unnatural practises, of confinement and restriction . . . even a suggestion of the mechanical and the automatic' (pp. 160–1).

This is a pitcture of Mrs Bromeroy and some peaple childron Lisning To Her read a storey.

Figure 8.1 *The excitement of reading!*

Books as children's friends

In order to explore this difference further, I will return to the analogy of friendship. Children need friends that they can interact with time and time again, they need to share the good times and the bad. Books described as free range, that is, high-quality, multi-layered texts, provide such opportunities. Amelia, aged four, sat with a copy of *The Teddy Robber* (Beck, 1991) every morning before school, for six months, just as she might have depended on one child for friendship. She read it over and over again, taking great comfort in its familiarity, and the happy ending. Eventually, she was able to make other friendships, but in times of stress she always returned to *The Teddy Robber*. Developing favourite texts is a key experience that all young readers should have, and is closely linked to the devlopment of tastes and preferences.

Brooke, whose Aunt had recently died, took *Granpa* (by John Burningham) home, not for herself, but for her mum. As she explained to me, 'It's so mummy will see that everything will be all right in the end.' An example of one friend helping another, and an example of how the youngest children can develop an understanding of how reading can support all of us. I have used many reading schemes during my career and cannot recall examples of any which would have provided such support. Battery books do not provide the sort of friends that stick around for long. They are with you for a short period of time, before you leave them and move on to the next. Lasting ties are not encouraged.

One of the important parts of friendship is the shared conversations that can exist. With your friends you laugh, cry and build a collection of joint memories, whilst all the time finding out more about yourself. Children's literature can provide such experiences. Alyck took *Owl Babies* by Martin Waddell home repeatedly, because he thought that Bill, the baby owl, was so funny. Other young children that I have taught have enjoyed *Owl Babies* because they feel that 'missing their mum' is legitimised in the story, and they strongly identify with Bill.

Children need friends that will help them learn, without fear of failure and with the knowledge that risk taking is a worthwhile activity. Friends encourage you to 'have another go', whether trying to ride your bike without stabilisers or to read *Each Peach Pear Plum* (Ahlberg, 1980) for yourself. Books such as those I have mentioned invite rereading because they offer opportunities to see the familiar and unfamiliar juxtapositioned in such a way as to make you want to read them again and again. Just like visiting an old friend, but playing a new game. Texts constructed especially for the teaching of reading may not provide such friendly support, especially if reading does not come easily. It is often difficult for children to recognise themselves in the text (or illustrations) and there may be no chance of trying out a new game until you have mastered the old one.

There is no doubt that the best friends are those that grow and change with you, not just those that were suitable for you when you were 5 or 8. This is also true of children's reading material. Liz Waterland (1992, p. 161) quotes Jim Trelease: 'If a book is not worth reading at the age of fifty, then it is not worth reading at the age of ten either.' Look at the books that you use in the classroom as if you were looking for friends. If you do not find them interesting and want to get to know them better, then why should the children? This is not to deny that there will be differences in opinion and in taste, but it's a good place to start.

I would hope that, encouraged by the adults with whom they work, children would develop a rich collection of good friends, to be remembered with affection and pleasure. Friends who teach them that reading is a pleasure for life, not a series of hoops through which they must jump. This chapter intends to introduce activities for using meaningful texts with children, that have been successful in my own early years classroom. It is not intended to be a definitive list of suggestions. Far from it! I hope rather that people would try one (or all) of the ideas out for themselves and be inspired to go on to discover more.

What young children need to learn about reading

It is important to accept that young children already know much about reading when they enter our classrooms. The activities outlined in this chapter, therefore, are designed to allow children to demonstrate what they already know, as well as educating them in new lessons about reading. Henrietta Dombey (1992, pp. 12–15) summarises the lessons that she feels children need to learn about reading; this is an abridged version of her list:

Attitudes

- pleasure and satisfaction: to see books as a powerful source of enjoyment, information and understanding;
- confidence: a firm belief that they will learn to read;
- concentration and persistence;
- toleration of uncertainty;
- tentativeness: a readiness to correct errors;
- reflexiveness: a readiness to look with a certain detachment at what they can do and have read, and at what they need to learn.

Knowledge and strategies – children need to understand:

- that the text is the same on each rereading and that the marks on the page tell you what to say;
- that language is composed of separable words;
- the conventions of the English language system;
- that words are made up of individual letters;
- the rules of English spelling;
- a reliable sight vocabulary;
- how to use their knowledge of the world and the content of books to aid word identification;
- how to use the information from the pictures (see Figure 8.2);
- how to use all these various devices together – orchestration.

HaNNaH andrstas The words Becos of The Pichets.

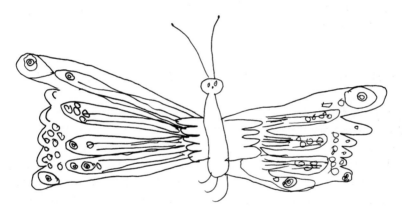

Figure 8.2 *Using information from the pictures*

I feel that the best way for children to learn these vital lessons is through the provision of a variety of rewarding experiences, provided by an educator who is enthusiastic about reading. Some lessons will, by necessity, be more explicit than others, but all will be crucial to the development of the children as readers. There is not room within this chapter to document all the ways in which it is possible to support the emergent reader. I feel that the activities outlined below show a variety of meaningful contexts in which most, if not all, the above lessons could be learned, both implicitly and explicitly.

Big Books

The theory behind using Big Books is well documented. Holdaway (1979), for example, working in New Zealand in the 1970s, looked at children who were already reading when they came to school, to find out what had made them successful. Many of the children had favourite stories that were read to them repeatedly. Gradually, the children were able to take on more of the reading for themselves, first by remembering the text and eventually being able to match words and phrases to the known text. Big Books were devised as a way of making stories available to a wider audience. Holdaway noted that all children were able to be successful at their own level, with this approach. Large groups were able to be involved in the shared reading of a familiar text. They provide a shared context for discussion and make it easy for all the children in a class to focus on the chosen text.

A favourite Big Book in my reception class was *This is the Bear* (Hayes, 1995). The children already knew the text extremely well, having heard the small version read out many times. The text rhymes and has marvellous pictures, features which help support the developing reader. Using this story in its outsize version helped to create a situation for the children to learn both explicit and implicit lessons about reading. Each time the Big Book is used, a similar format can be followed:

- Look closely at the cover, find features such as title, author, illustrator, publisher, publisher's symbol. If this is done on a regular basis, then the children will pick up the vocabulary surrounding books and authorship very quickly. They then use these terms for themselves, quite naturally.
- Have a look at each page, ignoring nothing. Some books contain beautifully constructed endpapers and in some cases, these tell part of the story (*Farmer Duck*, Waddell, 1991, for example).
- Look for dedications. To whom would the children dedicate a book?
- What initials would they use?
- Do the cover and the preceding pages tell the reader anything about the story that is to follow?

Developing comprehension skills

The teacher can then follow one of several paths. Skills of prediction and authorship can be encouraged by reading the story part of the way through and asking the children to decide what happens next. To extend this activity, ask the children to justify their reasons for suggesting particular outcomes. This provides an excellent opportunity for formative assessment of their ability to make deductions and create their own hypotheses.

Alternatively, the story can be read to the children, not necessarily without interruption, but with as few as possible, so that the children can get the most meaning from the story. This will be the first of many readings, so there will be plenty of opportunities for discussion. The idea is not to encourage passive listeners, an audience powerless to interrupt the reading instructor, but rather to encourage the children to join in and to question what they see and what they hear. This is more effective, however, when the children have heard the whole story through once and have a shared context for discussion.

There are many ways in which Big Books can be used to stimulate discussion. One of the most effective ways I have used is to organise the children into small talk groups and ask them to devise questions to ask about the story. This gives all children some opportunity to be involved in discussion about the text, and provides a safe context for talk for those who prefer not to speak in front of a large group. It also promotes close scrutiny of the text in a collaborative way, providing an ideal opportunity for children to discuss their reading and learn from one another.

As well as promoting comprehension skills, Big Books can be used to look carefully at features of print.

Looking at features of print

- Choose a particular letter. How many of this particular letter can the children find on one page, on a double-page spread?
- Can they find any words within words, e.g. is, in, the, and?
- Can they find two words with similar endings? (Particularly useful in a rhyming text)
- How many capital letters can they see? Whereabouts do they appear in the text?
- Introduce the children to the notion of the silent letter. Can any of these be found?
- Use the children's own names as a basis for the print search. Can Jodie find any words beginning with J? Can Matthew find at, the or he? My experience has shown that children especially enjoy the activities that involve their names and quickly learn features of not only their own, but also other people's names.
- Children can also be encouraged to devise similar questions of their own, so that this can become an independent as well as an adult-led activity.

Obviously, there is far more to becoming a critical and highly motivated reader than studying metalinguistic features of print! As educators, we want children to know that reading is pleasurable and that there is much to be gained from the rereading of old favourites. Again using Big Books, it is possible to demonstrate all of this to children and, at the same time, allow them space to air their opinions and perceptions about the books that they are reading. This is achieved by a combination of teacher questioning and, most importantly, providing the opportunity for the children to ask their own questions.

Looking beyond the text

- Children can be put into groups of two or three and asked to devise one question about the story (illustrations included).
- Encourage the children to focus on how the illustrations might be telling a different story to the pictures.
- Look carefully at the body language of the participants.
- Follow the actions of one character throughout the whole story. Use this tracking as a basis for studying character, motive and plot!

Looking beyond the text is especially exciting, as even with numerous readings of the same text, the children always spot something new. This was demonstrated when I discussed *This is the Bear* (Hayes, 1995) with a class of 5-year-olds. Briefly, this is the tale of a teddy bear who is pushed into the dustbin by a dog and mistakenly taken to the dump. He is found after a long search, by the same dog, and driven home to a hero's welcome! Questions devised about the story included:

> Why did the dog push the bear into the bin?
> How does the bear feel about being in the bin?
> How would you feel if you lost your teddy and couldn't get it back?
> Do you think that the dog is jealous of the bear?
> Do you think that the bear likes the dog?
> What's that dog thinking, Mrs Bromley?

I think that it is important to note that there were no questions of the type 'What colour is the van?' All the questions generated by the children were looking deep into the story to try and find out more about the characters in it.

Games and play

Whenever I have carried out such activities with my class, I have always told the children that it is part of a game; sometimes them against me, sometimes a collaborative guessing game. For example, individual words can be covered up with a small piece of card, while the children close their eyes. When they open them, they have to guess which word is covered. This promotes close scrutiny of the text and finger/voice match. Then, when the large group session is over, I would always make the suggestion that, if they wanted to play the games themselves later, then they could do so. All that needs to be provided is a Big Book, clipped to an easel, four chairs placed in a semi-circle around it and something to be used as a pointer.

This game was a particular favourite with Eleanor, Hannah and Rebecca, who would often take the opportunity to persuade other members of the class to come and take part as pupils, while they operated their own version of team teaching. Rebecca, the most experienced reader in the group, would ask questions like 'Can you find "the" on this page?' Eleanor, who was particularly skilled at memorising texts, would read the book to the rest of the group, pointing with the ruler as she did so. That left Hannah, who had an excellent grasp of initial sounds and was able to devise questions such as 'Can you find a word on here that begins with the same sound as "apple"?' I think that the pupils in the game were getting some excellent teaching from three young experts.

From watching the children play what in my class has become known simply as 'schools', it is apparent that the children reproduce and therefore reinforce the types of behaviour demonstrated by the teacher. Each time the game is played, it is never an exact copy of the previous game; new ideas are added and children negotiate and discuss the questions and the answers.

Developing children's awareness

The children in my class have also had the opportunity to share the Big Books available with their reading partners, children from a Year 2 class. At one session, I asked the children to reflect, in their pairs, on how Big Books might help them with their reading.

Here are some of their comments:

I like Big Books because you can always see the writing.

I think and my friend thinks that a Walker Big Book is good because you can see them better than you can see an ordinary book and you can see the pictures better.

Big Books help you to read properly because they have big words to help you read. (See Figure 8.3.)

It will help you write better. Reading will help you think better. It will help you to learn. It will help you think about the pictures.

Figure 8.3 *'Big Books help you to read properly because they have big words to help you read'*

As you can see, the children are very much aware of how the large format of the books encourages them to become participants in the shared reading process, allowing them to become even more involved than in a normal storytelling session. Talk is central to all the activities outlined above. They are operating in the zone of proximal development (Vygotsky, 1986) along-side a more experienced reader and their own knowledge, and learning potential will only become apparent if they are allowed to explore their knowledge through conversation. Through role-play (such as the game of 'schools') they are able to have the opportunity to act as the more able other, in the company of their peers. Self-esteem and confidence is built up this way, as well as there being room for errors to be made, without the ever watchful eye of an adult.

Group reading

Big Books are not the only way in which children can be encouraged to play with their reading! Group reading around multiple copies of the same text provides similar opportunities, if the right atmosphere for learning and risk taking is created.

Maisie Middleton (Sowter, 1994) is the story of an ordinary little girl who gets up one morning and despite attempting to rouse her parents, eventu-ally has to prepare breakfast for herself. It is a story that appealed to all the children in my class, possibly because they too would like to share some of Maisie's independence, however transitory. It was because of the popularity of the book that I chose it as a subject for group reading. All four children in the group had heard the story an equal number of times and could therefore bring some previous knowledge to the group situation.

During the session, the children listen to the story read out loud first, join-ing in if they wish. They then take it in turn to ask questions about each of the pages of the book, either to each other or to the adult present. I was sur-prised at how involved the children became with this particular text. I soon realised that I had underestimated its potential. The first page shows the exterior of Maisie's house, framed in an arch with a flower on the top. Eleanor began. 'I wonder who sleeps behind the blind with the stripes on?' she asked, and immediately the others joined in, speculating on the possible occupants of the house. Brooke was trying to imagine herself at the front door, stroking the cat and bringing in the milk. What to me had appeared to be a fairly simplistic picture provided the children with a rich source of dis-cussion for at least 15 minutes. I thought that we were never going to get any further into the book. Much knowledge was revealed in this discussion and many questions asked and answered. It's wrong to assume that it is always the adult that provides the answers. Thomas wanted to know why the milk was still on the doorstep, he was worried in case the sun turned it sour. It was Brooke who pointed out to him that as the blinds were still down, it must still be early in the morning. Eleanor also pointed out that the stars were still in the sky, so 'That's why the milk hadn't been taken in.' This discussion clearly demonstrated the children's speaking and listening skills, as well as their powers of reasoning and their ability to apply their knowledge of the real world to the imaginary world of the book. It also allowed them to develop ways of taking pleasure from the text that were in addition to those intended by the author.

While we were still considering the first two pages of the book, the children started to do something that I can clearly remember doing as a child. That was to pretend that they were in the book themselves. They began by deciding which room was which in Maisie Middleton's house and dividing them up amongst themselves. Space was also made for siblings and pets, ensuring links between the real world and the imaginary one. I felt that this incident demonstrated an enormous amount, not only about the children's understanding of the book, but also of their awareness of the possibilities that exist for any reader. (Another description of a child talking about Maisie Middleton can be found in Barbara Jordan's (1992) article 'Good for any age'.) I feel strongly that these lessons are as important as the lessons of sight vocabulary and decoding of text. It was very rewarding when, a few days later, Eleanor asked 'Can we play that pretending game again? You know, that one when we were in the book. That was really good.' Following the success of this activity, I built it into further group reading sessions, although the children did not need much direction from me. It was as popular with non-fiction texts as with stories, with children taking on the roles of knights and soldiers in one particular book.

Group reading of texts

- Try to provide a range of texts for this activity – include non-fiction, comics, etc.
- Use groups of texts by one author/illustrator, so the children can identify similar features.
- Promote discussion about the characters – who would the children most like/not like to be, etc.?
- Encourage and promote the use of puppets and props with the groups of books. A group of zoo animals with *Dear Zoo* for example (Campbell, 1995), or some astronaut and alien puppets with *Children of The Sun* (L'Hommedieu, 1996).

Reading out

This activity was actually devised by my class themselves, and was to provide a source of pleasure to them for many weeks, as well as giving me the opportunity to listen to them read, checking their sight vocabulary, acquisition of known texts and their understanding of what they were reading. Reading standards in the class improved dramatically as did listening skills and concentration spans. It was such a worthwhile activity that I would definitely introduce it to any new group of children that I taught.

The activity began when Rebecca came in one morning and asked if she could read *Daley B* (Blake, 1992), her favourite book of the moment, out to the rest of the class. It was agreed that she could, and later in the day, she read the book, with great expression and obvious understanding. The reaction from the rest of the class was extremely positive. Not only did they all, including the most restless children, listen attentively and with keen interest, but many of them offered to read out too. In fact, the whole activity snowballed. Children were allowed to read out either on their own, with a friend, or in a small group. This was to allow some of those children who were not quite brave enough to read by themselves to have the opportunity to participate in what became a very highly regarded activity.

The most popular grouping for the activity was a threesome. Within this group there would be one child who knew the text extremely well, one who knew it quite well, and one who was in the group to gain confidence and add to his or her knowledge of that particular text. This was a very good example of how children are able to achieve more when in the company of others than they could possibly achieve on their own. It provided great opportunities for the rest of the class to practise texts that were known to them already and add new texts to those that were familiar. Because the children were copying behaviour that they had seen in adults, many of them became adept at reading with the book held next to them, teacher-like, showing the pictures and questioning their very attentive audience.

I tried not to appropriate this activity, although I found this difficult, desperately wanting everyone to have a turn. One child in particular, Alyck, could not be encouraged to read out, however hard I tried to persuade him. This situation changed when his friend Sebastian wanted someone to read *Each Peach Pear Plum* out with him. He chose Alyck, who found it impossible to refuse his friend, even though it had been quite easy to refuse my requests. Alyck did read the book out with Sebastian extremely well, and this provided an enormous boost to his confidence and self-esteem. After this occasion, he frequently read out to the class.

Although I was involved in the activity as a non-participant observer, the children regulated the whole of the sessions themselves. Everyone who wanted to read out would leave the chosen book, with a named post-it note on the front, on a special chair, waiting for reading out time. They would question each other about the books that were read out and would comment on each others' reading. This was delightful to hear, and was only ever positive. Comments such as 'Your reading's coming along very well, Hayley' were never patronising, but well meant.

The teacher's role

It is important to realise that the three activities outlined above should not be young children's only experience with good-quality picture books. They should exist as part of a well-thought-out set of experiences designed to give children myriad opportunities to engage with the literacy heritage that surrounds them. As educators, we have the power to excite and inspire the children in our care and this should not be underestimated. Early years educators should make good use of and familiarise themselves with the rich variety of books that are published for young children, developing favourites of their own in order to be able to demonstrate to children, that it is OK to have tastes and preferences that are different from one another.

I believe quite passionately that the picture books of today will provide far more good friends for the children whom I teach than The Happy Venture Series ever did for me. However, in order to become known to children, these friends must first be invited into classrooms and introduced to children in ways that make them want to play with them, time and time again. As Henrietta Dombey (1992) states:

> All children need the skilled help of informed and sympathetic adults, who appreciate their strengths and weaknesses, have a clear idea of the goal ahead and engage the children's interest and commitment. They also need to encounter texts that are involving, manageable and satisfying, and give them a clear sense that they are making progress (p. 20). If all this occurs in ways that are exciting and inspiring, then young children will certainly acquire many 'friends for life'.

Pointers to supporting the emergent reader

- Take time to get to know a wide range of children's books yourself.
- Act as a role model for the children, demonstrating enthusiasm for and an interest in books and other reading materials.
- Encourage children to talk about what they have read, to you and each other.
- Plan for a wide range of reading experiences which include incorporating reading into children's play experiences. (puppet's, props, etc.).
- Develop effective and informative ways of monitoring the children's progress that truly reflect all aspects of the reading process, not merely the acquisition of sight vocabulary.

References

Dombey, H. (1992) *Words and Worlds: Reading in the Early Years of School*, NATE.

Holdaway, D. (1979) *The Foundations of Literacy*, Sydney: Ashton Scholastic.

Jordan, B. (1992) 'Good for any age – picture books and the experienced reader', in M. Styles, E. Bearne, and V. Watson (eds) *After Alice*, London: Cassell.

Vygotsky, L. (1986) *Thought and Language*, Cambridge, MA: The MIT Press.

Waterland, L. (1992) 'Ranging freely: the why and what of real books', in M. Styles, E. Bearne and V. Watson (eds) *After Alice*, London: Cassell.

Children's books mentioned in the text

Ahlberg, J. and A. (1980) *Each Peach Pear Plum*, London: Picture Lions.

Beck, I. (1991) *The Teddy Robber*, London: Picture Corgi.

Blake, J. (1992) *Daley B*, London: Walker Books.

Burningham, J. (1984) *Granpa*, London: Cape.

Campbell, R. (1985) *Dear Zoo* London: Puffin Books.

Hayes, S. (1995) *This is The Bear*, London: Walker Books.

L'Hommedieu, A.J. (1996) *Children of the Sun*, Child's Play (International) Ltd.

Minarik Holmelund, E. (1957) *Little Bear*, New York: Scholastic Book Services.

Seuss, Dr (1965) *Fox in Socks*, London: Collins.
Sowter, N. (1994) *Maisie Middleton*, London: Diamond Books.
Waddell, M. (1991) *Farmer Duck*, London: Walker Books.
Waddell, M. (1992) *Owl Babies*, London: Walker Books.

CHAPTER 9

'Penguins never meet polar bears'

READING FOR INFORMATION IN THE EARLY YEARS

Helen Arnold

Reading in some form is part of everyday life for nearly all adults. Many find satisfaction in reading fiction, but far more read for information, so frequently that they are unaware of it. They scan newspapers, absorb advertisements, signs, instructions and warnings. Car drivers do not always realise what skilful readers they must be.

It seems strange, therefore, that children have traditionally learnt to read almost exclusively from narrative texts. This is justified by the belief that response to story is inbuilt, that stories tell about events within children's experience, and that sequential (chronological) text is easier to predict and recall than non-sequential. Non-fiction elements were introduced in the higher levels of traditional reading schemes in the 1960s and 1970s, often called supplementary readers. Even then, these tended to be written chronologically, as history or geography or nature stories.

The assessment of such reading was invariably in the form of comprehension exercises. At upper primary levels 'higher order reading skills' were introduced; until one had mastered literal reading, one could not go on to reading for inference or appreciation. The main purpose of training in higher order reading skills was to prepare pupils for reading in the subject areas when they reached secondary school.

The idea of this hierarchical progression from fiction to non-fiction reading no longer holds. The national curriculum recognises the need to introduce children to reading for information at Key Stage 1. Publishers are now including non-fiction strands from the earliest stages, and there is a growing number of individually published texts in the best traditions of the picture book. Unfortunately many of these texts start with the wrong premiss, assuming that the function of this sort of reading is to include as many facts as possible. They are often not helpful to young readers. It is important to see how non-fiction reading fits into the young child's development, with the most important aim being to help towards concept formation.

Developmental aspects

Young children are intensely curious about the world around them, and from a very early age develop their own ways of classifying and categorising that world. Children probably experience more sharply and directly through their senses than adults. As we develop language to describe what we see and hear, we distance ourselves from the initial impressions. Once we have language it is very difficult to perceive without glossing what is seen with verbal description, response and comment. This is particularly so with regard to the disembedded contexts of reading and writing.

It is important not to push children too early into reading other people's verbalisations just for the sake of it. But it is good for them to realise gradually that there are many different ways of describing the world, some of

Figure 9.1 *The two strands of development*

which can be done only verbally because they involve things that are distant in time and space. Early literacy experiences develop in two main directions (see Figure 9.1), both equally important in the development of thinking and learning. Both may be equally motivating. Some children, indeed, will from the beginning be more interested in 'finding out' than in reading fiction. There is a place for developing both these strands by encouraging children to learn to read from non-fiction as well as story texts.

Life before school: The dinosaur phenomenon

I video-recorded Robert at intervals, not for educational purposes, but because his parents wanted a record of their baby growing up. Robert's mother would spread out a variety of toys and games, and he would choose what he wanted. In one of the early videos he did this by crawling towards them, because he was too young to walk or talk. Amongst the glossy toys was a rather elderly and dog-eared picture alphabet book (this was not a particularly literary family). Robert pushed the train, rolled the ball and crawled to the book. It engaged his interest. He did not eat it or throw it. He held it quite delicately and explored the pages, turned it another way up, pointed at one of the pictures. His mother said 'Duck'. 'Du—' attempted Robert, labelling dutifully. He stayed with the book for some time.

A later video shows Robert, now about two, with the same scenario, but no book on the floor. He exhibits his skill on the tricycle, builds with his bricks and clutches his rubber dinosaur. He walks deliberately to a shelf and removes a book from it, takes it straight to his mother on the settee, and climbs on to her lap. She reads the book to him and he points to the relevant pictures. Daniel, his baby brother, now part of the action, watches every movement from the floor.

At four years old, Robert does not play with any toys. He selects a dinosaur book almost immediately. Again he marches on to his mother's lap. He holds the book, surely turning the pages when he is ready. His mother reads the quite complex text, stumbling over some of the names. Robert seems to be able to pronounce them better than she does. She reads a description of the brontosaurus: 'That's the brontosaurus' points Robert. In fact, Robert knows all the names of the different dinosaurs, knows where their pictures are, and can tell his mother something about each of them. Daniel meanwhile looks on intently, and at one point tries to deseat Robert and climb on to his mother's knee with his own book.

A little girl of four sat by me on a plane journey. As the plane took off, she removed the safety instructions from the pocket and studied every picture carefully, telling herself what she thought each one depicted.

I watched a small boy tracing the letters of a notice in a public house carpark over and over again. It reminded me of how I did the same as a child with the name of my road – Seymour Road – helpfully embossed in metal on a low-standing notice.

Thalia (four and a half) found a small dead animal on the path. She was interested in animals, and had been to several nature parks. She answered her own questions:

'What is it?'
'A shrew? . . . No, because its tail is not long enough.'
'A mole? . . . No, its feet are too small.'
'A mouse? . . . No, it's not an ordinary mouse – its tail is too long . . .'
'SO . . . it must be a field-mouse.'

On her return home, her mother helped her to look in a reference book, and she was able to check with a picture that she was right.

These are apparently simple incidents. They occurred as part of children's experiences, not as part of teaching programmes. They indicate the vital interaction between adults and children. What is happening is actually complex. Children are turning their world into concepts, slotting them into schemata, understanding secondary symbolisation, assimilating and accommodating in true Piagetian fashion – all long before they start school. Their emerging reading skill is interacting with their conceptual development.

I believe that the way young children learn in the classroom should not only take into account such literacy experiences, but should try to utilise the same sort of motivation. (It is a pity that we do not really know exactly why dinosaurs are so universally motivating, as then we might solve all the problems of helping children to read for learning!)

Into school learning: bridging the gap

Although there are so many information books for young children on the market, I do not think that they are the only, or perhaps the best, way to introduce children to non-fiction. As I have indicated earlier, we are not asking children to read to collect facts like squirrels collect nuts. Some published information books, even for young readers, are packed with facts that are not expanded or easily connected with each other. How readers conceptualise information is as important as what they remember. It is difficult to store material that cannot first be linked with existing experience. It will be easier, therefore, to engage their active thinking through material with which they are already familiar, and through their own writing, than through reading other people's texts. Labels, notices and advertisements (termed 'environmental print' in the national curriculum) would serve this purpose admirably.

Using environmental print

A whole curriculum could be built around labels and notices. It is interesting to give children of different ages an assortment of food and drink containers (preferably empty!), asking them to sort them into groups in any way they wish. There is, of course, no RIGHT way, but there will probably be a progression from random sorting to personal preferences, to the stage when various properties are more conventionally taken into account. Can individuals or groups explain to one another why they have chosen their groupings?

Most food packets and tins have both visual and textual information that can be used for classification, comparison and evaluation. It would be valuable to compare two labels for similar products, for instance, chocolate biscuits or baked beans. Children could work in pairs and groups, discussing and recording first 'What's the same in the labels?' They might find that the weight is the same, that both products contain similar ingredients, or that the names are identical – chocolate chip cookies or baked beans.

In doing this, they would inevitably start noticing the differences, and these too could be discussed and recorded. For example, one label might emphasise economy, 'pennywise', and another novelty, 'NEW'. One might emphasise health-giving elements, the other the pleasures of eating. The children will, it is hoped, gradually realise that biscuits or beans which are basically the same products are promoted differently, to satisfy a range of consumers.

So, through looking at labels, often of their own choice, which they bring to school, children will gradually learn to classify and compare, and to read critically.

Environmental print in the street

It is a small step from the examples already given of children noticing the print of street names, to incorporating this curiosity into organised activity in and around the school. Bartlett and Fogg (1992), in their chapter called 'Language in the environment', give numerous practical examples of ways of looking and recording. Street names, shop names and house names are suggested as fruitful sources. An initial 'print walk' can be taken in an open-ended way, or with pre-planned categories to investigate. If open-ended, a very short walk with nursery age children will reveal what they notice if asked to find things to read. Will they notice the print on water hydrants and grids in the ground? Will they think that logos are words? Older children can collect house and street names and try to guess why they are so named.

Bartlett and Fogg point to the interest of shop names and show how they can be classified – owners' names, puns, alliteration, etc. For example:

> Fur, Feather and Fin: I think it is called Fur, Feather and Fin because it has everything that animals with Fur, Feathers and Fins need. The name also sounds good because all the first letters in the name are the same.
>
> (Bartlett and Fogg, 1992, p. 47)

Linking reading and writing

Research into emergent writing indicates how developing conceptual frameworks are revealed in the way children choose to write. Thus, by looking at their writing experiments we can see how they are internalising information in the early stages. Marie Clay (1982), Emilia Ferreiro (Ferreiro and Teberosky, 1982) and many other researchers, in different parts of the world, have found similar sequences of development.

> The child's written work also provides us with objective evidence of what the child has learned. We have an opportunity to see how the child organises his behaviour as he writes . . . if we see a child write a new word without a copy we can assume the capacity to synthesise information from several sources.
>
> (Clay, 1982, p. 210)

Two examples from my earlier snapshots of young children at home show how young children observe and categorise names. Ferreiro and Teberosky (1982) describe in detail the fascination emergent writers show with writing the names of objects and the way in which they distinguish between their written symbols and the picture of the object itself. Robert was already differentiating every dinosaur by its name. The recognition of house names, again, is derived from the desire to label everything. But there are repercussions which go beyond simple labelling. I remember, relating to my own experience with road names, my initial confusion when I found that my house had a number – 4 – and a name – Rufford, whereas the house next door was ONLY No.6 – no name! I learnt gradually that the same thing can have several names, and therefore, ultimately, that language defines multitudinously.

As we saw in our earlier examples, the next stage for most children is to want to make lists, combining their interest in naming with a desire to categorise.

> Until I began observing five-year-olds closely I had no idea that they took stock of their own learning. They spontaneously and systematically made lists of what they knew. They consciously ordered and arranged their learning.
>
> (Clay, 1982, p. 206)

The most common manifestation of lists in schools is the individual word-book, kept by most children as a spelling check. This is a useful way of helping children to be aware of alphabetical ordering, but they could also occasionally reorder those words in another way. Lists of words might be made that cluster round particular topics. Individuals might keep these books, or groups could be responsible for collecting words for areas within a topic. For example, if the ongoing topic was mini beasts, one group might collect words associated with spiders, another with snails, another with frogs. Or a different classification could be made, with groups collecting minibeast food words, breeding words, moving words.

I have tried to show here how two of the earliest features of emergent writing – naming and listing – are integral with the beginning stages of reading for information. Other features could be pursued to demonstrate more sophisticated levels of conceptual awareness at later stages.

Ways of reading

Readers of non-fiction should be flexible in the way they process text. Children need to be able to skim and scan and to read certain parts intensively. Reading aloud is not a useful way of approaching text in this case. Can young children use different techniques before they have learnt to read aloud fluently? The following excerpts from a discussion with Clara, who was seven, show that as soon as she became aware of the needs of reading to find out, she was able to apply flexible procedures with very little trouble.

Clara was shown *Writing and Drawing* (Bradshaw, 1988). This book poses questions in large print at the top of some of the pages, and answers the questions in the succeeding text. In this case the questions were masked with tape. Here the question was 'What is a ball-point pen?'

Teacher: Can you see where there is a bit that is covered up? There is a question under the tape. See if you can work out what the question might be. . . . It's got all the answers there to the question.
Clara: To do with pens.
Teacher: What sort of pens?
Clara: Biro pens.
Teacher: So what do you think the question might be?
Clara: How does it work?

They went on to a book about spiders.

Teacher: Look at this book. It's about spiders. I want you to think about what you know about spiders before we look at the book.

Clara is presented with a list of statements about spiders, to be filled in as 'TRUE' or 'FALSE' by guessing, without reference to the book. For example:

Teacher: It says here, 'Spiders are vegetarian – they don't eat meat'. Is that true or false? Are spiders vegetarians?
Clara: No . . . cos they eat flies.
(and so on through five more statements).
Teacher: Now go through the book and see if you can check from what it tells you whether you guessed right.

At this point Clara turned to the first page of the book and began to read it aloud.

Teacher: You won't have time to read the whole book. Look quickly through it and see if you can spot anything that helps you.

There was a long pause while pages were turned over. Then:

Clara: The thread DOES come out of its body.
Teacher: Where does it say that?
Clara: There.
Teacher: Right. Put a tick against that one.

Clara picked up the idea of silent scanning very quickly. Another ploy was tried with a book about signs and symbols:

Teacher: Now you need to look through this very quickly. I'm going to ask you some questions. It's a bit of a race. You won't have time to read all the book . . . you have to jump about a bit . . . . First can you tell me the page number which tells you about road signs?

Clara took three seconds to answer: 'Page 8 and 9.' Some questions related to pictures, some to text; they were not asked in page sequence. The longest time taken to find an answer was fifteen seconds, proof that it is possible to get the idea quite quickly, and to enjoy the fun of jumping about rather than slavishly reading every word.

Preparing to read books

The true/false? exercise is one way of engaging children's interest in what they are going to read about by linking new information with what they know already, known as focusing or priming. With young children a montage of jumbled pictures from books could be made into a large poster. The class or group then discuss with the teacher what the topic might be about. They would then be interested in finding the pictures again in the actual books.

Another method used with seven-year-olds was to divide the class into groups. In this case they were going to read books about different artefacts – bottles, bricks, knives and forks, bubbles. Each group was given a large piece of sugar paper. The scribe, after group discussion, wrote a list of 'what we know about . . .'. This was prior to seeing any books. In the next session, a similar list was made of 'what we would like to find out about . . .'.

When they came to reading their books, they focused on two things, whether they had been right in their assumptions, and whether their questions had been answered. Cries of glee came at intervals as they found they could tick items on the first list, or write in the answers to their questions on the second list. The lists were displayed on the wall throughout the project.

The teacher's role

Referring back to the accounts of young children with their parents, it is obvious that the carer's role was important in many ways. The parents in all cases were 'scaffolding' their children by putting them into situations where they could be active, interested learners, and supporting them in response to the children's own initiations. The adults' moves, although maybe unconscious, were subtle, unthreatening and enthusiastic. When children arrive at school, they may bring with them a different image of the new adult, their teacher, who is going to know so much more than they do and expect so much from them – to say nothing of the other children who will be trying to vie for that teacher's attention. The role of the teacher is bound to be more administrative, more aware of the need for total control, and more distant than the parents'. However, it is important that teachers and other early years educators should attempt to model ways of teaching on the natural contexts that have been encountered before. Above all, with reading for information, we must not give the impression that we already know everything, and that it is therefore not really necessary for our pupils to find things out independently.

The best way of working, therefore, is to model the different ways in which we find out from texts, showing exactly how we use an index, look up words, find key phrases, etc. Just as educators enthuse children in reading stories by reading to them with skill and enjoyment, reading to them from non-fiction books should also be introduced. We shall examine some scenarios in more detail to show how this might work in practice.

Polar bears

A reception class teacher introduced the topic of polar bears to the class, talking to them in the reading corner. She told them some facts, and showed where she had found them in two or three different books, holding the books up to show the pictures, and reading excerpts. As they discussed each point, she recorded it in a simple statement on the flip-chart. Then she gave each child a blank booklet cut out in the shape of a bear. The children were to make their own books, with a sentence on each page, using whatever information they wished. I sat by Jessica, watching her making her book. She received no more help from the teacher. Before writing on each blank page, she looked at the flip-chart and thought carefully.

She wrote:

    Page 1:   polar bears live in ice caves.
    Page 2:   polar bears hunt for fish.
    Page 3:   polar bears walk on ice.
    Page 4:   polar bears never meet penguins.

(This had interested the children greatly in discussion; they were excited by the fact that polar bears lived at one pole, and penguins at the other!)

There was a long pause at this point. There was one page left to fill, and Jessica had seemingly run out of ideas and information. But she still made no request to the teacher, and there was no panic. Eventually she turned to the blank page and made her last triumphant entry:

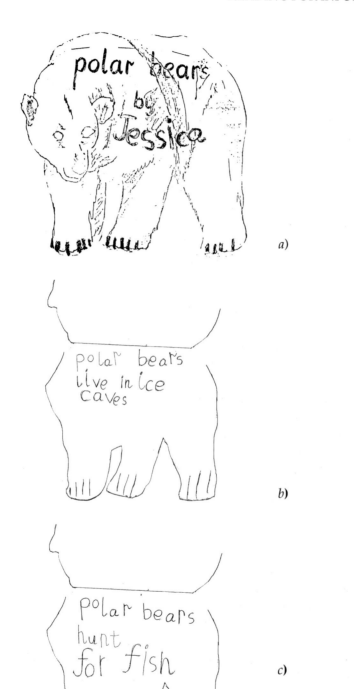

a)

b)

c)

Figure 9.2 *Jessica's book about polar bears: a) the cover, b) page 1, c) page 2*

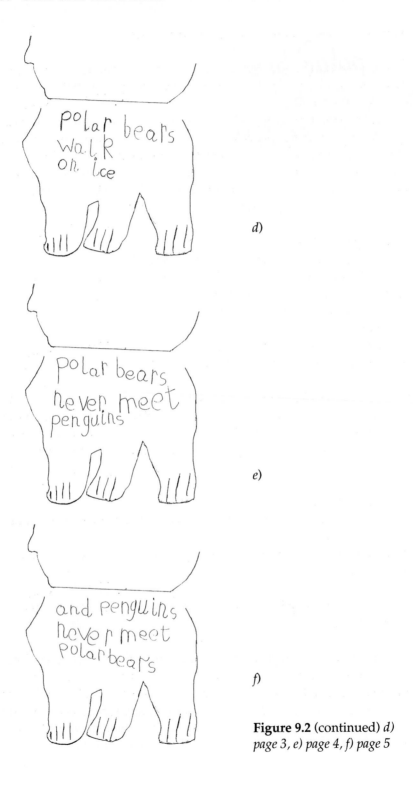

d)

e)

f)

Figure 9.2 (continued) *d) page 3, e) page 4, f) page 5*

Page 5:   and penguins never meet polar bears.

The controlled structure of the task enabled her to produce what was not only a beautiful syntactic reversal, linked correctly by 'and', but a neat piece of logical reasoning.

In this case the teacher introduced the class to specific books. There are very few non-fiction books which could be used independently from the beginning with young children. There are some, however, which lend themselves to be used as models, because they demonstrate different ways of presenting knowledge. It is important to select a few books for this purpose, which fulfil the following criteria:

- They should not be packed with facts.
- The illustrations should relate clearly to the text.
- There should not be extraneous fantasy or story elements.
- Language should be simple but not patronising.
- Close observation should be encouraged.
- The purpose of the book should be clear.
- Texts that ask rhetorical questions or give instructions that cannot practicably be carried out should be avoided.

One book which fulfils my criteria is _Minibeasts_ (Butler, 1991). Here the photographs are used to encourage the reader to look very carefully, and to compare with similar habitats in real life. The text gives clear definitions, and asks real questions, to draw on existing experience. The text facing the photographs of a stick insect on some twigs and a moth camouflaged on a piece of wood reads:

Where do minibeasts live?
Minibeasts live in many different habitats. They are very small and often hard to see.
Can you find the minibeasts in these pictures? There is a moth and a stick insect.

When animals can hide like this in their surroundings, we say they are camouflaged.

Each page in this book develops conceptually from the previous page. There is an index and a glossary, and words like 'camouflaged' will need to be explained. But it is the total content that should be explored carefully with the children, making sure that the questions are answered, and statements verified by checking with the photographs, leading on to taking the children out to look for minibeasts in their own environment.

One reading with the class will not, of course, be enough. I suggest that a book like this be tape-recorded, with the questions being asked in one voice, and statements in another, with pauses where indicated for the reader to look carefully at pictures. (This could well be an activity for a pair of Year 6 pupils.) The resource is there then for individual prolonged study.

What Makes a Bird a Bird? (Garelick, 1989) would be a suitable text to model with older children in Year 2 or 3. This book is built with an interesting conceptual structure. The pattern follows exactly Thalia's way of reasoning, quoted earlier. Each page hypothesises about the one question, 'How do we know that a bird is a bird?' and leads the reader through various possibilities.

For example, the suggestion that a bird is a bird because it flies is made on one page. However, this is rejected on the next page, because creatures other than birds fly. The mystery tour is an introduction to logical reasoning based on examples, hypothesis and classification. The very last page offers the solution: 'FEATHERS are the special things that MAKE A BIRD A BIRD.'

Where the Forest Meets the Sea (Baker, 1987) is a very different type of non-fiction book, in the tradition of the picture story. It would therefore be read to children first, to evoke intellectual and emotional response. A young boy describes his journey with his father to a tropical rain forest in North Queensland. The text is minimal; the illustrations are superb, built up into collages of the forest from natural materials, forming a wonderful three-dimensional effect. There are hidden elements in the pictures, which merge present and past. The boy says, 'I pretend it is a hundred million years ago' . . . 'I sit very still . . . and watch . . . and listen . . . I wonder how long it takes the trees to grow to the top of the forest!' There are no answers to these questions, but they are just what a young child would ask in similar circumstances, evoking wonder and dread. The book can obviously be read many times; older children could make similar stories with their own collages made from local materials, around an environment near their homes.

I am therefore suggesting that the introduction of reading for information in the early years will not be directed towards accumulation of knowledge as such, but to widening concepts about the environment, and towards encouraging ways of thinking that will include observation, hypothesising, comparison and classification, complementing the more personal response to fiction. Access will be through the children's own existing knowledge of environmental print rather than through graded reading schemes. The skills needed for reading non-fiction will develop from the beginning, in parallel with fictional reading. The children's writing of non-fiction text will be as important as their reading, and as far as possible will be for real purposes, to list, to record, to share with others, rather than to answer comprehension questions. Some texts of different types will be introduced. Even very young children will grow into this sort of reading, using active problem-solving and interaction with their educators. Through these experiences and processes they will come to realise that reading for information is just as imaginative and exciting as reading stories.

Pointers for reading for information in the early years

- Children can and should learn to read from non-fiction as well as fiction texts.
- Environmental print is the best introduction to reading for information.
- Children should not just be collecting facts, but building conceptual frameworks to categorise experience in different ways. The processes of comparison, classification and evaluation are part of this development.
- Adults scaffold and model ways of using information texts. It is important that parents and educators should share children's home and school early literacy experiences.
- The processes of learning to read and write are closely interlinked.
- Flexible reading for different purposes, including silent reading, can begin at an early age.
- A few good information texts should be selected and discussed in detail with children.

References

Baker, J. (1987) *Where the Forest Meets the Sea*, London: Walker Books.

Bartlett, R. and Fogg, D. (1992) 'Language in the environment', in R. Bain, B. Fitzgerald and M. Taylor (eds) *Looking Into Language*, London: Hodder & Stoughton.

Bradshaw, A. (1988) *Writing and Drawing*, Story Chest Stepping Stones, Walton-on-Thames: Nelson.

Butler, D. (1991) *Minibeasts*, Take One London: Simon & Schuster.

Clay, M. (1982) *Observing Young Readers*, London: Heinemann Educational.

Ferreiro, E. and Teberosky, A. (1982) *Literacy before Schooling*, London: Heinemann.

Garelick, M. (1989) *What Makes a Bird a Bird?*, London: Bookshelf.

Further reading

Mallett, M. (1994) *Reading Non-Fiction in the Primary Years: A Language and Learning Approach*, London: National Association for the Teaching of English.

PART C

The wider curriculum

CHAPTER 10

'How do I do this better?'

FROM MOVEMENT DEVELOPMENT INTO PHYSICAL LITERACY

Patricia Maude

How do you like to go up in a swing
Up in the air so blue?
Oh, I do think it the pleasantest thing
Ever a child can do!'

(from 'The Swing' in *A Child's Garden of Verses*,
Robert Louis Stevenson, 1885)

Introduction

The early years are exciting times both for children's physical development as they grow, changing in shape and size, and for children's movement development as they gain in body awareness and as they explore the vast range of available movement experiences within their environment. Through experimentation, trial, error and success, young movers progress towards coordinated, mature movement knowledge and performance. Not only is movement the main medium of exploration for the young child, but also physical activity is essential for normal growth, providing the necessary stimulus for normal development. As young children develop other abilities including language, observation skills, knowledge of the environments in which they live, and understanding of movement contexts, so they also become increasingly physically literate.

We, as educators, have a responsibility for ensuring that the children we teach are exposed to the widest possible world of movement. Within that world of movement children need to experience a varied programme of activity which both balances the demands made on different parts of the body and takes into account the maintenance and enhancement of strength, mobility and endurance, helping to ensure the development of sound physique and posture. Giving children worthwhile movement experience will also develop motor competence and encourage motor confidence and creativity. Confidence in movement is vital for self-expression, and articulate coordinated movement ability greatly enhances the development of self-esteem. One of the challenges for the early years educator is to capitalise on the vast movement experience that children have accumulated prior to starting school. Educators can then expose children to a rich and rewarding movement vocabulary from which they can increase physical knowledge and skill, build on that past experience and broaden their physical literacy.

In this chapter we shall examine some of the processes of physical development from birth through infancy and early childhood and will then explore motor development, by looking at ways in which the acquisition of fundamental motor patterns and movement experiences are achieved by the young child. We shall also consider the role of the child as a movement learner through play, the role of the educator as a facilitator and provider of movement knowledge and some suggestions as to what might constitute quality movement learning for children in their first years at school. In exploring what might constitute physical literacy in the life of the young child, we shall also consider some aims and content for the physical development and physical education curriculum in the early years, including the foundation stage and Key Stage 1 of the national curriculum in England.

Readers are encouraged to:

- review their knowledge of children's early physical development and motor skill acquisition;
- consider ways of extending children's movement vocabulary and movement memory;
- extend their ability to observe and analyse children's movement in order to give informed feedback on performance;
- provide an appropriate curriculum that emanates from children's play and that raises standards in children's movement competence;
- guide children in their entitlement to physical literacy.

Some processes of physical development

Pertinent to the learner and educator of movement are three key factors in the early physical development of infants, namely the principles of:

- cephalo-caudal development
- proximo-distal development
- differentiation

Cephalo-caudal development

This first principle of physical development is so named because it stems from the Greek word for 'head', which is *kephale*, and the Latin word for 'tail', which is *cauda*. It denotes the principle that development occurs from the head downwards towards the feet. This seems obvious, since the head houses the brain, which is the chief controller and regulator of all bodily functions. The brain also regulates the growth and development of the body. The head is the most developed part of the body at birth, having already achieved half of its adult length and the upper limbs, the arms, being near the top of the body, are quite well developed. The lower limbs, however, are relatively undeveloped and of relatively little importance, lacking in musculature, having achieved barely a fifth of their adult length. This principle of 'top-down' development will influence our planning and teaching when we are looking to ensure that the children we teach have acquired all the fundamental motor skills to enable them to be articulate movers in both the upper and lower limbs. We will expect that children will use their arms with increasing efficiency before they achieve equivalent efficiency in the feet, for example.

Proximo-distal development

The second principle refers to growth from the centre of the body outwards towards the extremities. This, too, is easily understood in the context of the significance of the central nervous system, which controls all messages from the brain, running down the spinal column and managing all the life functions of the infant. The vital organs, essential to survival, are housed in the centre of the body, with maximum potential for protection. By comparison, the early activity of peripheral limbs such as the hands is relatively insignificant! For example, the hands, the most distal elements at the farthest extremity from the centre of the body, are relatively inactive and non-instrumental in early life. Indeed, at this stage they are not structurally ready for action, since, for example, not all the bones in the wrists are differentiated. Before the wrists are fully prepared and ready to service the complex variety of movement demands that will be placed upon the hands when older, some of the wrist bones will separate and will develop appropriate musculature.

As with the principle of cephalo-caudal development, the principle of proximo-distal development is also important for the educator in creating a movement programme that takes account of the length of time necessary to achieve movement competence in those parts of the limbs that are relatively more distant from the centre of the body. Classroom learning can also be significantly dependent upon this principle, where, for example, the learner may not have achieved the moment of readiness to hold a pencil with the pincer grip (between the thumb and index finger) and feels more comfortable using the palmar grasp (pencil gripped between the palm and the fingers). The product of work produced using the palmar grasp is usually less accurate than that of the pincer grip with which it is possible to achieve greater control. However, the muscles of the hand need to be sufficiently strong to enable the child to sustain the more demanding pincer grip.

Differentiation

The third principle is that whereby the newborn child offers an apparently global response, whereas the more mature child is more discriminatory in response. For example, in response to a pin-prick on the hand, the infant cries, pulls the limb away and generally thrashes about, whereas the older child will withdraw the limb and may cry, but the adult is unlikely to do more than consider withdrawing the affected limb. As neurological development takes place and the child matures, so the ability to differentiate responses grows. This developing ability to discriminate responses with increasing maturity is an important element of learning for the early years child in school.

These three principles not only provide us with many insights into the process and rhythm of development of the infant, but also underpin many aspects of child development. They are particularly relevant as we move on to consider the movement (motor) development of young children. Movement is the lead area of functioning for the infant in acquiring information about the environment and in learning about self. The principles and processes of movement development therefore hold many of the keys for the educator in developing an appropriate movement curriculum for children.

Some processes of motor development

Motor development, along with other areas of development, follows the principles of cephalo-caudal, proximo-distal development and differentiation.

In relation to **cephalo-caudal development**, success is achieved in movement involving the upper part of the body before that involving the lower limbs. Control of the head, as in turning to look towards a stimulus and later lifting and holding the head, precedes management of the shoulders, to push up from front lying to raise the head. Thereafter further control of the trunk and hips enables the infant to learn to sit. This in turn precedes control of the hips, knees and ankles and later the feet and the increase in strength required for weight-bearing on the feet and for achieving the standing position, prior to learning to take the first step and later to walk.

The sequence of learning to walk, then, is significantly influenced by the principle of cephalo-caudal development. Although it is very rare that the mainstream educator of young children needs to be involved in teaching locomotion, this is a very significant sequence of development for some physically and mentally disabled children and for children with delayed movement development who are integrated into mainstream schooling. All early years educators will, however, be involved in developing and enhancing the efficiency and quality of this fundamental movement pattern and of the motor patterns that emanate from it, such as running, jumping and all other locomotion skills. The significance of cephalo-caudal development and its influence upon children's success in movement is of great importance both in the planning of the movement curriculum and in the general education of young children.

The equally logical principle of **proximo-distal movement skill development** can be observed as the infant explores the immediate environment and subsequently gains control over the arms, starting at the shoulders as the central or proximo part of the limb, before gaining controlled movement in the hands, the more peripheral or distal elements of the arms. Early exploration of the environment takes place through movement. Even from the relatively still supine lying position, the infant is seen to use the entire arm, flailing in the air, as if to swipe out and later to reach for objects in sight. In a similar way, apparently indiscriminate movement of the arms results in the infant discovering the mouth with the hands, and subsequent success is achieved in grasping at objects with both hands, followed by trying to put them into the mouth.

Much movement experience is gained using the entire arm as a single lever, with relatively little **differentiation** between the arm joints. It is not until distance from an object becomes significant that flexion of the elbow is used to shorten the arm, for example. Much later, when one hand rather than two is required to achieve a movement task, the infant is dependent upon the development of the wrist joint and the joints of the fingers and thumb having acquired appropriate structure and musculature. Significantly, the principle of readiness, by which the child is unable to attempt a more advanced procedure until the structure and musculature are sufficiently mature, dominates motor development. We thereby do not see the infant progress from two-handed grasping to the use of one hand until that readiness is in place.

The sequence of growth and development

This leads us on to consider the sequence of growth and development including motor development, which is invariable, from one infant to the next. Helpfully for us as educators, the order in which all infants acquire movement skills is the same, every child follows the same sequence. Normally, for example, infants learn to roll over, then to sit and later to stand before learning to walk (see Figure 10.1).

Similarly, in terms of sequential development, prior to acquiring the skill of hopping, children must gain the strength to fix the pelvis. so that it remains horizontal when holding the body balance over one foot. They then need the balance and coordination to transfer the body weight to that single foot before learning to take off and land on the same foot, usually to hop along before hopping on the spot.

Figure 10.1 *The regular sequence of motor development in infants. From Rathus (1988, p. 202)*

The fact that all children follow the same sequence of movement development is very helpful. However, the challenge for the educator comes from the knowledge that the rate of development is unique to each child; no two children, even in the same family, follow the same pace of development. In preparing movement programmes, therefore, we must take account, particularly in the foundation stage and Key Stage 1, of the need for some children to complete their learning of some fundamental motor skills.

Gross and fine motor skills

Linked with the three preceding principles of motor development is another invariable and not surprising feature of child development, that of gross and fine motor skills. The child achieves greater control in large (gross) body movement before managing control in smaller (fine) movements. For example, walking, jumping and running are more advanced in their performance and control at a relatively younger age than are drawing, cutting or colouring-in, where detailed management of the developing muscles of the wrist and hand can be extremely challenging for the young child. Since much learning activity in the classroom involves drawing, painting, writing, measuring, cutting, sticking, etc., the more mature the child's wrist and finger development and the stronger the musculature, the more successful will be the practical elements of the product and the least inhibition will have been experienced due to muscle fatigue. Some children's classroom behaviour may have been observed to be off-task or demonstrating lack of concentration, when the true inhibitor was lack of maturity in the structure and functioning of the wrist and hand, thereby disqualifying them from maximum participation. Since gross motor competence serves as a springboard for developing efficient fine motor skills, it is incumbent upon educators to provide frequent opportunities for young children to practise both gross and fine movement activities.

The importance of physical play

How better can provision for frequent gross and fine motor activity be made than through physical play? In developing a movement curriculum for young children, the notion of building upon play is a compelling aim. Physical play is important for:

- encouraging discovery of movement abilities;
- allowing for exploration of the movement environment;
- offering practice time to enhance fundamental motor skills and strengthen the cardio-vascular system and the muscles.

The provision of a stimulating environment, both for children's pre-school play and for developmental play during the school day is a matter for detailed planning for parents and educators of young children. In providing for gross motor competence, this might include:

- an adventure playground
- a secret garden
- a playground with suitable markings to encourage challenge in movement
- a tarmac area with wheeled toys including trucks, go-carts, tricycles, bicycles and other ride-on and push-along toys
- an indoor space with soft-play and gymnastics apparatus
- grass and hard areas with balls of various sizes and textures, beanbags, hoops, bats, velcro-catchers, targets and skipping ropes.

These and other home and school provisions can significantly enhance the movement-learning experience for young children.

The importance of play involving gross and fine motor skills is of paramount importance in children's movement development and must underpin the devising of the physical development and physical education curriculum. Indeed, the school curriculum should be founded upon the natural movement vocabulary of the playing child.

We rely on children arriving at school already articulate in movement, with mature movement patterns already established in the fundamental motor skills. On arrival at school, with a wealth of pre-school movement experiences, children should expect to draw from their existing movement vocabulary, using established and efficient movement patterns to enable them to participate fully in the activities on offer, to enjoy their learning and to be successful. My own experience would be that even where articulate movers arrive in school, reinforcement of mature movement patterns should continue to be a part of the curriculum, as the child grows, as body levers lengthen, strength increases and body awareness is enhanced. The child is in a state of readiness to become even more skilful and to acquire an even greater movement vocabulary and movement memory.

Developing an appropriate movement curriculum for young children

As a starting point for devising a movement curriculum we may ask ourselves what constitute the most useful movement skills that children bring with them to school? Certainly efficiency in all daily living tasks, including feeding, toileting, dressing and moving safely around the environment will enable the child to operate independently in school. Additionally, children bringing a range of the gross and fine motor skills that are needed for full participation in class activities, such as those previously discussed, have an advantage over children who are less experienced or whose gross and fine motor skills are less developed.

Many children also bring with them a rich movement vocabulary developed through play. The importance of play as a basis for all aspects of education cannot be overestimated, as has been ably discussed in this and other chapters within the present volume.

Aims of the physical development and physical education curriculum

Before deciding on the content of the physical education curriculum, we should explore what we might consider to be the aims of that programme. In order to enhance the child as a learner and to ensure that you, as the educator, offer the best possible provision for that learner, the following broad aims for the physical education curriculum for early years children need to be developed. These relate to physical and movement development, movement skill acquisition, confidence in movement, and physical literacy.

Physical development

- to stimulate growth
- to enhance physical development
- to provide healthy exercise

Movement development

- to build on existing movement vocabulary
- to develop coordination and body tension
- to extend movement vocabulary

Movement skill acquisition

- to develop fundamental motor skills to the mature stage
- to introduce new motor skills
- to increase knowledge of dynamics of movement
- to develop coordination
- to teach accuracy and efficiency in movement

Movement confidence development

- to teach movement observation skills
- to develop movement experimentation and expression
- to enhance self-expression
- to enhance self-confidence, self-image and self-esteem

Other aspects of physical literacy

- to teach movement observation
- to teach appropriate vocabulary for describing, explaining, discussing, assessing and improving the quality of movement
- to stimulate thought processes
- to expect quality work from children
- to encourage independence in and ownership of learning
- to learn respect in cooperation and competition
- to enhance positive attitudes towards health-related exercise
- to provide experiences that teach children to plan, perform and evaluate their movement learning
- to sustain feelings of enjoyment and well-being in physical activity

Are there other aims that should underpin a curriculum plan for early years children in movement development and physical education, such as providing stimulating, challenging and imaginative learning experiences for children? These can then be built into the curriculum, to ensure children's entitlement to be physically educated and to be physically literate.

The development of skilled movement

The route to the acquisition of skilled movement has been plotted by Gallahue and Ozman (1995). They name three progressive stages in skill learning:

1 The initial or rudimentary stage

This is the emergent movement pattern, or early experimentation stage.

2 The elementary stage

At this stage, in which coordination is improved, the movement is still incorrectly performed and incomplete, perhaps lacking in strength, mobility, balance or speed.

3 The mature stage

Finally the child achieves the mature stage in which all the elements of the movement pattern are integrated and in which the movement includes appropriate preparation, followed by the accurate action and ends with efficient follow through and recovery. At this stage the movement pattern also becomes integrated into the movement memory, to be called upon with ease.

Watch a professional cricketer throw the ball in from the boundary and compare that action with the overarm throw of the average 5-year-old and your mind's eye will no doubt provide ample evidence of potential for further development in the young child's achievement! (see Figure 10.2). Note the trunk flexion, rather than rotation.

Figure 10.2 *A beginning thrower. From Haywood (2001, p. 147)*

Figure 10.3 illustrates the movement development between a beginning and an advanced runner. With the advanced runner there is a much fuller range of leg motion and the thighs and arms drive forward and back rather than swinging out slightly to the side.

Bearing in mind that the elementary and mature movement patterns are normally achieved during the primary school years, the educator has considerable responsibility for recognising the three stages in the various fundamental motor skills of locomotion (walking and running), jumping (including taking off and landing) and projection (throwing, kicking) and in analysing the child's achievements, in order to improve performance.

Figure 10.3 *A beginning and advanced runner. From Haywood (2001, pp. 126–8)*

Recognising the moment of readiness in the child is a skill in itself to be acquired by the educator. Spatial and body awareness as well as appropriate maturing of the body structures and brain functioning are influential in attaining that moment of readiness. Have you ever tried to teach a child to ride a bicycle before readiness has been achieved? Holding the saddle, you walk or run along behind the bike growing ever more exhausted, as the child tries to stay upright and pedal, without success as far as independent balance is concerned. Put the bike away for a matter of weeks (or months if you or the child had been over-ambitious!) and then notice that when the child gets the bike out again he or she climbs on and rides away unaided. The frustration of anticipating readiness too soon is outweighed by the satisfaction of helping a child to be successful in enhancing a partially learnt skill or in acquiring a new skill!

The early years physical development and physical education curriculum

So, what should we include in our physical education curriculum that will meet our selected aims and provide satisfaction and rich movement experience for our young learners? In England, the curriculum guidance for the foundation stage provides an excellent section on physical development and the national curriculum for Key Stage 1 promotes experience in dance, games and gymnastics, with swimming as an option in either Key Stage 1 or Key Stage 2. These activities seem entirely appropriate for children whose pre-school movement experience has been made up of broad-based and varied play. Dance, games and gymnastics are also appropriate activities for children aged 5–7 years, as between them they offer the learner extensive movement vocabularies, opportunities to develop creative as well as functional movement and opportunities for exercise and the stimulus for physical development and growth. Through dance, games and gymnastics, the child can achieve the mature stage in fundamental movement patterns and can derive challenge, enjoyment, confidence and movement competence.

The range of movement vocabulary on offer can also be advantageous to the child with delayed movement development, who could be enabled to work within personal constraints and push out the boundaries of those limitations.

The child illustrated in Figure 10.4 has acquired by the age of 6 a sophistication of skill in kicking that is rarely seen in Key Stage 1.

The child seen in Figure 10.5, who is also aged 6 years, has achieved a quality of body and spatial awareness in leaping that should be our aim for all children in Key Stage 1.

Figure 10.4 *An advanced 6-year-old kicker*

Figure 10.5 *The leap*

For the normal child there need be no constraints beyond those imposed by the limitation of the developing body and brain, the confidence of the learner, and the bounds of reasonable safety imposed by the environment, the equipment to be used and the other children sharing the same space.

For me, the early years programme must be one of discovery and achievement, of valuing the learner, with evidence of excitement and satisfaction in learning. Can you recall an experience similar to that quoted above by Robert Louis Stevenson? Do you remember the effort of getting the swing started and then of discovering the knack of leaning back and then forward to increase the height of the swing and then the fear of going over the top, having seemingly swung too high? Do you also remember the pleasure derived from such play activities, as are recalled here by A. A. Milne?

He played with his skipping rope,
He played with his ball.
He ran after butterflies,
Blue ones and red;
He did a hundred happy things –
And then went to bed.

(from 'Forgotten' in *Now We Are Six*,
p.98, A. A. Milne, 1927)

Perhaps it is here, in the young child's physical play, that we should start observing in an attempt to discover the 'lifeworld' of physical literacy for young children. If we are to provide worthwhile learning experiences that challenge children, give them ownership of their learning and enable them to build on pre-school play experiences, we must seek out appropriate starting points. From these we can build upon:

- the fantasy and exploratory expressive play that becomes **dance** in twirling, galloping, leaping, reaching up and away and pausing
- the **games**-like play that involves chasing, dodging, catching, throwing, kicking and hitting
- the rolling, jumping, climbing, swinging and balancing play that
- becomes **gymnastics**.

We may need to take a closer look at what children actually do when they engage in physical activity and from our observation put ourselves in touch with the nature of children's physical development, before proceeding to influence that development by the pedagogical framework that we provide.

The role of the educator

One area of educator competence that is essential, in addition to that of children's physical and movement development, is knowledge of the progressions for, and techniques of, the basic skills to be developed in physical education. The remainder of this chapter attempts to illustrate what is involved here using an example from each of the areas of dance, games and gymnastics. Enabling children to leap, to catch or to do a forward roll, which are our three examples, requires a minimum level of technical knowledge, which can be acquired from observation, from personal experience, from demonstration or from videos, pictures or books.

Dance: learning to leap

Learning to leap involves transferring the body weight off the ground, from one foot to the other. Lead-up skills for children who cannot leap include the basic jumping skills of take-off and landing on two feet and on one foot (hopping), as well as focusing on stepping from one foot to the other. Striding (taking very long steps), trying to push off and make the knees straight to extend the stride length, is also an important lead-up skill. Many children who find leaping difficult take a run and then take off and land on the same foot, i.e. they do a sort of long, fast hop. Encourage these children to take long strides and to try to push off the floor, taking off from one foot, to do the step through the air and land on the other foot. Once the child can leap through the air from one foot to the other, the quality of the technique can be developed. Look for an upright body position, arms swinging to help elevate the leap, and then extending, probably sideways and symmetrically, to help control the shape in the air. Finally, look for height, distance, a clear shape in the air and a controlled landing.

Games: learning to catch

Learning to catch is best achieved by using a range of progressions, rather than by repeating experiences of failure, if it is clear that the child cannot catch the object being thrown. Progressions can be considered in at least two aspects:

1 **missile used** – size, weight, texture, shape, surface; encourage the child to choose a missile that is easy to catch, e.g. a velcro-catcher, a soft beanbag or a foam ball.
2 **receiving activity** – the progressions here are as follows:
   • receive from a slow roll sent along the ground towards the two waiting hands of the receiver
   • receive from an underarm feed with bounce so that the ball comes up to the waiting hands of the receiver
   • receive from an underarm throw.

The technique of the catch involves three phases:

1 **the preparation** – including the stance, arms extended towards the missile, the open-palmed ready position of the hands and the eyes watching the missile rather than the sender
2 **the action** – the hands closing around the ball, the arms bending or recoiling to control the impact of the missile
3 **the recovery** – in which the catcher regains a controlled position.

Gymnastics: learning to forward roll

As with the catch, there are many progressions that can precede practising the forward roll for children who cannot readily perform this complex roll. (The forward roll is made up of at least 17 flexions and extensions of joints of the body and limbs as it is performed!) Give children a vocabulary of other rolls that they can practise on the floor, on mats and on and from apparatus. Start with the log roll in which the child lies in a straight line and rolls over sideways. This roll can also be practised tucked. Rolling forward from front-lying on a low platform, by placing the hands on a mat to control the descent of the body on to the back of the shoulders, is often a helpful progression.

Teaching the ending of the forward roll prior to the whole roll can greatly encourage the less experienced child. By learning how to stand up from rocking on the back in a tucked shape often encourages the child to try out the complete roll. To do this the learner should keep the knees bent and rock forward to place the feet on the floor near the seat, while reaching forward with the hands and arms to help transfer the weight from the seat to the feet. The child is then ready to learn how to transfer the weight from standing on the feet to the hands and then on to the shoulders in a complete forward roll. This is best learnt going down a soft, gentle incline, such as a foam ramp on to a mat, before practising the whole roll on a mat.

These are some of the main teaching points for three basic skills. Other texts provide greater detail of these and other skills (see list at the end of this chapter). What else should be included within the pedagogical framework is a question to be answered by the competent curriculum planner, in devising an appropriate developmental physical education programme for young children.

Satisfying the 'skill-hungry years' of children in primary school and answering the myriad questions of these same children, such as 'How do I do this better?' is a constant and often insatiable challenge for the educator, just as it is the key question asked by children.

My own view is that this is not an insurmountable challenge. The educator who first observes and studies the life world of physical activity as experienced by the young learner engaged in natural movement development is well on the way to success. If the child is then put at the centre of the learning experience, then the educator can ensure that the joy of indulging in physical activity is sustained and enhanced as children mature and engage ever more skilfully and knowledgeably in the wide range of physical activities available.

Pointers for physical education and physical literacy in the early years

An effective physical education curriculum for the early years will help to cultivate in children movement that is skilful, articulate, creative and satisfying. In order to help young children to acquire motor skill competence and to develop their physical literacy, they need teachers and carers who have:

- acquired knowledge of the physical development of young children in relation to motor development and the achievement of mature motor patterns;
- learnt and understood the progressions for and techniques of movement skills;
- developed observation skills to enable them to assess progress and to give appropriate developmental feedback on the child's performance;
- built the physical development and physical education curriculum from natural movement and play;
- provided children with rich and frequent opportunities to explore movement and to practise and develop their movement vocabulary, movement memory and the quality of their movement.

Children will then be able to achieve their entitlement to be physically educated and to enhance all aspects of their physical literacy.

References

Gallahue, D. and Ozman, J. (1995) *Understanding Motor Development* (3rd edn), London: William C. Brown.

Haywood, K.M (2001) Lifespan Motor Development (3rd edn.) Champaign IL: Human Kinetics

Rafthus, S.A. (1988) *Understanding Child Development*, New York: Holt, Rinehart and Winston.

Further reading

Cooper, A. (1993) *The Development of Games and Athletic Skills*, Hemel Hempstead: Simon & Schuster.

Davies, M. (1995) *Helping Children to Learn Through a Movement Perspective*, London: Hodder Headline.

Harrison, K. (1993) *Look, Look What I Can Do*, London: Hodder & Stoughton.

Hopper, B., Grey, J. and Maude, P. (2000) *Teaching Primary Physical Education*, London: FalmerRoutledge.

Macintyre, C. (2000) *Dyspraxia in the Early Years*, London: David Fulton.

Maude, P.M. (1994) *The Gym Kit* (video and handbook), Cambridge: Albion Television and Homerton College.

Maude, P.M. (1997) *Gymnastics*, London: Hodder & Stoughton.

Maude, P.M. (2001) *Physical Children. Active Teaching*, Buckingham: Open University Press.

Physical Education Association (2003) *Observing Children Moving*, Reading: Physical Education Association of the United Kingdom.

Read, B. and Edwards, P. (1997) *Teaching Children to Play Games*, Physical Association of the United Kingdom.

Shreeves, R. (1998) *Imaginary Dances*, East Grinstead: Ward Locke.

Youth Sport Trust (2000) *TOP Dance*, Loughborough: YST.

CHAPTER 11

'Can I play the drum, Miss?'

MUSIC IN THE EARLY YEARS

Jane Edden

The task ahead

It would be altogether too easy to be deterred from teaching music to children. After all, in an investigation carried out in a College of Education, it was discovered that 'By a wide margin . . . music is the subject in which most students have the least confidence as teachers' and that 'Some students thought that they needed to have musical skills customarily associated with music specialists, e.g. piano playing, fluent music reading and an inside-out knowledge of the Classics' (Mills, 1989). This somewhat gloomy picture is offset, however, by those who have faced the challenge head on, and in one case, emerged with recommendations from the county music adviser as providing good practice in the classroom. A teaching head in Warwickshire (Dancer, 1991) who had 'never been on a music course of any kind', began her written guidelines with the words 'You don't need a piano, a guitar, a wonderful singing voice or a special room to enjoy music making with children.' Her commitment to 'bringing children into contact with the musician's fundamental activities of performing, composing and listening (DES, 1985, p. 2) in order that they 'can best discover something of its nature, its vitality, its evocative power and the range of its expressive qualities' (DES, 1985, p. 2), serves as an illustration for this chapter, which aims to outline the ways in which the world of sound can be presented to young children in an exciting, meaningful and yet non-threatening way. It is also hoped and expected that, during this endeavour, students and other early years educators may very well rediscover the key to their own previously lost world of sound. As such, the chapter will address the following:

1 the recognition, exploration and manipulation of sound and the beginnings of composition;
2 integrating musical activities into a broader framework;
3 the question of singing;
4 introducing rhythm and movement;
5 listening as part of a wider curriculum.

Exploring sound: Starting points

The simplest way of beginning an exploration of sound in the classroom is by helping children to develop the art of listening.

> Learning to listen – both to sounds around them and sounds that they can make themselves – is fundamental to children's music making. By encouraging children to think about these sounds, to be aware of them, to talk about them and to experiment with and manipulate them when they are in groups or by themselves, we provide a framework within which musical activities can take place and a real musical awareness can develop.
>
> (Davies, 1985, p. 8)

Through a series of questions, children can be introduced to some listening games in order to help them focus on the sound world around them.

What sound?

Listening game: What can you hear?

1 Ask the children to close their eyes and to listen to any sound they can hear within the room. Discuss with the children.
2 Next, ask the class what they can hear outside the room, but inside the building. Discuss.
3 Finally, ask them to listen to any sounds they can hear outside the building. Discuss.

As will be discovered, children will initially talk about any sound they hear regardless of its origin, but on repeated exposure to the game (it can be used as an infill at the end of a session, or as a contrast to a lively activity – no two playings will ever be the same!), it can be seen that the children are developing not only their powers of concentration, but also the ability to discriminate – two vital ingredients of the listening act.

The whole notion of games to explore musical learning is of significance. Storms (1983) suggests games are nothing new, but increasingly recognised as a valuable preparation for music education. He believes moreover, that games are a way of overcoming barriers for children and their educators alike – they can aid the personal, social and creative development of the children, while perhaps allowing the person lacking in confidence to explore ways of delivering music in the classroom.

It is important to give young children the opportunity on a regular basis to play some of these earliest listening games in order to develop their listening skills. It is worth remembering that an ability to listen is a crucial part of a child's whole development and essential for day-to-day life in the classroom! Something as simple as asking the children (with eyes closed) to wiggle their fingers when they hear keys being shaken will sharpen their concentration while aiding their motor skills.

Listening tape

Collect together on tape some household sounds, e.g. tap running, clock ticking, kettle boiling (it may be appropriate to group them together in order to enhance a topic – Water/Machines/Myself – early morning routine).

This could be used as a 'Guess the sound' game by itself as a classroom activity, or 'Match the picture to the sound' by providing visual representations of the sounds on the tape (such as those in Figure 11.1).

This could then become an individual listening task that could be set in an area with a small tape recorder and the picture cards – an activity that would contribute to the development of children's autonomy, while at the same time acquainting them with the operation of simple technology.

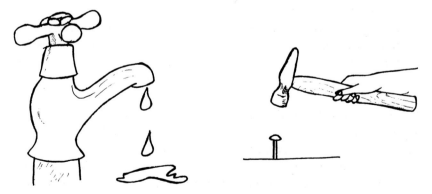

Figure 11.1 *'Match the picture to the sound'*

Once children have been given practice in listening skills, it is time to move on to ask the next question.

What kind of sound?

Listening game: Listen to my sound!

1 Gather together a collection of percussion instruments (if possible, an assortment of tuned and untuned, wood and metal).
2 Seat the children in a circle with an instrument in front of each child.
3 Ask the children to take turns in making one sound on their instrument, but only playing when they can no longer hear the sound made by the previous instrument.
4 Go round the circle, avoiding as far as possible any comments from the children. In this way full attention will be given to the sounds made and a sound picture will emerge.

A slightly different version of this game – How long does my sound last? – can be found in *Soundwaves* (Davies, 1985).

The discussion that follows the game can include a variety of questioning. A good way of beginning is to ask the children if they noticed if everybody waited until the sound had finished, thus focusing on their previously acquired skills (it is worth remembering, however, that an early entry may very well have more to do with over-enthusiasm than an inaccurate hearing!). Other questions might be:

1 Who thinks they had a longer sound? (e.g. metal instruments). Invite those children to play their sounds again.
2 Who had a shorter sound? (e.g. wooden instruments). Ask the class to listen to the differences between the two.
3 How do the materials affect the sound?
4 Can anybody change the sound they made? It may be necessary to demonstrate at this juncture. A particularly good point to make is how a drum can be played very quietly indeed (even with fingertips), thus putting paid to any preconceived ideas that it is always to be beaten as loudly as possible! It is also worth showing more imaginative transitions, e.g. how a long ringing note on a glockenspiel can be changed into something much duller and shorter by dampening it with one's hand.
5 What kind of sound is that? Can you describe it?

This last question is central. In setting up opportunities and games in which they can experiment and play with sound possibilities, children can be encouraged to respond in a variety of ways. For example, from the simple shaking of a maracca comes initially a recognition of the sound of a shaker. Through questioning, they can come to understand that they are making a series of 'fast' sounds. Furthermore, in encouraging them to talk about any related feelings or images that come to mind – 'It sounds like rain', 'It makes me scared 'cos I think of mice running' – they can use their imaginations to invent their own sound images.

Thus it can be seen that the exploration of sound with young children can elicit both a cognitive and an affective response, in addition to working hand in hand with the acquisition of language. Through this playful, experiential process with the raw materials of sound emerges a new vocabulary, neatly set out as the list of musical elements in the music national curriculum document:

pitch – higher/lower
duration – longer/shorter; steady pulse, beat, rhythm
dynamics – louder/quieter/silence
tempo – faster/slower
timbre – different types of sound
texture – different ways sounds are combined

and the use of the above within

structure – different ways sounds are organised.

Some of this technical vocabulary may seem daunting, but it is much less so for educators and children when the concepts have already been explored and described. The word 'timbre', for example, might be threatening in isolation, but when known to be dull or bright and, most importantly, recognised as the difference between the clashing cymbal or the one which falls with a thud to the floor, it is much more acceptable as part of a new vocabulary. Sound must be experienced before symbol to sow the seeds of joyous musical discovery. Gone are the days when the stave was taught in a vacuum without any meaningful purpose.

What makes the sound?

The third question addresses soundmakers, and it is important to remember that the child's first resource is his or her own body.

Listening ideas: My body

Get the children to listen to the sounds that they can produce themselves – this may well come out of a topic on 'My body'.

e.g.   playing with hair
       fingers on cheek – mouth open/mouth closed
       fingers in cheek – pops
       tapping/scraping teeth
       tongue clops/clicks
(see *Pompaleerie Jig* (Baxter and Thompson, 1978) for further ideas).

This only goes as far as the head! What can they think of for the rest of their body? What kinds of sounds are they making? What words can they use to describe the sounds they make? Encourage the children to listen first to their own sound, but then to the effect of the same sound made by the whole class – what do they think of when they have their eyes shut but are listening to the sound of 30 arms being lightly rubbed? Talk about the sound images that emerge.

Can they invent their own words for their very own soundmakers? If children are given permission at a young age to think creatively this will serve them well in every other area of life.

Listening game: Tropical storm

1 Stand the children in a circle.
2 Ask the children to very lightly rub the palms of their hands together. Gradually get louder.
3 Change to tapping two fingers against their palms.
4 Increase the volume and use the whole hand to clap.
5 Use the hands to slap the thighs.
6 Move the feet in quick succession.

The object of this game is to achieve a continuous increase and decrease in volume (no sudden lurches!) to represent the appearance and disappearance of a storm. It is an ideal opportunity to discuss *dynamics* with the children, and in particular the meaning of a *crescendo* and *diminuendo*. (It is only meaningful to do this because the children are experiencing it.)

Once the class have a grasp on the sequence of the actions, divide the circle up into four groups. The conductor (it could eventually be a child) then points to a group at a time to indicate when they start and move on to the next sequence. In this way the storm gradually increases in ferocity and will ultimately die away. Voices can be used (only use a few children at a time!) depending on how tropical the class want the storm to be. Keep this in reserve, however, for when the game has been played before, or possibly as an introduction to a discussion on the possibilities of the voice.

The voice

The voice is, of course, a very important soundmaker in its own right. Children should be given ample opportunities to use their voices inventively in order for them to appreciate that each have their own very special instrument with its own wealth of possibilities (Chacksfield and Binns, 1983, have some interesting ideas). The author appreciates that there are some amongst us who may feel very uncertain about exploring this area, but it is to be remembered that young children are a very uncritical audience and only welcome the opportunity to be allowed to make their own discoveries. As will be seen later, the larynx is a muscle that needs developing like any other.

Other soundmakers

Once children have been encouraged to use their voices, bodies and instruments in inventive ways, they can broaden their horizons by recognising that anything is a potential soundmaker. They might be asked to bring in any discarded packaging from home that can then be explored in exactly the same way as any other resource. An instant listening and response game can be conducted around different kinds of paper, for example. This may well fit into any kind of work on conservation or be linked with a blitz on litter!

'The freedom to explore chosen materials' (Paynter, 1978, p. 7) gives children the vocabulary with which to express themselves. If the word 'composition' (potentially threatening to some!) is to be seen as 'a way of saying things which are personal to the individual' (Paynter's definition of 'creative music' – an earlier description of the composition process), then by this stage children are ready to compose.

Combining sounds

Having had the experience of playing with sound, manipulating it to their own ends and realising that there is no right or wrong way, it is now time to give the children a framework in which to explore further. John Paynter has clear ideas about the role of the educator which might well be encouraging to many: the educator's role 'is to set off trains of thought and help the pupil develop his own critical powers and perception . . . as far as possible this work should not be controlled by a teacher' (Paynter, 1978, p. 7).

The simplest trains of thought, useful as starting points for composition, are action-packed pictures or picture books with a few words on the page (e.g. *Rosie's Walk*, Hutchins, 1968; *Dinner Time*, Pienkowski, 1980). After two or three readings of the story, the children can be asked to suggest some ideas for sound effects as illustration. This can emerge from discussion on characterisation and events, and use any sound sources the children consider appropriate (they may need to be reminded about their voice and body possibilities due to over-eagerness to play instruments!).

'The processes of composition in any art are selection and rejection, evaluating and confirming the material at each stage. It is essentially an experimental situation!' (Paynter, 1978, p. 7). So it is that the educator becomes an enabler and facilitator to help children explore, discuss and select the sounds they want. It is a case of constantly checking that they are happy with their choices. If, for example, they felt that the woodblock didn't sound 'bad' enough for the fox, the educator could open up a line of questioning on what kind of sound might sound more menacing – longer, shorter, metal, wood, vocal even? It is important to take time and for the class to listen with care to each others' suggestions (an ongoing reinforcement of the skill of listening). Maybe someone were to favour some longer sounds on the cymbal. This might be a forerunner of the processes of discrimination and refinement – 'Could we get louder then quieter?' Time will then need to be spent in fine tuning, until the children are satisfied with their results.

In the initial stages of this work, one would need to make this a whole-class activity, but ultimately small group work is desirable, as independent learning and social skills can come into play. The finished product can be committed to tape and played back to the children for appraisal. A series of questions can elicit to what extent the class are satisfied with their piece. Did it sound as they wanted it to sound? Is there anything they would like to change/improve upon? An opportunity for them to make further refinements is empowering and helps them to adopt the ownership of the work. Part of the role of the educator is to assist the children in taking a pride and a sense of responsibility for their creative acts. Encouraging positive comments to begin with before accepting constructive criticism can give the children a model with which to work.

We as educators can, during this critical listening time, be open to opportunities to reinforce any musical elements that might have been used. For example, Rosie walking over the haycock might have served well as an illustration of *pitch*, or a blend of voices/instruments and other soundmakers could have created a particularly interesting *texture*. If we can heighten children's awareness of what they have produced, we are making a substantial contribution to their musical development.

What then has the learning been in this compositional process? Over and above John Paynter's key summary, we can list the following:

1 *Social skills and cooperation*: taking turns, working together and sharing would have been in evidence (even more so when group work is begun).

2 *Motor skills and coordination of hand, ear and eye* would have been practised: e.g. holding a beater and playing at the right time.
3 *Imagination* would have been heavily engaged.
4 The children have been involved, not only as *performers* and *composers*, but as three different kinds of *listeners*: as composers – 'which sound is better for the splash?'; as performers – to each other; and finally as audience listeners – when they stand back and listen to the tape (and ultimately to their peer groups).
5 They have been introduced to the first stages of *appraising* their work.

Recording the sound

The final stage of the compositional process – finding a way to store the information on paper – can be an important breakthrough for adults and children alike in discovering its accessibility. In helping children explore pictorial representations of sound, the word *notation*, threatening for so many in the past, can have new meaning when expressed graphically. Figure 11.2 shows some early examples of starting points.

Figure 11.2 *Young children's graphical notation for music*

Figure 11.3 shows a full score in graphical notation, entitled 'Red Dragon's Cave', from 'Dewi the Dragon' by Gill Wilson (Edden *et al.*, 1989).

Before performing this, the children could look at, discuss and play each line separately, noting the obvious changes in *pitch* and *dynamics*, for example. For further reading in this area, see Gilbert (1981).

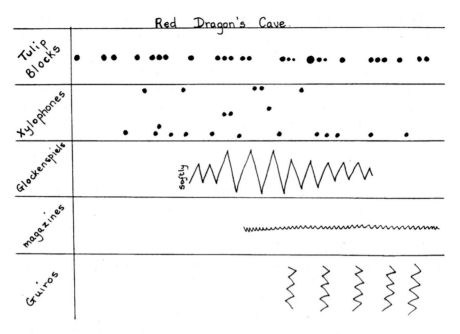

Figure 11.3 *'Red Dragon's Cave': a full score in graphical notation*

An holistic framework

It has been seen that composing, performing, listening and appraising skills can sit together very comfortably under the developmental umbrella of exploring sound. Such integration can be viewed as a model for working in an holistic fashion. Not only does this make sense from the child's perspective, but it can be most reassuring from our point of view to realise that music can be approached from any angle and in particular from our own strengths.

> Good primary school practice is based on teachers recognising the opportunities to fertilise work in one part of the curriculum with work in another. The unifying and integrating aspects of the arts give them a particular value in this respect.
>
> (Arts in Schools, 1982, p. 53)

Let us take an example. *Rosie's Walk* (Hutchins, 1968) can be read to the children as part of a topic on journeys. To give it musical depth, two elements are pre-selected to focus on, although this does not mean that others are not acknowledged! *Pitch, tempo* and *duration* all give particular scope (but it is hoped that during the course of the year all elements will be explored in some depth through various activities). Already, attention has been paid to pitch through Rosie walking up and down the haycock. Further endorsement of this might come at another time by showing children the xylophone and working with some high and low notes. Science can be introduced by carrying out pitch experiments with levels of water in bottles which could then be played like a xylophone. Geography can be covered by recreating Rosie's journey as simple mapping work for a classroom display, and maybe helping children map out their own journeys to school, that could then be used as scores for graphic notation. Language, of course, has been explored alongside the selected sounds.

Games can be played to reinforce the concepts and there are many useful books to explore. Mary York's (1984) choice is particularly appropriate in her book, *Gently into Music*, and *Hi Lo Dolly Pepper* (Clark, 1991) includes a comprehensive exploration of all the concepts together with some attractive graphic scores. Nursery rhymes like 'Hickory Dickory Dock' lend themselves ideally as a good illustration of both *pitch* and *tempo*. Stories like 'The Three Bears' and poems like 'The Four Friends' (in York, 1984) provide wonderful opportunities to consolidate the idea of *pitch*, but also feed into other areas of the curriculum. The flow chart in Figure 11.4 might be used not only as a model for any kind of comprehensive musical input to any topic, but as a basis for the kind of holistic framework that has been discussed.

Also not to be missed as valuable sources of topic ideas:

Topic Anthology for Young Children (Gilbert, 1991) – includes
   Water, Machines, Toys, Fairs and Circuses, Cowboys and Indians)
Music Through Topics (Clark, 1990)

The question of singing

One of the best links that can be made between topic areas and the musical elements is singing.

> For both children and teacher the importance of regular classroom singing is greater than realised. It can stimulate and calm the children, bring class and teacher together and provide an enjoyable controlled activity to balance the programme of a busy day. It develops the child's musical abilities and social skills whilst also acting as a valuable aid in reading and language development, in building basic concepts and in linking and extending other areas of the curriculum.
>
> (Gilbert, 1981 p. 15)

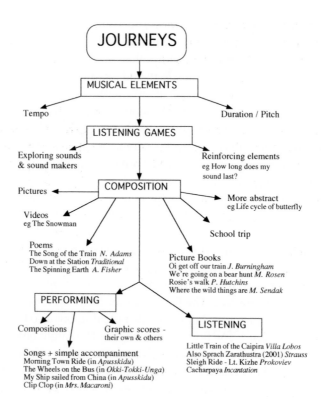

Figure 11.4 *Flow chart of musical activities related to the topic of 'Journeys'*

Ideally singing should be a daily activity and should fulfil a variety of criteria. Songs of different kinds will perform different functions.

Songs with repetition and action songs

These are particularly important to young children. The action song 'Jack in the Box' (Scott Wood) with its descending scale and its final leap 'Yes I will!' in answer to the question 'Will you come out?' is a perfect example of how to illustrate *pitch* to children. Some children might join in with a xylophone, stepping from high to low, while others could take it in turns to be Jack, and leap from low to high. Many songs can be used in this way to consolidate musical learning through a focus. Increasingly, there are books available that use songs in this kind of broader context. Try exploring other songs used to feature pitch and other elements in:

Game Songs For Infants (Richards, 1990)
Mrs Macaroni (Tillman, 1985)

Managing Music with Infants (Edden et al, 1989)
Gently into Music (York, 1984)
Hi Lo Dolly Pepper (Clark, 1991)

Two- and three-note songs

Children also need to be given opportunities to work with two- and three-note songs (e.g. 'Rain Rain', 'Bell Horses') to help them find their voices. Singing the register using the Soh–Me interval, or responding to a sung question can be of great value. Nicki Bennison and her intensive work with children at Central School Chichester proves how valuable this kind of work can be, and the success story of her choir (Sainsbury's Choir of the Year, 1990) is living proof that constant exposure to singing and making it a high-light of the school day can pay rich dividends. 'I believe that all children can be taught to sing if and only if somebody bothers to find their voice' (Bennison, 1991).

Singing with confidence

But what of those who have very low self-esteem when it comes to their own singing, and are fearful of leading children in song? There are no magic cures for this dilemma, but there are reassurances that can be given. The first of these is that young children are just grateful to have an opportunity to sing. They are not a critical audience. Be encouraged with older infants, moreover, to allow the stronger singers to assist in leading the class. There is a distinction to be made between those who are unwilling to sing in front of their peers but will 'have a go' behind closed doors, and those who have absolutely no confidence whatsoever. For the latter kind, pre-recorded tapes are a useful prop. The author has witnessed a very successful use of such a strategy in a situation where confidence was low, but a commitment to children's singing was high. Ten minutes before each break time, the teacher would gather the children from their various activities to sit together on the carpet and sing with the tape. It was a joyous sight, particularly in the light of the teacher's own perceived difficulties. It is important to realise that a willingness on the part of the unconfident educator to expose children to the joys of singing can be infinitely more beneficial than the 'expert' who quite erroneously blames a child for singing out of tune. After all, at 7 years old, only about 50 per cent of children can represent a given pitch.

Rhythm and movement

Another area which gives particular concern to early years educators is that of introducing rhythm to children. Yet simple activities can serve children well in this area. All children have had the experience of a steady beat (mother's heartbeat, rocking, knee bouncing) and, by the time they come to school, many have a developed sense of pulse. Helping children reinforce this skill by using body percussion to accompany simple rhymes, songs, jingles or any piece of recorded music with a steady beat is a good starting point.

Rhythm game: Follow my leader

1 Select a piece of recorded music with a strong beat.
2 Establish the pulse.
3 Ask the class to copy what you do – 'follow my leader'.
4 Use a variety of different body percussion to keep a steady pulse, e.g. tapping hands on head, shoulders, thighs; clapping, clicking, etc.
5 Alternate the actions.
6 If appropriate, invite a child to lead.

This game is not only helpful in terms of developing a sense of *pulse*, but improves concentration and is fun! It can also be used as a five minute 'filler' for those occasions when there is time to spare at the end of a session. Maybe the music that is selected (and this is certainly an opportunity to introduce the class to different genres) is chosen as part of the holistic framework, and can thus feed into an integrated curriculum.

Simple echo clapping, where the educator claps four beats (*pulse*) and the children follow, can move into an understanding of 'walking' beats – walk, walk, walk, walk – and can ultimately be drawn on cards as a demonstration of simplified crotchets (this is the very beginning of staff *notation*). The natural progression moves to clapping patterns (e.g. names, topic words, the words of a rhyme, e.g. 'Rain, rain, go away'). The following example demonstrates how children can begin to understand simple rhythm patterns in terms of walks, slow walks and runs.

Big   Chief Sit   ting Bull
(walk   walk   run   run   walk)

Hi   a   wa   tha   brave
(run   run   run   run   slow walk)

Paint ed   tee   pee   Ar   row head
(run   run   run   run   run   run   walk)

War   drums   grave.
(walk   walk   slow walk)

Each one of these lines forms a *pattern*, as opposed to a *pulse*, and a line said repeatedly becomes an *ostinato* (repeated pattern). This can be an exciting way of introducing simple song/rhyme accompaniment and the following can be used as a model for any simple song or rhyme.

Using an ostinato

1 Familiarise the children with the song or rhyme.
2 Select a short phrase from the words of the text, which lends itself to being repeated, e.g. Big Chief Sitting Bull/Rain, Rain'.
3 Ask the children to repeat it several times in rhythm.
4 Ask a small group to continue to do this while the rest of the class say the rhyme. This is vocal *ostinato* in action!

As a progression, try substituting the phrase with either body percussion or untuned percussion, asking the children to say the phrase silently in their heads. This internalisation helps develop musical memory. Linking patterns to words is a security and a learning tool for educators and children alike! It is important to state here that it is best to work only with the staff *notation* with which one is comfortable. It would be foolish to topple confidence that has gradually emerged in other areas by putting too much emphasis on delivering what might well be at the heart of our fears. This is in no way intended to undervalue the traditional form of recording music, but is much more an observation on unrealistic expectations.

Rhythm through movement

Many rhythmic ideas can be experienced through movement activities. 'Music is not heard by ear alone but the whole of the body' (Mothersole, 1921, p. 23). Movement is an ideal vehicle for consolidating learning while at the same time enabling children to make creative use of their energies. Games are a perfect medium to explore movement activities. Try the following:

Movement game: 'Journey of the animals'

1 Divide the class into four groups of different syllabic animals (cat, ti – ger, po – lar bear, al – li – ga – tor).
2 Send each group into a corner of the room.

3 Tap out each of the rhythms in turn, and encourage them to move to the secret cave in the centre by stepping out their pattern, when they hear their particular rhythm. (You may need to demonstrate first!) They must stop when they hear the pattern change.
4 When the children are secure with their rhythms, be more unpredictable in your sequencing!
5 Change the groups in order for them to experience all the patterns.

Some movement games need instrumental players: e.g. 'Charlie Chaplin went to France' and 'Punchinello' (Edden et al., 1989) both need a two-note drone (i.e. the same two notes played repeatedly throughout). Games to reinforce any of the musical elements can be led by someone without pianistic skills. With *pitch,* for example, children can be asked to 'walk tall' if they hear some high notes on the piano or move as low as they can when they hear low notes. This, of course, is further practice in listening skills.

Listening as part of a wider curriculum

In a world bombarded with sound, young children do not necessarily find listening as easy as in years gone by. There has already been discussion earlier in the chapter about the crucial role it plays in a child's musical development, and as such educators are encouraged to expose the child to a variety of listening activities. Affective responses can be made through the medium of paint or words (a 'journey' to South America to hear 'Cacharpaya', played by Incantation, is an ideal starting point here: 'How does it make you feel?', 'What can you imagine?'), although the cognitive response can be developed even at an early stage (Prokoviev's 'Sleigh Ride', for example, from Lieutenant Kizhe, features the sleigh bells the children may very well have on their music trolley. Can they hear them?). Attention to *tempo* can be given through Villa Lobos' 'Little Train of the Caipira', where they can hear the train increasing in speed, but they can also be asked if they think it sounds like a train, and why? We need to try and present a focus for listening and to take the musical questioning as far as we are able. Recorded music, it has been seen, can be played in a variety of different contexts all within a cohesive programme. Try finding a piece of music as a follow-up to children's compositions, or something relevant to the topic that could be used for movement purposes. If children can be in touch with live music (either attending concerts or inviting musicians into school) then it becomes an exciting, living reality.

Conclusion

It is hoped that after reading this chapter early years educators will come to see that whatever their own musical history might be, they have an important roles to play as enablers and inspirers of young children's music. If you can make music an integral part of the school day, you will be using your own and the children's creativity to build a new way of being for yourself and the children you teach. 'Every creative act involves a new innocence or perception, liberated from the cataract of accepted belief' (Arts in Schools, 1982, p. 22).

Pointers for early years music

- Don't assume you need to have had a traditional music training in order to facilitate young children's music making.
- Use simple games as a means of reinforcing a musical idea.
- Exploring sound and sound sources can stimulate the imagination while developing language skills.
- Look for any opportunities to reinforce the elements of music.
- When planning a topic look for ways in which music can be naturally linked with other areas of the curriculum, thus making it a daily and relevant activity.
- A song a day keeps the grumps away!
- Make music fun!

References

Arts in Schools (1982) *Principles, Practice and Provision*, London: Calouste Gulbenkian Foundation.

Bennison, N. (1991) *Singing is Central*, BBC2.

Dancer, A. (1991) 'Every child has a song to sing', *Times Educational Supplement*, 8 February.

Davies, L. (1985) *Soundwaves*, London: Unwin Hyman.

DES (1985) *Music from 9–16*, London: HMSO.

Gilbert, J. (1981) *Musical Starting Points with Young Children*, London: Ward Lock.

Mills, J. (1989) 'The generalist primary music teacher', *British Journal of Music Education*, 6, 125–38.

Mothersole, A. (1920) La Rythmique est-elle une lubie? *Le Rythme*, 5, 23.

Paynter, J. (1978) *Sound and Silence*, Cambridge: Cambridge University Press.

Storms, G. (1983) *Handbook of Musical Games*, London: Hutchinson.

Source material referred to in text

Baxter, A. and Thompson, D. (1978) *Pompaleerie Jig*, Exeter: E. J Arnold.

Chacksfield, M. and Binns, P. (1983) *Sound Ideas Books 1–6*, Oxford: Oxford University Press.

Clark, V. (I990) *Music Through Topics*, Cambridge: Cambridge University Press.

Clark, V. (1991) *Hi Lo Dolly Pepper*, London: A. & C. Black.

Edden, J., Edwards, R., Malcolm, A. and Wilson, G. (1989) *Managing Music with Infants*, Cambridge: Cambridge County Council.

Gilbert, J. (1991) *Topic Anthology for Young Children*, Oxford: Oxford University Press.

Hutchins, P. (1968) *Rosie's Walk*, London: Bodley Head.

Pienkowski, J. (1980) *Dinner Time*, London: Orchard.

Richards, C. (1990) *Game Songs For Infants* (available from Acorn Percussion Ltd, Unit 34, Abbey Business Centre, Ingate Place, London SW8 3NS.

Tillman, J. (1985) *Mrs Macaroni*, London: Macmillan.

York, M. (1984) *Gently into Music*, Harlow, Essex: Longmans.

Other source material

Birkenshaw, L. (1974) *Music for Fun, Music for Learning*, Toronto: Birk-Holt Rinehart & Winston.

Farmer, B. (1982) *Springboards*, Melbourne, Australia: Nelson.

Gamper, E. (1986) *Music with Mr Plinkerton*, Woodford Green, Essex: International Music Publications.

Maddocks, A. and Stocks, M. (1991) *Growing Up with Music KS1*, Harlow, Essex: Longmans.

Mills, J. (1991) *Music in the Primary School*, Cambridge: Cambridge University Press.

Wheway, D. and Thomson, S. (1993) *Explore Music through* . . . (9 subject areas), Oxford: Oxford University Press.

CHAPTER 12

'Oh, I'm just IN LOVE with those pots'

YOUNG CHILDREN'S ART

Jane Bower

Introduction

'It took me a lifetime to learn to draw like them.'

(Pablo Picasso in old age, at an
exhibition of children's drawings)

Why is art taught in schools? Why is it considered so important that it is a compulsory part of the curriculum?

Wherever you are as you read this, stop for a moment and look around you. If you are in a room, it is likely that everything in it has begun with an artist. Your clothes, the furniture, the weave of curtain fabric, the clock and other objects, the carpet pattern, and even your hairstyle have all been conceived, designed and executed by an artist of one kind or another. If you are sitting outside, the same applies – street furniture, benches, gardens and architecture have all begun in the mind of an artist. Without the creativity of art and design we would not only be static, but unable to function, and this form of creativity is inbuilt in every human from birth.

By the time a child begins attending school this inbuilt creativity is already being influenced by adult attitudes. It is for this reason that the teaching of art in the early years is so vital if we are to encourage children's understanding and expression of art to develop and grow richly and healthily, and not be stunted by lack of confidence, often unwittingly expressed by the most well-meaning of adults, including teachers.

Let us take drawing as an example. It is a familiar occurrence when a young child asks a parent, grandparent or other adult to draw them something, for the adult to reply, 'Oh, I can't draw', or 'I'm no good at drawing'. The same statements are frequently made by teachers or students on drawing courses, and by the time children reach the age of around 7, many are beginning to say the same thing.

I often ask adults and these older children whether a baby can draw. Most say it can. Some say a baby 'just scribbles'. I point out to them what the baby is doing. First, it has to learn to grasp a drawing tool and keep hold of it. Then it has to select the right end or part of the tool, and make and maintain contact with a surface, moving the tool along it. Finally, it has to see that this action causes a mark to be made. I ask them if they now think a baby's scribbles are drawing, and they decide that they are.

Why is it, then, that when a child first takes two steps and then falls down, we rush to tell our friends, but when this far more complex set of skills is achieved, we call it 'scribbling'? Conversely, why do we praise young children even for the most unformed drawings, saying 'that's lovely!' and yet denigrate our own efforts?

One of the first questions I put to adults is what they think drawing is. Most answers include words such as 'image', 'representation' or 'accurate portrayal'. Many also say that 'you need a pencil and paper'.

I begin to challenge their definitions. *Do* you need pencil and paper – would a finger in sand not be drawing? Does a drawing always have to look like something? Couldn't it be patterns, pleasing shapes or colours?

My definition of drawing is 'making marks with a tool on a surface', and this is how I begin with young children, just as, if you were approaching maths, you would start with learning the names and value of numbers, not try to tackle logarithms. If you happen to have a genuine talent for drawing, you must still begin at the child's level.

Who was the first artist? Many adults' and children's conception of an artist is a famous male painter. But an artist does not have to be any of these. Surely the first artist was the first person – and several of the earliest people have left examples of their art on rocks and cave walls. This for me proves that art is an inbuilt instinct and need, a natural form of human expression. Cave people had no formal tuition. They simply looked, with remarkable observational skills, and recorded what they saw.

> We have long come to realise that art is not produced in an empty space, that no artist is independent of predecessors and models, that he . . . is part of a specific tradition.
>
> (Ernst Kris, quoted in Gombrich, 1987)

Children need to realise this too – that they also are artists, part of a continuing culture.

Of course, drawing is only one of many artforms, but whether you are teaching art through clay, paint, fabrics or any other medium, the same principles apply.

As well as a necessary part of human existence, art is a subject that penetrates deeper. It feeds the soul. Without the arts our whole culture would collapse. It opens up for children beauty, emotion, expression, and the huge range and magic of colour, shape, texture and form. The following examples of ways to approach the teaching of art through various media were devised to maximise in the young child not only delight in exploring a material and learning the practical skills associated with it, but the sense of wonder that comes with creating something where there was nothing before; something entirely unique.

What should be covered?

When planning art teaching in the long term, the aim should be to give children both practical experience, and a deeper understanding of artists and their work.

The practical experience should offer children as wide a range of materials and techniques as possible, so that they become adept at choosing the right medium and tool for certain tasks, and begin to develop preferences and a deeper understanding. Ensure that there is a good balance between 2- and 3-dimensional work. The range might include:

- drawing (pencil, pastel, chalk, wax, charcoal, crayon on different surfaces);
- painting (powder, liquid, block; using brushes, fingers, other tools);
- printing (inks, paints; using fingers, card, vegetables, polystyrene);
- modelling materials (clay, plasticine, play dough, salt dough);
- textiles (fabrics, threads, wools; cutting, sticking, weaving, stitching);
- building (boxes, card, recycled materials, wood; various joining methods).

A diversity of stimuli should also be offered as starting points for artwork. These might include:

- natural forms (e.g. seedpods, woodgrain);
- made artefacts (machine parts, glassware);
- the imagination (a story, dreams);
- tactile stimuli (a rough shell, a smooth pebble);
- aural stimuli (taped music, percussion instruments);
- other artists' work (a bowl by a local potter, an Indian sari, a Monet reproduction).
- photographs (of architecture, moving water, clouds).

This list is by no means exhaustive and should also include opportunities for children to plan, design and discuss their work, evaluating and modifying it as necessary. The emphasis at this stage should be on exploring the materials, finding out what they can do; on discovering and delighting in the process rather than always concentrating on the end product.

> The aim of art education is not the production of works of art but the unity of the entire growing personality . . . an increase in (the child's) capacity to bring forth what is within him.
>
> (Lark-Horovitz, 1967)

This practical work should be consistently supported, complemented and illustrated by the work of other artists, so that children can relate what they are doing to what is going on, and has been going on for thousands of years, in the world of art around them. 'Other artists' includes yourself, potters, sculptors, weavers, wrapping paper designers and so on, famous or unknown. For example, if a child has just learned to make a firm join with clay, a pottery jug could be used to show them how important such joins are. If printing, a photograph of an early Aboriginal handprint would form a link between their own work and that of a past culture.

The three media and activities I describe below have been chosen to complement each other and to introduce a balanced range of the examples given above. Clay provides 3-dimensional experience, painting 2-dimensional, and textiles the possibility of either or both, depending on how the fabrics and threads are used.

Clay

Clay is one of the most beautiful and exciting materials for children of all ages, and my preference is to introduce it to them as early as possible. It is also one of the most inexpensive resources. Although there are several self-hardening or other varieties of modelling material available (all at a higher price!), nothing can match real clay for versatility and natural beauty of texture. Used correctly, it generates no mess, and neither a sink nor a kiln are required to achieve valuable results.

Choosing subject matter

To give children a recognisable object to model, such as a cat or a house, at too early a stage can pose a threat and a high risk of feeling a failure. ('Mine doesn't look like a cat.') It is important for children to first explore clay in an abstract way ('Can you make a curvy shape/a sharp shape?') to build up their confidence and knowledge of the material. The activity described below is designed to meet these criteria, and deliberately avoids any tools other than the fingers, so that children can discover the huge range of manipulation achievable with their own hands before investigating other possibilities.

Preparation

Before starting any work with clay, ask each child to apply a small dot of handcream to their palms, rubbing it in well (I call this 'putting on our invisible gloves'). This is recommended as a health and safety measure, and should become second nature to anyone working with clay. Potters' barrier cream is probably the most effective (available from educational catalogues) but any unscented handcream is fine.

Provide a mat for each child on which to rest their claywork. Deckchair canvas is by far the best, cut into 30cm squares. Hessian goes mouldy and makes an imprint; wooden boards warp easily and clay often has to be prized off them, whereas mats can be peeled cleanly from the work. One side of the mat can be used for grey clay and the other for red, and no washing or hemming is necessary. (When ordering clay, check that the two colours fire at the same temperature so that both grey and red pieces can be fired together, or mixed in the same model.)

Learning objectives

The suggested activity provides opportunities for children to learn in both practical and expressive ways:

- observing a natural form and responding to it;
- exploring a three-dimensional medium and experimenting with shape, form and space;
- expressing their feelings and ideas as they work;
- building up a knowledge of the visual and tactile qualities of clay and the vocabulary associated with it;
- using their own imagination to inspire their work;
- evaluating and modifying as they go along.

Introducing the clay

When first introducing clay to children, I make a point of bringing it in just as it comes – in the plastic bag. If it is presented to them ready rolled into a ball, much vital work is missed.

My first question is always 'What is clay?' Occasionally a child will know that it is earth or soil, but many will say 'plasticine' or 'play dough'. There is a teaching point here not to be ignored, because clay is the complete opposite of plasticine; it hardens in heat, whereas plasticine will melt.

When I ask 'Where does clay come from?' they often say 'a shop' or 'the factory'. Many are amazed when I say that it is from the ground. Where was it dug from? Why isn't it full of dirt, stones and worms? Why is it so heavy? Why does it have to be kept in a plastic bag? I ask the children to consider the colour of the clay. Not all clay is the same colour, because it is dug from different areas of the country.

Children love to watch the action of the clay cutter as I carve off chunks (you can make your own from two clothes pegs joined with a length of fuse wire or plastic thread). Any misconceptions that the clay is 'dirty' can be dispelled at this stage. It is beautifully clean, and smells of nothing. The size of the chunks should reflect the size of the pupils' hands – each chunk should be easy to control and not too big to pick up and handle.

Never have water on the table when working with clay. It is unnecessary and should only be introduced (and then in very small quantities) when children learn to join clay, at a much later stage.

Rather than launch into making something straight away, take the time when introducing the material for the first time to let the children explore the clay, find out its potential and simply take joy in it. One way to do this is to ask the children to wait until they all have their own piece, and then all touch it together, saying any words that describe the clay when they first feel it.

The first reaction from anyone is almost always 'It's cold.' 'Why does it have to be cold? Why must it not be allowed to get warm?' Other words such as 'squidgy' and 'soft' soon follow. It is never too early to develop the vocabulary associated with clay, so that words such as 'pliable' and 'moist' gradually come to replace 'bendy' and 'damp'. Such preliminary explorations and discussions serve not only to teach the children the properties of clay but begin to build up their fascination in it. To the children, clay seems to have almost magical properties, and for me its fascination never abates. You can bend it, squeeze it, break it, smear it; it can be turned into pottery, change its colour. . . .

Similarly, it is never too early to teach the skills needed to form a solid foundation for later work in clay. From their very first model, I teach children to wedge clay, explaining that it contains minute air bubbles, often far too tiny to see, which must be burst before any models can be made. (If left in, an air bubble can explode when fired in the kiln.) To wedge, the heel of the hand is used to tap the clay on all sides so that it forms a dense ball. After a few lessons, the children learn to put on barrier cream and wedge the clay before starting work.

A suggested clay activity – bony sculptures

Ask the children to hold their ball of clay in their stronger or writing hand. They are going to make it change its shape by giving it one, and only one, big squeeze. It is helpful if you do this too, so that you all squeeze together.

Apply as much pressure as possible and then carefully peel the fingers out and place the squeezed shape carefully on the mat.

What shapes can you see or feel? Where are there shadows and which bits have light on them? Do you think any other person could make a shape exactly like this one? Point out to the children that already each person's sculpture is unique because no one else has their fingerprints. Look closely to see them in the clay, along with the creases from the palms or marks from the nails.

Introduce a selection of clean bones to the children. Compare the shapes to the squeezed clay – are there any similarities? The shapes of our own bones in our hands have influenced the shapes of our sculptures. Now the selection of bones can be used to influence them further.

Encourage children to explore particular facets of the bones and develop their sculpture to incorporate or echo some of them. They are not changing their sculpture into a model of a bone, but rather aiming to subtly alter their sculpture to make it more bony.

For example, a ridge of clay formed between two fingers on the squeeze could be pinched thinner and sharper; a depression formed by the end of a finger could be pushed further until a hole is made through the clay. Areas could be smoothed with a thumb or left cracked to resemble the different textures found on the bones.

The finished sculptures can be displayed among the real bones, perhaps lit from one side with a lamp. Their shapes are often reminiscent of some of the work of Henry Moore, whose sculptures can provide inspiration for further sessions. The quotation in the title of this chapter was the response of a Year-1 boy on being shown ceramics by Mary Rogers.

Clearing up

When the claywork has been completed, children should not wash their hands in a sink, as the accumulation of clay dust will quickly block up the waste pipe. Instead, provide a bucket of warm water and paper towels for washing. Alternatively, have a couple of cloths in the bucket and pass the cloths around the class. The handcream applied earlier allows the clay to slip off the hands easily and there is no mess. The mats can be shaken over a bin, and the tables given a wipe.

Pour the water away outside, on to the nearest soil or garden. I was delighted when a 5-year-old described this as 'the clay going home'. It made a good opportunity to mention recycling!

Cross-curricular links

Clay offers a wealth of opportunity in science (observing how materials change when heated – particularly spectacular if you are glazing the work), history (the first pots made by people, how they shaped and fired clay and what they used clay vessels for) and geography (where clay occurs naturally in the earth, its properties and how it affects the environment).

Painting

> Virtually every activity in which the child engages contains an element of magic. With paint one can change a white paper into a blue paper. That is magic.
>
> (*Pre-School Play*, Jameson and Kidd)

As with clay, there is a time when paints should be used by the young child for pure play, for the joy of watching paper change colour and marks appear. But the way that paints are organised, handled and presented when undertaking a structured project will have an important effect on children's management of and respect for the materials, and their understanding of colour mixing. For the project below, ready-mixed liquid paints were used.

Preparation

Provide children with a sponge, a mixing tray (or plate), chalk and two brushes. The sponge should be dampened and squeezed out. It is used for wiping brushes, cleaning a place on the tray and mopping up any spills. (My aim is always to minimise any mess and to avoid the need for children to get up to change their paint water during the lesson.) The three primary colours and black and white are the only ones needed to mix any colours you need, and therefore the only ones I ever buy, although I do order two variants of each primary, such as a lemon and a chrome yellow.

Chalk is better than pencil for drawing – it won't show through the paint. Use the palest colour that will show on the paper. I provide both a large and a small brush (such as a size 12 bristle and a size 2 soft) so that the children have to make a choice. In this way they learn to consider what they are about to paint and what to expect from each tool. Teach the children to hold the brush like a pencil, on the fattest part of the wood.

Squeeze a small amount of each paint on to the child's tray. Trays should preferably be white to show up the paint colour clearly, and are better than palettes for colour mixing with liquid paints, as the children can pull colours directly into others across the surface, often making surprise discoveries for themselves.

Learning objectives

The main points I want children to learn when introducing paint, which I make again and again over the coming weeks until they become an automatic part of the children's practice, are:

- Do not mix one colour all over the tray. Because it is thin it will dry quickly and there will be no space for other colours.
- Whenever possible, paint light coloured areas first and move towards darker colours. This minimises the need to wash the brush.
- Wipe the brush on the sponge rather than always washing it in the water, or after doing so.
- Use as little water with the paint as possible – liquid paints are already mixed to the correct consistency.
- When eventually the water does need changing, ask the teacher to do it (have some filled replacements standing by) rather than carrying it yourself.
- Pale colours (yellow and white) are weak and you need a larger quantity of them; dark colours are strong and you need only a minute amount to change a pale colour.

The last point should be remembered when you are dispensing paint. As a general rule you need to give the child three times the amount of white and yellow and twice the amount of red as you do black and blue. The same amounts apply when you are ordering paint for the school – don't make the mistake of buying the same amount of each! It helps if you think of them as foods – white and yellow as, say, milk, and black as chilli powder.

As well as the above practical teaching points, there are other learning outcomes I aim to bring about:

- Good paintings are not always produced in one session; an artist will often need to work on a painting over a long period of time, rejecting, improving and developing ideas.
- An artist does not always find painting easy; it may involve struggling with problems, but there is always a way to solve them.
- You can often do something you didn't think you could do, and the feeling of pride and achievement on completion of a fulfilling piece of work makes all the problem-solving worthwhile.

A suggested painting project – snakes

This project began when a live pet snake was brought into the school. Having studied its appearance and movement, and learned about its habitat, we looked at the jungle paintings of Henri Rousseau and clear, close-up photographs of snakes, and discussed the different environments against which they appeared.

I asked the children to decide how their snake was to be positioned. We talked about placing it on the paper (in this case thick buff sugar paper, good for supporting lots of paint, about 42x62cm) so that its shape was balanced. I drew a tiny snake in the corner of the paper, and then a snake which filled the space. Which looked better? The children drew their snakes in yellow chalk, and I encouraged them to take care to keep the snake's body even, only tapering at the tail. The heads were drawn after looking closely at the photographs.

I then asked them to decide where their particular snake lived. Was it on a stony, shingly desert, or hot, sparkling sand, among big rocks, deep in a jungle, in a dark cave, or under the sea? They took their inspiration from the books I had brought in and from the Rousseau paintings.

The first two sessions were devoted entirely to the backgrounds. We looked at other reproductions of paintings to see how artists had made these full of interest. I told the children they should prepare the loveliest home they could for when their snake arrived in the picture. I pointed out that no great artists leave blank areas of canvas – the one exception known to me being

Gauguin, who at one stage was so poor he did not have enough paint to fill the corners of some of his Tahitian paintings.

I asked the children to tell me the colour they had in mind and how they thought it would be mixed. I then came round with the paint bottles and dispensed small amounts of the appropriate colours for them to mix, helping them if they did not know the combination. Doing this means a lot of travelling around, but is far less of a headache in the long run. When children need more paint, they put up their hands and tell me which colour they need.

The backgrounds provided a good opportunity for putting into practice the method of painting from light to dark. For example, a sandy background could start with pale yellow blobs, then a little red could be added to make a pale orange for more blobs, then a little blue to make a beigy brown, until gradually darker and darker blobs are added to the texture, without at any time needing to wash the brush.

Only when every bit of background was filled with paint in varied textures, shapes and colours, and had become interesting in its own right, were the snakes introduced. By now the children were itching to paint them, especially as I had been whetting their appetites with descriptions of how jewelled and brilliantly patterned we could make them.

We talked about what colours the snakes should be compared to the backgrounds. Would they be camouflaged, or show up brightly against them? Clean, large brushes were used to fill in the snake shapes with the child's chosen colour. Then the tiny brushes were used to paint contrasting, intricate scaly designs over the base colour. Children should be taught to stroke and not scrub with these, pulling the brush backwards from the paper, never pushing it forwards, and never letting the metal part of the brush rest on the paper. I encouraged the most minute detail to make a direct contrast with the textured, sweeping or bobbly backgrounds.

Finally, children used gold pens, metallic wax crayons and oil pastels to add the finishing touches – ferns growing between rocks, sparkling decoration on the snakes' scales, strange underwater plants, or tiny flowers blooming in the desert sand. The children (a mixture of reception, Years 1 and 2) worked on the paintings during five fairly lengthy sessions over a period of three months, working on other art projects in between some of the sessions.

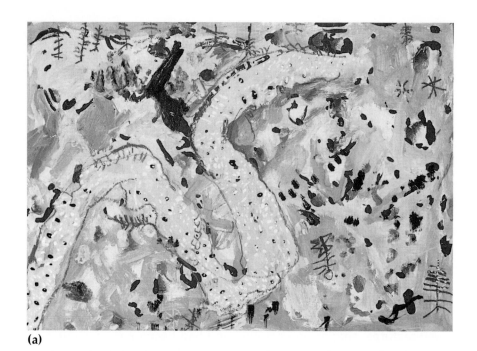

(a)

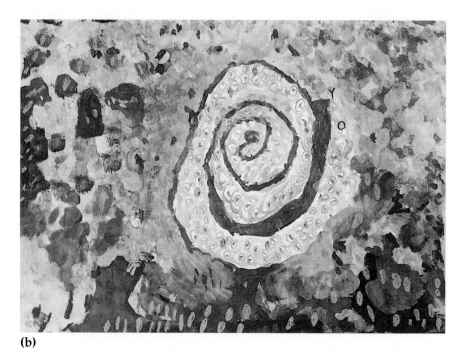

(b)

(c)

(d)

Figure 12.1 (a), (b), (c) & (d) *Snake paintings by Jenna Campbell-Butcher, Victoria Richards, Elizabeth Gunning and Miles Taylor, all aged 5 years, Horler's Pre-Preparatory school, Comberton Cambridge*

Cross-curricular links

The snake project provided valuable links with English (descriptive poems or prose about the snake and where it lives, building on vocabulary and a set of instructions for looking after art materials); geography (hot countries, different habitats); science (reptiles, what they eat, how and where they lay their eggs, what conditions they need) and maths (numberwork based on sequence patterns such as those painted on the snakes).

Textiles

I think of stitching as mark-making or a form of painting with wools and threads. With the right combination of equipment, teaching techniques and subject matter it can be taught successfully to very young children.

Preparation

For very first stitches, begin by fixing small (7cm) circular rubber embroidery rings into a roll of stockinette (dishcloth fabric obtainable on a roll from household or car stores). The stockinette comes doubled, and should be used like this, as a single layer is very easily ripped.

Unroll the cloth and fix all the rings you need in it before cutting. If you try to cut pieces to fit in the rings they will curl up and be impossible to manage. Cut round the rings with sharp scissors, leaving about 2cm around the edges. Any less, and it will jump out of the ring; any more, and the child will catch it with the needle and sew it underneath.

Threading the needle

Use blunt-ended, large-eyed metal needles or bodkins for first stitches. You can show even the youngest children how to thread them – they will enjoy trying and will often succeed. Teach them to find the end of the ball of wool and put it on their nose. Holding the ball in their other hand they should unwind it slowly until the elbow is straight (this is good manipulative practice in its own right!) and cut the wool near the ball. Doing this, which is the traditional way for tailors to measure thread, ensures that the wool will be a comfortable length for the child to use.

Discourage licking the wool, or trying to poke it through the needle as if it were thread. Instead, fold it around the needle top, pinch it off between finger and thumb (I tell the children to try and hide it, like a little secret) and poke the eye of the needle over the almost-hidden pinched loop before pulling it through. There is great excitement when this is managed alone for the first time.

The stitching process

Show the children how to use their thumb and forefinger 'like a bird's beak' to hold the needle. All the other fingers on that hand should be used to grip the wool in the needle eye, forming a fist so that it can't escape. I call this 'trapping the mouse'. As you poke the needle through the fabric and hold it as it comes out the other side, say 'bird's beak', and as you pull the thread through and grab it with your remaining fingers say 'trap the mouse!' Children soon get used to this sequence and enjoy it.

Starting and finishing

I never tie knots in the end of the wool. It only means that queues of children will form for this to be done, and more importantly it tends to make them yank the wool, knowing the knot will stop it, rather than drawing it through carefully. Similarly, never tie the wool into the needle. Not only will it prevent the wool from being pulled through some fabrics, but it also gets in the way of them learning the correct procedure for holding and manipulating the needle described above.

Instead, show children how to leave a loose end on the back when they first pull the wool through (I call this 'the mouse's tail') and this gradually teaches them not to pull too tightly. Later, teach them 'fastening off' – two tiny stitches in the same place on the back.

When first beginning stitching, select a subject which lends itself to simple mark-making with wools. For example, water or fire offer more freedom and are far less threatening than 'my initials' or 'a cat'.

Try looking at photographs of fireworks exploding, or watching a real sparkler (held by an adult in a gloved hand). Ask the children to choose suitably coloured wools (I store these in separate baskets, each holding a different colour range) and then make stitches on the 7cm rings of dishcloth. As they grow more confident you can give them small challenges – 'Can you make a long stitch/a tiny stitch/a stitch that is loose so that it stands up like a loop?' On one such project I showed the children how to snip these loops at the top when the firework stitching was completed. The children described these as 'jumping-up sparks'.

Learning objectives

My aim is that children should learn:

- that stitching is a form of recording from first-hand observation, and that it offers tactile and textural 2- and 3-dimensional possibilities which can be used to mimic or represent objects or materials;
- to take delight in the variety of colours and textures fabrics, wools and threads offer and to begin to understand what they can expect from them;
- to learn to manipulate relevant tools correctly and safely.

A suggested textile project – pizzas

Pizzas make an excellent first project for many reasons. They are round, which means that a circular embroidery ring to hold the fabric taut forms an ideal frame, and they have a beige-coloured dough base for which the dishcloth fabric is perfect. They are not neat and tidy, but are covered in randomly shaped and positioned foods, so that even children who find cutting and sticking extremely difficult can have success, and they offer a range of textures, shapes and colours so that a variety of fabrics can be used.

This project was devised to give children a range of experiences and techniques including collage, stitching and beadwork. Initial stimulus for discussion is important – looking at photographs of pizzas from packets and in recipe books, studying a selection of raw ingredients used for toppings, a visit to a local pizza house to make pizzas, or making pizzas in school. Discuss the shapes, colours, textures and how foods change when they are cooked; how the cook chooses to place the ingredients on the pizza so that there is a bit of everything everywhere, and how the toppings overlap each other.

The pizzas illustrated began with the children choosing a fabric they thought was suitable for one chosen ingredient. A good way to do this is for them to carry a pizza photograph from the packet over to the fabrics (which, like the wools, I store in different colour ranges) and hold it against different pieces until they find a close match. There is good opportunity for developing vocabulary here ('Is this piece paler or darker than the mushrooms? Is it shiny or matt? Do you think we need a richer brown?', etc.)

I encouraged the children to cut several examples of the same topping (e.g. sliced mushrooms, strips of green pepper) and place them in a balanced but random position on the stockinette background before gluing them. For this I gave them a small dab of Copydex on a plastic dish, and showed them how to use the glue-spreader vertically to apply the tiniest dab (we called it a 'whisper of Copydex') on to the background rather than the cut-out shape. The shape was then stuck on to the dab. The huge advantage of Copydex is that so little is needed, and although it holds immediately, the pieces can be peeled off and repositioned. There is also no washing up – the dried residue can simply be peeled off leaving a beautifully clean dish or spreader. If on the hands or table, children can just rub the surface, whereupon the Copydex turns to solid rubber and can be thrown away. But do protect clothes – it is difficult to remove from them without a chewing-gum stain remover.

The same procedure was followed for the other toppings, and gradually the pizzas filled up with red pepper, ham, pepperoni, anchovies and numerous other delicacies. The children then used wool stitching in different yellows to stitch on grated cheese. I encouraged them to bring the needle up in blank areas of the dishcloth, and keep the stitches about 2cm in length. They enjoyed the effect of the yellow wool against other colours as they stitched over the toppings.

Thinner green thread and smaller stitches were then used to sew on sprinkled herbs. This was good preparation for sewing on the beads, because to do this a thinner needle is needed to sew through the hole in the bead, and I wanted the children to have some experience of manipulating these smaller needles and finer thread. There was great excitement over the beads. I found some real dried sweetcorn (on a necklace in a charity shop) and some oval black beads for olives. The latter had very large holes and some children were able to cut a tiny sliver of red or green felt to slip through the hole after sewing the beads on, to make stuffed olives. We decided that the beads were not shiny enough for black olives, so as a final touch the children took turns to paint them with a layer of clear nail varnish.

Finally the pizzas were removed from the frames and mounted on the backs of paper plates with the frayed edges wrapped underneath. The plates gave them a domed shape reminiscent of a real pizza.

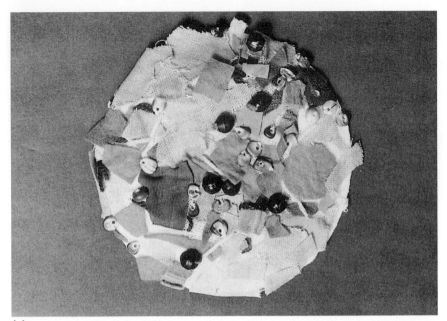

(a)

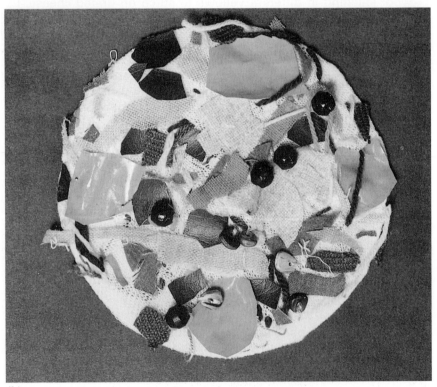

(b)

(c)

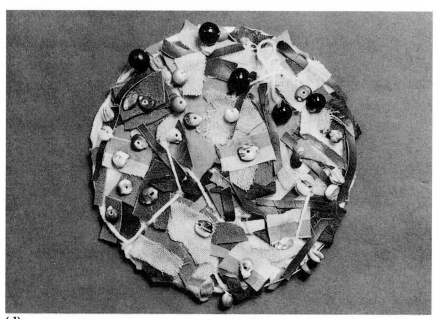

(d)

Figure 12.2 (a), (b), (c) & (d) *Sewn pizzas by Sam Harrison, Byron van Deventer, Tatiana Hoecklin and Tiffany Worrall all aged 5 years, and aged 4 years, Horler's Pre-Preparatory school, Camberton Cambridge*

Cross-curricular links

The above project provides links with design technology (designing pizzas, cooking, designing menus), different writing styles (setting out a recipe, describing the taste and texture of a hot pizza), science (how foods change in heat), and geography (origins of pizzas, where the ingredients grow, which plants fabrics and threads are made from, where wool comes from).

Pointers for art in the early years

- Children should be helped to realise that art is a necessary part of our culture and inheritance, and that humans have an inbuilt instinct to create.
- Children should learn through as wide a range of stimuli, media and techniques as possible, exploring, discovering and delighting in their variety.
- Children should be encouraged to plan, design, discuss, evaluate and modify their artwork.
- Children should see that they, too, are artists.
- Sound organisation and practical management of materials bring about better results and a safer classroom environment.
- The way the teacher respects, handles and stores art materials, and responds to art, gives a strong message to children.
- Art is interwoven with every other curriculum area.

References

Gombrich, E.H. (1987) *Art and Illusion*, Oxford: Phaidon Press.

Jameson and Kidd, *Pre-School Play*, (Publisher and year of publication unknown).

Lark-Horovitz, B (1967)*Understanding Children's Art for Better Teaching*, Colombus, OH: Charles Merrill.

Recommended books

Davidson, R. (1993)*What is Art?*, Oxford: Oxford University Press.
   (Written by the owner of a Cambridge art gallery, this lavishly illustrated, easily read book helps children and teachers find out what art is for, and covers all arts and crafts, stimulating wonder and appreciation.)

Edwards, B. (1993)*Drawing on the Right Side of the Brain*, London: HarperCollins.

(Fascinating and readable book detailing practical ways to unlock the human ability to draw).

McQueen, D. (1998) *Art and Craft Skills – Painting* (Adviser – Jane Bower), London: Franklin Watts.
(Colourful, practical book giving a wide range of painting techniques and ideas for children.)

Mein, A. (1995) *The Art of Annemieke Mein*, Tunbridge Wells: Search Press Ltd.
(Beautifully detailed photographs of stunning 2- and 3-D textile forms based on the natural world. Children find the work breathtaking.)

Rogers, M. (1984) *On Pottery and Porcelain*, Sherbourne: Alphabooks.
(Beautifully made handbuilt pots, mostly based on natural forms, to inspire children.)

CHAPTER 13

'How many toes has a newt?'

SCIENCE IN THE EARLY YEARS

Penny Coltman

Rich in first hand explorations, science in the early years can be seen as one of the most dynamic areas of the early years curriculum. The intention of this chapter is to consider some of the factors which can support the development of secure scientific concepts and process skills in young children. The desirability of accessing and building upon existing ideas and understandings will be discussed, together with some practical implications of this approach. In addition the aim of the chapter is to endorse the value of both real and imaginary contexts in promoting learning as they encourage children to see both purpose in their activities and usefulness in their new-found knowledge and capabilities.

On entering an early years classroom to observe a science lesson the sight I saw was 20-something children, draped in various pieces of fabric and seated in a large circle. My initial reaction was to suppose that a mistake had been made; the class was not carrying out a science activity after all, but was engaged in a rehearsal for some sort of performance. A closer look, however, revealed that this was a lesson about observing and describing the properties of materials. The children were absorbed in a role-play activity in which they had been carried away to a distant land by a magic carpet. In true Arabian Nights fashion they had been transported to the palace of a king who had been cursed. Unable to see or feel beautiful objects, the king was dependent upon the children to tell him about the wonderful things that they had brought for him. Only by helping the king to sort the materials they had brought into various enchanted circles (each labelled with different, descriptive vocabulary) could the children help to lift the dreadful curse.

This lesson, planned and led by a talented trainee teacher, was magical in more ways than one. It showed a rare appreciation that although science may be viewed as a progression towards an understanding of perceived realities, the teaching of science in the early years can and indeed should adhere to those principles which are understood to promote any effective learning in young children, not least of which is a substantial use of imagination.

Working with children's ideas

If we accept a holistic model of learning in the early years, then the notion of science as an independent curriculum subject becomes somewhat spurious. As children learn in a wide-ranging, multi-disciplinary manner they constantly explore the phenomena and workings of their world and make increasing sense of their findings. The interpretations that children make may be anomalous, based on literal constructions or idiosyncratic connections, but nevertheless such ideas are remarkably resistant to change, and children will hold on to them even when subsequent experiences provide conflicting evidence (Driver, 1983).

This awareness of the potential variety of ideas that young children may bring with them to the classroom leads to a constructivist approach to the teaching of science, which involves a constant cycle of accessing and modifying children's ideas. Harlen (1999) describes constructivism as a model in which learning is seen as changing pupils' own ideas into ones consistent with the scientific view. A key element of teaching any aspect of science through this approach is consequently the range of strategies used in eliciting responses from children which illuminate existing understandings.

Rachel Sparks Linfield and Paul Warwick discuss some of the ways in which children's ideas can be accessed in their chapter on assessment, Chapter 5, but it is worthwhile here to consider some additional strategies for gaining insights into children's thinking. Conversation is certainly a powerful tool, especially when children feel comfortable in the company of the interviewer. It can be even more enlightening to place children in role for the purposes of assessment. When in role children respond with confidence. In role anything is possible. In a realm of fantasy there are no right or wrong answers – anything goes. The children on the flying carpet at the beginning of this chapter were at that boundary beyond which imaginative worlds become at least a temporary 'reality', so intense was their captivation. Such scenarios allow and encourage children to venture ideas within a safe context. The bounds of possibilities are known to become elastic as anything goes in a fantasy world.

Similarly children can be placed in role as directors. Such devices are now commonplace in mathematics lessons in which children correct the counting errors made by a cuddly but inept puppet, thus demonstrating their own proficiencies. It is not hard to see how this strategy could be transferred to science as the same character, for example, plans his meals or plants his garden. Lesley Hendy, in Chapter 6 about the value of dramatic activity, describes a similarly effective lesson in which children give advice to Mrs Pig about the relative merits of the various materials her children have chosen to use to build their houses. The skilful presentation of this context gives an urgency to the response reminiscent of the 'It's behind you!' moments in a pantomime, guaranteed to motivate and enthuse young learners.

Collaborative storytelling can be used in much the same way. In a recent lesson the class teacher started to tell a class of 6-year-old children a story about themselves. They had gone on a school trip and become hopelessly lost, eventually finding themselves in some dark and mysterious caves. All the members of the class were woven into the story, delighting the audience as references were made to their own characteristics. The storytelling then became much more interactive, with children confidently adding details to their own adventures; at this point the assessment purpose of the activity became clear. The teacher was exploring children's ideas about the variety of light sources. As the story progressed through the gloomy tunnels, each child in turn was encouraged to find new ways of providing light:

Teacher: As the children turned around the corner they could hardly see their way, but luckily Robert found a . . .
Robert: A torch!
Teacher: This made all the difference, but unfortunately the batteries in the torch were not strong, and the children had not gone far when the torch went out. Fortunately Elli found a . . .
Elli: A candle!

Language and science

One of the difficulties in making assessments about children's understandings is that conceptual development and language development may not be in step. Science is a discipline that is heavily dependent on precise definitions; indeed one of the indicators of progression in science is the use of increasingly sophisticated and refined vocabulary. In the early years children's attempts to describe or explain a phenomenon may well be open to misinterpretation as they search in vain for the most appropriate language to use. An example of this is often encountered when young children, playing outside on a sunny day, use the word 'reflection' to describe the shape they see on the ground. It may indeed be the case that there is some confusion of concepts, and that children have the idea that the ground is somehow behaving as a mirror. Alternatively it may be that in the search for a word to describe the observation, children have used one that they have found useful before in describing 'an image of themselves'. In other words, use of inappropriate language cannot always be assumed to indicate a genuine misconception, but may be more indicative of the problem many will have faced when trying to order a drink in a foreign language. We use the best word available in our limited vocabulary – and it may not prove to be quite as accurate as we would like! Such difficulties are evidence not of *misconceptions*, but rather of concepts which are still unrefined. Further experience of both mirrors and shadows will be needed before the two words are understood to relate to distinct and unrelated phenomena.

Further illustrations of children's ideas can be found in the reports published by the SPACE (Science Processes and Concept Exploration) project which was a joint project between the Centre for Educational Studies, King's College and the Centre for Research in Primary Science and Technology, Liverpool University (SPACE, 1990–94). Many examples are cited, and often the source of misconception or confusion is explored. Young children, for example, frequently expressed the idea that an object is seen because of something coming from the eyes. Osborne (1995) describes how this idea is extended by children to imagine that the eyes direct some ray towards objects to make them visible and goes on to cite examples of everyday speech which implicitly reinforce this notion; we 'look at' books, 'cast our gaze', 'have looks thrown at us' or even 'look right through people'. We might also speculate on the effect of cartoons such as those in which superheroes send laser beams from their eyes in order to see in the dark or zap the enemy.

Another example is commonly found as young children describe materials and appear to demonstrate misconceptions over the use of the words 'soft' and 'smooth'. If we try to clarify the meaning of the word 'smooth' the difficulty becomes apparent. This is a problem of definition. An explanation, for example, of the word 'smooth' is almost certain to focus on negatives. A smooth surface does not have bumps, it is not rough and it is not creased or crumpled. This is a confusion that only experience will resolve. As children handle hard pebbles that are smooth or soft knitted fabrics that are soft but textured, the distinction between the two terms becomes less ambiguous. So as questioning reveals a greater insight into children's understandings the importance of language development in early years science becomes ever more apparent.

Rosemary Feasey (Feasey, 2000) lists three major challenges of language development in the early years which are relevant to science:

'• to introduce language that is directly related to immediate, concrete, everyday, hands-on experiences;
• to move children on, so that they are able to use the same scientific language in a wider range of contexts that are removed by time and space;
• to develop scientific language that is conceptually based, that is, linked to ideas that may be difficult to understand, for example, the movement of particles in dissolving and changes of state.

If children are to move from concrete to abstract in their thinking, or from generic to specific language, they must be given the opportunity to manipulate and experience objects, materials and phenomena and to talk about them (see Figure 13.1). The basic words of naming and describing become the tools of the future. The everyday contexts of making a collage of shiny, curly or transparent materials, or of using paints of different textures and thicknesses, provide rich contexts for the development of this vital language. As adults talk about activities, explaining or questioning, the use of new language is modelled in an appropriate and secure context. As vocabulary is introduced it is helpful to draw attention to it, encouraging children to repeat and enjoy the new words. Using new language in questions then helps to consolidate and ensure understanding:

Figure 13.1 *May, aged 3, explores materials as she makes a batch of dough*

Can you think of something that is shiny to use for the robot's buttons? What sort of material do you think we should use for the baby fairy's bed?

Developing skills

Science is a subject with two complementary aspects. The exploration of areas of knowledge encountered; materials, natural sciences or physical processes provide the contexts for the development of skills, such as observation, questioning, communication and using measurement, which in turn will facilitate the acquisition of knowledge. Later in the primary phase the skills of science will be combined to form investigations, but in the early years they will largely be developed independently. An analogy can be made with the way in which children learn to play a team game such as football. Skills such as kicking and aiming a ball, passing and receiving, must be practised before a team game can be played. Eventually these will all be drawn together, but only with a great deal of adult direction. It will be some time before children are ready to organise themselves into coherent teams. In the same way the skills related to scientific exploration, which will eventually be woven together, need to be separately honed. Later they will be brought together as children carry out their first investigations, but the structure of these will be heavily teacher directed. Careful teacher guidance, gradually involving greater degrees of pupil initiatives, will allow the investigation process to become internalised, until by the end of the primary phase, or thereabouts, children are ready to plan and carry out fair tests with independence and confidence.

The first stage in the field of measurement, for example, is language which categorises by size: big, little, thick or thin. Progression is seen as children begin to use comparative vocabulary; smaller, taller, etc. By the end of their reception year most children have begun to use arbitrary units, introducing a quantitative aspect to their measuring skills. The length of a table can be measured in toy cars and the weight of a teddy can be determined by counting the conkers which will balance it. Stories such as that of the king whose new bed is measured by the strides of carpenters of vastly differing sizes are used to help children to understand the limitations of such methods, and the conkers and shells will soon be replaced by uniform units, such as plastic cubes, counters or dominoes. This is then the precursor to the introduction of standard units. Over the remaining primary years children will then become adept in measuring using increasingly sophisticated resources, to ever finer degrees of accuracy.

Daisy, featured on the front cover of this book (and in Figure 13.2), is 4

Figure 13.2 *Daisy investigates a newt*

years old. She is able to count small numbers fairly accurately and knows something about measure. The newt, pictured with her, was perhaps unfortunate enough to be discovered during an outside play session. Daisy gently held the animal on her hands, carefully examining it from every perspective and expressing great delight as she noticed its tiny feet. 'I can see its toes' she said. 'I am going to count them.' Then she spotted a cardboard teaching clock on the ground nearby and carefully placed the newt in the middle of it. 'Look,' she announced emphatically, 'The newt weighs ten!'

The role of questioning

The brief interaction described demonstrates that Daisy is confident in making observations. She is able to look closely and to talk about what she sees. In addition she is confidently exploring the idea of quantifying her observations. She is also able to apply the knowledge she has already gained of animals, to inform her exploration of the newt, looking for legs, toes, eyes and, less successfully, ears. As Daisy makes such connections between new and previous experiences she will gradually develop and refine her understandings and will begin to be able to make reasoned assumptions.

Early years curriculum guidance tends to place great emphasis on the importance of encouraging children to ask questions. The thinking behind this is presumably to foster the sense of enquiry that will lead to cognitive and conceptual developments as illustrated by Daisy. However, children need no encouragement to be curious; they spend their lives in exploration and experimentation. Observation in an early years setting, however, generally provides fewer instances of children asking questions than might be anticipated. Part of the reason for this may be that the concepts that children are encountering and developing, by reason of their newness, are rarely within their confident linguistic grasp, as previously discussed. To formulate a question also requires a degree of familiarity with possibilities gained by experiences that are as yet beyond young learners. So the role of questioner in the early years classroom could be described as one predominantly to be adopted by the educator rather than the children.

We now have to accept that children's explorations alone are not going to result in the acquisition of secure and accurate concepts. We can take a child to water, but that will not make him learn!

> Sand and water play is often promoted and justified as supporting children's learning in science, but we can easily overestimate what young children learn through these activities. In fact our expectations are often contradictory. While we fail to recognise the quality or significance of the child's observational skills in their day-to-day interaction with the world, we nevertheless expect them to discover phenomena whenever we make the relevant resources available to them.
>
> (Siraj-Blatchford and MacLeod-Brudenell, 1999: 33)

Learning in relation to specific objectives will occur only when the adults supporting an activity are clear about the learning intentions of that activity, and promote relevant conversations, rich in carefully framed questions. This questioning can support learning in a number of respects:

- It presents a linguistic role model, showing children how to frame appropriate questions.
  'I wonder what would happen if . . .' 'How could we . . . ?'

- It can present a model of autonomous learning which is characteristic of science. If we want to find something out, then we can do something about it. Children are shown how to be pro-active learners.
  'What do you think the snails would feel like?'

- It directs children's attention to those activities and aspects of activities which will lead to teaching opportunities.
  'Where do you think the water has gone?'

- It can reinforce new vocabulary.
  'What else do you think the magnet might be attracted to?'

- It can promote thinking and problem solving skills
  'How could you change the bubble mix?'

- It can help children to make connections between new and existing experiences.
  'What do you think has happened to the chocolate? Think about the ice cubes we watched yesterday.'

Questioning is also one way of introducing ideas that gently challenge children's existing cognition, leading children towards new understandings. This is sometimes described as creating 'dissonance', and it is particularly effective when the new thinking opens up, in a manner which is clear to the learner, new possibilities and/or explanations (Harlen, 1999).

Here is an example to illustrate this. Daniel was attempting to balance a short, flat piece of wood on top of three cones. He carefully lined up the three cones in a row and placed the piece of wood on the top of them. When the wood immediately fell down, he checked that the linear arrangement of the cones was as straight as could be, and then tried the balance again.

Daniel's teacher then replaced the piece of wood with a cube and asked Daniel whether he could use the cube and cones to build a model rocket. Both the chosen context and the constraints of the blocks available now strongly suggested that the cones should be arranged in a group under the cube rather than in a line. As Daniel arrived at this conclusion, and successfully balanced the cube on the cones, he discovered the concept of a tripod. His previous understanding, that linear arrangements are generally more likely to be successful, was challenged and found wanting. Armed with his new discovery, he returned to the original piece of wood, arranged the cones in a tight group and successfully managed the balance. A further element of metacognition, as Daniel showed an awareness of his learning and its potential usefulness, was seen as he was later observed taking great delight in applying the idea of tripods made from cones or pyramids to the constructions he created during free play. New possibilities had been created not only for methods of achieving balance, but for the cones and pyramids themselves which had previously been used exclusively to decorate or punctuate the tops of towers. (For more details see Coltman, Anghileri and Petyaea, (2002.)

The importance of purposeful science

Writing about ways of helping children become confident mathematicians, Whitebread (2000) cites the observation that mathematics is often bereft of any real, meaningful or supporting context as a prime feature contributing to difficulties experienced by young children. Children complain that mathematics 'isn't about anything'. Sadly, in many instances the same criticism could be levelled at the teaching of science. Too often children are taught procedures or pieces of knowledge, but are not presented with opportunities to use them in any meaningful way. They consequently have little or no appreciation of the value of their learning or the possibilities for its use. There is no notion of the model of teaching and learning suggested by a popular brand of electrical goods: 'The appliance of science'.

Failure to provide opportunities for children to use their learning prevents them from demonstrating anything other than superficial understanding. The development of secure concepts is manifest when children are able to show metacognition, transferring learning to new situations, as Daniel used the tripod. Annie, aged 6, demonstrated this beautifully when she announced after a lesson on simple circuit building: 'I know what I could do – I could put landing lights on that plane I built' (see Figure 13.3).

Creative tasks can also support learning by providing a focus for relevant conversation. As children weave with fabric samples they will discuss texture, colour, thickness, flexibility and appearance. The selection of materials for a woven seascape or tapestry of autumn colours invites discernment and gives real purpose to discrimination. As they make salt dough models of faces children will use the vocabulary of features and expressions and will describe the feel of the dough as they manipulate it in their hands and the

Figure 13.3 *Annie's drawing shows how she used her knowledge of circuits to add landing lights to a plane made from a construction kit*

forces used as it is stretched, flattened and squeezed. Motivation and engagement and consequent meaningful learning are again promoted by the goal of the finished artefact.

The manufacture of artefacts is an underrated route to assessment. As children make things they demonstrate their knowledge not only by the conversation elicited by the task, but also by their representations. Children constructing imaginary animals, for example, will happily discuss the location in which it might be found, the appearance of its legs, head and wings and whether or not it can run, swim or fly. Less obvious ideas are explored: Can this animal talk or sing? What other animals might it like to live with? Would you want one in your garden? In this way children are not only demonstrating an appropriate use of subject-related vocabulary as they name and describe features, but are also communicating a broader understanding of interrelationships, structure and function.

Using the outdoor environment

One particularly encouraging aspect of early years curricula is the developing emphasis on the use of the outdoor environment. By exploring the natural world around them children encounter a wealth of constantly changing phenomena illustrating an infinitely diverse range of concepts. Science is placed firmly within a real, relevant and vibrant context that is familiar and yet constantly changing and endlessly fascinating. It is through such explorations that the attitudes of responsibility and respect towards both the living and non-living environments can be engendered, as children learn to look closely, to 'not disturb' and to handle with care.

Simple trails can be set up that encourage children to develop awareness of a range of environmental features and the use of different senses and methods in making observations. Sensory trails have stations which encourage children to explore experiences: 'Shuffle the leaves with your feet. What can you hear?' 'Rub a leaf between your fingers. Enjoy the lovely smell.' Other trails invite the use of apparatus: 'Use a mirror to look around the corner. Can you see the spider's web?' 'Look at the moss through a magnifier.' The joys of such discoveries are compounded by opportunities to share findings with others, and it is not hard to imagine how such ideas can be built into opportunities for children to plan and make trails for others to enjoy.

As schools develop ideas of the 'outdoor classroom' many are including permanent and semi-permanent features to encourage children to enjoy and care for school grounds. Many schools now have gazebos and outdoor working tables to facilitate outdoor, learning and mazes, tunnels and huts made from living willow wands are sprouting in profusion. Wildlife areas vary from formally designated sites, with fences, pond and seats to a log in an unmown patch of grass with a tree swathed in knitting wool: 'What can you add to the weaving tree?'

But desirable as these may be, environmental education is not dependent on anything so structured, and as always it is often the simplest of ideas which are the most effective. The construction of a 'playground for a mouse' or a 'rain shelter for a fairy' are examples of the types of activities, which foster imagination and creativity and remain in memories for a very long time. Intense concentration is evident as children select natural materials for their tasks, supplementing them by sequins, twisted aluminium foil goblets or a smooth, round pebble placed as a throne, and rich and relevant conversation flows. This is 'materials chosen for their uses' in the real sense, with a purposeful context leading to autonomous and self-directed learning as children meet their own self-imposed challenges.

The following passage is taken from the book *The Hundred Languages of Children* (Malaguzzi, 1996) that accompanies a remarkable touring exhibition presenting a series of projects carried out by children in Municipal Infant–Toddler Centres and Pre-schools in Reggio Emilia, Italy. It epitomises a pedagogical approach that is based on an enquiring and aesthetic appreciation of the natural world and the importance of listening to children. Both uncertainty and amazement are valued as integral to any learning and especially to learning in science. The smallest of everyday contexts is seen as rich in opportunities for scientific enquiry and deduction. This excerpt describes what happens when a group of children explore a puddle:

> The children's excitement . . . becomes astonished and vociferous when they notice the play of light, of colours, of transparencies in the puddle and the reflection of their images and that immediate part of the world around them which the puddle mirrors back at them. From that moment on the game opens up and expands, changes level, and draws in all the children's intelligence. And this intelligence stimulates children's observations, thoughts, and intuitions, and leads the children closer and closer to convincing laws of physics and perception, even when – and perhaps above all – they use their intelligence playfully to contemplate situations and even worlds that are turned upside down, with everything this implies.
>
> (Malaguzzi (1996, pp. 88-9)

Pointers for early years science

- Science is a creative area of learning which can be taught through rich, imaginative contexts.
- Educators must take into account the diversity of children's previous experiences and the consequent variation in their understandings.
- Language development is a crucial consideration in effective science teaching.
- Each of the process skills related to scientific investigation has its own strands of progression and should be separately addressed.
- The educator has a vital role in promoting scientific enquiry through questioning.
- Children should have opportunities to use newly acquired skills and knowledge in practical and purposeful contexts.

References

With special thanks to Lydia Toumazou, whose lesson is referred to at the beginning of this chapter.

Coltman, P., Anghileri, J. and Petyaea, P. (2002) 'Scaffolding learning through meaningful tasks and adult interaction', *Early Years*, 22, 1.

Driver, R. (1983) *The Pupil as Scientist?*, Milton Keynes: Open University Press.

Feasey, R. (2000) 'Children's language in science', in M. de Boo (ed.) *Science 3–6 Laying the Foundations in the Early Years*, Hatfield: ASE Publications.

Harlen, W. (1999) *Effective Teaching of Science. A Review of Research*, Edinburgh: SCRE Publications.

Malaguzzi, L. (1996) 'Puddle Intelligence', in T. Filippini and V. Vecchi (eds) *The Hundred Languages of Children*, Reggio Emilia, Italy: Reggio Children.

Osborne, J. (1995) 'Science from a child's perspective', in S. Atkinson and M. Fleer (eds) *Science with Reason*, London: Hodder & Stoughton.

Siraj-Blatchford, J. and MacLeod-Brudenell, I. (1999) *Supporting Science, Design and Technology in the Early Years*, Buckingham: Open University Press.

SPACE: *Science Processes and Concept Exploration* (1990–94) King's College, London and Liverpool University Press.

Whitebread, D. (2000) 'Teaching numeracy: helping children become confident mathematicians', in D. Whitebread (ed.) *The Psychology of Teaching and Learning in the Primary School*, London: Routledge/Falmer.

Further Reading

de Boo, M. (ed.) (2000) *Science 3–6 Laying the Foundations in the Early Years*, Hatfield: The Association for Science Education.

CHAPTER 14

'Maths – is that a kind of game for grown-ups?'

UNDERSTANDING NUMBER IN THE EARLY YEARS

Annie Owen and Laurie Rousham

'Maths – is that a kind of game for grown-ups?' asked 3-year-old Mark. He had heard the visitor say he 'did maths' and wasn't sure what it was. Unfortunately, Mark's rosy pre-school view did not survive his encounter with school mathematics, yet his guess comes closer to the reality of the professional mathematician. Young children love to count, to put shapes together (which will fit, which will balance) and to put their dolls and other toys in order. This they do to explore their world, usually without prompting. Adult mathematicians work in a similar way, exploring their world in a way not very different from pre-school children's play. They try things out and if they don't work they try something slightly different. If they do work, they get excited and write about it in an academic journal (not that different from running to tell Mummy!). Why is it that the majority of us lose that sense of wonder and of fun?

Instead, mathematics has become an area of great concern to teachers, parents and the general public. For many, their own learning of the subject ended with feelings of confusion or failure. Adults pass these feelings on to young children through such statements as 'I could never do maths' or 'I hated maths!', but teachers of the early years can also have a more directly negative effect.

When we feel insecure, whatever the situation, we play safe. A drowning person will not use a swimming stroke he has only just learnt to get himself to dry land. Less dramatically, a cook will not experiment with a new recipe if important guests are expected. Similarly, there is a temptation in the classroom for the teacher who feels insecure mathematically to fall back on traditional procedures and teaching methods.

Unfortunately, most traditional methods are very didactic in style and regard the young child as a blank sheet on to which the teacher writes mathematical knowledge. Hilary Shuard put this very well in the 1985 Horizon television programme *Twice Five Plus the Wings of a Bird* for the BBC:

> We've had very much in mathematics education the idea that the child is an empty vessel and you pour in mathematics. Often I think we have thought of the child as a rather leaky vessel and mathematics has flowed out as well as in!

Such an approach will not only ignore the understanding a child already has about mathematics but also assumes that all children will learn the subject in the same way, in the same order and at the same rate. A short time spent in an infant mathematics class soon shows the deficits in this model of learning! Shuard continues:

> But I think that, if we are to be more successful in helping children to learn mathematics, we need to see them as people who think about their experiences and build on them. . . . We are coming to see children as mathematical thinkers in their own right, trying to develop their thinking, and we need to provide the experiences from which they can build mathematics for themselves.

This so-called 'emergent' approach, which begins with the child and not with the mathematics to be learned, is the focus of our chapter. It is a methodology which has developed gradually from the days of the Nuffield Mathematics Project (1968), through the recommendations of the Cockcroft Report (1982) and the guidance of the PrIME (Primary Initiatives In Mathematics Education) project (1986–89), and is reflected in the *Curriculum Guidance for the Foundation Stage* (QCA, 2000):' effective teaching requires: Practitioners who help children to see themselves as mathematicians, and develop positive attitudes and dispositions towards their learning.' The National Curriculum also emphasises mathematical process, that is the need for children to ask their own questions, to explore them and to form their own conclusions. Whitebread (1995) has produced a useful review of the essential elements of this 'emergent mathematics' approach together with the psychological research evidence about children's learning which crucially underpins it. In this chapter, we have concentrated on the area of *number*, this being the area causing most concern to the new teacher, but the issues which we raise are pertinent to all areas of mathematics. The chapter is organised under two headings:

- *Understanding, knowledge and application:* How do children come to understand number concepts, know important number facts and learn to use their understanding and knowledge to solve number problems?
- *Learning factors and the teacher's role:* How can we facilitate this understanding, knowledge and learning?

Understanding, knowledge and application

Trying to untangle the three areas of understanding, knowledge and application may be seen by some as fruitless. Each is vitally important and all are interdependent and supportive. Understanding addition without ever being able to remember such number bonds as 5+3=8 would be extremely limiting. Knowing multiplication tables without understanding what multiplication is would be pretty meaningless. Solving a multiplication problem is impossible without a recognition of the operation required and is tedious if the answer cannot be easily remembered or computed.

However, the failure to recognise the distinction between these three elements will lead to poor teaching and hence poor learning. Although the children may see their mathematical experiences holistically, the teacher needs to keep the distinctions in the forefront of his or her planning in order to ensure balance. Overemphasis on rote learning of facts and procedures produces children who cannot adapt or use their knowledge. Traditional drill and practice methods are notorious for such failure. Children who understand what they are doing but have poor memory skills are less handicapped, as there are always other ways to reach an answer, but the tedium of relying on elementary procedures is very demotivating. Such an approach gave the 'discovery' learning of the 1960s such a bad reputation.

Therefore, let us take a short look at each area separately.

Understanding

The world of pre-school children is full of numbers. Whether setting the table, feeding the ducks, sharing their sweets or building with blocks, they are involved not just in counting and pre-counting skills but are also making assumptions about how numbers work. They begin to see partitions in numbers (e.g. their six building bricks can be split into three red and three blue or perhaps four green and two yellow – the beginnings of addition and subtraction), to recognise that sometimes sharing doesn't work exactly (you can't share five sweets between yourself and your sister, but you can share four and give one to the dog), and other simple beginnings of pattern and structure.

Take the 'Five Little Ducks' rhyme:

Five little ducks went out one day
over the hill and far away.
Mother duck said, 'Quack, quack, quack, quack'
but only four little ducks came back.

On the surface, this is a 'counting back' rhyme, but subtraction can be introduced through such questioning as 'So, how many little ducks have gone altogether now?' (two, say), 'How many has mother duck got left?' (three). 'So, what is five little ducks take away two little ducks?' Martin Hughes (1986) found that children as young as age 3 can add and subtract small numbers, as long as the problem is one which has meaning for them. His book, *Children and Number* is an essential read for anyone involved in early years education.

Children do not always need adults to spark thinking in this way. They can automatically make connections and form their own conclusions. They cannot always verbalise them in a form adults recognise, as they lack formal mathematical language, and their assumptions are often incorrect. However, they slowly build up their own personal view of the world of numbers, their properties and their interconnections. Take Tim (aged 5 years, 6 months), who was playing with a calculator and wrote down spontaneously the addition sums reproduced in Figure 14.1.

At this point he brought his paper to an adult and asked 'What's the next number?' Tim was exploring within a free play situation. He clearly knew how to recognise and write 100 and this was most likely his starting point. (It is worth reflecting on the fact that the National Numeracy Strategy (DfEE, 1999) does not expect children to work with 100 until Year 2, 1000 until Year 3 and 10,000 until Year 4!)

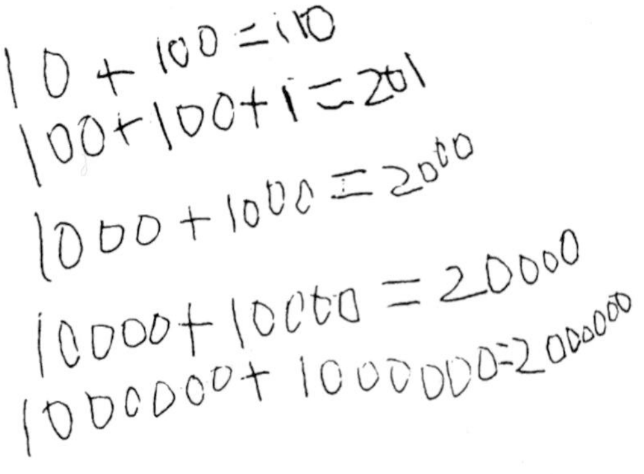

Figure 14.1 *Addition sums produced by Tim (aged 5 years, 6 months) while playing with a calculator*

Barbara Jaworski (1988) views this type of activity from a constructivist stance, quoting two principles of knowledge and learning:

1 Knowledge is actively constructed by the cognising subject, not passively received from the environment.

2 Coming to know is an adaptive process that organises one's experiential world; it does not discover an independent, pre-existing world outside the mind of the knower.

Teachers of mathematics at all levels know only too well that, no matter how careful their explanations, children can misunderstand a concept, make incorrect connections or just plainly 'fail to learn'. Unless they can incorporate the new idea into their existing view of mathematics (what constructivists would call their schema), and hence make sense of it, children are very unlikely to take it on board. The old adage 'you can take a horse to water but you can't make it drink' fits perfectly! Look at the example in Figure 14.2, in which a 6-year-old is counting the sides (edges) and corners (vertices) of some plastic shapes, a fairly common activity. Dean has filled in a teacher-prepared grid.

As you can see, Dean appears to be able to count corners correctly, but not sides. What might be going on here? Well, one point of view might be that we already knew Dean isn't very able and this proves it. Alternatively, he could be making mistakes out of sheer wilful naughtiness. Fortunately, his

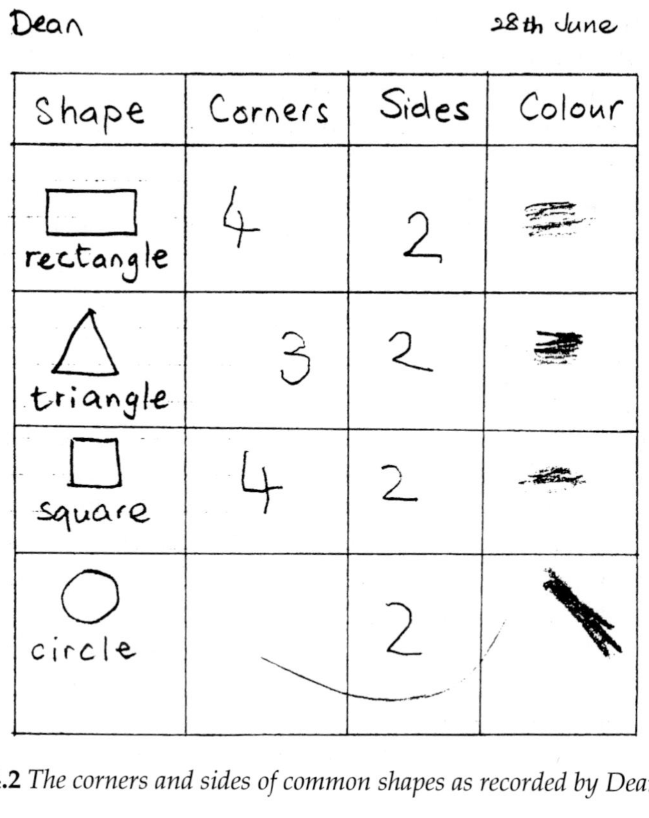

Dean   28th June

Shape	Corners	Sides	Colour
rectangle	4	2	
triangle	3	2	
square	4	2	
circle		2	

Figure 14.2 *The corners and sides of common shapes as recorded by Dean, aged 6*

teacher chose not to operate on the basis of either of these views, and instead opened negotiations with him to try and see what he was thinking.

Teacher: Dean, I'm not sure this is right, is it? Do all these different shapes have two sides?

Dean: (Belligerently) Yes.

Teacher: Well, can you get your shapes and show me the two sides?

Dean: (Returning with his set of plastic shapes) Look (holding triangle in one hand and using his other hand to point, he places his index finger in the centre), one . . . (turns shape over) . . . two.

If Dean had been told to 'Go away and do it properly' or to 'Go back and think again' he would perhaps have begun to believe that maths is some strange activity with its own rules that do not accord with common sense. And from his point of view he would have been exactly right! It may be experiences like this that demoralise and undermine the initial confidence with which young children approach mathematics and we have included this exchange to illustrate how sensitive one needs to be in responding to 'mistakes'.

Often children's errors are the best indicators of their thinking and of how conceptual development is coming along. The biggest problem with this 'negotiability' approach is that of teacher time: all teachers are busy and it is difficult to investigate individual pupils' mistakes as thoroughly as we would like. We have all certainly been guilty of saying 'No, go back and do it again' on occasion, particularly if we were trying to attend to another group or hear readers at the time! Nevertheless we recommend negotiation to you whenever you can manage it.

Knowledge

As previously stated, there are mathematical facts and procedures that it is useful for children to know if they are to be confident and competent mathematicians. The controversy comes in deciding which are essential and which can be seen as optional. Being able to multiply a three-digit number by a two-digit number may be seen as useful in a junior child (and in fact can be used to promote understanding – particularly of place value), but not exactly essential in these days of cheap calculators. Also, the teacher must decide when to encourage the children's own methods and when to teach the standard algorithm (as required eventually by the National Numeracy Strategy). At a simpler level, take subtraction facts and the following short conversation (pupil is in reception):

Teacher:	What's twelve take away seven?
Pupil:	(Five-second pause) Five.
Teacher:	How did you do that?
Pupil:	Well, I knew that two sixes make twelve, so if I took one six away it would be six. But it's twelve take away seven, so that would be one more than six. But like I said before, um, twelve take away six would be six, so it would be one less than six, so it must be five.

The teacher's eventual aim for the pupil is that he or she be able to recall automatically the number fact 12–7=5, and will most likely be engaging the pupil in practical activities involving counting out twelve objects, removing seven (counting again) and finally counting the remainder. The pupil may also be encouraged to use his or her fingers and count backwards. Much consolidation and practice will be done to ensure that the pupil eventually attains the required 'instant recall'. Yet this child is thinking on a much more sophisticated level, and needs encouraging to build on that present ability. The failure to do so can lead to lack of self-confidence (as teacher always does it in only one way, then my way must be wrong) and boredom. Ian Thompson (1992) describes children as old as 10 and 11 relying on simple counting strategies to solve arithmetic problems, most likely because they lack the confidence to do it any other way. Our own experiences of researching top juniors' knowledge and application of multiplication facts shows that less able children constantly revert to counting strategies when in a stressful situation (e.g. being interviewed by a stranger!).

To show the crippling effects of lack of confidence in maths, look at the following subtraction, done by 7-year-old Katy, who has made a very common error, and the subsequent discussion with Laurie.

$$\begin{array}{r} 23 \\ -18 \\ \hline 15 \\ \hline \end{array}$$

Laurie:	Hello, can I talk to you about what you are doing?
Katy:	Yes.
Laurie:	What are these? What do you have to do?
Katy:	You have to . . . you have to take this away from that.
Laurie:	Tell me about this one. What numbers are these?
Katy:	Twenty-three . . . take away eighteen.
Laurie:	Twenty-three take away eighteen. Right. So how did you do it?

Katy: Well, you say eight take away three is . . . five, and two take away one is one. That's how I did it.

Laurie: Good. I see. Um . . . why do you take the top number away from the bottom here, and then you take away the bottom one here . . . that's what I was wondering.

Katy: That's . . . that's just what you have to do.

Laurie: How do you know when to do what, that's . . .

Katy: (interrupting)You have to always take away the smaller number . . . away from the bigger number, that's why.

Laurie: Why do you have to always take away the smaller number, do you think?

Katy: I don't know, that's the way my teacher told me to do it.

Laurie: But why do you think?

Katy: (laughs) Teacher told me to do it!

Laurie: And . . . this answer, fifteen, twenty-three take away eighteen leaves fifteen . . .

Katy: Oh, it isn't right, I know it isn't right.

Laurie took mercy on Katy at this point, but she was a bright child who knew perfectly well that the answer she had written down was wrong. Parents sometimes ask 'Why do you spend all this time trying to get them to understand, why don't you just TELL them?' Katy's example illustrates why 'because that's the way my teacher told me to do it' is an inadequate reason for doing a sum a certain way. This sort of difficulty does not arise so often when children are encouraged to devise their own methods, perhaps because then they expect to make mistakes and correct them as they go along, adapting their processes as they meet harder numbers and so on. It is a great pity that in many mathematics classrooms, children are so afraid of making mistakes that they will cheerfully write down answers they know to be nonsense. This does not seem to happen so much in other subjects. It is the notion which attaches to maths, that it must be done at great speed but without making any mistakes, that bedevils the teaching of it.

Application

Ever since universal education began, there have been complaints that children cannot apply their mathematical knowledge to varying contexts. When the curriculum is delivered in separate bundles, called subjects, as in almost all secondary schools and now in the majority of primaries, children fail to make connections between them and cannot identify the required mathematical processes even when they have only very recently studied them (Brown and Kuchemann, 1976). Employers complain that mathematics graduates lack application skills, secondary science teachers complain that pupils cannot draw graphs (though they magically produce similar ones in their maths lessons) and primary teachers are familiar with the blank stare when children are given word problems (what is it asking me to do?).

The thematic method

From the time of the Nuffield Project and until the advent of the Literacy and Numeracy hours, British primary teachers attempted to improve the situation through thematic teaching, but many found mathematics difficult to build into their topics. Most have now abandoned the task completely, teaching mathematics as discrete from the rest of the curriculum. At the other extreme, some have sometimes produced links that are so weak that both the mathematics and the topic have suffered. For example, a popular theme within history teaching is that of shopping, which on the surface offers many opportunities for cross-curricular work. When the mathematics is analysed, however, the units are usually too difficult (e.g. using number bases different from our own – not a good idea if the children are still struggling with base 10) or are inappropriate (imperial units no longer forming part of early years mathematics). One solution is to simplify the numbers by giving incorrect prices or measures, but what does this do to the historical accuracy? And can we really say that the mathematics is being applied to a real situation? Similarly, at Key Stage 2, a recent pack of cross-curricular material on the Egyptians included a maze inside a pyramid that a cat must solve in order to reach a mouse. Certainly, this is a mathematical skill worth developing, but it gives children erroneous messages about the structure of the inside of the pyramid!

Cross-curricular themes do exist which contain rich mathematical opportunities – for example, shopping in the present day:

- Items can be sorted – edible/not edible; animal/vegetable; liquid/solid, etc.
- Articles can be compared by weight or weighed if the children are ready.
- Packages can be explored for the packing properties, or cut open to look at the nets.
- Layouts of supermarkets can be explored – plan the best way around with a particular list of items.
- Prices can be entered into a calculator, or into a computer and then printed to make their own till receipts.
- Tallies can be made of when parents shop, who goes with them. etc.

All these have relevance to children, and all the mathematics is worth doing. If the mathematics does not grow naturally out of a topic, and hence has no real purpose, then it is better left out.

Mathematics as a theme

An alternative to both the thematic method and the context-free method is to follow a theme which is particularly rich mathematically and which runs concurrently with other classroom topics. For example, the title 'Bigger and smaller' (Burton et al., 1990) provides impetus to look at how numbers grow (as Tim was doing in our example on page 286), to explore number patterns (early algebra) and shape patterns, to get a better feel for the concepts within measurement and to represent growth pictorially (data-handling). Hence, the mathematics curriculum is united.

Such a topic supports an emergent approach – the teacher cannot be sure where the child will take the investigation and hence cannot dictate in advance the methodology – and can be used to encourage children to devise their own methods of calculation and problem-solving.

Whichever thematic approach is employed, opportunities arise for problem-solving within a context which will interest and hence motivate the children. Mathematics without a context is not only dry for young children, but is also harder to visualise and hence harder to engage with. Visualisation and practical engagement also help children to decode the mathematical language, finding equivalent everyday alternatives.

Real contexts

Even better is to use a real context from the children's environment. For example, if a new playground is to be laid out, children can investigate different arrangements. If a picnic or party is planned, the children can plan the sharing out and the cost – using a calculator, please, not doctoring the numbers! If a party is not planned, organise one for the (mathematical) purpose. You are the teacher, who can make things happen! Suggest to them that they invite the local over-60s club in for a tea party, or their parents, or just another class. Of course, even the most energetic teacher cannot make things happen every day, and hence real problem-solving, as such an approach is often called, cannot be the only method used. With practice, however, you can get into the habit of using the available environment whenever possible to practise the mathematics you have already taught. This is not a time to 'teach' new knowledge, rather a chance for children to enjoy being creative with what they know, and to learn through playing around with numbers. So, for example, you might say:

> I wonder how many bricks there are in this school. How could we find out?

No starter is infallibly successful, but this one has often produced fierce enthusiasm and much incidental learning. Children have all sorts of suggestions as to how to do it. Calculators and clipboards and anything else they want should be provided. We have seen this done with children who were too young to have met multiplication yet, and who began simply by counting every brick in one outside wall. They began to realise that the task was going to be a daunting one, but wanted to persevere. After some time, one pair came running up in tremendous excitement so the whole group (half a class in this instance) was quickly assembled to hear what they had to say – it was obviously very important!

> Look, look, you don't have to count all the bricks! You count how many in a row and if it's twenty-seven, you see how many rows there are and it's that number of twenty-sevens!

They had not been taught multiplication so, faced with a great need, had simply invented it for themselves. Not all of the rest of the group really understood what these two were saying, but some did. It also provided a very useful experience later, when multiplication was being introduced formally: we all built little walls out of bricks and the original pair proudly explained their discovery again.

Another time, this class enjoyed some mathematical play on the parquet floor of the hall. We began the activity by drawing squares of different sizes with chalk on the floor, then counting to see how many of the little wooden rectangular blocks had been enclosed. The original idea was to see whether anyone spotted a relationship between the sizes of squares and the number of blocks, but this didn't happen. Maybe it was too ambitious, but in any case the children quickly subverted this purpose by drawing all sorts of different shapes. It didn't really matter that they did this: they had a very enjoyable time and recorded their findings in all kinds of different ways.

The impact of the activity was shown by the paintings they produced on the following and subsequent days, based on the patterns of the rectangular blocks but with lots of different arrangements and colours. The only drawback to what had been a relaxed morning of maths came when the caretaker saw what we had done to his highly varnished floor. When doing this again, we experimented using frames made from paper and with string, but nothing had quite the same appeal. They just enjoyed drawing all over the floor, so we went back to doing that, but being always much more careful to clean it off before the caretaker got in! Your children will nearly always enjoy activities invented or inspired by you more than the ones invented by the writers of books, however eminent, so be bold and experiment, while remembering the caretaker.

Games and puzzles

Equally motivating are games and puzzles with a mathematical content. Children are hopefully already enjoying card games and board games at home and during wet playtime at school. Most of these require counting and number recognition – both symbolic (numeral) and iconic (pictorial) – and only slight adaptation is needed to introduce addition, subtraction and higher order concepts. Usually, such games are used to reinforce and prac-tise skills already acquired, though concept formation can happen spontaneously as children make their own connections. Little investigations and puzzles can be introduced too:

- What do the opposite sides of a dice add up to? (partitioning of 7).
- What is the difference between the opposite numbers on a dice? (sub-traction). What sort of numbers are these? (recognition of odd numbers). Why do we only get this sort of number? (connections between odds and evens).
- Can you put two dice together so that all the touching numbers add up to make the same? (addition, trial and error).
- Are you a lucky person? Do you get a 6 more often than other numbers? (probability).

Competition need not be a negative element – for many it can add to the enjoyment – but if a game is to be played competitively then the teacher needs to choose partners carefully. A bad ability match can lead to a poor experience for the loser. One way around this is to introduce a large element of luck independently from the mathematics, though this can reduce the amount of time available actually to do mathematics. Alternatively, aim for cooperative games or large group efforts. Student teachers are often sur-prised by the willingness of children to help one another even within a competitive situation.

Puzzles are an excellent way of introducing mathematical problem-solving. Children who are already interested in numbers will enjoy mathematics for its own sake, but others need motivating and hopefully the intrinsic interest will grow. As with all problem-solving, discussing the results and strategies is very important. Young children find it difficult to explain their methods formally, but informal chat with their peers about what to do next, what would be a good 'next move' is an important step along the way.

It is difficult to do justice to this very wide subject in a single chapter, and we therefore recommend that those wishing a more in-depth coverage read *Mathematics with Reason* by Sue Atkinson (1992). This excellent book pro-vides many useful ideas alongside examples of children's work.

Learning factors and the teacher's role

If we therefore regard the child as an active learner – choosing what to learn and what to reject, making their own mathematics rather than ingesting ours – then what role is there for the primary teacher? Obviously, children cannot create for themselves the body of knowledge we call mathematics, nor can we afford to let them develop only in certain areas of the subject. We have a responsibility to the children not only to expose them to the fascination mathematics can engender but also to equip them for the adult world. Teachers by necessity exert control over the curriculum by the questions they ask the child, by the experiences they provide for concept formation and the challenges they set for application of those concepts. We become their guides and their mentors.

In order to fulfil this role to the best of our ability, it is vital to keep in mind some important factors: language, visualisation, differentiation and, finally, self-respect and personal responsibility.

Language

Mathematics has to some extent its own language – a combination of what are often referred to as Ordinary English (OE) and Mathematical English (ME). Our explanations and discussions with the very young begin with OE, as otherwise the language would be meaningless, but ME needs to be introduced gradually and continuously. There are a few myths in this regard, for example, the idea that young children cannot cope with large proper names for mathematical concepts or objects. We are told by some that infants cannot cope with such words as 'subtract' and that therefore 'take away' is better, yet these very same children have no difficulty remembering and using names like Diplodocus or Brontosaurus! It is important to use both the correct language and also a variety of language as there is therefore less room for misunderstanding. 'Take away' represents only one aspect of subtraction. 'Difference between', 'more than' and 'less than' are others in which nothing is being removed. What one must be careful to avoid is confusion, and hence these different aspects – with their correct language – are not tackled all at once.

There is also the danger of misunderstanding through the ME word existing with a different meaning within OE. A good example of this occurred when one of our students asked a group of infants if they knew what volume was. Up went one hand very firmly, but on asking the student was told 'It's the button on the remote control that makes things louder!'

To aid children's learning of ME, much discussion is required, both teacher–pupil and pupil–pupil. The latter will often use everyday alternatives, but this in itself helps as children draw connections between the new concept and the familiar. A more formal situation such as show and tell, or pupil feedback during the plenary of a Numeracy hour, where discoveries and achievements of the day are shared by individual children with the rest of the class, encourages them to use ME correctly. For a fuller discussion of language issues in mathematics please read *Maths Talk* by the Mathematics Association (1987).

It is vital to keep in mind language confusions when trying to assess children's mathematical knowledge. When a local education authority set up a working group to try to devise assessment items that would avoid language difficulties, they opted for a minimalist, orally presented script which was to be very closely adhered to, for example:

> I will read out some questions and I want you to write down just the answer to the question. You will have plenty of time.
> Write down the answer to:
> 1 One more than seven   (pause)
> 2 Two less than ten   (pause)
> 3 Three more than eight.

On taking in the work, they discovered that several children had written:

1 No
2 Yes
3 No

Well, one isn't more than seven and two is less than ten! This illustrates the dangers of trying to avoid language difficulties by avoiding language. Far better to take a language-enriched approach than an impoverished one. Always simplifying 'difficult' words or even, as here, cutting them out completely is not helpful to children in the long run. Discussion should be a vital part of maths, and expanding a child's mathematical vocabulary is as important as it is in other areas of the curriculum. So, accept responsibility for promoting your children's powers of expression in mathematical situations as you would in any other.

Many teachers of young children will go to enormous lengths, and use hundreds of words, to avoid using a precise term like 'parallel'. It would be better, and less patronising, to introduce the term, defining and explaining it when the opportunity arises, even if you think that the children are too young. Better still would be to do this, then make a point of using it correctly yourself a few times over the course of the next few days. Children are brilliant little learners and we underestimate their potential far too frequently in the early years.

Visualisation

Young children cannot work easily in the abstract, and learn to do so only gradually. If they cannot visualise the situation, they will most likely fail to understand it. Martin Hughes (1986) describes an experiment with pre-school children to investigate their conservation of number, a concept of which Piaget had thought them incapable. When the questions were couched in contexts which were familiar to the children (using teddy stories), and hence that they could visualise, then far fewer children failed to conserve number.

The following is an account by a teacher in a CAN school (see Note, page 300-1) of a discussion with a 7-year-old boy.

> Daniel was finding as many ways as he could to make 8. He had filled a page of his book with fairly short examples (like $10 - 2$, $6 + 4 - 2$, and so on). Now he was using a calculator to produce long, interesting strings of numbers, using the calculator to keep a check on the running total.
>
> Looking over his shoulder, I could see that he was able to range up into thousands and below zero into negative numbers and still end up with a number sentence that equalled 8. I said to him 'Don't you ever think that you'll never be able to get back to 8?'
>
> He looked at me scornfully and said 'I can always get back to 8.'
> 'How can you be sure that you'll always be able to get back to 8?'
> 'I can get back to 8 any time I want to. See this (the calculator) is like a video recorder.'
>
> I was genuinely puzzled by this. 'What do you mean?'
> 'You see this (the addition key) is, like, "play". Now this one (multiplication) is like fast forward. The take-away key is rewind, and this one (division key) is fast rewind.'

Children like Daniel have years of experience of putting videotapes into video recorders and running them backwards and forwards to find the recording they want. While they are doing this, the four-digit display of the tape counter reels past their eyes, from 0000 to 9999. Some machines even show negative numbers. Daniel was relating this familiar vision to the school work he was doing with his calculator.

It is important always to keep in mind the 'child's eye' on the world. Talking to children informally – as they arrive at school, in the playground, etc. – helps the teacher to get to know how they think, what interests them and what are their common experiences. An infant teacher cannot afford to keep a distance between herself and her pupils.

Another aid to visualisation is practical activity. All infant schools use practical, or 'structured' apparatus for mathematics to a greater or lesser extent. It makes explanations easier, it helps the children keep a check of their progress, and it provides a pictorial image of the answer that can be used for assessment (very helpful with children who are not yet recording formally). Nowadays, it would be unthinkable to teach mathematics without this hands-on experience, and we would never wish to discourage such activity, but a word of warning is necessary. It is possible for children to learn a practical procedure by rote – similar to a standard written algorithm – and work through the stages with little understanding of what they are doing or why. Such children find it very difficult to transfer from the practical method to the mental or written forms as they can make no connections. The visualisation is not happening – they are only going through the motions. Unless the practical manipulation builds on their previous understanding – and if at all possible is a method devised by themselves – then it will be no more meaningful than playing 'Simple Simon Says'. This is equally true of computer work, calculator methods, etc. Without a solid understanding of how children think and learn, these aids become gimmicks and finally are unfairly discredited.

Differentiation

Every child has the right to an education delivered at a level that is within their grasp and that challenges them, pushing them ever forward. Easy to say, but far less easy to deliver to a large class of small children. Groupings by ability are a part solution, though even with a group size of only two, we can find significant differences between children.

Open-ended working is a different way to tackle the problem, which provides more opportunity to learn from one another and more room for discussion. At a very simple level, this can mean the difference between asking children to solve such sums as $2 + 7$ or $9 - 3$, etc. and asking them instead to find all the partitions of 9 they can (as in how many different ways can they put 9 cows in two fields). The latter can easily be extended – choose your own number of cows, choose the number of fields – saving teachers from producing endless, repetitive worksheets. In this way, consolidation and practice (a vital element of learning if such number bonds are to come to be known) is kept interesting. It can also tell you much more about the children's abilities as they will explore and push forward their own frontiers, sometimes into areas the teacher might not have thought of.

Figure 14.3 shows a 6-year-old's attempt at partitioning money. Notice how he begins each section by finding solutions using only one type of coin. He is obviously comfortable with this, and needs further activities leading to exploring multiplication and division. This piece of work also tells the teacher that this child has a well-developed feeling for pattern (10p being made with 2,1,2,1,2,1 . . . 1) and works fairly systematically (starts with the larger coins, looks for equal additions, and then moves on to mixed coins). Quite a lot from a small piece of writing, and perhaps too presumptive, but the class teacher will base her assessments on many such items from one child.

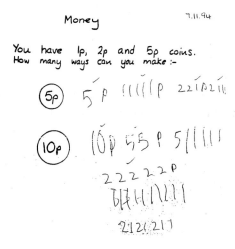

Figure 14.3 *A 6-year-old's attempt at partitioning money*

Self-respect and personal responsibility

Finally, while planning mathematics for young children, we cannot help but consider our wider role in young children's personal development. We need to help them become effective, autonomous learners; they must also learn to work cooperatively, to listen to others and to respect others. None of this is possible without an element of self-respect, and this will not come about unless their work and their responses in mathematics are respected by the teacher. They need to know that you are genuinely interested in the work they do, the things they say, and the way they are thinking as they try to solve their problems. 'Tell me about this: how are you getting on? Is it difficult and what are the difficult bits?' are better interactions than simply marking things right or wrong. Children also need praise; they need appropriate work that they tackle with some success and they need to see their own lives, interests and experiences valued and reflected in the business of the day.

These are, of course, issues which pervade the whole curriculum, but there is a specific role for mathematics. In the outside world, the popular image of a mathematician is of a white male – probably wearing glasses and equally likely to have a calculator in his pocket or be sitting at a computer. These images give subtle messages to children about what is appropriate behaviour for them, causing disaffection which becomes manifest from upper junior children onwards. Because the effects are not evident at the infant stage does not mean that the damage has not begun. In reception classes, boys can be seen dominating the construction tables. Teachers often have to engineer time specifically for girls, rather than having free choice time, as construction work is vital for their growing understanding of shape and space. As boys are more likely to be bought calculators and computers by their parents than are girls, teachers need to monitor carefully girls' attitudes to these aids, and to ensure girls use them as much as necessary.

It is well known that girls on average are neater than boys, and hence do better at standard arithmetic work – they can at least get the tens and units in the right columns! – but this may be more a reflection of teacher attitude than any innate difference between the sexes. Close monitoring of teacher–pupil interaction shows girls being praised for neatness, while boys are praised for creativity. The children respond with whatever will gain your approval.

Conclusion

Teachers entering the profession at the start of the new millennium do so at an exciting time. Dogma on all sides has been tempered by experience and to some extent the appearance of the national curriculum and the national numeracy strategy provide's a breathing space for us to sit back and re-evaluate mathematics teaching and learning. People are again questioning what education is really about and mathematics is no exception. It can be an exciting time if we allow it, and much depends on our new recruits. Get in there and experiment – you have nothing to lose and a great deal of professional satisfaction to gain!

Note

CAN is an acronym for the Calculator-Aware Number curriculum project that was a part of Hilary Shuard's much larger PrIME project, already referred to earlier in the chapter (Shuard et al., 1991). Schools that joined the project agreed to make a calculator permanently available to each child, allowing them to use it at any time they chose, and undertook not to teach any standard 'right' way of doing the number operations for addition, subtraction, multiplication and division. There were many exciting results that are reported in the readings at the end of this chapter, but noteworthy here is Daniel's confidence and sense of ownership of what he was doing. An enhanced ability to do calculations mentally was another result, probably because of increased understanding of place value and the way the number system works, which of course are built into the calculator, thus making it a very powerful teaching tool. For a fuller discussion of meaningful calculator use, see Rousham (1995).

Pointers for early years number work

- Children are mathematical thinkers in their own right, and have already made many connections and conclusions before they start school.
- Educators need to be aware of children's perceptions about mathematics (through observation and discussion) so that they can build on the children's correct understandings and help them amend their misunderstandings.
- In order to understand mathematics, and be able to apply it to solve differing problems, it needs to be couched in understandable language and within a context which is relevant or interesting to the child.
- Educators can provide appropriate experiences (through, for example, play, investigations or practical tasks) and encourage children's thinking through discussion and exposition, but children maintain control over what and how much is learnt.
- Mathematics has its part to play in children's personal development. Their attempts must be respected, no matter how trivial to the adult observer and no matter how they perform compared to their peers.

References

Atkinson, S. (1992) *Mathematics with Reason – The Emergent Approach to Primary Maths*, London: Hodder & Stoughton.

Brown, M. and Kuchemann, D. (1976) 'Is it an add, Miss?', *Mathematics in School*, 5, 5.

Burton, L., Harvey, R., Kerslake, D., Street, L. and Walsh, A. (1990) *HBJ Mathematics*, London: Collins Educational (HarperCollins).

Cockcroft, W.H. (1982) *Mathematics Counts*, London: HMSO.

DfEE (1999) *The National Numeracy Strategy*, Suffolk: DfEE.

Hughes, M. (1986) *Children and Number: Difficulties in Learning Mathematics*, Oxford: Basil Blackwell.

Jaworski, B. (1988) '"Is" versus "seeing as": constructivism and the mathematics classroom', in D. Pimm (ed.) *Mathematics, Teachers and Children*, London: Hodder & Stoughton.

Mathematics Association (1987) *Maths Talk*, Cheltenham, Gloucestershire: Stanley Thornes.

Nuffield Mathematics Project (1968) *Mathematics Begins (1); Computation and Structure (2); Computation and Structure (3)*, London: W & R Chambers and John Murray.

QCA (2000) *Curriculum Guidance for the Foundation Stage*, Suffolk: DfEE.

Rousham, L. (1995) 'CAN calculators make a difference?', in J.Anghileri (ed.) *Children's Mathematical Thinking in the Primary Years – Perspectives on Children's Learning*, London: Cassell.

Shuard, H., Walsh, A., Goodwin, J. and Worcester, V. (1991) *Calculators, Children and Mathematics:The Calculator-Aware Number Curriculum (CAN)*, London: Simon & Schuster.

Thompson, I. (1992) 'From counting to calculating', *Topic: Practical Applications of Research in Education*, 7, 10, 1–6.

Whitebread, D. (1995) 'Emergent mathematics or how to help young children become confident mathematicians', in J.Anghileri (ed.) *Children's Mathematical Thinking in the Primary Years – Perspectives on Children's Learning*, London: Cassell.

CHAPTER 15

'PLEASE can we have another bit?'

INFORMATION AND COMMUNICATIONS TECHNOLOGY (ICT) IN THE EARLY YEARS: AN EMERGENT APPROACH

John Siraj-Blatchford

Socio-constructivist perspectives in early childhood education (Sayeed and Guerin, 2000) recognise the importance of viewing play as an activity where children are developing their confidence and capability for interacting with their cultural environment. If we are to provide for an appropriate, broad and balanced education in the early years we must first think about children playing, but then we must also think about the particular subjects of that play. In recent years the application of Information and Communications Technologies (ICT) has brought about fundamental changes to our culture, and the legitimacy of its place in the curriculum can therefore be hardly doubted.

Since computers were first introduced into UK primary schools in the early 1980s an ever wider range of information and communications technology (ICT) products has been developed for use by young children. Some of these have been found appropriate for use in pre-schools, and other new products have been developed specifically for this age group. But given the relatively high cost of computers and computer software, and the even greater investment in training that is required to use them effectively, it is important that we make critical and informed choices regarding their use.

There are six commonly cited benefits in applying ICT in the early years. It has been argued that:

- Computers offer a means of teaching basic skills more efficiently.
- Computers have been employed widely in schools and industry, and it is

therefore important for children to begin to develop the computer keyboard and mouse skills that will increasingly determine their future success in these new technological environments.

- Children working at the computer benefit from the experience of collaborating with their peers.
- Programmable toys and screen images provide motivating real and virtual objects for the child to 'think with' (Papert, 1982).
- Early play and experience with ICT supports the development of enduring positive dispositions to the subject.
- Technology provides a range of powerful compensatory tools to be applied in educating children with special educational needs.

Learning the basics

A range of software products have been developed to support early learning in a wide range of subject areas. These include drill and practice programmes designed to support the development of number and letter recognition and basic phonic skills. Popular examples include *Baileys Book House* (Edmark) and *Oxford Reading Tree*. Programs such as *My World Animal Sort* and *Freddy Teddy* also support children in developing sorting and sequencing skills. A good example of an early drill and practice programe of this sort is *Millie's Math House* (Edmark). This CD includes 'Make a bug', 'Number machine' and 'Bing/bong'; a program that encourages children to complete patterns that the program makers claim to: 'empower children to recognise other patterns in music, mathematics, art, and science and to make better sense of the world.' While an optional free-play mode is included in this program it also provides a very clear demonstration of the behaviourist teaching approach (learning approach based on behaviour modification) that is inherent in many of the programs of this genre. If children get a right answer, they are rewarded by some amusing action sequence and/or tune. If they make a mistake the options are gradually reduced until they are forced to make the 'correct' response. This is an approach that is widely considered inappropriate in British early childhood settings as it runs against the grain of the dominant 'play and discovery' philosophy of early childhood education.

When children interact with this kind of software their interaction is often especially absorbing and extended. Products should therefore be carefully reviewed to ensure that they are suitable. There are flaws even in some of the most popular programs. To take one notable example of this, 'Sentence builder' (*Stickybear's Reading Room*) allows the children to create their own sentences, the computer animates them, prompts them to read it and then plays their recording back:

The program has 86 nouns and 48 verb phrases but it is interesting to note that while the software refers to an astronaut, an acrobat, clown, diver, and 29 animals – there are no children included. The people that the child might identify with are therefore all adult and they are also stereotypically male – and this is compounded by the artefacts – bulldozers, garages, motorcycles, submarines and rockets that are included. There are no prams, shopping trolleys, department stores and kitchens.

(Siraj-Blatchford, 1998)

The verb phrases are restricted in that it is possible for the astronaut to move in a wide variety of ways: He can fly, jump, even skip . . . but he cannot sit, talk, laugh, cry or hug anyone. The program has an inbuilt bias towards boys. As the US National Association for the Education of Young Children (NAEYC) Position Statement on Technology suggests:

> The teacher's role is critical in making certain that good decisions are made about which technology to use and in supporting children in their use of technology to ensure that potential benefits are achieved. Teachers must take time to evaluate and choose software in light of principles of development and learning and must carefully observe children using the software to identify both opportunities and problems and make appropriate adaptations. Choosing appropriate software is similar to choosing appropriate books for the classroom – teachers constantly make judgments about what is age appropriate, individually appropriate, and culturally appropriate.
>
> (NAEYC, 1996)

The use of an inappropriate teaching method can have a devastating effect upon a child's learning dispositions. There is evidence to suggest, for example, that excessive early drill and practice in the teaching of reading can undermine a child's dispositions to be a reader (Katz, 1992). Yelland (2002) usefully cites Negroponte (1995) in this context:

> In the 1960's, most pioneers of computers in education advocated a crummy drill-and-practice approach, using computers on a one-to-one basis, in a self-paced fashion, to teach those same God-awful facts more effectively. Now, with the rage of multimedia, we have closet drill and practice believers who think they can colonise the pizzazz of a Sega game to squirt a bit more information into the heads of children, with more so called productivity.
>
> (Negroponte, 1995, pp. 198–9)

Computer keyboard and mouse skills

Many early years teachers prioritise the development of basic mouse and keyboard skills and software such as *Switch on Original; Picture Building* (Brilliant Computing) is often used specifically for this purpose. School suppliers and toy shops provide a range of other apparatus and equipment designed to satisfy the same needs. Yet, if we look back to the early days of educational (or industrial) computing, one of the most obvious changes has been in precisely these areas. The first computer introduced into many primary schools was the Sinclair ZX81 (see Figure 15.1). Programs were stored on cassette tapes that took a long time to load. None of the early computers had a mouse and written commands had to be typed on to the screen – the 'drag and drop' facility that was first introduced by Macintosh had yet to be developed. We have come a long way since these early days . . . but they weren't actually that long ago and that is something we really need to think about. Future developments are difficult to predict but looking back on the manner of developments so far it is clear that computing in the future will be faster and easier to access.

Figure 15.1 *The Sinclair ZX81*

Touch sensitive screens have already replaced other means of control in a variety of handheld devices, and the likelihood of the infants of today operating a mouse in their future employment seems extremely doubtful. New technologies are being constantly developed and voice recognition systems are becoming increasingly sophisticated. The future of the QWERTY keyboard seems even more bleak. The odd layout of the QWERTY keys was initially designed to slow down the typist to avoid the typewriter 'hammers' colliding and locking together as they were thrown against the ribbon and paper. That keyboard is already a technological anachronism.

Children do need to access the technology that is currently available, and the point that I am making here is not that we shouldn't support them in initially gaining that access. We should provide them with the best possible access to the technological tools currently available. But what we shouldn't do is present that as a central objective of early years ICT education.

Most new desktop computers arrive with an instruction book that warns the user about some of the ergonomic difficulties associated with extended exposure to the screen, and in operating the keyboard and mouse. The dangers of developing repetitive strain injuries (RSIs) and carpal tunnel syndrome have been well documented. The recommendations for appropriate posture should therefore always be followed as far as possible. Yet this is often extremely difficult to achieve in a classroom, and in pre-schools the difficulties may actually be insurmountable. Young children vary greatly in height and the provision of suitable furniture is often beyond the resources of playgroups and nurseries. In these circumstances the identification of alternative patterns of usage and means of access becomes crucial.

A major advantage of using a touch screen is that children's interactions with the computer are often relatively short, and the equipment may be set up to be accessed by the child from a standing position. This overcomes many of the ergonomic problems alluded to above. Software such as Fisher Price's *Toyland* and the *Winnie the Pooh Toddler* (Disney) lends itself very well to these purposes. One of the games featured on the CD involves 'Popping balloons for Pooh', a game where the child is encouraged to 'help Pooh and his friends get down from an awfully high place' by popping balloons! As each balloon is popped it sounds out the letter, number, colour or shape that it is decorated with. The game therefore enhances the educational environment (supporting the development of emergent literacy and numeracy) without making that the central function of the activity.

Collaboration

While the extended use (e.g. in excess of 40 minutes or an hour at a time) of desk-top computer keyboards is therefore not to be recommended in early childhood, there are still a great many early years programs available that can be used to encourage collaborative activity (see Figure 15.2).

Figure 15.2 *Good early years software encourages collaboration and joint attention*

As Light and Butterworth (1992) have argued 'joint attention' and 'children learning to share' and/or 'engaged jointly' provides an important source of cognitive challenge for young children. In collaboration children articulate their thinking, sharing their understandings and bringing to consciousness many ideas that they may still be only beginning to grasp intuitively (Hoyles, 1985). Collaboration is also considered important in providing opportunities for cognitive conflict as efforts are made to reach consensus (Doise and Mugny, 1984), and it has been recognised as important in facilitating the co-construction of potential solutions in the creative processes of problem-solving (Forman, 1989). Some of the best programmes also provide context for work away from the screen. For example a screen 'bug' designed in 'Make a bug' (*Millie's Math House* – see Figure 15.3) may be subsequently constructed using play dough or found materials.

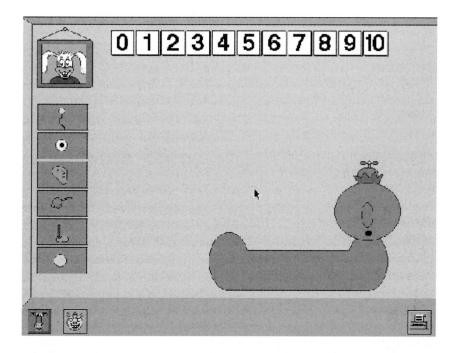

Figure 15.3 *'Make a bug', from Millie's Math House*

Adventure games and simulations are also popular and old favourites such as *Grannie's Garden* (Formation) and *Albert's House* (Links Education) are now being supplemented increasingly by programs such as *Pirate Ship* (Fisher Price). There are also a wide range of graphics programs on the market that can be applied collaboratively. Early word processing packages have also been used to good effect at times (*First Writer, My World*).

Manipulables

At one time it was thought that many of the activities associated with computers would not encourage creativity and in fact required only that the child press buttons. The manipulation of virtual objects on a screen was seen as a weak substitute for the manipulation of real three-dimensional objects, artefacts and toys. But as Yelland (2002) argues, the potential of computers to enable children to encounter and play with ideas has been increased and products such as *Logo* and *Kid Pix* (The Learning Company) provide a means by which children can create objects and play with them in a variety of ways. In such environments the children often spontaneously discover mathematical ideas and engage in interactions with other learners that would not have been possible without the technology.

Most early childhood educators believe that young children learn best by investigating with their senses, but a common concern early has been that children are not ready to work with computers. In discussing developmental issues surrounding the use of computers in childhood education, Silvern and McCary (1986) suggested that two conditions should be met for an activity to be concrete. The first is that the material used in the activity should be manipulated easily and the second is that 'the results of the manipulation must be directly verifiable by the manipulator'. Using these criteria, concrete uses of the computer may be identified, and by concrete activities children are given the chance to use the task assigned to them for developing their experience.

But as Clements and McMillen (1996) have stated, 'What is concrete to the child may have more to do with what is meaningful and manipulable than with its physical nature' (p. 273). Clements (1994) has also highlighted the unique characteristics of computer manipulatives and suggested that they include:

- flexibility;
- the ability to change arrangement or representations;
- the storage and availability of configurations;
- recording and replaying children's actions;
- linking the concrete and the symbolic and providing feedback;
- dynamic linking of multiple representations;
- focusing the children's attention and increasing motivation.

While most of us are very much aware of the ways in which ICT has revolutionised *communications*, its parallel effects in *control* technology are often forgotten. This is unfortunate because its probable that the vast majority of the computers with which we interact on a day-to-day basis are dedicated to these purposes alone. Microprocessors are now routinely incorporated in a vast range of devices. They are also incorporated in a growing number of children's toys. In the UK, programmable toys are now commonly available to children as 'symbolic objects to think with' (Papert, 1982). A floor 'turtle' such as Swallow Systems' *Pixie* (Swallow Systems) is controlled by the child by giving it program instructions: Forward, back, left, right. These instructions make the turtle move and in the process children use their thinking skills to explore, take risks and apply their prior knowledge in new and creative ways. Many experts believe this can enhance their cognitive development. *Pixie* is exceptionally simple to control and provides a very good starting point as an 'object to think with'. 'The Jelly bean hunt' in

Trudy's Time and Place House (Edmark) provides an appropriate and popular screen-based alternative (see Figure 15.4).

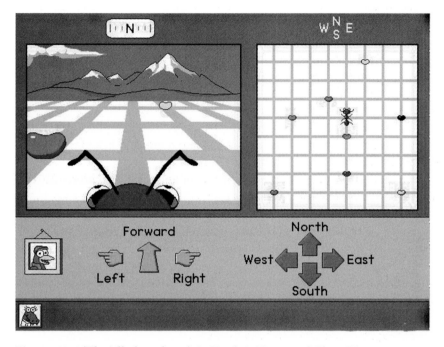

Figure 15.4 *'The jelly bean hunt'*, *in* Trudy's Time and Place House

Symbolic play, and sociodramatic play in particular, is seen as the characteristic mode for this age group, and by inference the most appropriate vehicle for learning (Anning and Edwards, 1999; Vygotsky, 1978; Wood and Attfield, 1996). ICT research conducted as a part of the children's awareness of technology (CHAT) project (see www address on page 320) has shown that the manipulation of symbols and images on the computer screen may actually represent a new form of symbolic play, which the children seem to treat every bit as 'concretely' as the manipulation of any alternative blocks and small-world toys:

On-screen images were 'grabbed', scolded, fingered and smacked, with dramatic effect, as part of the small-group interaction with the software. In some instances, they took on an off-screen life of their own, as children continued the game the computer had initiated, away from the machine. 'Food' items were one of the favourite symbols for adoption, particularly by the morning 'girls' group':

Tabitha says 'click'; Alice says 'That won't do anything'; there is group glee when they succeed. All three evolve a highly physical and interactive game away from computer: for several minutes they pretend to eat the cheese on the screen, with lots of lip-smacking and appreciative noises and role-play – 'Oh god, it's all gone and I didn't get any!'. Annabelle skilfully uses the mouse to remove cheese from screen into the limbo of a black border (unconscious control, very skilled). Tabitha says, 'PLEASE can we have another bit?' All three are standing and role-playing: Alice even wipes her fingers on her jumper after 'eating'.

These three, and other girls, frequently 'grabbed' apples and pears from the screen, begged each other to share them, and licked their lips appreciatively after pretending to eat them.

(Brooker and Siraj-Blatchford, 2002)

Developing technological literacy and positive dispositions to ICT

'I'm a rocket scientist', one engineer complained to me. 'I design missile systems, but I can't figure out how to program my VCR'.

(Norman, 1995)

As Norman (1995) has argued it is inevitable that as technology has developed we have all come to know less and less about the inner workings of the systems that are under our control. This is as true of adult experiences of technology as it is of children's experience. In the face of these changes, we need to consider carefully what our educational priorities should now be. We also need to consider what it actually means to 'understand' a technological product. When technology was mostly mechanical we could see the internal workings and we could see the effects of our actions. But increasingly their operation and design are invisible and abstract, so that if we are not to be entirely alienated from the technology around us we need to redefine what it means to be technologically literate. It is this sort of argument that provides the rationale for including educational provisions for children learning about the 'uses of technology' in the foundation stage curriculum.

Many early childhood applications do provide a parallel with adult applications. Children are now introduced to a wide range of computer software on CD-Roms and in addition to all of those referred to above; they come to apply software encyclopedia and a range of word processors, spreadsheets and databases in school. In the early years hardware and software applications have been developed specifically with the intention of encouraging children to 'play' within adult ICT contexts. For example, the *Playskool Store* (Hasbro) checkout unit clips on to the keyboard providing a point of sale shopping simulation that incorporates a working till, bar-code reader, etc. (see Figure 15.5). When we apply technology in this way in the early years we may describe our perspective as one supporting an 'emergent technology curriculum'.

Figure 15.5 *The Playskool Store checkout unit*

An 'emergent technology curriculum' is in many ways just like an emergent literacy curriculum. Teachers who teach emergent literacy encourage 'mark making' as a natural prelude to writing. In emergent technology we should encourage the 'childs application' of technology and support them in sustaining the application over time. Teachers who teach emergent literacy *read* a range of different kinds of text to children. In emergent technology we should introduce the children to 'new applications'. We should provide them with the essential early experiences that they must have if they are to go on to understand and be empowered by technology in their later lives.

These early experiences will include playing with a range of different technological artefacts and software products (real and pretend telephones, cameras, computers, etc.). They will also include drawing children's attention to the uses of technology in the world around them. We can also encourage 'technology play' in the nursery, setting up office play environments, supermarket checkouts and bank cash points for children to integrate into their play. Teachers who teach emergent literacy provide positive role models by showing children the value they place in their own use of print. In emergent technology education we can do the same by talking about technology and involving children in the development of our own collaborative technological applications. We can set up a computer database to keep a check on the books and other resources that we use. We can use the computer for our own purposes, sharing our experiences of its use with the children. In doing so we will encourage children to develop an emergent awareness of the nature and value of these resources as well as positive dispositions towards the kind of technological applications that they will experience in the future.

Many of those promoting emergent literacy see parent and teacher 'modelling', that is teachers and parents providing good role models to be the most important factor in developing children's capability. They therefore encourage parents to read to their children and ensure that the children see them reading for their own purposes. This is backed up by numerous large-scale research projects which show that the single most influential factor in determining children's future academic success in the early years is parents reading to children and taking them to the library regularly (Sylva et al., 2000). This in turn is related to social class and other factors – but the primary determinant seems to be the parents' behaviour; change that and it will compensate for social class differences in academic achievement! So the real challenge is to provide children with strong models of technology so that they develop positive attitudes and beliefs about the importance of the subject; that, more than anything else, is what will influence their motivation to engage in it in the future.

Play is a 'leading activity' (Leontiev, 1981; Oerter, 1993), and as van Oers (1999) has suggested, when children consciously reflect upon the relationship between their 'pretend' signs and 'real' meanings they are engaged in a form of semiotic activity that will provide a valuable precursor to new learning activities:

> learning activity must be fostered as a new special form of play activity. As a new quality emerging from play activity, it can be argued that learning activity has to be conceived as a language game in which negotiation about meanings in a community of learners is the basic strategy for the acquisition of knowledge and abilities.
>
> (van Oers, 1999, p. 273)

From this theoretical standpoint I want to argue that we should be providing opportunities for children to play with technology and to play at being technologists. It is commonplace for children to play at being mummies, daddies, as well as a wide range of traditional roles such as those of soldiers, doctors, nurses and firefighters. In the UK, pre-school suppliers and toy shops produce 'dressing-up' clothes to promote this kind of play. All we need to do is to provide the props and encouragement to include technology in all of this as well. For some practitioners this may seem to be prescriptive, but as Vygotsky argued:

> In one sense a child at play is free to determine his own actions. But in another sense this is an illusory freedom, for his actions are in fact subordinated to the meanings of things and he acts accordingly:
>
> (Vygotsky, 1978, p. 103)

Special educational needs

Experience in the UK and abroad suggests that computers may actually be maintaining, and may even be exaggerating, educational inequalities. Some children benefit from having frequent use of computers in the home, and boys tend to be encouraged to use them much more than girls. Girls' and boys' software preferences differ and it is all too easy for the children who have the most experience and capability to dominate the computer's use. ICT provides no panacea for educational inequality; everything depends upon the choices that are made to provide technology that is appropriate to each child's unique special needs, learning styles and individual preferences:

> For children with special needs, technology has many potential benefits. Technology can be a powerful compensatory tool – it can augment sensory input or reduce distractions; it can provide support for cognitive processing or enhance memory and recall; it can serve as a personal 'on-demand' tutor and as an enabling device that supports independent functioning. The variety of assistive-technology products ranges from low-tech toys with simple switches to expansive high-tech systems capable of managing complex environments. These technologies empower young children, increasing their independence and supporting their inclusion in classes with their peers. With adapted materials, young children with disabilities no longer have to be excluded from activities. Using appropriately designed and supported computer applications, the ability to learn, move, communicate, and recreate are within the reach of all learners. Yet, with all these

enhanced capabilities, this technology requires thoughtful integration into the early childhood curriculum, or it may fall far short of its promise. Educators must match the technology to each child's unique special needs, learning styles, and individual preferences.

(NAEYC, 1996)

In our recent study of early computer use by bilingual children (Brooker and Siraj-Blatchford, 2002) we found that the nursery computer provided accessible language forms that were being exemplified and supported through visual cues and animations, and that these were frequently repeated:

Instances of language learning, and practice, in response to the software, were regularly recorded. The computer often provided a shared focus and experience for children who didn't share the same spoken language, and this undoubtedly contributed towards the development of the very positive, collaborative, and language enriched multicultural learning environment that we observed.

(Brooker and Siraj-Blatchford, 2002)

Conclusions

We began this chapter by identifying six reasons that might be given for introducing the computer into early education: they might be used to teach basic skills more efficiently; prepare children for the future in schools and employment; encourage collaboration and positive dispositions towards ICT; provide objects for the child to 'think with' ; and/or provide for special educational needs.

In the subsequent discussion of each of these areas, the UK early learning goals and statutory requirements of the national curriculum were put to one side. But if we consider the early learning goals carefully we can see that they actually address a very similar set of concerns:

- use computers to support their learning;
- find out about and identify the uses of technology in their everyday lives;
- use programmed toys to support their learning.

Early Learning Goals (DfEE, 1999)

The evidence shows that when they are given the freedom to play with appropriate software young children are active in constructing their own learning at the computer, and in scaffolding each other's learning. As the UK foundation stage curriculum suggests, young children should be encouraged to begin to develop a knowledge and awareness of the common uses of ICT. As I have argued above, there can be few places better to start this process than in early childhood sociodramatic play. This is also the sort of integrated ICT provision that is promoted by the *Developmentally Appropriate Technology in Early Childhood* (DATEC) project (www.ioe.ac.uk/cdl/datec). DATEC has involved a two-year collaboration between practitioners and academics in the UK, Sweden and Portugal and provides early childhood guidance and exemplar material. This information is now freely available from the project website (see below).

We all have a contribution to make in providing a better ICT education for young children and in doing so we should always be acutely aware of the influence of the wider environment, and of role models in particular on young children. In our work and interactions with children we should demonstrate confidence and competence with technology. As Pluckrose (1999) has suggested young children learn a great deal from the models that are provided for them:

> Watch a nursery child put on a pair of high-heeled shoes and a Sloane Ranger hat and toss a giant sized handbag over her shoulder. Listen to the language. Admire the walk. Then, take time to reflect upon the inter-pretation of her world through her eyes, marvelling that one so young is able to 'read', so meticulously, the adults who people her world.
>
> (Pluckrose, 1999: 113)

If we show that we value the new technology and confidently control it then children will be encouraged to develop the same attitudes. But if we present them with models that are disempowered and helpless in the face of technology we take the risk of encouraging just the same in them.

Pointers for early years ICT

- Beware of over using drill and practice software with young children.
- How children access software (QWERTY keyboard; mouse) will change and should not be a central objective of the curriculum.
- Ergonomics are important; consider using touchscreens with the children standing or programmes that encourage activity away from the computer as well.
- Use software which encourages collaboration.
- Manipulating objects on-screen in a meaningful context pro-vides valuable opportunities for symbolic play.

- Using computers should be part of a wider 'emergent techno-logy curriculum'.
- Children should be provided with opportunities to engage in sociodramatic play with all kinds of technology.
- Teachers should positive models showing how they use tech-nology.
- Used thoughtfully, technology can empower children with spe-cial educational needs and support their inclusion.

References and bibliography

Anning, A. and Edwards, A. (1999) *Promoting Young Children's Learning from Birth to Five*, Buckingham: Open University Press.

Brooker, E. and Siraj-Blatchford, J. (2002) ' "Click on Miaow!" how children of 3 and 4 experience the nursery computer', *Contemporary Issues in Early Childhood* 3, 2 (ISSN 1463–9491) http://www.triangle.co.uk/ciec/

Clements, D.H. (1994) 'The uniqueness of the computer as a learning tool: Insights from research and practice', in J.L. Wright and D.D. Shade (eds) *Young Children: Active Learners in a Technological Age*, Washington, DC: NAEYC, pp. 31–50.

Clements, D.H. and McMillen, S. (1996) 'Rethinking concrete manipula-tives', *Teaching Children Mathematics*, Jan, 270–9.

Department for Education and Employment (DfEE) (1999) *The National Curriculum Handbook for Primary Teachers in England, Key Stages 1 and 2*, London. HMSO:

Doise, W. and Mugny, G. (1984) *The Social Development of the Intellect*, Oxford: Pergamon Press.

Dweck, C.S. (1991) 'Self-theories and goals: Their role in motivation, per-sonality, and development', in R. Dienstbier (ed.) *Perspectives on Motivation: Nebraska Symposium on Motivation*, Omaha, NB: University of Nebraska Press, pp. 199–236.

Foreman, E. (1989) 'The role of peer interaction in the social construction of math-ematical knowledge', *International Journal of Educational Research*, 13, 55–69.

Hoyles, C. (1985) 'What is the point of group discussion in mathematics?', *Studies in Mathematics*, 16, 205–14.

Katz, L.G. (1992) *What Should Young Children Be Doing?* ERIC Digest, Urbana, IL: ERIC Clearinghouse on Elementary and Early Childhood Education, Chicago, IL: University of Illinois.

Leontiev, A. (1981) *Problems of the Development of Mind*, Moscow: Moscow University Press.

Light, P. and Butterworth, G. (eds) (1992) *Context and Cognition: Ways of Learning and Knowing*, Hemel Hempstead: Harvester-Wheatsheaf.

National Association for the Education of Young Children (1996) 'NAEYC Position Statement: Technology and young children – ages three through eight'. *Young Children*, September, pp. 11–16.

Negroponte, N. (1995) *Being Digital*, Rydalmere, NSW: Hodder & Stoughton.

Norman, D. (1995) 'Designing the future', *Scientific American*, September, p. 159.

Oerter, R. (1993) *The Psychology of Play: An Activity Oriented Approach*, Munich: Quintessenz.

Papert, S. (1982). *Mindstorms: Children, Computers, and Powerful Ideas*, Brighton, Sussex: Harvester.

Pluckrose, H. (1999) *The Caring Classroom: Towards a Learning Environment*, Nottingham: Education Now Books.

Sayeed, Z. and Guerin, E. (2000) *Early Years Play: A Happy Medium FOR Assessment AND Intervention*, London: David Fulton Publishers.

Silvern, S. and McCary, J. (1986) 'Computers in the educational lives of children: Developmental issues', in J. L. Hoot, *Computers in Early Childhood Education*, Englewood Cliffs, NJ: Prentice-Hall, pp. 6–21.

Siraj-Blatchford, J. (1996) *Learning Science, Technology and Social Justice: An Integrated Approach for 3 to 13-year-olds*, Nottingham: Education Now.

Siraj-Blatchford, J. (1998) 'Design, technology and the use of computers in the early years', in I. Siraj-Blatchford (ed.) *A Curriculum Development Handbook for Early Childhood Educators*, Stoke on Trent: Trentham Books.

Siraj-Blatchford, J. and MacLeod-Brudenell, I. (1999) *Supporting Science, Design and Technology in the Early Years*, Buckingham: Open University Press.

Siraj-Blatchford, J. and Siraj-Blatchford, I. (2001) *KidSmart: The Phase 1 UK Evaluation: Final Report (2000–2001)*, IBM United Kingdom Ltd., unpublished white paper.

Sylva, K., Melhuish, E., Sammons, P., Siraj-Blatchford, I. and Taggart, B. (2000) *Effective Provision of Pre-school Education Project – Recent Findings*, Presented at the British Educational Research Conference, Cardiff University, September 2000.

van Oers, B. (1999) 'Teaching opportunities in play', in M. Hedegaard and J. Lompscher (eds) *Learning Activity and Development*, Aarhus: Aarhus University Press.

Vygotsky, L. (1978) *Mind in Society: The Development of Higher Psychological Processes*, Cambridge, MA: Harvard University Press.

Wood, E. and Attfield, J. (1996) *Play, Learning and the Early Childhood Curriculum*, London: Paul Chapman.

Yelland, N. (2002) 'Reconceptualising schooling with technology for the twenty-first century: images and reflections', *Contemporary Issues in Early Childhood* 3, 2 (ISSN 1463–9491). http://www.triangle.co.uk/ciec/

Software reviews, further information and guidance on appropriate technology in early childhood is available on the *Developmentally Appropriate Technology in Early Childhood* (DATEC) project website: www.ioe.ac.uk/cdl/datec

The *CHAT website* can be found at: www.ioe.ac.uk/cdl/CHAT

Other useful Internet addresses

Teacher reviews of a wide range of early years software are available on:

http://www.teem.org.uk
http://www.becta.org.uk
http://www.ucc.uconn.edu/~wwwpcse/wcool.html
http://hometown.aol.com/wiseowlsw/index.html
http://freespace.virgin.net/kindergarten.software/

Other sites:

http://www.open.gov.uk/dfee/nursery.htm
http://www.earlyexcellence.org
http://www.naeyc.org/default.htm
http://www.letsfindout.com
http://www.cyberkids.com
http://www.disney.go.com
http://www.teacherxpress.com
http://www.parentsonline.gov.uk
http://www.pin.org.uk/
http://www.ioe.ac.uk/cdl/CHAT/index.htm

CHAPTER 16

'Mrs Rainbow told us what things were like when she went to school'

HISTORY IN THE EARLY YEARS

Sallie Purkis

Y ou may think that learning history has no place in early years education. Lively young children, full of energy, seem essentially part of the present, curious to explore the living world around them, nurturing their imagination on stories, particularly those with just a touch of magic and unreality in them. How could the past, which is dead and buried, have any relevance for them?

In this chapter we will consider how we can justify the place of history in teaching and learning in the early years, the skills, knowledge, understanding and attitudes that can be developed through learning history, appropriate resources and activities to promote learning, and how progress can be planned and monitored. We will identify where activities with a historical theme link to the early learning goals for the foundation stage and to the programme of study for Years R, 1 and 2 in the national curriculum as well as addressing the contribution it can make to sound practice and effective teaching and learning.

You may not like the suggestion that 'subjects' should be part of an early years curriculum. Until recently, many practitioners found themselves unable even to use the word 'history', putting forward three main arguments in favour of leaving it aside until the child was much older. Unfortunately these views revealed serious misconceptions about what the subject we call history actually is, but it is worth listing them in order to get them out of the way:

- History is a series of facts and dates that have to be memorised.
- It can only be learned by children who can read history books.
- Young children cannot understand the concept of time, so it is pointless to introduce it in the early years.

In the light of experience, understanding and practice, most modern teachers reject these arguments and recognise the close links between the real discipline of history, which will be examined below, and effective teaching and learning. Exciting classroom displays, learning environments that stimulate further investigation, and resources like oral history, objects and pictures have enabled teachers to capitalise on the opportunities for developing skills and concepts across the curriculum, including those relating to numeracy and literacy. Many schools, through their history guidelines and policies have identified what exactly it is they want the children to learn and how they can evaluate, assess and celebrate children's progress and achievement.

What is history?

History is not a body of knowledge about what happened before we were born and not a series of facts that can be learnt by heart. While some events can be dated with a fair degree of accuracy, others cannot. The discipline of history is about analysing the fragments of evidence that people, once alive and with similar human needs and aspirations to our own, left behind. We consider the evidence and have opinions about what it means. From these opinions, history is constructed and the past reconstructed.

Historians, archaeologists and museum professionals reconstruct the past, but so do film makers, novelists and advertisers. Ordinary members of the public have their own way of interpreting the past when they join the Sealed Knot and put on a performance of a Civil War Battle, dress up to attend an Elizabethan Banquet or make bread on a kitchen range in one of the reconstructed communities like the Beamish site in County Durham. Some reconstructions are more accurate than others and debate often rages between heritage purists, conservators, and leisure and tourist interests. Professional historians revise and reinterpret the work of a previous generation, by looking at new evidence or posing different questions. All these examples highlight the fact that there are no incontrovertible right answers about the past. History is a subject where questioning and hypothesising lie at the heart and where the simple questions are the ones we all want answered whether we are five or fifty.

Some of these key questions in history are as follows:

- When did these people live?
- What were their lives like?
- How did they feed and clothe themselves?
- What were their homes like?
- What technology did they know about?

- What was the same or different about them and us?
- What happened to them?
- When did things change?
- Why did things change?
- How did things change?
- How do we know?

You will not expect all these questions to be relevant for the youngest children, but each of them can be explored at different levels of understanding. They are a framework around which investigation of the past can be structured. For example, we would expect older children and adults to answer the first question with a date, a century or a period, such as Tudor; in the early years we might be satisfied with the all-pervasive 'in the olden days', but quite soon a more accurate response, such as 'before we were born', 'in the past' or 'twenty years ago' can be applied. The important point to keep in mind is that the methods used by a historian or archaeologist are entirely consistent with the best teaching practice in the early years. The key words are **exploration, investigation** and **problem-solving**. Learning objectives should enable the children to both describe and explain the past.

Is history relevant?

When I asked some early years teachers if they would include history in their schemes of work, even if they were not forced to by the national curriculum, I received positive responses. They gave a number of reasons:

- The importance of subjects concerned with questions like those above.
- The interest value of taking a 'detective' or 'investigator' approach.
- The opportunities for starting with the children's knowledge of themselves, their families and communities but the potential for extending their horizons, to learn about other people – the product model of the curriculum.
- The links with other areas of the curriculum, through the development of skills, understanding and attitudes – the process model of the curriculum.

They recognised the role of history in the growth of self-esteem, personal identity and social identity. As one early years coordinator commented, 'The sort of history we do is their history and it's a good introduction to a lot of other subjects.'

They further justified it by reference to the children when they first arrive at school. They have enormous energy, but they are usually egocentric, unpractised in looking beyond themselves and in some cases, bring anti-social attitudes towards others. Part of the educational objectives of educators in the early years are to help them look beyond themselves, integrate in a group and develop tolerance and social skills. History has a role to play in this programme. The growing awareness that each of us has a past as well as a present and a future extends knowledge of self and is a psychologically healthy sign of developing maturity. Knowledge and understanding of history can help answer the two key questions: Who am I? and Where am I? In the early years, most practitioners think that personal and local history is the most important.

Learning opportunities

History has a language of its own, the language of time, but it is also a vehicle for developing skills and concepts across the curriculum. It helps explain change, similarity and difference, not in a scientific way but in terms of human experience. In the early years, it is the learning process, linked to activities and experiences, which should take priority over any knowledge objectives. Figure 16.1 shows the basics of history as a subject. As you look at it, you may like to think about the teaching strategies and resources that would engage four-, five- or six-year-olds in any of the processes and skills listed in the diagram.

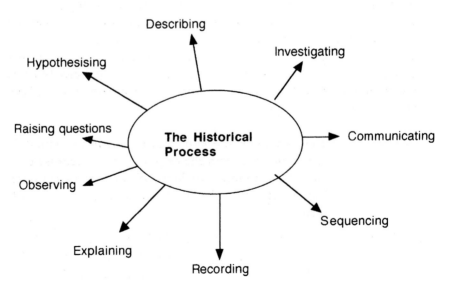

Figure 16.1 *The historical process*

The diagram is also an affirmation of the central place that talk has in early years classrooms, particularly when teaching about the past. Although the aim is to let the children do most of the talking, it is the teacher who must ensure that there is something interesting to talk about, initiate and sustain the quality of the language and steer discussion from mere observation and description to investigation and hypothesis. By understanding what history actually is and the uncertainty about conclusions, you will feel comfortable as a teacher when the children raise questions which may not have an immediate answer. Hopefully you will feel able to positively encourage them to pose questions that they would like to know about the topic, object or picture under discussion. As they grow older, they will become familiar with the framework of historical questions, providing there is an agreed policy about their importance in all classes in the school, and will be able to draw up their own historical questions, like those listed above.

You would not, of course, expect all children at every stage to go through the whole range of processes in Figure 16.1, but it is a framework to keep constantly in mind when planning activities in history so that you will not fall into the trap of thinking that repeating what the teacher says, describing and recording are the only objectives to plan for.

Practical implications of the process model

Let's imagine that an adult, perhaps someone's granny, volunteers to come into the classroom to show the children something old, such as a stoneware hot water bottle. How could even very young children be drawn into the process of learning history? Here are some suggestions for putting the historical process into action. As you read them, think of the opportunities the activity provides for extending the children's vocabulary to include historical language (see below, page 328).

Observing   The hot water bottle would be carefully passed round the group, handled with the help of an adult because of its weight. The children would probably notice the screw top, but might need to have the flat bottom pointed out to them.

Describing   Vocabulary would probably include words to describe the colour (brown, grey), the weight (heavy) and the feel (cold). The length and girth could be measured.

Questioning, investigating	The children might ask what it is, where it came from and how it was used. The owner might have a story to tell about how it came into her possession and pointing out the function of the flat bottom, the place where the hot water was poured and how it was secured.
Hypothesising	The children could be asked what they thought it was like to have a hot water bottle like this to warm the bed and why it was necessary. Some children may make guesses about the material from which it is made. Further discussion will develop from those who think it is made of stone or rock. They may also have opinions about why we do not still use them today.
Sequencing	This would be possible only if you had some modern hot water bottles in the classroom (and the children knew what they were). Some may have the cuddly-toy type of warmer which is heated in a microwave oven; others may recognise the traditional rubber bottle.
Explaining	It is an object from the past, when there was no heating in bedrooms. It was last used in the Second World War, more than fifty years ago, when rubber was not available.
Communicating	The children may have more questions or express their opinions about the hot water bottle. All teachers know that it is impossible to predict, with accuracy, just what the children will notice and want to comment on.
Recording	The hot water bottle can be drawn or photographed, with the owner holding it. Four-year-olds will make an impression of the object but five and six-year-olds will be able to write some sentences about the bottle and what they have learnt about it. The contributions can be displayed with the object or made up into a book.

You will see how this activity and the framework for learning can be easily adapted to discussion of something like an old toy in Year 1, helping to answer the question posed in the QCA Scheme of Work 'How are our toys different from those in the past?' (QCA,1998).

Attitudes

When the teaching and learning is appropriately planned, history has an important contribution to make in the promotion of attitudes to learning and to other people. Figure 16.2 shows some of these.

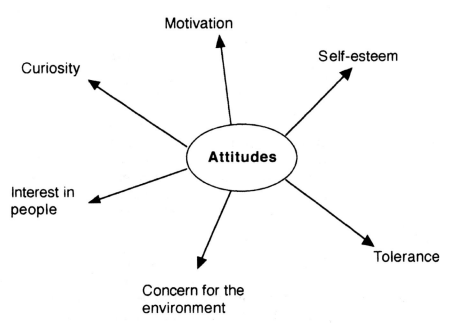

Figure 16.2 *Attitudes promoted by history*

You will not find it difficult to foster interest, enjoyment and curiosity through work in history, providing you provide an active hands-on approach. As a teacher you will find yourself drawn into the excitement of historical detective work, handling objects and listening to reminiscences and able to pass on this enthusiasm to the children. Some of the other attitudes, however, may have to be deliberately selected and identified in your curriculum planning.

Unfortunately, there is evidence that even small children come to school with values and prejudices towards other people and the environment which are intolerant and anti-social. They include racist attitudes that have been learnt from adults and older siblings at home and in their neighbourhood. They will find that these have no place at school. Of course, education cannot put right the ills in society, but since history is not a subject that deals in fantasy or make-believe but in the lives of people who have actually lived, one can argue that it has a responsibility to put the case for making reasoned and informed judgements, based on evidence.

Historical language

Language empowers, and in order to explain human experiences in the past, with accuracy, the children need to be equipped with vocabulary which encodes meaning. We will begin with the consideration of the language which describes time. There are many ways in which children grow to recognise and understand the passing of time. Talking accurately about *yesterday*, *today* and *tomorrow*, progressing to *last week*, *this week* and *next week* and then to some understanding of *seasons*, *months*, regular events that happen every year like their *birthdays*, the *summer holidays* and various *festivals* lay the foundation for describing the past, which is a very big concept indeed for the youngest children. Historical time has its own labels such as *year* and *century*. Where these are a measurement they can be part of the mathematics programme, but unfortunately history also has a series of subject-specific labels, such as *Victorian*. Experience shows, however, that by the age of seven, most children enjoy using the right label and can show that they know what it means, so there is no need to shy away from using the correct terms. It is not in the children's long-term educational interest to persist with labels like *the olden days*. They are perfectly able to learn to use *the past* and even the subject label *history*. *Before* and *after* are other concepts that become working components of the young child's vocabulary as they to learn to recognise the sequence of stories and of numbers.

Many teachers introduce historical sequencing by using the photos of the children or their mums when they were babies and discussing how they have changed. A simple timeline can be used to count back in years and language such as 'When I was a baby', 'When I was two, three or four'. These help explain the passing of time at the young child's level.

The other aspect of historical language that it is appropriate to develop before the age of seven is the vocabulary to describe old things and age. A brainstorming session with colleagues and friends or a check in a thesaurus will reveal a list that can be used to challenge and extend children's language development. Words like *old-fashioned*, *ancient*, *antique*, *decayed*, *worn-out* all have slightly different meanings. They are applied to some things, such as people but not to others, like buildings. You would not expect everything to be introduced to all children at one time, but knowing what they mean and when they are applied are an essential basic in teaching and learning about the past.

The last group of words are about the key concepts in history – *change and continuity; similarity and difference; cause and consequence*. Of these change and difference most frequently feature in early years history. It is important however that you always discuss their binary opposites – continuity and similarity – at the same time. Life in the past may have been different in degree from our own, but what is similar across the barriers of time and culture are human needs for food, clothing, shelter, security and belief. Change does not occur at the same rate in all societies.

It is important not to pass judgement too hastily on other times and cultures or to use pejorative or evaluative terms like *primitive* or *civilised*. There are still too many people in the world today who do not have access to running water or electric light. Emphasising difference between ourselves and people in the past can be another major pitfall. Care must be taken not to stereotype, but to acknowledge and respect difference. Everyone did not have servants in Victorian times and the Tudors did not all dress like the privileged courtiers whose portraits give us an image of the age.

Continuity is also wide open for discussion. The evidence from the past is all around us. Some of us inhabit houses and schools built a hundred years ago. They have been changed and brought up-to-date over time, but they remain a living and tangible link with the past. In Britain we frequently celebrate the past, and this includes the popular Victorian school day in primary schools. Even though the concepts of continuity and change are subtle, many young children are able to grasp difficult concepts. What they lack, unless you help provide it, is the language to articulate what they know and understand. It is important to have a framework of language and concepts listed in your school policy document for history, to raise awareness among staff and parents of the stages of knowledge and understanding that will help you support and monitor each child's progress.

Resources

Collecting resources to use in teaching history is not difficult or expensive and we can conveniently classify them under four headings:

People
Pictures
Objects and buildings
Books

We might also include music, but this needs other sources such as an old radio or record player to make it meaningful. Popular songs also have a place under the heading of people, particularly when they come as part of an older person's memories.

What follows is a discussion of issues related to the use of these various resources which I have illustrated by reference to a delightful local history project carried out by children at Harborne Infant School, Birmingham (Mauser and Reid, 1990).

People

Oral history or reminiscence is one of the approaches most valued by early years educators. Its merit is that it is a contribution to history at school which children and families can make themselves. It is accessible and language-based, and need not come as English, if some groups within the class all have the same mother-tongue. It is easy to organise if you call on the school community and their contacts first. You do not need to restrict yourself to finding someone elderly or retired since everyone has a life story to tell and even 'young' people are old to a five or six-year-old. Oral history is a winner in the classroom and makes an impact because it brings in a perspective on the past that is immediate, personal and alive. The Mrs Rainbow referred to in the title of this chapter was a real person (see Figure 16.3), even though her attractive name could have been a fictional invention.

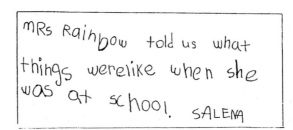

Figure 16.3 *Mrs Rainbow told us what things were like when she was at school*

When the children meet or interview someone, it is not necessary or desirable to draw up a rigid questionnaire, which might only result in stilted answers as you want to encourage the visitor to tell their story as a narrative. However, I am assuming that you will focus the session around a topic and that you will have discussed this with the interviewee so that you can tell the children before they arrive the purpose behind the interview. Most people can easily talk about their school days, their family life, their homes and journeys they have made. The children at Harborne Infant School interviewed past teachers about their memories of the school. The children asked questions reflecting their own interests, such as:

What time did school start and finish?
Did you have dinner at school?
What was your favourite dinner?
Did you have drinks at school?
What lessons did you have?
What games did you play with your friends in the playground?

Having more than one contribution on the same theme can be a positive bonus, since you will have different versions of the past which the children can discuss, describe, compare and explain. For example, everyone had a childhood, but the experiences they talk about will depend how long ago it was, where it was, the size and extent of the family, gender and social class.

The oral history interview becomes more valuable in association with other historical sources such as photographs, objects or places. The history of the school, for example, will make more sense for little children if they can walk round the building, look at old school photographs and listen to what it was like ten, 20 or 50 years ago from a former pupil or member of staff.

If you have a particularly good interviewee, one who talks to the point and at the children's level, you may decide to record it, saving the cassette for another occasion. This sounds useful, but you are unlikely to get the same attention from the children listening to a tape, unless they are also part of it, as you will from a real person in the classroom. It is also possible for the children, perhaps working in pairs, to make transcripts of their interviews (see Figure 16.4).

Pictures

Pictures of unfamiliar people and places from the past are also invaluable. They too will make the past accessible, something to look at, talk about and compare. The advantages of using old photographs or paintings of familiar situations such as shopping or travelling are obvious and enable the

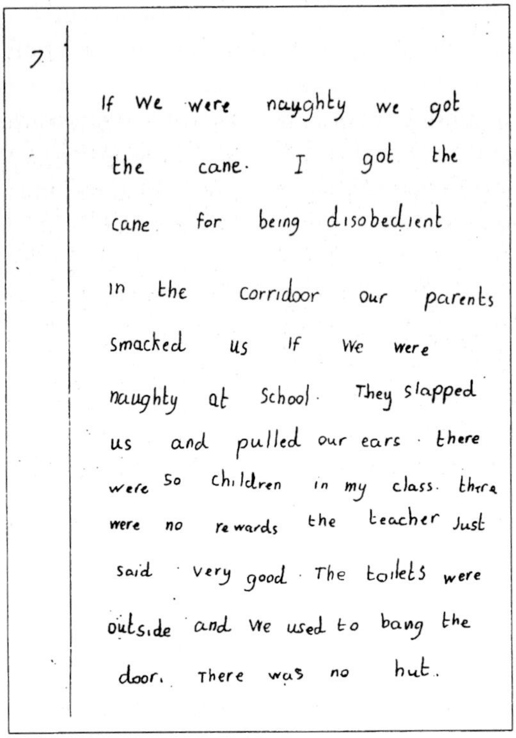

> 7.
>
> If We were naughty we got the cane. I got the cane for being disobedient in the corridor our parents smacked us If We were naughty at School. They slapped us and pulled our ears. there were so children in my class. there were no rewards the teacher Just said very good. The toilets were outside and We used to bang the door. There was no hut.

Figure 16.4 *Transcript of an interview with an ex-pupil of Harborne Infant School*

children to work out for themselves what was the same and what was different about then and now. Figure 16.5 shows a good example of this kind of comparison from the Harborne Infant School project.

Most county libraries and local museums collect old photographs and can supply prints. You will want to select clear images, such as scenes of the milkman with his horse and cart or the ice-cream vendor on his tricycle, but there are often family groups in collections, which have unfortunately become separated from the families to which they once belonged. These show details of clothes, hair-styles, gardens and objects, and have the kind of detail in them which will enable children to pick out features about the past for themselves.

Objects

Objects can be collected as a result of an appeal to parents and friends as well as from car boot sales and charity shops. Like the invitation to come into school for an oral history interview, parents and friends can be asked to

MRs Porters Room

1923   1989

The desks have changed.
In the old photograph there are
Flowers and there aren't any
Flowers in the new photogrph.
In the new photogrnph the boys have
    different shoes then the
ones in the old photograph.
they both have a radiotor.
Mrs porters classroom has changed
a lot. the windows are the
same. The old photograph was taken
in 1923 and the new
photogrnaph was taken in 1989

Figure 16.5 *The use of an old photograph of a familiar situation*

bring in an old object to talk about, as described in the section about the hot water bottle above. Objects collected by you can be touched and handled and presented to the children as mystery objects, something similar to the *Antiques Road Show* situation. They can be valuable contributions to topics like light, food and homes and put on display with their modern equivalents.

The environment outside the classroom

You will find good examples of museum visiting with early years pupils in the teachers' guides (Forber, undated and 1990) listed at the end of the chapter from the Ironbridge Gorge Museum. The success of the visits described here was almost certainly because the children were able to enter a reconstructed domestic environment; they could understand the context and make comparisons with their own experiences. A poor museum experience, for example, where objects are in high glass cases, or where a lot of reading is involved in order to understand the display, is not really worth the effort with very young children.

It is crucial that you make contact with a curator or education officer and assess the learning outcomes yourself, before booking a visit. The children will need to be well prepared and to have practised the skills such as close observation of objects, sketching and labelling they will need to use in the museum. You do not want to have a class of tired, restless children on your hands, particularly in a public space, so go prepared to look closely at one area, painting or object, not the whole museum. Where you do have a suitable museum near your school, consider building visits, activities and areas into your whole school policy for history, so that the children can consolidate any early years experience as they progress up the school.

Buildings

You may be in an area of old buildings, even at school in one! If your ancient building does not present any hazards, such as road safety, then it provides an ideal resource for many of the skills discussed earlier in the chapter, for accurate use of historical vocabulary and for drawing up a diagram of historical questions about the building. In terms of schools, the oral history potential is enormous, as can be seen from the work done at Harborne Infant School. However, oral history is of no use in either Ironbridge or in a castle, although both can become suitable places for young children to learn.

Books

Books also have a place in resources for teaching history in the early years. Familiar stories like *Grandpa* by John Burningham, *The Sandal* by Tony Bradman and Philippe Dupasquier, and *Peepo* by Janet and Allan Ahlberg are about history and, since the national curriculum began, some good history information books for Key Stage 1 have been written (see list at the end of the chapter). The best bring a past perspective to familiar infant themes and use historical sources like oral history, pictures and objects to bring the past alive.

A variety of resources will contribute to the quality of teaching and learning in the early years, but cannot guarantee it. Resources are of use only when used in a planned scheme of work with a definite purpose in mind.

Activities

Activities for the children can be divided into experiences that you provide or tasks which may be used for assessment. Whatever you choose will depend on the child or group and the skills, attitudes, concepts and knowledge you select. Below are listed some suggested activities for young children which can be adapted to particular historical projects.

Activities related to play

- Dressing up can be fun and related to the past by reference to pictures or oral memories.
- Food can be made following favourite dishes parents and older friends ate when they were children.
- Feely boxes can also be used to identify again the old objects like flat irons or candlesticks that have already become familiar from a classroom display.
- Kim's game – objects on a tray that you have to remember – will require both concentration and memory and again make your resources work for you in different situations.

Nursery songs and stories

- Many nursery songs and rhymes like 'Ride a Cock Horse', 'Three Blind Mice' or 'Baa Baa Blacksheep' describe an aspect of life in the past and explain what has changed.
- Stories like those listed above and from different cultural traditions are a rich source of cultural and ethnic heritage.

Using vocabulary

- Objects can be drawn and described. Make a set of cards with some of the historical vocabulary listed above and encourage the children to put the objects in a time order and use accurate vocabulary about them.

Sorting

- Sort the objects, with modern equivalents into categories, such as age or ownership, e.g. *indoors, outdoors; men, women, children; town, country, seaside*.
- Sort them, by relating them to a room where they were used, e.g. *kitchen., classroom, parlour* (discuss the label and how it has changed).
- Sort them into the material from which they are made, constructing descriptive phrases which can later be incorporated into sentences, e.g. *the felt hat, the leather suitcase, the iron kettle*.
- Sort them into categories for display in the class museum. Write the labels and invite parents and other children to visit the museum.

Detective work

- Make time for the children to make guesses about objects, pictures and buildings.
- Provide the opportunity for them to pose their own questions such as 'I would like to know . . .'
- Test out their guesses about an object, picture or building on another group of children. Can they work out the original from the guess?
- Introduce a collection of objects as a detective exercise by inventing a story about Granny's suitcase and what the contents tell us about her life.
- Use old photographs to 'work out' three things about the people or places in the past. What was *different* about their lives and ours? What has changed?

Time and sequence

- Use buildings around the school – you can take your own photographs of them when you go on a walk – to provide practice with sequencing activities. To begin with you might just use two categories, *now* and *then*, or *past* and *present*, but some children by the age of seven will be able to sort objects and buildings into centuries.
- Put all sorts of pictures, such as postcards that can be bought cheaply from museums, to put *homes, clothes* or *transport* into a time order.
- Use paper timelines from the publishers, strips of paper or washing lines and pegs to arrange the children's drawings or photographs of the locality in a chronological order.

Change

- Use pictures, objects, buildings and oral history to work out not only *what* has changed but *why* and *how*. (You will see that there is a hierarchy about these questions, which could be presented as a worksheet, moving from what can be seen to analysis and comparison. The questions demand thought and deduction, not just a retelling of information that has been given by the teacher.)

Oral history

Information generated in an oral history interview can be used in many ways:

- Make a book with the interviewee and their memories as the subject.
- Discuss why the book is a history book, or non-fiction book. What is the difference between the story of Mrs Rainbow, who actually came into school, and Mairi Hedderwick's fictional story of *Katie Morag and the Two Grandmothers*?

In the olddays the toliets used to be by the junior gate but now thay are by the hall and not by the gate. This is what I think it might have looked like.

Figure 16.6 *The Harborne Infant School toilets 'in the old days'*

- Use part of the book to transcribe the actual words spoken by the visitor. Compare these with the account members of the class wrote about what she said.
- Draw pictures based on what the visitor told them (see example from Harborne Infant School in Figure 16.6).
- Round up the book with a special section on change, e.g. the *visitor* then and now, the *area* around the school and *how things were done*. This moves the task on beyond description to explanation and analysis.

Raising standards in teaching and learning

The past decade has seen an explosion of government initiatives to codify and monitor standards of teaching and learning for all children over the age of three. These include *Curriculum Guidance for the Foundation Stage* (QCA, 2000), revision of *The National Curriculum* (QCA, 1999) and *A Scheme of Work for Key Stages 1 and 2: History* (QCA, 1998). They all recognise that the process of learning transcends subject boundaries and identifies skills and attitudes, whatever the content of the topic. They also provide a measure of every child's entitlement to the same education, whatever their circumstances.

The early learning goals

Taking the approach outlined above, historical experiences and activities can be a vehicle for advancing both the underlying principles for early years education and for enriching the areas of learning. The foundation stage document includes a specific recommendation to use the local community and environment as a source for learning. The local community will be the main resource for oral history and discussion of old buildings in the local area will lead to greater understanding of the children's immediate surroundings. Activities suggested in the personal, social and emotional development area of learning include examples of interaction with other people and a growing sense of belonging in a place, a family and a community. The use of questions, vocabulary extension, connecting ideas, understanding and explaining and solving problems all come within the communication, language and literacy remit. Awareness of the differences in age between different generations becomes an early mathematical concept and importance is placed on the use of tangible objects in understanding the world in which we live. Those things used by previous generations and how they have changed will contribute to knowledge and understanding of the world. Many of the examples of what children can be asked to do at the nursery end of their education can easily be transposed to include activities with a 'past' or 'change' dimension.

The national curriculum

History is included as a specific subject at Key Stage 1. The attainment targets for levels 1 and 2 suggest activities that will develop skills, attitudes and understanding. They expect that children will develop and refine their vocabulary of time and that they will be given experiences with historical sources that suit their age and ability. Difference, change and discussion about why things happened in the past are also part of the programme of study, which is also explicit about the kinds of topics which teachers should introduce. These include family history as well as stories about the lives of significant individuals – teachers are offered a free choice on this one; there are many select people associated with their own local area, commemorated in street names or in local memorials. Events from the past can also be presented in a narrative format and can be used as a structure to explore reasons why things happened as they did. Teachers are again free to choose, and many have selected relevant and exciting events that have some meaning in the local context. The schemes of work published by QCA provide examples of the three content strands. They are not statutory, and creative teachers can adapt them. Even within the constraints of a legal document it is possible to promote quality teaching and learning in history at Key Stage 1. Experience shows that few children find any difficulty in reaching the norm for their age, level 2, by the time they are seven.

Pointers for teaching history in the early years

- Be aware of the contribution history makes to the growth of personal and social identity.
- Ensure that activities and discussion promote investigation and enquiry.
- Develop language relating to time and open-ended discussion, which helps children explain as well as describe the past.
- Collect and display resources which children can handle (objects), talk about (books and pictures) and listen to (memories of older people, old rhymes and songs).
- Have a policy for history which identifies progression in skills, knowledge and understanding, and which promotes positive attitudes to history.

Acknowledgements

I am grateful to Diane Humphreys, early years coordinator at Arbury Primary School, Cambridge, for talking over many of these findings with me.

References

Forber, D. (ed.) undated, *Under-Fives and Museums: Guidelines for Teachers*, Telford: Ironbridge Gorge Museum Trust.

Forber, D, (ed.) (1990) *Primary Schools and Museums: Key Stage 1*, Telford: Ironbridge Gorge Museum Trust.

Mauser, M. and Reid, S. (1990) *Harborne Infant School Local History Project*, Birmingham: Education Department, Birmingham City Council.

QCA (1998) *A Scheme of Work for Key Stages 1 and 2: History*, London: QCA.

QCA (1999) *The National Curriculum*, London: QCA.

QCA (2000) *Curriculum Guidance for the Foundation Stage*, London: QCA.

Further reading

Cooper, H. (1995) *History in the Early Years*, London: Routledge.

Hazareesingh, S., Kenway, P. and Simms, K. (1994) *Speaking about the Past: A Resource for Teachers*, London: Trentham Books.

Pluckrose, H. (1991) *Children Learning History*, Oxford: Blackwell.

Purkis, S. (1991, revised 2000) *A Sense of History: Key Stage One Teachers' Book*, Harlow: Pearson Education.

Purkis, S. (2000) *A Sense of History: Key Stage 1 Coordinator's Handbook*, Harlow: Pearson Education.

Wright, M. (1992) *The Really Practical Guide to Primary History*, Cheltenham: Stanley Thornes.

CHAPTER 17

'If the world is round, how come the piece I'm standing on is flat?'

EARLY YEARS GEOGRAPHY

Dianne Conway and Pam Pointon

What is geography? Why teach geography?

These are questions asked by many early years educators who are not geography specialists. Comments such as 'I'm hopeless with maps!' or 'What can I do? There are no hills or mountains round here' are heard by those responsible for ensuring geography is taught in our schools. So, what is geography?

> Geography explores the relationship between the earth and its peoples. It studies the location of the physical and human features of the earth and the processes, systems and inter-relationships that create and influence them. The character of places, the subject's central focus, derives from the interaction of people and environments.
>
> (Curriculum Council for Wales, 1991)

That geography is such a wide-ranging subject that attempts to make connections between the earth sciences and the social sciences is its strength (which other subject tries to connect the human and natural worlds to the same extent?) – but also its difficulty in common-sense understanding. How many people, if asked to explain what geography is, would refer to Trivial Pursuit knowledge of countries and their capital cities, naming of capes and bays, listing of major rivers and mountain ranges? Locational knowledge is obviously an important element of geography, but if it is merely factual recall then the potential contribution is sadly diminished.

The current, more sophisticated approach includes a much broader view of what geography is about and a more active style of learning that engages children in observation, investigation, analysis and interpretation and encourages their development as young geographers. At the heart of the subject is its focus on both people and places through active exploration of their immediate environment. Their growing sense of 'their own special places' and curiosity about 'other places' is influenced by a range of experiences – both direct and vicarious through film, television, stories, music, computer games, CD-ROM, etc. as illustrated in the useful model by Goodey (1973).

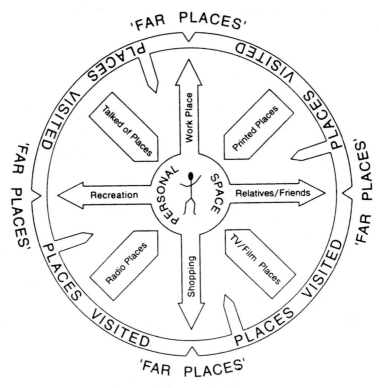

Figure 17.1 *Goodey's (1973) model of geographical experiences*

Developing learning experiences that extend young children's knowledge and stimulates their curiosity about the wider world is important. The starting point, however, needs to be their perception of their own personal space. This is unique to them and their perceptions may be influenced by a range of variables including age, gender, class, ethnicity or disability. Young children are able to articulate thoughts and feelings about places that have meaning for them and can forcefully express their likes and dislikes of particular features in their environment, as shown by this conversation between two 6-year-olds on a visit to the city:

I don't think I'd like to live in those flats. I wouldn't have a garden to play in. I think those small houses over there would be better.'

'Oh no. I'd rather live in the flat. The view would be great and there would be a lift to go in. Those houses are very small and squashed together.'

The argument continued along similar lines for quite a while. The group were able to appreciate that everyone has their own point of view and that these views may differ. They were able to see that sometimes there are no right or wrong answers.

Broad aims for geographical education

Geography for Ages 5 to 16 (DES, 1990) sets out the following broad aims for geographical education. It should:

- stimulate pupils' interests in their surroundings and in the variety of physical and human conditions on the earth's surface;
- foster their sense of wonder at the beauty of the world around them;
- help them to develop an informed concern about the quality of the environment and the future of the human habitat;
- and thereby enhance their sense of responsibility for care of the earth and its peoples.

These broad aims need to be achieved through a range of teaching objectives which may be subdivided into those concerned with skills, knowledge and understanding, and values and attitudes (see Figure 17.2).

Geographical enquiry

Pupils should not be primarily passive recipients of information but should be given adequate opportunities to carry out practical investigations, to explore and express ideas in their own language . . . and to reflect on other peoples' attitudes and values.

(_Geography from 5 to 16_, DES, 1986)

Involving young children in effective enquiry helps them to understand geographical concepts, develop geographical skills and explore the importance of values and attitudes in making sense of an increasingly complex and rapidly changing world.

Skills

- *Graphicacy* – the making, using and reading of maps; using globes and atlases; use of photographs, diagrams, graphs

- *fieldwork and enquiry skills* – observation, investigation, analysis and interpretation of primary and secondary sources

Values and attitudes

- an interest in other people and places

- awareness and appreciation of cultural and ethnic diversity within UK and beyond

- concern for quality of environments

- concern to value and conserve resources

- awareness of different perspectives on environmental issues

Knowledge and understanding

- general locational knowledge

- specific locational knowledge, e.g. local area, contrasting localities

- understanding key concepts:

    location – where is this place/feature in relation to other places/features?

    patterns – what is this place like? how are its building, parks, shops, etc. organised?

    relationships – connections between different elements within a place, e.g. where people live and where people shop, etc.

    processes – underlying reasons/causes for patterns and relationships which exist in the environment (local and global scale) and how they change over time

    similarity and difference – how is this place/feature similar/different to other places/features?

Figure 17.2 *Aims for geographical education*

	Key questions	**Activities**
Initial perception	What is it? What do I feel about it?	*Exploring* the beach – a sensory walk *Describing* – is it warm/cold/exciting/dull
Description and definition	What is it like?	*Collecting* – pebbles/rocks/sand/shells Taking photographs, drawing pictures *Observing/counting* – different shops, building
Analysis and exploration	How do people use the beach? Why do they go there?	*Analysing* activities *Analysing* postcards *Explaining* why the seaside is a good place for these activities

This partial enquiry sequence could be followed by:

Collecting artefacts – children bring into school pictures, souvenirs, postcards, photographs of seaside resorts.
Comparing similarities and differences – using artefacts and personal experiences, are all the seaside resorts the same? If not how do they differ?
Questioning/finding out about a contrasting resort – children discuss what they would like to find out about a Spanish holiday resort. In groups they construct four or five questions to ask. Children invite a visitor who has been to a Spanish holiday resort and ask questions: e.g. What is the beach like? What sort of food do you eat? What do people do there? What is the weather like? What sorts of shops ae there?

Figure 17.3 *Exploring the seaside: a geographical enquiry. Geography in the National Curriculum: Non Statutory Guidance for Teachers Curriculum Council for Wales (1991), p. 42*

What does enquiry involve?

- asking questions
- planning an investigation
- carrying out the investigation
- evaluating the conclusions

Enquiries can be of different lengths (one lesson to a whole term), of different foci (an issue, a place or a theme) and at different scales (local to global). Identifying geographical questions can be a useful initial stage in planning an enquiry. There are seven key geographical questions which provide a framework for enquiry, each question can be a focus for an entire enquiry and further sub-questions developed:

- Where is this place?
- What is this place like?
- Why is this place as it is?
- How is this place connected to other places?
- How is this place changing?
- What is it like to be in this place?
- How is this place similar to or different from another place?

A sample enquiry is shown in Figure 17.3 (*Non-statutory Guidance for Geography'*, Curriculum Council for Wales, 1991).

This next section offers a range of learning activities and useful resources for developing the young geographers' understanding of their world. The case study of 'Teddy's Visit' usefully highlights how an enquiry approach can be used to explore the local area and develop a real sense of place.

Developing map skills through play

All children enter school with some understanding and use of mapping skills. These skills have developed informally, directly from children's experiences. They are the result of activity and movement in and familiarity with the environment. These skills include an ability to:

- remember and find where objects are at home, e.g. their toys
- remember where features are in the local area and take or direct you to them, e.g. the swings
- find their way around their immediate environment, e.g. home, classroom, familiar play area

- talk about going to places that are some distance away, e.g. the seaside, my gran's, on a train, to London.

The most successful work will build on each child's spatial awareness and understanding and will acknowledge their experience in movement and spatial language. Much of it arises spontaneously out of traditional good practice in the early years classroom. It is important to recognise these opportunities to develop mapping skills and to think carefully about how to help children understand more from activities they naturally enjoy. Many of the activities outlined below happen in early years classrooms as a matter of course.

Using spatial language

It is important to emphasise the _where_ in talking with children, encouraging them to be precise about direction and location in relation to themselves, others and objects around.

- Encourage children to use locational vocabulary: it's behind . . ., it's next to . . ., it's in front of . . ., rather than it's there.
- Play games such as 'I spy' in which children have to name objects and the clue may be 'it's beside a table in front of the window next to the flowers'.
- When directing children to a resource in the classroom give them directions using direction words: 'go past the bookshelf, turn left, it is next to the red table'.
- Play games in pairs where the children have to give directions to identify objects or make journeys round the room.
- Encourage the children to give directions. Ask 'who knows where the . . .?' If telling is difficult ask children to show others where things are.

Thinking about distances

Mapping is about how far away things are. The children should be encouraged to think about distances and to make comparisons.

- When giving directions use positional vocabulary: 'it's near the table', 'it's on the other side of the room from . . .'.
- Make comparisons of longer and shorter around the classroom and school.
- Ask 'is it further to walk to the cloakroom or to the hall?' Ask the children to find out if they are correct.
- When making journeys talk about whether you are 'getting nearer' the destination and 'further away' from the starting point.

Using miniature world play

The activities outlined above can all be introduced and developed further and developed further by using play equipment found in all early years classrooms.

- The wet sand can be transformed into a landscape with model houses and trees for playpeople to live in.
- Playmats of road layouts and farm layouts are representations of reality in pictorial form. They allow children to look down on a landscape and make journeys.
- Construction toys on various scales can be used to model environments in which journeys can be made.
- The doll's house provides another miniature environment where positional language can be encouraged.
- Programmable toys such as 'Pip', 'Roamer' or 'Floor Turtle' can be used to make journeys and create environments.

Using plans and pictures

Photographs taken looking vertically down on objects and places interest young children. Take photographs of objects looking vertically down: the bin, chairs, toys, everyday objects, manhole covers – anything you see.

- Send the children off to find the object in the photograph.
- Draw the shapes of the object on card and ask the children to match the shape to the photograph.
- Encourage the children to draw their own overhead or bird's eye view of classroom objects.

These activities lead easily into discussions about a bird's eye view of school or the locality and the introduction of vertical aerial photographs and plans of the school building.

Using maps

Young children are fascinated by maps of any sort. Many children enter school with experience of a variety of maps:

- the weather map on television;
- pictorial maps from theme parks, holiday resorts, zoos, forest rails, etc.;
- maps on postcards;
- the road atlas and maybe a street map.

The early years educator can build on this experience by introducing a wide variety of maps including the more conventional ones (see the list in Figure 17.4).

street maps	building plans
postcard maps	road maps
maps in adverts	road sign maps
housing estate maps	house plans
tourist area maps	town centre maps
Ordnance Survey maps	trail maps
railway maps	bus route maps
room plans	storybook maps
board game maps	atlas maps
textbook maps	guidebook maps
wall chart maps	teacher drawn maps
maps drawn by children	picture maps
land use maps	'antique' maps
resort maps	sketch maps
playmat maps	newspaper maps
building site plans	globes
teaching pack maps	walkers' maps
aerial photomaps	airline route maps
jigsaw maps	mazes
theme park maps	tea towel maps
underground maps	

Figure 17.4 *Types of maps to show young children*

A school should have copies of Ordnance Survey (OS) maps of the locality:

1: 50,000 – 2cm on the map represents 1km on the ground.
1: 25,000 – 4cm on the map represents 1km on the ground.
1: 10,000 – 1cm on the map represents 100cm on the ground.
1: 2,500 – 1cm on the map represents 25cm on the ground.
1: 1,250 – 1cm on the map represents 12.5m on the ground.

Maps can be included in many activities. The youngest children will need help with orientation. Even if this is difficult, just handling the map is worthwhile.

A school plan can be used for journeys around school, for familiarisation or to carry messages. Groups of children, under the supervision of an adult, can be asked to try and follow a route marked on a school plan as a treasure hunt or an adventure game.

Street plans or Ordnance maps can be used for walks in the local environment or planning the route the postman might take to deliver letters to the children's homes.

Aerial photographs of the local area both vertical and oblique can be used alongside local conventional maps. Encourage children to talk about what they see in the picture, and to recognise from where it was taken.

Pictorial maps and theme park maps from holidays and weekend visits are usually attractively presented and give children lots of ideas for creating maps of their own.

The road atlas is often one of the most popular books in the book corner. It gives exciting opportunities for discussion amongst the children. Unfortunately many atlases quickly fall apart. Regular requests to parents for their out-of-date road atlases, particularly the hardback ones, need to be made. The following observations were made while watching a mixed Year 1/Year 2 class working with atlases:

> One 7-year-old was observed engrossed in the atlas for quite a long time. When asked what he was doing his reply was, 'I'm planning the route for my holiday in Cornwall.' When asked to show the teacher the route, he proceeded to find Cambridge and work his way through the atlas following the instructions to move to the next page until he arrived at the page showing Cornwall. A discussion followed about the different road colours shown on the map and he was able to pick out the motorways.
>
> Another group of children were to be found poring over the atlas after a coach trip to a small village 15 miles from school. They had identified the correct page and were soon able to find the village. They then spent a while trying to guess which route the coach had taken.
>
> The children discovered for themselves the index and how to use it. They very quickly learned how to look up the name of a place that they knew or had visited and find the correct page in the atlas.

The Map of the British Isles is familiar to most young children even if they do not know exactly what it is. It is seen on the weather forecast regularly. A video of several weather forecasts is a useful tool not only when thinking about the weather but also when learning the countries of Great Britain. Most weather forecasters mention and point to the countries as they make their forecast.

> The children enjoyed looking at a British Isles wall map and soon learned to spot the nearest large town, the nearest major river and

where it reached the coast. They asked about the shading on the map and could think of places where there were hills and mountains.

A globe creates a great deal of discussion and is a source of fascination to young children. Every classroom should have access to one (see Figure 17.5).

A world map can be used for discussing places children have visited and countries in the news.

Making maps

Drawing is another way of representing and trying to understand movement, location and distance. Many drawings done by young children show relationships between features, for instance, parts of the body or homes and streets. Map work should involve drawing, painting, making collages and modelling.

Figure 17.5 *'If the world is round, how come the piece I'm standing on is flat?'*

- Children could draw or paint their route to school. They should be encouraged to remember landmarks and other details (see Figure 17.6).
- Drawings can be made of layouts created with playmats and construction toys such as Lego.
- 'Junk model' representations of the classroom, parts of the school, or the locality can be made. The children can finger walk routes and talk about them or even record them on paper.
- Children could be encouraged to make their own playmats and miniature worlds to use with Playmobile or Lego people and cars.
- Many children are inspired by the idea of making treasure maps.

Using stories

Children's stories often involve journeys and things happening in places, e.g. *Rosie's Walk, Little Red Riding Hood* and many more. Stories need not be confined to storytime! They can be used as a source of geographical

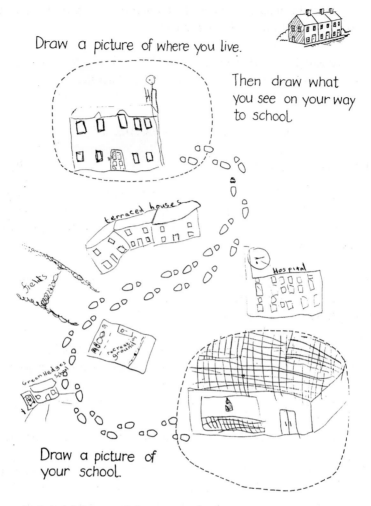

Draw a picture of where you live.

Then draw what you see on your way to school

terraced houses

fields

Hospital

recreation ground

Green Hedges

Draw a picture of your school.

Figure 17.6 *A child's map of the way to school*

information to set alongside fieldwork or mapping activities. They introduce young children to people, places and ideas. They contribute to children's understanding of and participation in the world around them. They help to foster children's curiosity about their changing world, e.g. *Where the Forest Meets the Sea*.

- Some stories have maps provided by the author or artist. These can be enlarged so that the route can be followed while the story is read.
- If there is no map either you or the children can create one, either small individual ones or a big wall frieze.

- The story could be acted out, creating an imaginary map or using furniture to represent the physical environment.

More ideas for using stories can be found in *Place in Story-time* by Nicholson (1994). Suitable stories are listed at the end of this chapter.

Using the local environment

Observational walks

Most children, and indeed many adults, are not used to observing their environment closely. It is a good idea to encourage observation when out and about on any visit. Observation skills can be taught as fun activities to the youngest children.

- The children have to identify the location of photographs taken around the classroom or around school grounds.
- Photographs of the locality can be used in a similar way.
- When out on a walk children can look for various items of street furniture, post boxes, telephone boxes, bus stops, road signs, traffic, etc. Make sure that the numbers involved are not too large and that the space to record or tally their results is large enough.
- The children might look at physical features: rivers, hills and farmland or buildings of different types and their use.
- Children can be asked to observe the quality of the environment and to discuss their likes and dislikes about places. They could be asked to list significant problems and their locations, such as dogs fouling footpaths, litter in the park and fumes in the street. After identifying the problem they could suggest what action could be taken to improve the environment.

Choosing a context for a local geographical study

The same principles apply to selecting a geographical theme as to any other area of study.

- Is it relevant and accessible to the children?
- Does it offer the opportunity to work from firsthand experience?
- Does it build on previous experience and knowledge?
- Will it enable the children to ask questions and search for answers?
- Can it be adequately resourced?

Young children should begin their geographical study in their immediate environment around themes such as our school, our village, journeys, where I live, homes, a place to live or people who help us. For the older Key Stage 1 children many of these themes can be extended to include localities further afield, i.e. the nearest city or a smaller village.

Many of the practical ideas given earlier in this chapter can be used in these themes. A geographically based theme usually allows study in a cross-curricular way. There are opportunities for work in all areas of the curriculum. Below are two examples of cross-curricular projects that can be included in any locality study.

The Picnic

This project involves the children asking questions and considering various possible solutions. It gives opportunities to cover areas of maths and technology as well as geography. There is also some consideration of health issues.

- Where shall we go for our picnic?
- How shall we get there?
- Which route will we take?

A local map is found. The children discuss various local picnic spots. They consider transport and maybe costs. A route is planned.

- Could we go by one route and return a different way?
- Whose route is the quickest or the most interesting?

Then comes the most important set of questions:

- What food shall we eat?
- Which foods are good to eat on a picnic?
- Where can we buy the food we need?

The children plan a walk to the local shop to find the answers. They return with some answers but also with more questions:

- How much of everything do we need to buy?
- Can we bake some cakes and biscuits ourselves?
- What will we put our picnic in?
- Could we design a lunch box?

A list of food is drawn up and the children decide what they would like. The data are gathered and sorted into a shopping list. A request is sent home for the money to cover the cost of the shopping. Recipes are found, ingredients listed, help with cooking is requested. Now there are more questions:

- When shall we go on our picnic?
- When shall we make the cakes?
- When shall we buy the ingredients to make the cakes?
- Can we buy all our food then?
- If not, when do we need to buy the other food for the picnic?

Then it's off to the shop again for the cooking ingredients.

- Perhaps we could find a different route to the shop?
- How long does it take?
- Is it a longer route than last time?

The baking is done. More shopping lists are planned and prepared so that every child can do some of the shopping. It is a good idea to warn the shop that 30 young shoppers will be coming. Try not to choose a busy time of day or delivery day. With 15 lists prepared, 30 children set off to the shop clutching their shopping bags and money.

- What do I do first when I go into the shop?
- How can I find what I want?
- How much does it cost?
- Where do I pay?
- Do I get any change? How much?

On the day of the picnic the bread is buttered, sandwiches and drinks are made. Then 30 excited children carrying lunch boxes and maps set off for the picnic spot. If it is a local park or playground there could be a discussion about the play equipment, more observation work, and consideration of the quality of the environment. As a follow-up task the children could be asked to design their own play area and maybe make a model.

By using books like *Sam's Sandwich* and *Sam's Snack* by David Pelham, the children can be encouraged to write and create their own such books.

Teddy's Visit

This activity is rather like a story that unfolds and develops as the weeks go by. The ideas for activities have all been tried out by a mixed Year 1/Year 2 class. Some activities can be used by younger children.

The story begins one morning when a small suitcase or bag is found on a chair in the classroom. It has a large label saying: 'Please look after this bear.' Inside is a small teddy bear. He has a map and a message with him saying that he is lost and needs help to find out which country he is in and to mark his location on the map (see Figure 17.7).

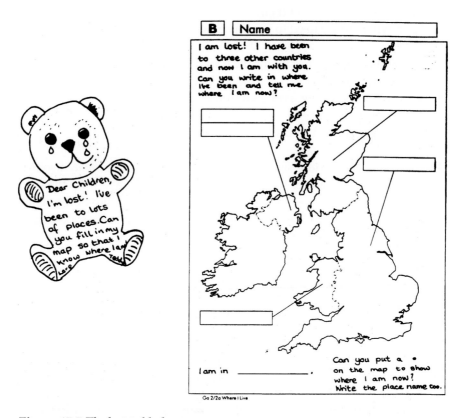

Figure 17.7 *The lost teddy bear*

The map is photocopied and everyone tries to help Teddy out. Teddy spends time with each group as they work.

The next day there is another message from Teddy saying he would like to be shown around the school. So groups of children armed with route maps take him around. On another occasion he asks the children to write about themselves so that he can get to know them. His next request is to be taken on a walk around the neighbourhood. Another session with the maps and some route planning to make sure Teddy sees all the important parts of the area around school. Teddy is carried carefully in various pockets. He must not get lost again! He might even request a picnic as a treat, and so we get into planning a picnic as discussed above.

Then one morning Teddy is not in his bag. He has left a note (see Figure 17.8) to say he is hiding and the children are to follow the instructions to find him but they must keep his hiding place a secret.

Hello, I'm Yellow Teddy.

I am hiding in your classroom. Can you find me? Follow the instructions and see if you can find me. Mark where you went on the map.

Start at the tape recorder -

forward 5 steps
turn left
forward 2 steps
turn right
forward 2 steps
turn left
forward 4 steps
turn left
forward 5 steps
turn right
forward 3 steps
turn left
forward 4 steps

Open the door.

Can you see me?

SSHH....Don't tell anyone.

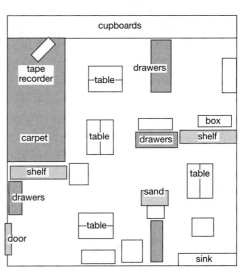

Figure 17.8 *Instructions to find Teddy*

This game can go on for several days with different hiding places. The children can devise their own instructions to new hiding places. Eventually Teddy grows tired of the classroom and asks the children to take him home to their house to play. But before they can take him they must be able to fill in their address on his label, just in case he gets lost again! While he is visiting them they are asked to do some tasks:

- read Teddy the storybook in his bag;
- get a grown-up to read the harder storybook to them both;
- write Teddy's diary so he can remember his visit;
- draw a route map of how to get back to school. He might get lost!

Teddy might accompany the children on other trips and visits that the class make. If it is possible he might request a ride on a train or a bus. During his stay, of course, he likes to hear stories about teddy bears, either real books or those stories written by the children. In the end Teddy receives a letter inviting him to visit a relative in another country. So out come the maps. Teddy is helped to plan his journey, his bag is labelled and then one night he disappears.

> The class became very involved with Teddy. They were enthusiastic about the tasks he gave them. They were very concerned when he really did get lost! On one walkabout he was dropped in a puddle and was left out to dry on a radiator overnight. The caretaker thinking he had been left by a younger child put him in the lost property bin. The search the next day was frantic. Teddy was well hugged when he returned.
>
> The children were particularly keen to take Teddy home. They learned their addresses quickly. His diary was carefully written. The parents played their part well and shared the children's tasks. Teddy was included in lots of the children's activities: parties, November 5th fireworks in the city, TV, computer games and meals out. There were lots of talking opportunities the next day. Even the shy children had something to say.

So geography is fun. It is happening and probably has been happening in early years classrooms for many years. Young children are fascinated by their surroundings and have the capacity to build upon natural learning experiences. Through topics like those outlined above, young children will learn from firsthand experience that there is a relationship between people and places and that they themselves can have an influence on the environment. It is important to recognise that many of the things we do have geographical possibilities. A geographical topic gives good opportunities for cross-curricular work in many subjects.

Pointers for early years geography

The following key points are important to recognise and remember when planning for geographical activities in early years classrooms:

- Young children are already active geographers.
- It is important to explore feelings about places as well as developing skills.
- Opportunities should be provided for young children to explore known and unknown worlds through play, stories, maps, photographs, etc.
- Enquiry is central, especially though not exclusively through fieldwork investigations.
- There is a wealth of resources available locally for developing geographical awareness.

Stories involving journeys or places

The Three Bears (1985), Murdock, H., Ladybird.
Jack and the Beanstalk (1987), Hunia, F., Ladybird.
Hansel and Gretel, in *Classic Fairy Tales* (1993), Cresswell, H., HarperCollins.
Red Riding Hood (1988), Southgate, V., Ladybird.
The Three Pigs (1989), Southgate, V., Ladybird.
The Gingerbread Man (1966), Southgate, V., Ladybird.
Dick Whittington (1986), Southgate, V., Ladybird.
Town Mouse and Country Mouse (1982), McKie, A., Ladybird.
Three Billy Goats Gruff (1984), Traditional, J.M. Dent.
Fantastic Mr Fox (1970), Dahl, R., George Allen Unwin.
Winnie-the-Pooh (1926), Milne, A.A., Methuen.
Where The Forest Meets the Sea (1987), Baker, J., Julia MacRae Books.
Window (1991), Baker, J., Julia MacRae Books.
Don't Forget the Bacon (1978), Hutchins, P., Picture Puffin.
Rosie's Walk (1992), Hutchins, P., Picture Puffin.
Our Village (1988), Yeoman, J. and Blake, Q., Walker Books.
The Little Prince and the Great Dragon Chase (1994), Kavanagh, Simon & Schuster.
Penguin Small (1992), Inkpen, M., Hodder Children's Books.

Finn Family Moomintroll (1950), Janssen, T., Ernest Benn.
Enchanted Wood (1991), Hawkesley, G., Tree House Children's Books.

References

Curriculum Council for Wales (1991) *Geography in the National Curriculum: Non Statutory Guidance for Teachers*, CCW.
DES (1986) *Geography from 5–16 Curriculum Matters 7*, London: HMSO.
DES (1990) *Geography for Ages 5–16*, London: HMSO.
Goodey, B. (1973) *Perception of the Environment: An Introduction to the Literature, Occasional Paper No. 17*, Birmingham: University of Birmingham Centre for Urban and Regional Studies.
Nicholson, H.N. (1994) *Place in Story-time*, Sheffield: Geographical Association.

Further reading

Foley, M. and Janikoun, J. (1992) *The Really Practical Guide to Primary Geography*, Cheltenham, Gloucestershire: Stanley Thornes.
Geographical Association: *Primary Geographer* (quarterly magazine published specifically for non-specialist primary teachers, available from Geographical Association, 343 Fulwood Road, Sheffield, S10 3BP).
Hulme, B., James, F. and Kerr, A. (1995) *A Sense of Place*, Twickenham: Belair.
Marsden, B. and Hughes, J. (1994) *Primary School Geography*, London: David Fulton.
Milner, A. (1994) *Geography Starts Here*, Sheffield: Geographical Association.
Palmer, J. (1994) *Geography in the Early Years*, London: Routledge.
Wiegand, P. (1992) *Places in the Primary School*, London: Falmer Press.

The way
forward

CHAPTER 18

Whatever next?

FUTURE TRENDS IN EARLY YEARS EDUCATION

Mary Jane Drummond

In this chapter I will explore the proposition that the ways in which we think about young children can and do affect the ways in which we provide for their learning and support their development. To put it another way, what we know about children, or think we know, shapes what we do for them in the name of education. I will examine some ways of thinking about children, and children's learning, taken from recent accounts of early years classrooms (and other settings) and try to show how we might take steps to reorganise and reshape our thoughts, our assumptions and our expectations. Future developments in early years education will, I believe, spring from the efforts of educators who prioritise the serious work of thinking about children's learning, and thereby achieve an enhanced understanding of children and childhood.

Teachers teaching and children learning

One of the most challenging and entertaining books I have ever read about children's learning is *GNYS AT WRK: A Child Learns to Write and Read* (Bissex, 1980). It is a detailed, vivid, firsthand narrative account of how 5-year-old Paul became an accomplished writer and reader; what makes it different is not just its puzzling title (taken from a notice Paul pinned over his workbench-desk at the age of 5 years, 6 months) but its insider's viewpoint: the author, Glenda L. Bissex, is Paul's mother. She was also, when the story began, an educator studying for her master's degree in education. One afternoon, when she was trying to read, Paul wanted to play with her.

Frustrated in his attempts to make her put down her book, Paul disappeared for a few minutes, returning with a piece of paper, on which he had printed, with rubber stamps from his printing set, the letters RUDF (Are you deaf?) His mother was dumbstruck and, in her own words, 'Of course I put down my book.'

The bulk of the book comprises Bissex's regular observations of her son's acts of writing and reading, illustrated with copious extracts from the written material that Paul produced over the six years of the study: there are excerpts from stories, lists, notices, books of jokes, report cards for his pets (including marks for PEING) and, in due course, when he starts school (at 5 years, 10 months) his first written texts from the classroom, sadly stilted, after the richness of his earlier output. For example, at 6 years 10 months at school he writes: 'This is my reading book', whereas at 6 years, 5 months, in just one day at home, he had written four newspapers, complete with cartoons, news, advertising and weather (THE SAFTERNEWN IT'S GOING TO RAIN).

Bissex's commentary and conclusions are based on her privileged position as both mother and educator. With a kind of binocular vision, she sees some disconcerting truths about how educators intervene in children's learning. In one memorable passage she writes:

> We speak of starting with a child 'where he is', which in one sense is not to assert an educational desideratum but an inescapable fact; there is no other place the child can start from. There are only other places the educator can start from.
>
> (Bissex, 1980, p.111)

I hope I am not alone in finding this insight an uncomfortable one. Bissex seems to me to be suggesting, all too credibly, that educators do (sometimes? often?) start in 'other places', and that the consequences for children's learning are frequently undesirable. Furthermore this suggestion seems to be an alternative version of the proposition with which I began: that how we think about children – or 'the child' – is of crucial importance in how we educate them – or him, or her. And this proposition, however we phrase it, raises questions worth worrying about. If early years educators do not, as Bissex suggests, start 'where the child is', with a coherent and principled understanding of the child's learning, then where do they start? And why? Can we learn to move closer to a more desirable starting point? What would it look like? What do we really mean by this 'educational desideratum', or an enhanced understanding of children?

My suspicions that Bissex is telling us something important about teaching and learning are based on two distinct sources of evidence: first, my own experiences as an educator and observer in early years classrooms and other settings for young children, and second, written accounts and research studies of what early years educators actually do, and how they conceptualise the relationship between teaching and learning.

My own firsthand experience tells me that, all too often, my carefully prepared activities, my lovingly drawn-up topic webs, my finely adjusted schemes of work, have failed to connect with children's pressing intellectual concerns, or with their energetic and enquiring minds. My observations in other classrooms have, over the years, confirmed my awareness of what I think of as 'the curriculum gap', the distance, sometimes a hair's breadth, sometimes a yawning chasm, that stands between what educators teach and what children learn.

If there is such a gap, and I am certain that there is, at least some of the time, in every setting for young children, I am equally certain that it cannot be attributed to malice or apathy in the hearts and minds of early years educators. Nor do published studies of children's early experiences at school (Wells, 1987, or Hughes, 1989, for example) resort to the language of blame to account for what they see in classrooms. These authors do not mince words in identifying the mismatch between the educators' benevolent and educational intentions and the children's learning. But nor do they suggest that educators deliberately disable learners, or consciously create dysfunctional learning environments. So what is going wrong? And what can we do to put it right?

Some of the evidence suggests that part of the problem lies in the weakness of the language in which we describe and justify our work. In an early study of infant teachers' thinking (or, rather, a study of what infant teachers are prepared to say about their work to investigative sociologists), Sharp and Green (1975) report an interview with 'Mrs Carpenter', a teacher of a vertically grouped class of rising-fives to rising-sevens. The discussion turned to the need for structure in teaching.

The interview proceeded as follows:

Interviewer: How do you mean?

Teacher: I mean we all, well, I have a little plan but I don't really... I just sort of, mmm, try and work out what stages each child is at and take it from there.

Interviewer: How do you do this? How does one notice what stage a child is at?

Teacher: Oh we don't really know, you can only say the stage he isn't at really, because you know when a child doesn't know but you don't really know when he knows. Do you see what I mean? You can usually tell when they don't know (long pause). (There was a distraction in the interview at this point.) What was I talking about?

Interviewer:	Certain stages, knowing when they know –
Teacher:	– and when they don't know. But even so, you still don't know, when they really don't (pause) you can't really say they don't know, can you? . . . That's why really that plan they wanted wouldn't have worked. I wouldn't have been able to stick to it, because you just don't . . . you know when they don't know, you don't know when they know.
Interviewer:	How do you know when they don't know?
Teacher:	How do I know when they don't know? (pause) Well, no, it's not so much that you don't know. I know when they're not ready to know, perhaps that's a better way of putting it.

(Sharp and Green, 1975, p.168)

The disarming candour of these statements should not blind us to the poverty of the understanding they express. This teacher, for all her good intentions, which I am willing to take for granted, is unlikely to be able to start 'where the child is'. She does not, on the evidence of this interview, have a way of explaining, even to herself, what it is that the educator knows when she or he knows where a child is, or what it is that the educator must then do with that knowledge.

Sharp and Green's work has been succeeded by other enquiries, less ideologically driven, but reaching similarly worrying conclusions. For example, Bennett et al. (1984) investigated the match between tasks and pupils, and identified a chronic weakness in educators' skills of diagnosis. In this carefully planned and cautiously quantified study of 'the quality of pupil learning experiences', the researchers found that more than half the observed tasks were badly matched to the child's level of understanding and achievement. High attainers were regularly underestimated and low attainers overestimated (p.65).

The diagnostic skills of a group of 17 experienced infant teachers were studied in detail. As part of an inservice course, they were asked to examine transcriptions of some of the mismatched tasks recorded in the early part of the study. They were invited to discuss what seemed to be going on, to hypothesise about the children's understanding, and to explore any questions raised by the observations. The authors report that the teachers were extremely unwilling to respond to the classroom material in this way. 'They saw all problems as self-evident . . . (they) made no use of the notion of hunch or hypothesis . . . all problems were to be solved by direct teaching' (p.197). It seems as though these teachers' prime concern was with the quality of teaching, and that they had correspondingly little interest in learning.

Evidence from studies such as these suggests that there is indeed a problem. The professional language of the early years educator does not seem to be robust enough to frame adequate or effective descriptions of children and their learning. It is, I believe, not just the looseness and vagueness of the words we use that let us down, but a more fundamental issue. Starting 'where the child is', for all its familiarity as a slogan, as an 'educational desideratum', is simply not the best place to start; it is not an effective way of conceptualising the enterprise of early years education.

'To have' and 'To be'

I am influenced in this suggestion by the work of Erich Fromm, sociologist and psychoanalyst, who suggested in *To Have or To Be?* (1976) that the human condition in general is suffering from the dominance of western society's desire 'to have', at the expense of our understanding of what it is 'to be'. Applying this distinction to early years education, to its curriculum, its pedagogy, and its most idealistic aspirations, suggests to me that there is a need to re-emphasise our understanding of what children are, rather than where they are, or what we want them to have. Since, as Fromm says, 'there is no being that is not, at the same time, becoming and changing', it follows that, if we know what we want children to be, in the first four or five years of their educational lives, then we are likely to be effective in helping them to become the well-educated 7 or 8-year-olds who will move into the next stage of their education. We will be well placed too, during their years of early education, to support to the utmost their present 'powers to be', another of Fromm's memorable phrases (in *Man for Himself*, 1949).

Since reading and rereading Fromm, I have been drawing on his concept of children's 'powers to be' in my thinking and writing, and I am slowly becoming convinced of the strength of this starting point in thinking about the future of early years education. This vital phase of education has, until recently, straddled the statutory/pre-statutory divide. Now the years from 3 to 5 have been retitled the foundation stage, and educators are being encouraged to think of this period as a distinct phase of education. By the time they enter Key Stage 1, 'foundation stage children' will have been living and learning for five solid years, in their homes, and in a bewildering variety of other settings. But both before and after the children's fifth birthdays, we, their educators, are still at liberty to think about them in ways that match our philosophy and our principles. In Key Stage 1, and in terms of teaching, coverage and content, we will, for the foreseeable future, be working with the core and foundation subjects and religious education. In the foundation stage we will be working within the terms of the QCA document *Curriculum Guidance for the Foundation Stage* (2000). But in terms of children's learning, we are still at liberty to think for ourselves, using the QCA's early learning goals as a support, not a substitute, for our own thinking work. And I am arguing here that we cannot do better than to think in terms of what we know for certain about children's powers – their powers to do, to think, to feel, to know and understand, to represent and express. There is no compulsion on us to think of children in the early years as, exclusively, students of mathematics, literacy, science and so on. There are, if children's learning is our priority, more effective ways to be their educators than by surrendering our own powers to think to the guidance we have so generously been offered.

By way of encouragement, we might turn to an exciting curriculum document from New Zealand, which sets out guidelines for the education of children from birth to 6 (the age of starting school). The Maori title of their bilingual document, *Te Whariki*, refers to a traditional hand-made mat, which can be woven in an infinite variety of patterns; it represents the idea that the planned curriculum, based on commonly agreed goals and principles, can have a different pattern for every kind of early years service, in every individual early years centre. This in itself is a stimulating approach from the perspective of this country, but even more challenging is the set of ideas embodied in the five goals that constitute the heart of the guidelines.

These goals are:

- **well-being**
  (the health and well-being of the child are protected and nurtured)
- **belonging**
  (children and their families feel a sense of belonging)
- **contribution**
  (opportunities for learning are equitable and each child's contribution is valued)
- **communication**
  (the languages and symbols of their own and other cultures are promoted and protected)
- **exploration**
  (the child learns through active exploration of the environment)

Early years educators in New Zealand, in whatever kind of setting, are invited to commit themselves to these goals for children; some of them may seem to go almost without saying, but others are well worth thinking about more carefully. The goal of well-being fits securely within the British tradition; we are still proudly conscious of the legacy from the great pioneers of early education – Rachel and Margaret McMillan, for example, working in the back streets of Bradford and Deptford to bring health and hygiene into the lives of young children (Steedman, 1990). The goal of communication is equally likely to receive general assent from early years educators here, though it may be some years yet before our Department for Education publishes its curriculum guidelines in two languages. But the goals of belonging and contributing are radical departures from our familiar ways of thinking.

In these goals, it seems to me, the New Zealand educators are setting out their aspirations for children's 'powers to be'; they are explicitly prioritising their belief that children can, and should, be members of a harmonious community, in which they have a place, to which they can make a contribution. This is a way of thinking about young children, and the education they deserve that, I believe, we might enthusiastically try for ourselves.

The New Zealand representation of children's powers set out in *Te Whariki* reads easily enough across on to a model of children's learning that is proposed in a series of questions set out in *Making Assessment Work: Values and Principles in Assessing Children's Learning* (Drummond, Rouse and Pugh, 1992). In this discussion pack, the authors argue that effective assessment is predicated on the educator's principled understanding of the purposes of early years education. Practitioners are invited to ask themselves about their aspirations for children. What do we want our young children:

- to do?
- to feel?
- to think?
- to know and understand?
- to represent and express?

Answering these questions, is, I believe, part of the way forward for early years education in this country. And there are, fortunately for us, many sources to which we can turn to support us in our thinking. In this volume too, other authors have written of their personal experiences of children's powers, and the versatility and enthusiasm of children's learning in appropriately structured environments. There is a healthy emphasis, throughout this collection, on the range of children's powers, and an accompanying emphasis on the context – children's play – in which so many of these powers are exercised.

Play and imagination

This emphasis on play is an important element in the argument to be made for a distinctive approach to early years education. But it is also a particularly challenging part of the task that lies ahead. Every early years educator, it is safe to assume, has at some time been made painfully aware that the importance of play in educational settings is not universally acknowledged. Although numbers of recent publications have taken up the challenge, and defended the educational value and outcomes of play, perhaps we have put too much professional energy into defending the contentious verb 'to play', which in some quarters is used as the polar opposite of the verb 'to learn' – see Michael Fallon's notorious speech about pre-school play groups, for example.[1] Perhaps we would do better to emphasise 'play' in its noun form, and to construct our arguments around a full description of what, in the context of play, children think, feel, do, understand and express. What kinds of thinking and feeling characterise play? Are they important? Might it not be easier to make a case for the imagination, or for empathy, or for experiment and exploration, than for play?

In making such a case as an in service educator, working with practitioners from settings across the foundation stage, I have found it salutary to see the confidence and the zeal with which other educationalists, outside the early years community, argue a position that I find thoroughly convincing. Mary Warnock, for example, moral philosopher as well as educational reformer, argues in *Schools of Thought* (1977) that the imagination is good in itself. Being more imaginative, like being more healthy, needs no further justification (p.153). In *Imagination* (1976), Warnock makes even bolder claims:

> I have come very strongly to believe that it is the cultivation of imagination which should be the chief aim of education, and in which our present systems of education most conspicuously fail, where they do fail . . . in education we have a duty to educate the imagination above all else.
>
> (p.9)

She characterises imagination as the human power 'to go beyond what is immediately in front of (their) noses', and, in a telling phrase she has borrowed from Coleridge, as the capacity to 'see into the life of things'. It is a power which is not only intellectual: 'its impetus comes from the emotions as much as from the head.' Imagination is both necessary and universal; as part of human intelligence it needs educating, and this will entail 'an education not only of the intelligence but, going along with it, of the feelings' (p. 202).

The need for high expectations

Warnock's aspirations for the human condition, even in this briefest of summaries, seem to me to illuminate some exciting possibilities for children's early learning. If we can recognise, as I believe we can, the young child's powers to think and to feel, we can see clearly the weight of our responsibility to educate, to exercise and strengthen those powers.

In recent years, there has been considerable interest in an approach to early years education practised in the Emilia-Romagna district of Italy. A touring exhibition of their work, *The Hundred Languages of Children*, which has visited the UK twice in recent years, testifies to the extraordinary richness of their early educational provisions. 'The cornerstone of our experience', says Carla Rinaldi, until recently the Director of Services to Young Children in the region, is an understanding of children as 'rich, strong and powerful'. She spells out what this means:

> they have . . . plasticity, the desire to grow, curiosity, the ability to be amazed, and the desire to relate to other people and communicate . . . . Children are eager to express themselves in a plurality of symbolic languages . . . (they) are open to exchanges and reciprocity as deeds and acts of love which they not only want to receive but also want to offer.
>
> (Edwards, Gandini and Forman, 1993, pp. 101–2)

There are interesting parallels here, I think, with the New Zealand educators' categories of belonging and contributing. But the Italian educators are not exclusively interested in the social dimension of learning; they go on to describe a central feature of their provision, the atelier, a creative workshop, rich in materials and tools, in which children from birth to 3, as well as from 3–6, become masters of 'all the symbolic languages' (such as painting, drawing and working in clay). In the atelier, 'children invent autonomous vehicles of expressive freedom, cognitive freedom, symbolic freedom and paths to communication' (ibid., p. 120). In the atelier, surely, they are exercising the powers that Warnock describes: 'to see into the life of things' – and not just to see, but to represent and express what they see.

The Reggio Emilia approach to early childhood provision has, I am arguing, much to teach us in this country. I am not suggesting that we should follow their prescriptions to the letter, or that we should swallow, wholesale, their priorities and perceptions. But I am convinced that their way of seeing children, from birth, as strong to do and feel, skilled in learning, powerful in communicating, has profound effects upon the curriculum they provide, a curriculum that is sensitively and challengingly matched to the children's developing 'powers to be'. Their expectations of what children can do, and think and feel, are, to English eyes and ears, extraordinarily high. But the children in their settings rise to these expectations, as they explore both the world that is opening out in front of them, and their own interior worlds of feeling and imagination. As one reads the detailed accounts of their cross-curricular projects, given in Edwards' book, and in a growing number of other publications (for example, Gandini and Edwards, 2001), one wonders what these Italian educators would make of some of the experiences provided in early years settings in this country.

My own observations of 4-year-olds in their first terms in primary school in several local authorities suggest that, in some classrooms, children's powers are seriously undervalued. The demands made on the children – to follow instructions, to complete worksheets, to cut and stick and colour in, as required by their educators – do not do justice to the children's energetic and enthusiastic minds. In one classroom, as part of a local authority evaluation programme (Drummond, 1995), a child was observed using a template to draw a shape representing a T-shirt on a square piece of wallpaper. The T-shirt was one of twenty similar cutouts, destined for a frieze of teddy bears, who were being changed from their winter outfits to their summer clothes as part of the classroom topic on The Summer. The child followed his teacher's directions as best he could, but the scissors were far from sharp and the wallpaper prone to tear. After some frustrating minutes had passed, the child looked up at the teacher who was leading this activity and said, 'I can sew, you know.' I take this child's comment seriously, as a gentle – even forgiving – admonition to his educators. It is as if he were telling them to think again, to question their motives in asking him to perform this meaningless and unrewarding task. It is as if he were pointing out, most politely, that his powers to think, and do, and feel, were not being nourished or exercised by a curricular diet of templates and teddy bear friezes.

Bennett et al. (1984), we have already noted, found evidence that teachers both overestimated and underestimated children's abilities to complete language and number tasks. One particularly interesting finding from this study is that the problem of underestimation, when the task set was too easy for a child, seemed to be 'invisible to teachers in classrooms'. (p.49). The teachers in the study did not identify any tasks as beneath the child's attainment level, not challenging enough, or as a waste of a child's time. Bennett et al. explain this finding by reference to the emphasis placed on procedure, rather than product, in number and language tasks. When teachers saw children correctly following these procedures (using full stops in their writing, for example, or carrying a ten in an addition task), they 'did not compare the child's product with his actual level of understanding' (p.63). They appeared to be satisfied with the children's compliance with the procedures they had been taught. This explanation seems reasonable enough, but it may be only half of the story. If one piece of the puzzle is excessive concern for procedures as defined by the educator, then another, equally important, element in the picture is a serious lack of concern for what children can do for themselves. It appears that the teachers in this study were not interested in the possibility that the children could do more than was required of them. They seemed to be blind to children's inventiveness, their individual ways of seeing, their personal explorations into the unknown.

By contrast, in another classroom in the evaluation study cited above (Drummond, 1995) a group of young children spent 25 minutes absorbed in water play. The nursery nurse had, at their request, added some blue dye to the water, and the children were intrigued by the different shades of blue they could see: paler at the shallow margin, and darker at the deepest, central part of the water tray. One child was even more interested in another, related phenomenon. He spent nearly ten minutes of this period of water play observing his own shoes and how their colour appeared to change when he looked at them, through the water and the transparent water tray. The child seemed to be fascinated by what happened when he placed his feet in different positions; he leaned intently over the tray to see what colour his shoes appeared to be at each stage. He did not use the words *experiment* or *observation*, but that was what he was engaged in, nonetheless. After each trial, he withdrew his feet into the natural light of day, as if to check that they retained their proper colour. Had the dye stayed in the water, where he had seen it put, or had some of it seeped out, into his shoes?

At the end of the morning session, the teacher and nursery nurse announced that it was time to tidy up. The children worked together to empty the water tray of the sieves, funnels and beakers they had been using. They took out the jugs, the teaspoons and the ladles, emptied them, and put them away. When they had nearly finished, the boy stopped and asked aloud, of no one in particular, 'How do we get the blue out?'

I think this is a remarkable question, showing as it does this young scientist's mind at work. Only further conversation with him would reveal his present understanding of the concepts of light, colour and reversibility; but his question is incontrovertible evidence of his urgent desire to find out how the world works, how its regularities and unpredictabilities can be accounted for. It is evidence too of his already firmly established knowledge that, as an active member of the world, he can experiment with it, act on it, question it, and reflect on it, on the way to understanding it.

This child's powerful question offers his educators exciting opportunities for development, but only if they respond to what he can do, and is doing. If they focus on what he does not know, or does not fully understand, they will miss the chance to feed and exercise his growing powers to hypothesise and experiment. The way they conceptualise this child's question – as genuine enquiry, or unthinking ignorance – will directly affect the experiences they go on to provide for him.

Conclusion

I have been arguing that the way forward for early years education is in a re-examination of some of our taken-for-granted assumptions and expectations. If educators, without any ill-will, think of young children as immature, incapable, illiterate, or ignorant pupils, then the experiences and activities they provide will not give children opportunities to prove themselves for what they really are: accomplished learners, passionate enquirers, loving companions. The primary classroom and its predefined tasks, the early years setting and its learning goals, will simply not be spacious enough for the exercise of children's powers *to be*: to be scientists, artists, citizens, dramatists, moralists, constructing and reconstructing the world.

But if early years educators can free themselves from any notion that because the children they work with are the youngest children in the system, not yet ready for the heavy demands of Key Stage 1, they are therefore the least capable, and least competent, then the future looks bright. There is then a real possibility that we can provide experiences, time and space, food and exercise, for learners who are already, long before they start school, capable, competent, imaginative and eloquent.

The founder and, for many years, Director of the Reggio Emilia programme is the late and much revered Loris Malaguzzi. In a long interview about the principles underpinning their developing pedagogy he describes how, in Italy too, pressure from later stages of education threatens to distort and deform early years practices.

> If the school for young children has to be preparatory, and provide continuity with the elementary school, then we as educators are already prisoners of a model that ends up as a funnel. I think, moreover, that the funnel is a detestable object, and it is not much appreciated by children either. Its purpose is to narrow down what is big into what is small. This choking device is against nature.
>
> (Edwards et al., 1993, p. 86)

But Malaguzzi is optimistic, visionary even, in his determination that early years education will not choke or be choked. His fundamental position is a succinct summary of the argument I have proposed here: 'Suffice it to say that the school for young children has to respond to the children.' I have suggested that for settings for young children to do this, our starting point must be a thorough understanding of what children are, in order that we can support their being and becoming. And if we can achieve such an understanding, we will be well placed to share in the glory of Malaguzzi's vision of the future. 'The continuing motivation for our work,' he claims, is 'to liberate hopes for a new human culture of childhood. It is a motive that finds its origin in a powerful nostalgia for the future and for humankind' (ibid., p. 88)

Note

1. Michael Fallon, then Minister for Schools, spoke to the National Primary Conference of the NAHT on 1 November 1991. His speech included these words:

> At worst, this kind of practice (topic work) turns primary schools into pre-school playgroups where there is much happiness and painting but very little learning.

References

Bennett, N., Desforges, C., Cockburn A. and Wilkinson B. (1984) *The Quality of Pupil Learning Experiences*, London: Lawrence Erlbaum Associates.

Bissex, G.L. (1980) *GNYS AT WRK: A Child Learns to Write and Read*, Cambridge, MA: Harvard University Press.

Drummond, M. J. (1995) *In School at Four*, Hampshire's earlier admissions programme, final evaluation report. Spring 1995, Hampshire County Council.

Drummond, M. J., Rouse, D. and Pugh, G. (1992) *Making Assessment Work. Values and Principles in Assessing Young Children's Learning*, Nottingham: NES Arnold/National Children's Bureau.

Edwards, C., Gandini, L. and Forman, G. (1993) *The Hundred Languages of Children: The Reggio Emilia Approach to Early Childhood Education*, Norwood, NJ: Ablex Publishing Corporation.

Fromm, E. (1949) *Man for Himself*, London: Routledge & Kegan Paul.

Fromm, E. (1976) *To Have or To Be?*, London: Jonathan Cape.

Gandini, L. and Edwards, C. (eds) (2001) *Bambini: The Italian Approach to Infant/Toddler Care*, New York: Teachers College Press.

Hughes, M. (1989) 'The child as learner: the contrasting views of developmental psychology and early education', in C. Desforges (ed.) *Early Childhood Education*, British Journal of Educational Psychology Monograph Series No. 4, pp. 144–57.

Ministry of Education (1996) T*e Whariki: Early Childhood and Curriculum*, Wellington: Learning Media.

Qualifications and Curriculum Authority (2000) *Curriculum Guidance for the Foundation Stage QCA/DfEE*.

Sharp, R. and Green, A. (1975) *Education and Social Control: A Study in Progressive Primary Education*, London: Routledge & Kegan Paul.

Steedman, C. (1990) *Childhood, Culture and Class in Britain: Margaret McMillan, 1860–1931*, London: Virago.

Warnock, M. (1976) *Imagination*, London: Faber and Faber.

Warnock, M. (1977) *Schools of Thought*, London: Faber and Faber.

Wells, G. (1987) *The Meaning Makers*, London: Hodder & Stoughton.

INDEX